Abnormal Psychology

HARPERCOLLINS COLLEGE OUTLINE

Abnormal Psychology

2nd Edition

Timothy W. Costello, Ph.D.

Joseph T. Costello, Ph.D.

HarperResource
An Imprint of HarperCollinsPublishers

This book is dedicated to Genevieve, wife and mother, whose courage, patience, and good spirit in the face of severe Parkinsonism have been an inspiration to her husband and six children, and to Doreen, whose love and support counted so much in the writing of this book as it does in so many other facets of her husband's life.

An American BookWorks Corporation Production

Project Manager: Judith A. V. Harlan

Editor: Thomas Quinn

Library of Congress Cataloging-in-Publication

Costello, Timothy W.
  Abnormal psychology / Timothy W. Costello, Joseph T. Costello.
    p.   cm.
  Includes bibliographical references and index.
  ISBN: 0-06-467121-6   (pbk.)
  1. Psychology, Pathological—Handbooks, manuals, etc.
I. Costello, Joseph T., 1951–   . II. Title.
  [DNLM: 1. Mental Disorders—outlines. 2. Psychopathology—
outlines.   WM 100 C8415a]
RC454.C665 1992
616.89—dc20
DNLM/DLC
for Library of Congress   90–56016
                                                        CIP

Contents

Preface

This outline presents a descriptive and interpretative summary of the field of abnormal behavior covering in a systematic and comprehensive fashion material usually set forth in one semester or one quarter courses in abnormal psychology. Since it includes full discussions of the main points presented in the principal current texts in the field, it may be used in a supplementary way as an efficient method of reviewing course material.

The outline begins with a discussion of the differences between the abnormal and normal, traces the history of humanity's efforts to understand and deal with psychological disorders, and analyzes modern theoretical perspectives on the development of the human personality and the causes of mental illness.

Prior to examining the principal mental disorders it describes the strengths and weaknesses of the official system for classified mental disorders, the *Diagnostic and Statistical Manual, IIIR*. It then considers in detail the methods psychologists use to assess and classify abnormal behavior.

The outline completes its presentation of introductory concepts as it examines treatment methods derived from the principal theoretical perspectives in the field of abnormal psychology: the psychodynamic (including the psychoanalytical), the humanistic and existential, the cognitive/behavioral, and the biogenic perspectives. The outline describes each of the major psychological disorders identified in *DSM IIIR*. It includes a complete listing of the mental disorders as classified in *DSM IIIR* (including numerical coding).

Students will find that the outline's mode of presentation makes for simplified reading of the material and, as well, makes for efficient and logical review in preparation for examinations. Each chapter introduces and outlines the material of the chapter; each major section identifies the sub-topics to be discussed; a summary at the end of each chapter restates the main points of the chapter. The outline includes a glossary of technical terms and suggested readings for each chapter.

In preparing this outline, the authors had in mind its usefulness not only to the college student, but also to the general reader, as well as practioners in the fields of personnel, teaching, law, social work, religion, nursing, and the medical specialties. They hope that for those groups it will provide a ready compendium of accurate and up-to-date factual material about abnormal behavior. Particular care has been devoted to the index for this purpose.

The authors gratefully acknowledge help received in bringing this outline to publication. Judith A.V. Harlan, the Project Manager, always found a cheerful, sensitive, yet motivating way to keep the authors on track and on time (mostly). George Stricker and Tom Quinn reviewed various chapters of the manuscript for psychological content; they will, we trust, be able to see how their suggestions have been integrated into the text. M.R. Kline painstakingly edited the manuscript and helped the authors to smooth their prose. The staff of Executive Word Processing professionally saw the manuscript from first draft to "word perfect" completion. We owe much to: Ann Marie Herrington, Deborah Soviero, and Miriam Chua, who typed and edited the entire manuscript.

1

The Field of Abnormal Psychology

A national study reports that one person in seven living in the United States will, at some time in his or her life, require professional help for a psychological disorder. Those disorders take many forms. They range from relatively quiet symptoms that principally affect only the individual with the disorder, to behavior that seriously impinges upon the rights of others; from mild symptoms to more extreme symptoms to symptoms that are bizarre.

The average person is vaguely aware of the problem, perhaps has experienced a mentally ill person in his or her family; but, for the most part, holds opinions about abnormal behavior that are based on bits of information or erroneous reports. Common misconceptions about abnormal behavior are that it is incurable or inherited; that the mentally ill are dangerous; that abnormal behavior is always bizarre; that mental illness comes from weakness of will or immoral behavior. Those statements are either totally false or apply in only limited ways. Apart from misconceptions, for many individuals, even the question, "How does one distinguish between normal and abnormal behavior?", is a puzzling one.

Abnormal Psychology is that branch of psychology that concerns itself with establishing criteria to distinguish abnormal from normal behavior; describing the various types of abnormal behavior; searching out the causes of abnormal behavior; seeking means of treating it; and finally, with finding ways to prevent it. More formally, we can define abnormal psychology as the scientific control of behavior that is not considered normal.

This chapter examines the basic aspects of abnormal psychology, answering, in a beginning way, questions newcomers to its study often have in mind: How does one distinguish between normal and abnormal behavior? How prevalent is mental illness? What causes mental illness? Why professional help is necessary? Where such help can be found? Who is professionally qualified to offer help?

WHAT IS NORMAL? WHAT IS ABNORMAL?

"Normal" and "abnormal," as applied to human behavior, are relative terms. Many people use these classifications subjectively and carelessly, often in a judgmental manner, to suggest good or bad behavior. As defined in the dictionary, their accurate use would seem easy enough: normal—conforming to a typical pattern; abnormal—deviating from a norm. The trouble lies in the word *norm*. Whose norm? For what age person? At what period of history? In which of the world's many cultures?

Goodness as a Criterion of Normal

Equating normal with good behavior and abnormal with bad behavior also has its problems. Some questions that must be asked are these: Good or bad by whose values or standards? Under what circumstances? Is assertive behavior bad because it is disconcerting, and compliant behavior good because it is easy to accept? Is behavior at variance with paternal practice bad, and model behavior good? Is aggressive behavior always bad?

Psychologists who work in the field of abnormal behavior, usually referred to as clinical psychologists, have come to grips with those problems and offer more objective criteria.

Two Basic but Different Concepts of Normal and Abnormal

Social science offers two ways of distinguishing between the normal and abnormal. One emphasized by sociologists and anthropologists considers the question meaningful only as it applies to a particular culture at a particular time: abnormal is that which deviates from society's norms. The other, stressed more by psychologists, sets as the basic criterion the individual's well-being and the maladaptiveness of his or her behavior. One we will call the criterion of deviance; the other, the criterion of maladaptive behavior.

ABNORMAL DEFINED AS DEVIATION FROM SOCIAL NORMS

The criterion of cultural relativism—that is, deviation from society's norm's—provides an easy way of identifying abnormal behavior: If behavior differs in a significant way from the way in which others in the same society typically behave, it is abnormal. Cultural relativism bypasses the question of whether or not there are sick societies whose values are pathological, contravening, as they might, basic human rights. When such a sick society changes radically— as, for example, Germany did after World War II—does that make all the previously conforming individuals abnormal and all the resistive, nonconforming individuals now normal?

Another problem faced by the cultural relativists is the question of whether or not there are any types of abnormal behavior whose observable symptoms cut across all cultures. Emil Kraeplin (1856–1926), whose *Textbook of Psychiatry*, published in 1923, provided a basis for classifying mental illness that is still used today, felt that depression, sociopathy (fixed patterns of antisocial behavior) and schizophrenia were worldwide disorders, appearing in all cultures and societies.

There is no question that cultural factors color the symptoms of any mental illness, nor is there question that some mental illnesses appear more frequently in some cultures than in others. But most psychologists question the usefulness of social acceptability as a meaningful criterion for sorting out abnormal behavior from normal behavior.

MALADAPTIVENESS AS A CRITERION OF ABNORMAL BEHAVIOR

To reject cultural relativism requires that the individual or the society make a value judgment—one not necessarily defensible scientifically—that some values are intrinsically good in themselves. American society, at least since the Declaration of Independence (and the Western world has followed suit), has made such an initial judgment, that the well-being of the individual is such a good and that assuring the well-being of the individual assures the well-being of society. With that value in place, instead of acceptability by the society, behavior that promotes an individual's growth and well-being is considered normal behavior, and behavior that maladaptively prevents that growth or significantly limits it, is considered abnormal.

Such a criterion does not do away with all subjectivity in evaluating the normality of anyone's behavior, but it does put that decision in the hands of those who will use the objectivity of science to evaluate whether any given behavior is adaptive and normal or maladaptive and abnormal. "Well-being" here is given a broad definition: not merely survival, but growth and fulfillment, which are paths to self-actualization.

The well-being perspective allows room for the conforming behavior necessary for group cohesiveness and for deviant behavior, as it may stimulate the society to reexamine itself and its goals, so long as it is not irreparably self-damaging. It includes a concern for the family's well-being and a mission to work to eliminate those social problems that can erode a society's well-being, such as racism, discrimination and poverty.

SPECIFIC CRITERIA FOR JUDGING MALADAPTIVE BEHAVIOR

Using maladaptiveness as a criterion of abnormality has its own problems. It is the rare person whose behavior is never maladaptive—who never becomes angry in a self-damaging way, who never takes one alcoholic drink more than is sensible, never feels depressed or anxious. In evaluating the maladaptiveness of behavior, psychologists take account of the frequency of the behavior and the extent to which it impairs necessary functioning, especially in interpersonal relations and in occupational pursuits. They also take account of severely stressful life situations that the individual may face or catastrophic events he or she may have lived through. Those factors may cause a transitory spell of maladaptive behavior.

There are certain categories of behavior that suggest the presence of psychological disorders that may benefit from psychological treatment. All those disorders, in one way or another, are maladaptive in that they threaten the well-being of the individual. A description of them follows.

Long Periods of Subjective Discomfort

Everyone goes through periods of psychological discomfort: worry about the severity of a loved one's illness; fearful anticipation of a challenging assignment; aggrieved feelings after an unfair criticism. But those feelings are transitory, and they are related to real or threatened events. When such feelings as anxiety and depression or frenetic behavior persist, month after month, and appear to be unrelated to events surrounding the person, they would be considered abnormal and suggestive of psychological disorder.

Impaired Functioning

Here again a distinction must be drawn between periods of transitory inefficiency and prolonged inefficiency, between inefficiency whose cause can be identified—and inefficiency over a prolonged period which seems to be inexplicable. Important examples that would be considered signs of an abnormal psychological condition are as follows: frequent job changes without apparent justification or frequent loss of jobs; prolonged performance notably below the individual's potential, the most common examples of which are the very bright student who gets only low or failing grades or the brilliantly talented person who fails in one effort after another.

Bizarre Behavior

Here is not meant unconventional behavior that is carried out for some reason that can be understood by others—for example, performances imposed on freshmen as part of an initiation rite or behavior carried out to gain attention or to achieve notoriety. An older generation will remember goldfish swallowing and flagpole sitting. Silly, but most people understood the motivation. Today, unusually dramatic hairstyles may be another example.

Bizarre behavior indicative of abnormality has no rational basis, is unconnected to reality, and seems to suggest that the individual is disoriented. Such behavior indicates serious mental illness. The psychoses (the most serious of mental disorders), to be described later, frequently bring on hallucinations (baseless sensations): hearing voices when no one is present, for example; or delusions, which are beliefs that are patently false, yet steadfastly held by the psychotic individual. An example is delusions of grandeur in which an individual believes he or she is a great historical character who is long dead.

Disruptive Behavior

What is meant here is impulsive, seemingly uncontrollable behavior that regularly disrupts the lives of others or deprives them of their rights. Such behavior is characteristic of several psychological disorders. The antisocial personality disorder to be described later has, as one of its principal characteristics, conscienceless and apparently purposeless, aggressive or exploitative behavior.

All of the described behaviors are maladaptive because they directly affect well-being by blocking growth and fulfillment of the individual's potential or do so indirectly and, in the long run, by seriously interfering with the well-being of others.

PREVALENCE OF ABNORMAL BEHAVIOR

In considering the extent of mental illness, a distinction is drawn between prevalence, which is the number of individuals suffering a mental disease at a given time, and incidence, which reports the rate at which a specified disorder appears in the population in a stated period of time. Incidence, for example, would report the lifetime risk of developing a specified mental illness for individuals grouped by age or sex. *Associated risk factors* is another term used in reporting incidence, an example of which would be the lifetime expected occurrence of mental illness for individuals with relatives having a mental illness.

Abnormal behavior (mental or psychological illness, as we will call it in this book) brings unhappiness and discomfort to well over one hundred million American adults; in addition, 12 percent of school-age children are classified as clinically maladjusted, and 3 to 6 percent of the aged suffer with organically caused mental disorders. The social costs for hospitalization and mental health care and the lost income resulting from enforced unemployment and absenteeism are so high as to be inestimable.

Prevalence of Specific Disorders

Later chapters will describe in detail the variety of psychological disorders: here we can say that a description of the mentally ill would include 11 to 16 percent of the American population of approximately 250 million people who suffer from alcohol dependence, the most widely prevalent form of mental disorder, and 8 to 23 percent of that population who suffer phobic (fear) disorders, the second most prevalent disorder. Depressive episodes and drug abuse or dependence each accounts for more than five percent of the general population. One percent, or 1.4 million people, suffer from schizophrenia, an especially severe form of mental disorder.

Age and Sex Differences

There are both sex differences and age differences in the types of mental disorders suffered. Although men and women in equal numbers experience mental disorders, they differ in the kinds of mental illnesses affecting them. Alcoholism affects 24 percent of the male population, but only 4 percent of females. Women are more prone than men to suffer depression and anxiety. Drug dependence occurs most frequently in the age group of eighteen to twenty-four years of age; depression and alcoholism develop during the age span of twenty-five to forty-four years of age. Disorders of thinking are most prevalent among the aged.

PRINCIPAL FACTORS CAUSING ABNORMAL BEHAVIOR

Here in this introductory chapter, we can take only a broad-brush approach to describing causative factors in mental illness. There are three concepts that are important for the student to grasp in considering the development of psychological disorders: stress, coping mechanisms and vulnerability. It is the interaction among those elements that will determine the development of mental illness. Detailed descriptions of causative elements can be found in chapters describing specific disorders.

Stress

Stress is a set of emotional tensions accompanied by biological changes (principally of the autonomic system; that is, sweating, heart pounding, blood pressure changes) caused by a threatened external event. In milder forms, it causes worry and fretfulness. The experience of some level of stress is a frequent event in everyone's life. When the stressing external event is extreme or prolonged, such as a serious automobile accident or an earthquake, or when it imposes prolonged frustration of an important human need or a bewildering conflict in which a decision is required, a major adjustive effort is required of the individual. That demand may push the individual into a breakdown of adaptive responses and cause the appearance of abnormal behavior. Whether that breakdown occurs at all, and whether it is mild or extreme, depends on the existence of previously learned adaptive behavior or, in its absence, on the presence of a tendency to depend upon defensive coping mechanisms. Existing vulnerabilities predispose the individual to the possibility of mental disorder in extremely stressful situations.

Coping Mechanisms

Faced with a stressful event or set of circumstances, a person may rise to the challenge by directing behavior primarily at dealing with the stressful event—that is, by task-oriented behavior— or the person may become defensive and call on unconsciously operating coping mechanisms, which are commonly called defense mechanisms. A coping mechanism is defined as a process of changing the meaning or significance of an event to protect the self from psychic pain and/or psychological damage. Much maladaptive or abnormal behavior is the result of defense-oriented, rather than task-oriented, behavior.

Vulnerability

Whether or not individuals respond adequately to stress depends upon their vulnerability, or susceptibility, to the development of psychological disorders. There are, of course, "soft spots," or vulnerabilities, in the personalities of all people; but when they are significant or multiple, they can predispose the individual to break down and exhibit maladaptive behavior.

There are two principal causes of vulnerability: genetic causes, in which faulty genes create predispositions to mental disorder; and early life experiences that provide faulty parenting or other inadequate learning opportunities.

WHY PROFESSIONAL HELP BECOMES NECESSARY

Despite expert opinion that psychological disorders (along with physical disorders) are most effectively treated at the earliest sign of significant emotional disturbance, many people, for one reason or another, delay treatment, deluding themselves that palliatives or self-help approaches will cure the illness. In most cases, it requires some relatively powerful influence to bring an individual to the therapists's office.

Troubled individuals finally enter therapy as a result of one of three kinds of influence: personal discomfort; the pressure of relatives or friends; the demands of community or legal authorities.

Personal Discomfort

Most people who seek professional psychological help are suffering from physical or emotional discomfort. Many discomforting, even frightening, physical symptoms stem from or are made worse by emotional disorders. Among them are asthma, ulcer and hypertension; among the physical symptoms are chronic fatigue, heart palpitations, stomach complaints, and pain. Often, the effective stimulus motivating the individual is the family doctor, who has ruled out physical causes for a disorder and suggests that the person seek psychological or psychiatric assistance.

Emotional symptoms, particularly intense anxiety or spells of depression, may become so painful or alarming that they overcome whatever reasons the person may have had for delaying treatment. Many clinicians feel that a client must be experiencing notable psychic pain to persist with therapy and to respond to it.

The Influence of Family and Friends

The behavior associated with abnormal behavior may be more painful to family members or friends than to the disordered individual. Examples are abuse of alcohol, assaultive behavior, emotionally draining dependence, or exploitative behavior. Sometimes, desperate to change things, family or close friends will bring pressure on the individual to seek help. That pressure may benignly be brought to bear in a heart-to-heart talk; but strong methods are also used: threats by a spouse that he or she will leave, or by a parent that the house will be locked against the individual unless treatment is sought; previously supportive friends may simply desert the individual.

The kind of pressure used to induce the individual to enter therapy will, of course, have an effect on the individual's responsiveness to treatment, sometimes causing an indifferent attendance at therapy sessions with little emotional involvement; or, in other situations, causing a panic-stricken demand that the therapist do something to help.

The Influence of Legal or Community Authorities

Psychological disorders can produce behavior that is so antisocial or disruptive as to call the individual to the attention of community authorities; a social worker to whom the family has become known, a clergyperson who has tried to help; or, in extreme cases, the police or other legal authorities. With that kind of intercession, the pressure to seek therapy is powerful. How that power is brought to bear will also have an effect on the individual's attitude toward therapy.

SPECIALISTS WHO PROVIDE HELP

Throughout later chapters, we will consider the variety of help, called therapies, available to those with psychological disorders. The first step in that process is an assessment of the individual's condition. That process leads to a diagnosis, which enables the clinician to fit the psychological troubles of the individual into a specific category of mental illness. That diagnosis gives the clinician an initial understanding of some of the elements in the individual's illness and enables the clinician to plan a course of treatment.

There are three professions that provide those helping services, either as a team or, more frequently, individually. They are psychologists, psychiatrists, and social workers. The academic and experiential training they receive, although different for each of the professions, prepares them, in ways relevant to their training, to offer psychological help in a skilled and responsible fashion. Beyond that primary group of mental health professionals, there are other professionals and paraprofessionals who offer specialized ancillary services, but not psychotherapy. They ordinarily work in association with psychiatrists or psychologists.

Psychologists

These professionals, who are trained to make psychological assessments and to provide psychotherapy, will carry one of three titles: clinical psychologists, counseling psychologists, and/or school psychologists. Only three categories of psychologist are trained to offer professional help for psychological disorders. Ordinarily, in four or five years of post-baccalaureate schooling, they acquire a Ph.D. (Doctor of Philosophy), which is a scientific degree preparing the individual for research, as well as for clinical practice; or a Psy.D. (Doctor of Psychology), an applied degree providing training principally for psychological practice. Before obtaining their degrees, both groups complete a supervised, one-year applied internship.

Clinical psychologists specialize in working with those who suffer psychological disorders; counseling psychologists, in addition to assessment and therapy, also offer consultation on vocational and career problems; school psychologists work mostly with children who are having school problems, the source of which may be emotional problems. All states require those three types of psychologists to pass a licensing or certification test.

Psychiatrists

These professionals are medical doctors who, after completing their medical education, spend three years in residence, under supervision, in a mental health facility. After that training, they may choose to become board certified by passing an examination. Only physicians can write prescriptions for drugs or admit an individual to a hospital or undertake biological forms of therapy.

Psychoanalysts may be psychiatrists, psychologists, or social workers who have completed a program in psychoanalytical theory and practice, a type of program usually offered by psychoanalytical institutes which, within the psychoanalytical framework, may differ one from another in their theoretical orientation. As part of their training, they undergo a personal psychoanalysis.

Psychiatric Social Workers

These professionals are social workers who have completed a two-year post-baccalaureate program in a school of social work. Some may continue on for a doctorate degree. Their training emphasizes skilled assessment, interviewing, and treatment in individual or group settings.

Other Professionals and Para-professionls

These ancillary aides include psychiatric nurses who, beyond their R.N. (Registered Nurse) degree, have had special training for working with mentally ill individuals in psychiatric hospitals; psychiatric attendants, a paraprofessional group, who work in the psychiatric wards of psychiatric hospitals; and skill therapists, who put into effect the suggestions of the principal therapists to provide recreational, artistic, dance, music, or occupational activities (largely crafts). They hold such titles as occupational, dance or music therapists.

Settings in Which Mental Health Therapists Work

A large number of mental health clinicians—that is, psychologists, psychiatrists, and, increasingly, social workers, work in private practice, either singly or in groups. Clients or patients are referred to them by family doctors, clergy, social agencies, or by former clients. Other things being equal, the Yellow Pages of the telephone directory is not a suitable source for selecting a clinician.

Other mental health professionals practice in outpatient settings, usually sponsored by mental health societies or other social agencies, or are attached to a hospital staff. General hospitals and psychiatric hospitals may sponsor outpatient psychological service; but most frequently, they provide service only for hospitalized patients.

Abnormal Psychology is that branch of psychology that establishes criteria distinguishing normal from abnormal behavior, describes the various types of abnormal behavior, searches out the causes of it and seeks to find means of treating or preventing it.

Psychologists set maladaptive behavior, that is, behavior that interferes with the individual's well-being and psychological growth, as the overriding criterion for diagnosing abnormality. They do not consider behavior that deviates from society's norms as necessarily a sign of abnormality.

There are four principal criteria for considering behavior maladaptive: long periods of personal discomfort; impaired social, educational or occupational functioning; bizarre or disruptive behavior.

In assessing the problem of mental disorder, social scientists speak of prevalence (the total number of individuals in a specific category suffering a mental disorder) and incidence (the rate at which mental disorders, usually of a particular type, will occur in a specified population during a stated period of time).

The principal factors causing mental disorders are stress, failure to learn adequate coping mechanisms, and vulnerability (such as defective genes or deficient early personality development).

People seek professional help because of personal discomfort, the urging of family or friends, and the influence of legal or community authorities.

There are four professional groups that offer help to victims of mental disorders. They are psychologists, psychiatrists, social workers and psychiatric nurses. They are assisted by other professional groups, such as occupational therapists, and such paraprofessional groups as psychiatric ward attendants.

Selected Readings

Chesler, P. 1972. *Women and Madness*. Garden City, N.Y.: Doubleday.

Cleckley, H.M. 1976. *The Mask of Sanity*. St. Louis, MO: Mosby.

Comas-Diaz, L. and E.E. Griffith (Eds.). 1988. *Clinical Guidelines in Cross-Cultural Mental Health*. New York: Wiley.

Corey, G., M.S. Corey, and P. Callahan. 1984. *Issues and Ethics in the Helping Professions*. Monterey, CA: Brooks/Cole.

Cowen, E.L. 1982. "Help is Where You Find It: Four Informal Helping Groups." *American Psychologist* 37: 385-395.

Goffman, E. 1959. *Presentation of Self in Everyday Life*. New York: Doubleday.

Kaplan, B., Ed. 1964. *The Inner World of Mental Illness*. New York: Harper Row.

Kiesler, C.A. 1982. "Public and Professional Myths About Mental Hospitalization." *American Psychologist* 37: 1323-1339.

2

History of the Problem of Abnormal Behavior

The problem of mental disorder is probably as old as humankind. Recorded history reports a broad range of interpretations of abnormal behavior and methods for correcting it, which have generally reflected the degree of enlightenment and the trends of religious, philosophical and social beliefs and practices of the times. It is not surprising that earlier efforts to deal with the problem were fraught with difficulties and that the evolution of a science of abnormal psychology has been painfully slow. This has been the case for two reasons.

First, the very nature of the problems caused by abnormal behavior has made it a "thing apart," arousing fear, shame, and guilt in the families and communities of those afflicted. Hence, the management of the mentally disordered has been turned over to the state and the church, which have been the traditional guardians of both group and individual behavior. Second, the evolution of all the sciences has been slow and sporadic, many of the most important advances having been achieved only against great resistance. While this has been more typical of abnormal psychology than of other disciplines, the difference is only relative. In reviewing the historical account that follows, one should not be too critical; although it is true that in earlier times the abnormal person was misunderstood and often mistreated, the lot of the "normal" individual was not a much happier one.

PRIMITIVE PERIOD

Archaeological findings suggest that some types of mental illness must have been recognized as far back as the Stone Age. Skeletal remains from that period reveal that attempts were made to relieve brain pressure by chipping away an area of the skull. Though the procedure was similar to the operative technique now known as trephining, there is serious question as to whether it was based on any knowledge of brain pathology. It seems more likely that the operation was performed in the belief that, in this way, an avenue of escape was provided for "evil spirits." Our knowledge of primitive "psychiatry" does not go beyond speculations suggested by such skeletal remains.

PRECLASSICAL PERIOD

Although primitive superstitions persisted into and beyond the Classical period, history shows that attempts were being made before the golden ages of Greece and Rome to find a more rational approach to the understanding and treatment of the mentally disordered.

In the Orient

About 2600 B.C., in China, some forms of faith healing, diversion of interest, and change of environment emerged as the chief methods for treating mental disorders. By 1140 B.C., institutions for the "insane" had been established there, and patients were being cared for until "recovery." In the writings of physicians in India around 600 B.C. are found detailed descriptions of some forms of mental disease and epilepsy, with recommendations for kindness in treatment.

In the Middle East

Egyptian and Babylonian manuscripts dating back to 5000 B.C. describe the behavior of the mentally disordered as being due to influences of evil spirits. Aside from the practice of trephining (opening the skull), treatment was restricted almost exclusively to the ministrations of priests and magicians. Biblical sources indicate that the Hebrews looked upon mental illness as a punishment from God and that treatment was principally along lines of atonement to Him.

CLASSICAL PERIOD

As in all areas of scientific and social thought, in the era of classical Greece and Rome, important strides were made toward a more reasonable and humane treatment of the mentally ill, and the first glimmer appeared of a medical approach to the problem.

In Greece

Some of the more significant assumptions of Greek thought have been confirmed by modern research, and much of the terminology of modern psychiatry (as, indeed, of medicine and science in general) is a legacy from this period. The humane, rational approach to mental illness that emerged during this era was due largely to the findings of the following men.

PYTHAGORAS (CIRCA 500 B.C.)

Before 500 B.C., priest-physicians combined suggestion, diet, massage and recreation with their more regular prescriptions of incantations and sacrifices; but in all treatment, the guiding motive was appeasement of good or evil spirits. However, Pythagoras was the first to teach a natural explanation for mental illness. He identified the brain as the center of intelligence and attributed mental disease to a disorder of the brain.

HIPPOCRATES (460–377 B.C.)

The "Father of Medicine" held that brain disturbance is the cause of mental disorder. He emphasized that treatment should be physical in nature, urging the use of baths, special diets, bleeding, and drugs. Hippocrates taught the importance of heredity and of predisposition to mental illness. He related sensory and motor disturbances to head injuries. Anticipating modern psychiatry, he also realized that the analysis of dreams can be useful in understanding the patient's personality.

PLATO (428–347 B.C.)

This Greek philosopher manifested keen insight into the human personality. He recognized the existence of individual differences in intelligence and in other psychological characteristics, and he asserted that man is motivated by "natural appetites." To Plato, mental disorder is partly moral, partly physical and partly divine in origin. He described the patient-doctor relationship in the treatment pattern, believed that fantasy and dreams are substitute satisfactions for inhibited "passions," and introduced the concept of the criminal as a mentally disturbed person.

ARISTOTLE (384–322 B.C.)

Aristotle accepted a physiological basis for mental illness, as taught by Hippocrates. While he did consider the possibility of a psychological cause, he rejected it, and so strong was his influence on philosophical thought that for nearly two thousand years, his point of view discouraged further exploration along these lines.

ALEXANDER THE GREAT (356–323 B.C.)

Alexander established sanatoriums for the mentally ill, where occupation, entertainment, and exercise were provided, practices which were continued during the later Greek and Roman periods.

In Rome

The Romans, for the most part, continued to follow the teachings of the Greek physicians and philosophers in their treatment of mental illness. Greek physicians, the most outstanding of whom were Aesclepiades, Aretaeus, and Galen, settled in Rome, where they continued their studies and teaching.

AESCLEPIADES (124–40 B.C.)

This Greek-born physician and philosopher was the first to differentiate between acute and chronic mental illness. He developed mechanical devices for the comfort and relaxation of mental patients; he opposed bleeding, restraints, and isolation in dungeons. Whereas his predecessors had considered both delusions and hallucinations under one heading ("phantasia"), Aesclepiades differentiated between the two.

ARETAEUS (FIRST TO SECOND CENTURIES A.D.)

Aretaeus was the first to suggest that mental illness is a psychological extension of normal personality traits. He believed that there existed a predisposition to certain forms of mental disorder. One of his original thoughts (placing the seat of mental disease in the brain and the abdomen) foreshadowed the psychosomatic approach to medicine.

GALEN (A.D. 129–199)

Galen's contribution to medical science, though of great value in one respect, served to retard development in another. Like Hippocrates, who lived seven centuries earlier, he gathered and organized an enormous amount of data concerning mental and physical illness and conducted studies in the anatomy of the nervous system and its relation to human behavior. He recognized the duality of physical and psychic causation in mental illness, identifying such varied factors as head injuries, alcoholism, fear, adolescence, menopausal changes, economic difficulties and love affairs. On the other hand, like many others of his time, he permitted his concern with teleology (having to do with purpose in nature) to becloud his scientific conclusions. He felt impelled to assign specific divine or astrological influences to this or that organ of the body. Since his prestige was great, for centuries after his death, progress was encumbered by controversies over the metaphysical aspects of his contributions and, thus, independent thinking in the medical sciences was delayed until well into the eighteenth century.

In Arabia

The last faint echo of the efforts of the classicists to conquer the problem of mental disorder was heard not in the West, but in Arabia, where Avicenna (A.D. 980–1037) and later, his follower, Averrhoes (A.D. 1126–1198), maintained a scientific approach to the mentally ill and urged humane treatment. Elsewhere, as we shall see, a return to primitive notions prevailed.

MEDIEVAL PERIOD

With the dissolution of the Graeco-Roman civilization, learning and scientific progress in Europe experienced a grave setback. Ancient superstitions and demonology were revived, and contemporary theological thinking did little to discourage the "spiritistic" approach to the problem of mental illness. Exorcism (expelling an evil spirit) was considered imperative; accordingly, incantations were regarded as a legitimate adjunct of medicine. Even the application of perfectly rational techniques had to be accompanied by the pronouncement of mystical phrases.

The best physicians of the time were given to the use of amulets. Alexander of Tralles (A.D. 525–605), for example, who stressed the importance of constitutional factors and related them to specific types of mental disorder, and who studied frontal lobe injuries and noted accompanying changes in behavior, treated colic by the application of a stone on which an image of Hercules overcoming the lion was carved.

The Dancing Mania

At intervals from the tenth to the fifteenth centuries, the dancing mania, also referred to as "mass madness," in which large groups of people danced wildly until they dropped from exhaustion, was seen in Europe. In Italy, the condition was called "tarantism" because the mania was thought to be due to the bite of the tarantula, a venomous ground spider. Elsewhere in western Europe, the mania was called "Saint Vitus's dance." It is difficult to say whether these seemingly epidemic manifestations have been greatly exaggerated in the telling. It has been suggested that a large number of people may have been suffering from various forms of chorea. Fear of this unexplained disorder may have risen to a mass suggestibility and hysteria which mounted unchecked and which subsequently have been recorded as a single clinical entity.

Witchcraft: Belief in Demonology

The period from the fifteenth to the eighteenth centuries comprises a sorry chapter of history with respect to the fate of the mentally ill. Their afflictions were generally ascribed to possession by the devil; and treatment, consisting chiefly of attempts to "cast out the demon," was hardly distinguishable from punishment. The "Black Death" (bubonic plague) had ravaged Europe in the fourteenth century, and the resulting depression and fear rendered whole people highly susceptible to the ministrations of witchcraft. The humane, scientific approach to the mentally ill (for that matter, to all illness) was indeed at a low ebb.

Late in the fifteenth century, the plight of abnormal people was intensified by the publication of *Malleus Maleficarum, The Hammer of Witches which destroyeth witches and their heresy as with a two-edged sword,* by Henry Kraemer and James Sprenger, of the Order of Preachers. Their book, appearing in 1484 and fortified by an approving papal bull of Innocent VIII, was to be the handbook of inquisitors for two hundred years. The bull authorized inquisitors to proceed according to the regulations of the Inquisition; ecclesiastical courts ferreted out persons thought to be "possessed of the Devil"; the unfortunates were then turned over to civil authorities to be tortured or executed. Sprenger and Kraemer met some early resistance from cooler heads in the church and community but soon won support from people already imbued with a fear of witchcraft; their crusade caught fire and thereafter spread throughout both Roman Catholic and Reformed centers in Europe. So widely held was the belief in witches that the persecution of witches continued off and on for the next three centuries. In America, the most notorious trials for witchcraft occurred in Salem, Massachusetts, in 1692.

Institutional Care of the Mentally Ill

Symbolic of the kind of institutional care afforded the mentally ill during the late medieval and early Renaissance periods was that seen at "Bedlam." (The name is a contraction of Bethlehem.) As early as 1400, the monastery of Saint Mary of Bethlehem in London began caring for lunatics; in 1547, the monastery was officially converted into a mental hospital. Because of the inhumanity of the treatment there, "Bedlam" has come to stand for anything that is cruel in the management of the mentally disturbed.

But this era was not entirely without examples of tolerance and mercy. The shrine of Saint Dymphna at Gheel in Belgium (established in the fifteenth century) not only lent solace to thousands of afflicted persons who visited there, but also grew gradually into a "colony" that was dedicated to the care of the mentally ill. Its work still goes on, and Gheel is regarded as the model for similar colony plans elsewhere.

RENAISSANCE PERIOD

Although the mentally disturbed became engulfed in the morass of superstition and inhumanity, in certain countries of Europe voices were raised in the cause of reason by enlightened men of religion, medicine, and philosophy. Their efforts during this period can well be described as "lights in the darkness."

In Switzerland   Paracelsus (Theophrastus von Hohenheim), (1493–1541) rejected demonology, recognized psychological causes of mental illness, and proposed a theory of "bodily magnetism," a forerunner of hypnosis. Like Hippocrates, he suggested the sexual nature of hysteria. However, like so many otherwise reasonable men of his time, he laid great store on astral influences, assigning to various planets control over specific organs of the body.

In Germany   Heinrich Cornelius Agrippa (1486–1535) fought against the hypocrisy and bloodthirsty application of the edicts of the Inquisition. A scholar and later advocate of the city of Metz, Agrippa was persecuted and reviled for his views. He died in poverty. Johann Weyer (1515–1588) was a physician who studied under Agrippa. In 1563, he published a scientific analysis of witchcraft, rejecting the notion of demon causation in mental illness. His clinical descriptions of mental disorders were remarkably concise, uncluttered with opinions and theological illusions. Weyer is regarded by some as the "Father of Modern Psychiatry."

In England   Reginald Scot (1538–1599) published a scholarly, painstaking study entitled *The Discovery of Witchcraft: Proving That the Compacts and Contracts of Witches and Devils . . . Are But Erroneous Novelties and Imaginary Conceptions*. But James I ordered the book seized and burned, and published a refutation of Scot's views.

In France   Saint Vincent de Paul (1576–1660) urged a more humane approach to the mentally ill. He emphasized the fact that mental disease differs in no way from bodily disease. In the hospital which he founded at Saint Lazare, he put into practice what he held to be a basic Christian principle, namely, that we are as much obligated to care humanely for the mentally ill as for the physically ill.

EIGHTEENTH TO TWENTIETH CENTURIES

The transition from the demonological to the scientific approach to mental illness was not accomplished overnight. In France, for example, capital punishment for convicted "sorcerers" was not abolished until 1862. The first general trend toward specialized treatment of the mentally ill probably came in the wake of the social, political, economic, and scientific reforms that characterized the latter half of the eighteenth century.

In France

Soon after the Revolution, Philippe Pinel (1745–1826) removed the chains from the inmates at Bicetre and provided pleasant, sanitary housing along with walkways and workshops. Later, at Salpetriere, he introduced the practice of training of attendants. Jean Esquirol (1772–1840) continued Pinel's work; through his efforts, ten new mental hospitals were established in France.

In England

William Tuke (1732–1822), a layman and a Quaker, interested the Society of Friends in establishing the York Retreat in 1796. Through his urging, special training was instituted for nurses working in this field. John Conolly (1794–1866), founder of a small medical association which later became the British Medical Association, was mainly responsible for the wide acceptance of nonviolent measures in the treatment of the mentally ill.

In Germany

Anton Muller (1755–1827), working in a hospital for mental diseases, preached humane treatment of the insane and protested against brutal restraint of patients.

In Italy

Vincenzo Chiarugi (1759–1820) published his "Hundred Observations" of the mentally ill and demanded humanization of treatment of the deranged.

In Latin America

The first asylum for the "insane" in the Americas was San Hopolito, organized about 1570 by Bernadino Alvarez in Mexico City, but it is difficult to say whether it was really more than a place of confinement. Elsewhere in Latin America, the earliest mental hospitals began to appear in the 1820s. As late as 1847, visitors to Mexico and Peru reported that "lunatics" were displayed for the amusement of the populace, who paid for the exhibition (as had been done at Bedlam three centuries earlier).

In the United States

In Philadelphia, the Blockley Insane Asylum was opened in 1752. The only other institution for the mentally disturbed in the United States before the nineteenth century was the Eastern State Lunatic Asylum in Virginia, opened in 1773.

Humanitarian treatment of the mentally ill was encouraged by Benjamin Rush (1745–1813), who is generally accepted as the "Father of American Psychiatry." Rush organized the first course in psychiatry and published the first systematic treatise on the subject in the United States. In the latter half of the nineteenth century, Dorothea Lynde Dix (1802–1887) carried on a militant campaign for reform in the care of the mentally ill. She was responsible for a more enlightened attitude and improved programs in twenty states; in New York, her efforts resulted in the State Care Act of 1889, which did away with confinement of the mentally disturbed in jails and almshouses. Her influence was felt also in Canada, Scotland and England.

At Utica State Lunatic Asylum (now Utica State Hospital), an Association of Superintendents of American Institutions for the Insane was formed in 1846; the name was changed to American Medico-Psychological Association in the 1880s. It finally became the American Psychiatric Association of today. Its professional scientific publication, originally called the *American Journal of Insanity,* has been published continuously for over a hundred years.

In the early years of the twentieth century, Clifford Beers (1876–1943) described his experiences as a mental patient in the book *A Mind That Found Itself.* The wide distribution of this volume stimulated public interest in a movement to improve conditions in mental hospitals and gave rise to the formation of the National Committee for Mental Hygiene, in which Beers played an active role. That organization was later incorporated, along with other smaller groups, into the National Association for Mental Health.

In the Western World: National and International Efforts

The mental hygiene movement spread throughout the Western world. During the first half of the twentieth century, a variety of national and international organizations were established to aid in the development of improved facilities for the mentally ill. In recent decades, there has been a trend toward public acceptance of both humanitarian and scientific approaches to the problem of mental abnormality. This new attitude has been reflected in the activities of world organizations such as the World Health Organization, UNESCO, and the World Federation of Mental Health, as well as in those of innumerable national and local public and private agencies. (For a discussion of modern treatment approaches, see chapters 6 and 7.)

THE MODERN ERA: DEVELOPMENTS IN PSYCHIATRIC THOUGHT

The development of psychiatric thought and the subsequent contributions to the understanding of mental abnormality during the eighteenth to twentieth centuries may be summarized under two headings: organic interpretations and psychological interpretations.

Organic Interpretations

The importance of brain pathology in the causation of mental illness was recognized by Albrecht von Haller (1708–1777), who sought corroboration of his beliefs through postmortem studies. In 1845, William Griesinger (1817–1868) published his *Pathology and Therapy of Psychic Disorders*, in which he held that all theories of mental disturbances must be based on brain pathology. The psychiatrist Henry Morel (1809–1873) attributed mental illness to hereditary neural weakness. Valentin Magnan (1835–1916) investigated mental illness occurring in relation to alcoholism, paralysis, and childbirth.

Perhaps the most influential figure in psychiatry in the latter nineteenth and early twentieth centuries was Emil Kraepelin (1856–1926). In 1883, he published a textbook outlining mental illness in terms of organic pathology; in particular, the disordered functioning of the nervous system, a point of view which oriented his approach to the general problem of mental disturbances. He described and classified many types of disorders and provided a basis for descriptive psychiatry by drawing attention to clusters of symptoms. Kraepelin evolved a theoretical system that divided mental illness into two large categories: those due to endogenous factors (originating within the body) and those due to exogenous factors (originating outside the body). His classification remained substantially unchanged until a few years after World War I. Kraepelin made notable contributions to psychiatry, but his approach to mental illness was that of an experimentalist, and, consequently, he studied disease processes as entities in themselves rather than as the dynamic reactions of living individuals.

In 1897, Richard von Krafft-Ebing (1840–1902), a Viennese psychiatrist, disclosed experimental proof of the relationship of general paresis (a psychosis) to syphilis (see chapter 16). In 1907, Alois Alzheimer established the presence of brain pathology in senile psychoses. In 1917, Julius Wagner-Jauregg (1857–1940) inoculated nine paretic patients with malaria, with consequent alleviation of their condition. These and other discoveries during the early twentieth century lent strong support to the believers in the organic approach to mental illness.

Psychological Interpretations

Despite the achievements of the organically oriented investigators in certain limited areas, very little progress was being made in treating mentally disordered patients. As early as the first decades of the eighteenth century, vague and uncertain theories (e.g., mesmerism) had postulated psychological causation.

MESMERISM

The development of a psychological interpretation of mental illness can be traced from the early works of France Anton Mesmer (1734–1815). Mesmer developed and applied a technique he called "animal magnetism." He attributed his cures to the control and alteration of "magnetic forces" which he believed to be the causes of mental disease. One English physician, John Elliotson (1792–1868), used mesmerism in surgery. Another, James Braid (1795–1862), studied the process and concluded that it was a purely psychological phenomenon whose chief characteristic was suggestion, and in 1841 he termed the process "hypnosis." Ambroise-Auguste Liebeault (1823–1904) and Hippolyte-Marie Bernheim (1840–1919), two French physicians practicing at Nancy, investigated the influence of suggestion in inducing a hypnotic state. They concluded that both hypnosis and hysteria are due to suggestion. Jean-Martin Charcot (1825–1893), a French neuropsychiatrist, disagreed with them, believing that hypnosis was dependent upon physiological processses as well as upon suggestion. He insisted that persons capable of being hypnotized were hysterical.

THE DEVELOPMENT OF PSYCHOANALYSIS

The foregoing observations laid the groundwork for the accomplishments of the psychologically oriented scientists: Janet, Breuer, Freud and others.

Pierre Janet (1859–1947) developed the first psychological theory explaining neurosis. Using hypnosis as his investigating technique, he did extensive research on hysteria, and his work did much to attract attention to the psychological point of view in mental illness.

In Vienna, Josef Breuer (1842–1925) in 1880 successfully treated hysteria with hypnosis and observed that the release of pent-up emotion resulted in the removal of symptoms. This discovery served as a point of departure for the development of psychoanalysis. However, in Vienna, a colleague of his, Sigmund Freud (1856–1939), who was a physician and neurologist, was less successful with hypnosis and thus worked out the "cathartic" method in which free association and dream interpretation are used to uncover dynamic and unconscious material. Freud's technique and his theory are the cornerstones of the psychoanalytic school (chapter 3).

The differences in the organic and psychological points of view that were present in the early history of abnormal psychology continue to form the backdrop of this field of scientific endeavor. The question of the relative importance of organic and psychological factors in the causation of mental illness remains unanswered.

*P*sychological disorders, expressing themselves in a variety of maladaptive behavior patterns, different, to some extent, from one time period to another and from one culture to another, have beset men, women and children for as long as we have any record of humankind's existence. Interpretations of those disorders and ways of caring for the psychologically disordered have, over the centuries, rested on superstition, religious beliefs, the speculations of philosophers and, to some extent, on common sense and compassion.

The earliest record of any physical mode of treatment is found in the skeletal remains of primitive humans, which reveal holes chopped into certain skulls from the prehistoric period, presumably to release the evil spirits within.

In the earliest periods for which we have historical records (about 2600 B.C.), faith healing, diversion of interest, and change of environment emerged as the chief methods of treating mental disorders. In Egypt and Babylon, manuscripts dating back to 5000 B.C. attribute mental disorders to evil spirits. In India, around 600 B.C., medical records describe some forms of mental disorder, including epilepsy.

During the Grecian classical period, Hippocrates, the "Father of Medicine," held that brain disturbance was the cause of mental disorder. While Plato considered mental disorder partly moral, partly physical and partly divine in origin, Aristotle followed Hippocrates and shaped medical thinking for centuries to come by attributing mental disorder to physiological influences.

During the medieval period, with the dissolution of earlier civilizations, ancient superstitions and demonology were revived to explain the abnormal behavior of the disordered. Remnants of that way of thinking about mental disorder continued to be influential until the late seventeenth century, when "witches" were burned at the stake in Salem, Massachusetts.

The foreshadowing of the modern approach to mental disorder appears during the Renaissance Period in the work of exceptional individuals in the major countries of Europe.

The social, political, economic and scientific reforms accelerated by the Industrial Revolution in the late nineteenth century introduced radically new ways of understanding and treating the mentally disordered. Pinel in France, for example, removed their chains; William Tuke, an English Quaker, introduced psychological training for nurses working in the field; in North and South America, psychiatric hospitals were established; and in the United States, Benjamin Rush, the "Father of American psychiatry," published the first psychiatric textbooks.

Among other advances during this period in understanding the nature of mental disorder were Krafft-Ebing's experimental demonstration that general paresis was caused by the syphilis spirochete and Alzheimer's establishment of brain pathology as a senile mental disorder, which has since been named Alzheimer's Disease. In the early twentieth century, Wagner-Jauregg inoculated nine paretic patients with malaria and thereby provided a treatment for the disease. Those findings lent strength to an organic interpretation of mental disorders. Kraepelin generalized that point of view by providing a systematic classification of mental disorders which he attributed to a malfunctioning of the brain.

Recognition of the influence of psychological elements in causing mental disorders can be traced to Mesmer, who considered that "magnetic forces" caused mental disorders; James Braid, in examining Mesmer's work, concluded that the influences he described were psychological in nature, largely the result of suggestion provided in a hypnotic-like trance. That finding was elaborated upon by Liebeault, Bernheim and Charcot, who concluded that both hypnosis and the mental disorder then called "hysteria" were caused by suggestion.

Building on those insights, Pierre Janet developed the first psychological theory explaining neurosis. In 1880, Breuer successfully treated hysteria with hypnosis. That early work blazed a path for the profound insights of Sigmund Freud, whose work is described in chapter 3.

Selected Readings

Alexander, F.G. and S.T. Selesnick. 1966. *The History of Psychiatry*. New York: Harper & Row.

Allridge, P. 1970. "Hospitals, Madhouses and Asylums: Cycles in the Care of the Insane." *British Journal of Psychiatry 134, 321-334.*

Beers, C. 1970. *A Mind That Found Itself*. (Rev. ed.) New York: Doubleday.

Bromberg, W. 1937. *The Mind of Man*. New York: Harper & Row.

Campbell, D. 1926. *Arabian Medicine and Its Influence on the Middle Ages*. New York: Dutton.

Deutsch, A. 1949. *The Mentally Ill in America*. 2nd ed. New York: Columbia University Press.

Fine, R. 1979. *A History of Psychoanalysis*. New York: Columbia University Press.

Selling, L.S. 1943. *Men Against Madness*. New York: Garden City Books.

Zilborg, G. and G. W. Henry. 1941. *A History of Medical Psychology*. New York: Norton.

3

Psychodynamic, Humanistic, and Existential Perspectives

Abnormal psychology has moved a great distance from the sometimes primitive interpretations of abnormal behavior offered in past centuries. Its advances have been considerable, even when compared with those of the early years of the twentieth century. Although much scientific work was done earlier, particularly in identifying biological causes of abnormal behavior, dramatic new understandings of abnormal behavior begin with the work of Sigmund Freud. Soon after Freud's work, from a different direction, came the behaviorism of John B. Watson and the influential body of research by B. F. Skinner, which established on a rigid empirical basis the behavioral perspective. Most recent to arrive as explanations of human behavior are the cognitive, humanistic, and existential points of view.

Today the student of abnormal psychology will find broad areas of agreement among psychologists about causation and treatment of abnormal behavior, but the student will also find various schools of psychology that bring different perspectives to their interpretations of abnormal behavior. No doubt, as these schools of thought become, in future decades, a part of the history of psychology, there will evolve a unified understanding of most complexities that still exist in the field.

It is not now possible to find a complete explanation of either the causes of all abnormal behavior or the best means of treatment by viewing human behavior through any one of the human perspectives. For that reason, many clinicians in the field take an eclectic point of view, selecting from each of the schools the insights that increase understanding and promote effective treatment. In this book, we follow their example and have chosen an eclectic perspective.

The existence of differing models for studying and understanding human behavior parallels developments in all sciences. Differing interpretations of phenomena exist, for example, in physics or astronomy, until a brilliant scientific breakthrough develops, out of years of research effort, to provide new insights and to unify thinking. That was Einstein's contribution to physics, and Freud's contribution, in earlier years, to psychology. But even such quantum leaps forward can be subject to revision by later research, as is some of Freud's and Einstein's thinking today.

This chapter examines the psychodynamic perspective traceable to Freud's work in psychoanalysis, but will also consider deviations from it by the neo-Freudians and the humanistic and existential schools. The chapter that follows this one considers the behavioral/cognitive perspectives and the biological perspective.

THE PSYCHODYNAMIC PERSPECTIVE

Although, as chapter 2 suggests, early indications of a psychodynamic approach to abnormal behavior begin to appear in the late nineteenth and early twentieth centuries, the full sweep of the perspective comes out of the clinical practice and writings of Sigmund Freud, whose work began in the latter half of the nineteenth century and ended in 1939. His profound contributions have been extended and modified by early disciples and thereafter by the neo-Freudians and by the ego psychologists.

Basic Concepts of the Psychodynamic Perspective

Key to an understanding of the perspective is an understanding of the word *psychodynamic*. From the dictionary comes this definition: "an emphasis on the interaction of the various psychic or mental forces that influence behavior." Psychoanalysts and other psychodynamic theorists specify that definition to say, "the interactions of the psychic forces and processes developed during childhood that influence adult thinking, motives and behavior."

Almost universally, members of the psychodynamic school identify three basic concepts underlying the psychodynamic perspective: psychic determinism; unconscious motivation; the role of childhood experiences.

PSYCHIC DETERMINISM

Psychodynamic theorists believe that although we have a sense of freely choosing what we will think about, desire and do, much of our behavior, as a matter of fact, is determined for us or at least strongly influenced by earlier life experiences.

UNCONSCIOUS MOTIVATIONS

Motivational forces operate, to a considerable degree, at an unconscious or, at most, preconscious level. The psychodynamic theorists hold that the full basis for significant behavior, especially for motivation, is largely unknown to the affected individual. This belief significantly influences psychotherapeutic techniques, which are discussed in later chapters.

CHILDHOOD EXPERIENCES

The individual is most vulnerable to influences from the environment during the early years of life. For these reasons, most, but not all, psychodynamic thinkers believe that critical dynamic forces influential throughout the lifespan of the individual are developed during the early years of childhood. This principle of the psychodynamic perspective also has an important influence on treatment approaches, especially on psychoanalytically oriented treatment.

Sigmund Freud: Psychoanalytic Theory

Because of the originality of Freud's thinking and his continuing influence on modern psychological thinking and practice, this chapter gives special attention to the details of his psychoanalytic theories.

There are four principal aspects of psychoanalytic theory: the three levels of consciousness; the structural components of the human mind; psychosexual development; the defense mechanisms.

THE THREE LEVELS OF CONSCIOUSNESS

Freud described three levels of consciousness: perceptual consciousness, the preconscious, and the unconscious.

Perceptual Consciousness. At any moment, the individual attends to—that is, is consciously aware of—only a small number of items or events. This awareness Freud called the perceptual consciousness. An example of the perceptual consciousness follows: an individual may be aware of the content of a book he or she is reading, yet hears the phone ring, and perhaps with less sharpness, is aware of the person sitting across the table.

The Preconscious. This level of consciousness comprises those events or facts not in the center of attention, yet readily retrieved from memory: an experience in class yesterday, a forthcoming appointment, luncheon fare two hours ago.

The Unconscious. The largest mass of memory of past experiences, impulses and data lies at the unconscious level. There are two types of unconscious material: the first are those that have been forgotten, for whatever reason; the second those that, because of conflict and the anxiety they produce, are repressed and actively excluded from consciousness. Ordinary forgotten events, such as the exact price paid for last year's textbook or a difficult-to-understand theory in chemistry, gradually fade out of memory and have little subsequent influence on personality. But repressed items live on and show up in a variety of covert ways: dreams, fairly well-disguised fantasies, slips of speech, motivated recall under hypnosis or drugs and, for some people, in a variety of psychological disorders. They are among the most influential forces in mental disorders, according to psychoanalytic theory.

THE STRUCTURAL PROCESS OF THE HUMAN PERSONALITY

The human personality in psychoanalytic theory is structured by three kinds of dynamic and interactive processes. Freud makes clear that they are neither objects or places, but ways in which personality expresses itself. The three are the id, the ego and the superego.

The Id. The word *id* itself comes to us from the original German word, *es,* meaning "it," by way of Latin, which translates "it" as *id*. Formally defined, it is that division or process of the psyche or personality associated with instinctive impulses and demands for immediate satisfaction of primitive and essentially biological needs.

According to Freud, this energy comes from one of two basic instincts within the id, one of which he named *eros*. The energy derived from the eros is *libido*. The other major instinctive force within the id is *thanatos,* or the death instinct, to which Freud and his disciples have attributed only a small role in affecting human behavior.

In the first few week of life, all the organism's activities motivated by the id process, instinctive and biological, seek immediate and uninhibited gratification. As maturing takes place, the libido, the id's source of energy, provides life-furthering power and driving force for later activities that are part of psychological growth and biological survival. The id process operates raw and unrestrained under the demand of the pleasure principle, which seeks immediate gratification of impulses and immediate reduction of tension. A comparison frequently used is that the id behaves like an extremely spoiled child. This primitive irrational process is labelled primary process thinking.

The Ego. Under the influence of the id process, individuals know no limits to what they will do, and thus would eat whatever they please, express aggressions indiscriminately, and find sexual satisfaction without social or moral limitations.

Ego, from the German word *ich,* by way of the Latin word *ego,* means "I." The ego is that part of the self that operates to some extent at a conscious level, most immediately controls behavior, and is most in touch with the real world. The ego allows expression of the id but only in ways that meet the requirements of reality, and thus it operates in accordance with the reality principle.

Freud uses the example of horse and rider to describe the possible interactions between the ego and the id. He puts it in these words: "The horse supplies the locomotive energy, while the rider has the privilege of deciding on the goal and of guiding the powerful animal's movements. But only too often, there arises between the ego and the id the not-precisely-ideal situation of the rider being obliged to guide the horse along the path by which it (the id) itself wants to go."

The ego process can begin to function in this way only when children's maturing reaches the point at which they can use reason to allow thought, memory, evaluation and planning to control behavior. The individual under the influence of the ego process behaves in a way to minimize negative results from the influence of the id. The increasing control of behavior exacted by the ego process is a maturing form of behavior and is called secondary process.

The Superego. The superego loosely resembles the conscience. It comprises values, ethical standards and concepts of what is right and what is wrong, almost all of which have been acquired from parents. The superego is formed out of the child's resolution of the Oedipal or Electra complexes (to be described later).

The superego, like the id, develops with only limited relation to reality. Typically, instead of allowing reality to provide boundaries for its development, it aims for an ego ideal which sets unrealistically high standards for the suppression of id impulses.

With the development of the superego, some time around the age of six or seven, the child's personality expresses itself under the influence of three forces: the id, made up of pleasure-seeking impulses, all unconscious; the ego, the only one of the forces in direct contact with reality; and the superego, the strong voice of conscience.

The ego then works as a kind of gatekeeper in seeking outlets for id impulses that the superego will not taboo.

PSYCHOSEXUAL DEVELOPMENT

Freud divided the child's personality development into five stages: oral, anal, phallic, latency and genital. In each of the first three stages, the pleasure-seeking behavior of the id is associated with an area of the body— the mouth, the anus and the genital region, which have been called erogenous zones. As the child goes through each of these three phases, it faces conflict between personal demands for gratification and the restrictions of reality—for example, the child is asked to give up the nipple or bottle, but still desires its satisfactions; toilet training places limitations on anal satisfactions; during the phallic phase (notice the masculine emphasis Freud gave this naming process), the child is taught that any attention paid to the genital area is "naughty." The latency period is a period of respite, giving the child a time of quiet and freedom from sexual tensions of the earlier periods. How the child resolves the conflicts and frustrations of the early three phases shapes the adult personality, particularly in the psychosexual areas of life.

Freud's use of the words *sex* and *sexual* can lead to misunderstanding of what he meant by the pleasures to which he attaches those words. The words have broad application to any pleasurable psychic feelings, as well as to genital intercourse and fantasies about sex.

The Oral Stage. At birth, the child is equipped to suck the nipple or the bottle reflexively and thus is, from the beginning, naturally equipped to obtain food and find oral pleasure. As the neural system matures, the child is able to do much more with his mouth: mouthing objects, biting, chewing, rolling food around in it. The child soon develops special feelings for a number of objects: a pacifier, a security blanket to suck on or chew, his or her thumb, and many more. The psychologically significant conclusion Freud drew was that experiences with these early oral satisfactions shape later personality traits. For example, a child whose oral needs are not adequately satisfied may turn, later in life, to overeating, heavy smoking, or even alcoholism. Such traits as tenacity, disruptiveness or acquisitiveness, in psychoanalytic thinking, may be shaped by early oral experiences. The first year of life marks off the oral stage.

The Anal Stage. During the second year of life, the child's id strivings for pleasure focus on the anus. All of a sudden, toilet training becomes an important influence of later personality traits. Early in life the child finds pleasure in retaining and expelling the feces and finds pleasure in the reduction of the tensions that accompany bowel movements.

Those representatives of reality, parents, insist on surrounding anal activities with rules. The confrontation is a sharp one, and the frustration imposed, and the resulting testing of will with parents, can be a more disturbing one even than weaning. The discipline of voluntary control of pleasurable impulses is a first-time experience for the two-year-old. How parents approach this training activity will, Freud states, have significant effect on later personality traits. Too strict a regimen, for example, can lead to what has been called the anal personality, characterized by stinginess, obsessiveness and excessive concern with cleanliness. Too little control can lead to tolerance of mess and sloppiness. When such overconcern with the experiences of particular psychosexual phases develops, Freud speaks of the freezing of development, to which has been given the name *fixation*.

The Phallic Stage. During this third phase of the child's psychosexual development, between the third and fifth or sixth year, the child seeks pleasure from stimulation of the genitalia, expressed in much relatively innocent masturbatory behavior. The child is soon again confronted with another first-time demand, that he or she give up pleasures that are not reflexively produced but brought on by voluntary stimulation of the child's own body. This confrontation does much to direct children's attention to their own body. With that focus, self-identity, a sense of independence, and willfulness lead to a kind of narcissistic preoccupation.

The phallic stage is of special importance because during it, the Oedipus complex develops. How children resolve that complex will affect, in significant ways, their sexual adjustment in later life.

The story of King Oedipus, originally a Greek legend, has become a part of the mythology of most countries of the Western world. King Oedipus, after a great struggle, finds that in that struggle he has killed his father and has married the Queen, his mother. Crushed by grief and guilt, Oedipus gouges out his own eyes. Freud uses that metaphor to describe the young boy's psychosexual experiences toward the end of the phallic stage. The metaphor for girls is the Electra complex, the story of a daughter who avenges her father's death by killing her mother and her mother's lover.

Under the influence of the Oedipus complex, the boy in the late years of the phallic stage falls incestuously in love with his mother. The guilt and fear arising out of those impulses generates castration anxiety, a fear that his father will punish him for his forbidden impulses. That anxiety, under normal circumstances, is resolved as the incestuous impulses are repressed and kept unconscious. In accomplishing this, the boy, instead of continuing to fear a war with his father, joins the "enemy" in a process of identification through which the boy internalizes (makes part of himself) the values and sentiments of the father and incorporates them into his own behavior, even to the external mannerisms of his father.

Under the influence of the Electra complex, the girl experiences a similar set of consequences. As she comes to realize that she has been born without a penis, penis envy develops. That envy seems to impel her toward incestuous desires for her father. Freudian psychoanalysts would say her reasoning is that if she cannot have her own penis, she can make up for that loss through possession of her father. Her response to the guilt and fear aroused in her by her forbidden wishes cause her to declare peace with her mother and to identify with her.

The Period of Latency. Once the Oedipus and Electra complexes are resolved at age six or seven, the child's sexual impulses become latent. The libido seems at rest, and the narcissistic preoccupation with self disappears as the child turns to the outside world. During this period, there is time for learning and the acquiring of social and technical skills that serve as steps toward maturity.

The Genital Stage. With the arrival of puberty, the adolescent experiences a new stirring of sexual impulses, but not now directed narcissistically toward his or her own body. The child's interests are now aroused by other people. The child has arrived at the foothills of maturity. Altruistic love and tenderness gradually prepare the individual for mature sexual behavior. Dependence moves toward independent resourcefulness, and the ability to master work skills.

ANXIETY AND THE DEFENSE MECHANISMS

Freud distinguished three kinds of anxiety. Realistic anxiety, which modern psychology calls fear, arises out of the presence of danger in the real world. That danger may result from a physical hazard—for example, military combat or being trapped in a burning building. But it may also be psychological in nature; for example, tensions resulting from real-life frustration or irresolvable conflict. Neurotic anxiety, in Freud's thinking, arises out of concern that unconscious impulses, particularly sexual and aggressive ones, will gain the upper hand in a conflict between the id and the ego. Moral anxiety arises out of concern that behavior will violate one's personal standards or conscience (a conflict between the ego and the superego). The experiences of anxiety (any one of the three types described by Freud) is a disquieting trial, from which the individual attempts to escape, often through the use of defense mechanisms.

Defense mechanisms are the unconscious attempts of individuals to protect themselves from threats to the integrity of the ego or self and also to relieve the tension and anxiety resulting from unresolved frustrations and conflicts. All people employ these self-deceptive measures to some extent, attempting in this way to maintain their self-esteem and soften the impact of failure, deprivation, or sense of guilt. It must not be assumed that defense mechanisms invariably signify abnormal personality structure. Such mechanisms frequently result in gains for the individual using them; their reactions may be a constructive form of adjusting. Excessive dependence on defense mechanisms to block out significant aspects of the individual's personality indicates abnormal modes of adjustment. The principal defense mechanisms are described below.

Compensation. Using this mechanism, individuals devote themselves to a given pursuit with increased vigor in an attempt to make up for some feelings of real or imagined inadequacy. The compensation may be direct or indirect. *Direct compensation* refers to the generation of an intense desire to succeed in an area in which one has experienced failure or inadequacy. The classic example is the effort of Demosthenes to become an outstanding orator because of his early childhood speech disabilities; the very existence of this frustrating handicap provided the motivation to work more intensely to overcome it. *Indirect compensation* consists of the effort to find success in one field when there has been failure in another. This is seen in the vigorous efforts frequently made toward social achievements by students who fail to make their mark in academic circles or on the athletic field. *Overcompensation* is compensatory effort which is made at the expense of a well-rounded and complete adjustment to a variety of life's demands.

Denial. In this mechanism, an individual avoids painful or anxiety-producing reality by unconsciously denying that it exists. The denied reality may be a thought, a wish or a need, or some external object or condition. Denial may take on verbal form in an occasional statement that something is not so or in a compulsively repeated formula which is resorted to as a means of keeping the thought, wish, etc., out of consciousness. In an extreme form, such a denial may result in complete loss of contact with surrounding reality.

Displacement. The mechanism employs a process in which pent-up emotions are redirected toward ideas, objects or persons other than the primary source of the emotion. Displacement may occur with both positive and negative emotions. For example, feelings of love which cannot be expressed openly toward a married member of the opposite sex may be displaced toward a child of that person. Another way in which displacement may be shown is by changing the channel of expression for the emotion; for instance, physical aggression may be inhibited but expressed verbally.

Dissociation. Here is a defense mechanism in which a group of mental associations are separated or isolated from consciousness and operate independently or automatically. The end result may be a splitting of certain mental content from the main personality or a loss of normal thought-affect relationships. Examples are amnesia, development of a multiple personalty (see chapter 9) and somnambulism (sleep-walking).

Fantasy. In this mechanism, daydreaming or some form of imaginative activity provides escape from reality, with satisfaction obtained through imagined achievements or, occasionally, even martyrdom of some sort. A certain amount of daydreaming, especially in the earlier years of life, must be regarded as normal. As a preparation for creativity, fantasy is not only desirable but even essential. But fantasy becomes a dangerous and sometimes disabling mechanism if it is consistently preferred to reality and is indulged in as a method of problem-solving.

Identification. In using this mechanism, the individual enhances his self-esteem (or believes he or she is) by patterning behavior after another person. This may be done in fantasy or in real life. Employed in moderation, identification may be both helpful and stimulating, and it frequently leads to superior achievement. Used to excess, it may deny the individual gratification of his or her own personality needs.

Internalization. Those who employ this mechanism take into their own psychological makeup the values, beliefs or ways of thinking of another person, frequently a parent or other admired figure.

Projection. Individuals using this mechanism protect themselves from awareness of their own undesirable traits or feelings by attributing them to others. In its function of self-deception, this mechanism is particularly harmful to healthy personality development since it blocks self-insight.

Rationalization. This is a common mechanism in which individuals justify inconsistent or undesirable behavior, beliefs or motivations by providing acceptable explanations for them. A "sour grapes" reaction, in which one denies wanting what one has failed to obtain, is a common example.

Reaction Formation. This is a mechanism in which impulses that are not acceptable to consciousness are repressed (kept unconscious) and, in their stead, opposite attitudes or modes of behavior are expressed with considerable intensity. For example, overprotestations of sincerity or of willingness to help may often mean the very opposite. Scrupulosity (overconcern about the morality of one's behavior) may stem from unacceptable desires.

Regression. Confronted by anxiety, threat or frustration, an individual retreats to an earlier and psychologically more comforting level of adjustment. Mild regression is seen in the return of an older child to babyish mannerisms upon the birth of a sibling. The infantile behavior of some psychotics (see chapter 13) is an expression of extreme regression.

Repression. Here the individual prevents dangerous or intolerably painful or guilt-producing thoughts or impulses from entering consciousness. Repression is essential for the existence and operation of all the other defense mechanisms. It should be distinguished from *suppression,* which is the conscious control of unacceptable impulses, feelings and experiences.

Sublimation. Here unconscious and unacceptable desires are channeled into activities that have strong social approval. The unacceptable desires, in Freudian theory, are sometimes sexual in nature, and their expression may be sublimated as creative effort in music, art and literature. Other areas of life that provide avenues for sublimation are social welfare, teaching and the religious life.

Undoing. In this defense mechanism, individuals symbolically act out in reverse (usually repetitiously) something they have done or thought which is unacceptable to them. Through this behavior, they strive to erase the offending act or thought and with it the accompanying sense of guilt or anxiety.

BREAKDOWN IN DEFENSES

The function of a defense mechanism is to maintain the integrity of the ego and thus to keep the individual in a state of psychological equilibrium. When the stress is too great for the personality to resist, defenses are weakened, and the personality begins to disintegrate. This process is called *decompensation*. In decompensation, individuals may at first attempt to use other measures. They may, for example, pass from superficial rationalization to severe projection. The decompensation may produce a panic state of anxiety as the individual is confronted with the breakthrough of unconscious material. From a psychological point of view, the final stages of decompensation for some individuals may be florid psychotic reactions.

OVERVIEW OF FREUDIAN CONCEPTS

Because Freud's work created a major scientific breakthrough in our understanding of both normal and abnormal behavior, and because it continues to provide the framework for psychodynamic thinking, this chapter has presented Freud's thinking in detail. After a brief critique of Freudian concepts, the chapter continues with his description of normal and abnormal adjustment.

Limitations of Freud's Work

Freud's development of psychoanalytic theory suffers two critical limitations. In the first place, the structure he outlined, the developmental states described, and the conflicts experienced are largely unverifiable—a criterion for all scientific work. Beyond that, modern study disputes many of Freud's statements about infancy and childhood.

Secondly, Freud's professional experience was severely limited in the kinds of contacts he had with human behavior. Except for his own family experiences, he spent no time studying the behavior of infants or children. Even his clinical practice was limited to the kind of clients he had opportunity to study. They were principally upper-class men and women in early and middle age and were all drawn from the highly-stylized Viennese culture. Both limitations narrowed his views as to the nature of all the influences operating on the human being's psychological development. As a result, later psychoanalysts and others with a psychodynamic point of view have modified significantly his theories about human development.

The Freudian Concept of Normal Development

Freud taught that both normal and abnormal individuals were subject to irrational forces. The personalities of both normal and abnormal individuals are formed, according to Freud, out of childhood experiences occurring before the age of six. They differ only in the nature of those experiences and in the effect they have had on the formation of personality.

The essential distinction between normal and abnormal for Freud was in the balance achieved by normal individuals in the influence of id, ego and superego. There is, in the normal individual, greater strength in the gatekeeping function of the ego.

The Freudian Concept of Abnormal Development

For Freud, the neurotic individual (now called anxiety-based disorder; see chapter 8) is one in whom spells of overwhelming anxiety have created the need to become overdependent on personality-warping defense mechanisms. Damaging early childhood experiences are the source of the anxiety. The result is severe impairment in functioning and the development of severely uncomfortable symptoms.

Psychosis (described fully in later chapters) develops from a severe weakening of the ego, either from extreme underdevelopment in early life or from later life experiences. The result is a breakdown of the personality's defense system, with resultant overpowering anxiety as id forces become dominant. Associated with this development is loss of orientation, incoherence of speech, and delusions and hallucinations in which voices are heard issuing destructive demands.

EARLY DISSONANT VOICES

Although Freud's original concepts evoked doubt or strong opposition from contemporaries, his work also attracted a number of brilliant and influential students, two of the foremost of whom were Carl Jung and Alfred Adler. In later years, other clinicians with an initial Freudian perspective made their own powerful contributions to ways of thinking about human development, all of them markedly different from Freud's. This chapter examines briefly the contributions of the two most influential of Freud's students, Jung and Adler, then the contributions of Harry Stack Sullivan, Karen Horney, Erik Erikson and Margaret Mahler.

Carl Gustav Jung (1875–1961)

Among the voices dissonant from Freud's, Carl Jung stands alone because, although accepting the Freudian unconscious, he added to it the existence of a collective unconscious. It comprises a variety of archetypes, or universal ideas, with which we are born. The child does not have to learn fears of darkness, fire or death, for example; he is born with those predispositions. Jung moved away from the concept of libido with its emphasis on sexual energy and hypothesized the existence of a spiritual instinct. He gave much more emphasis than did Freud to the importance of religion, mythology, mysticism and the occult.

Alfred Adler (1870–1939)

Adler departed from orthodox Freudian teaching in three important directions. He disagreed with what he felt was Freud's undue emphasis on the libido or sexual drive and substituted for it an aggressive drive for dominance. He also placed much less emphasis on early childhood experiences, believing instead that psychological difficulties had their roots in the immediate social context surrounding the individual. And finally, Adler assigned a social responsibility to the individual. To attain maturity, the individual must, Adler taught, give up his self-absorbed power struggle and focus on service to others. In moving away from the biological emphasis of Freud, Adler accented the importance of self and gave it a creative function which enabled the individual to work out his lifestyle.

In popular thinking, Adler is perhaps best known for his concept of the inferiority complex, a feeling of inadequacy which stirs up compensatory strivings for power and dominance.

LATER MODIFICATIONS OF FREUDIAN VIEWS

Four clinicians independent of Freud but psychoanalytically trained suggested further modifications in orthodox Freudian thinking. They are Karen Horney, Harry Stack Sullivan, Erik Erikson and Margaret Mahler.

Karen Horney (1885–1952)

In her influential book, *The Neurotic Personality of Our Time,* Horney presented what was perhaps her most significant modification of Freudian theory. Here she presented the case that neurosis was a response to the values of industrial society, which pressed for competition and materialism, leaving the individual with anxieties about aggression and an overweening interest in seeking affection, but an incompatible inability to express affection.

Behind this proposition there was her understanding of the nature of neurosis, which was, for her, a disturbance in human relationships, expressing itself in basic anxiety, the result of having to face a hostile world. Its cause lay in bad parenting, whether too strict or too indulgent, negligent or too concerned, and led to neurotic strategies of adjustment, such as helplessness, hostility or isolation.

Harry Stack Sullivan (1892–1949)

Sullivan's contributions to the newly developing psychodynamic/psychoanalytic perspective were twofold: the importance he assigned to the self concept, and his willingness to use psychoanalytic therapy in the treatment of psychotics, an approach that Freud considered of little value. Sullivan believed that personality could not develop apart from the social context in which it operated and is perceived. He defined psychological disorders as those that occurred in social relationships. The self concept, he stated, evolves principally out of the appraisal of the self by others. When those appraisals are hostile, the individual blocks them out of consciousness by denial. When this warping of reality in the self concept becomes extreme, Sullivan believed, psychological disturbance, neurosis or psychosis result.

Sullivan was the first analyst to use psychoanalysis successfully with psychotic individuals. Much of that success came less from the theory behind it than from the non-confrontational, warm and supportive approach Sullivan took to those he treated. Sullivan's style in therapy has become a part of the modern psychodynamic perspective.

Erik Erikson (1902–1990)

Erikson brought to psychoanalysis a strong anthropological orientation, which gave his concepts a heavily social emphasis and also a more hopeful point of view than Freud's. He saw personality development as taking place over eight stages. At each stage, there was a challenge to be faced, largely psychological in nature. As individuals face each challenge successfully, they work out what Erikson called their ego identity, an integrated, unique and autonomous sense of selfhood. Each stage offers the individual a chance to eradicate earlier damaging experiences. Personality formation does not end with childhood, but continues on through the adult years. In influencing personality, Erikson added the influence of teachers, advisers, friends and others to that of parents.

Margaret Mahler (1897–1985)

Mahler offered major changes in Freud's theories that have significantly affected the psychodynamic way of thinking about human behavior. A major contribution was her development of the theory of object relations, objects here meaning persons to whom the individual becomes emotionally attached, principally the child's caretaker, usually the mother. Mahler describes the movement toward psychological maturity and the formation of the awareness of self as a process of separation (that is, from the mother) and individuation (that is, in the child's independent development). That process comprises a series of stages of the child's experience in mother/child relationships. Gradually, as children first experience separateness from mother, the changing ups and downs in that relationship conclude as they internalize (make part of themselves) the image of the mother. This step, object constancy (as she calls it), finally stabilizes the relationship. Any tendency on the mother's part to rush or delay the natural process of separation causes problems in personality development.

AN OVERVIEW OF THE PSYCHODYNAMIC PERSPECTIVE

As the individual theorists whose contributions we have just described, beginning with the concepts of Jung, moved further and further away from the emphasis of Freud, the importance of interpersonal relationships has become a central feature of the psychodynamic perspective. For the student desirous of understanding the modern psychodynamic interpretation of abnormal behavior, a good summary statement is the following:

> Abnormal behavior can best be understood by studying the individual's past and present relationships with other people. Begin by assigning principal weight to the child's interpersonal relations with parents, and then continue on through the life of the person's interpersonal relations with siblings, grandparents, teachers, early and current friends. It is that set of relationships that offers the best understanding of his or her personality and any pathology that may be present.

HUMANISTIC AND EXISTENTIAL PERSPECTIVES

With theoretical roots extending, for the humanistic group, back to William James (1842–1910), Gordon Allport (1897–1967) and Gardiner Murphy (1895–1979), and for the existential school, back to nineteenth century philosophers Soren Kierkegaard (1813–1855) and Martin Heidegger (1889–1976), and with only slight connections to psychoanalytic ways of thinking about human behavior, two separate groups of theorists, working individually, have developed ways of looking at the human personality, normal and abnormal, that can conveniently be discussed under the headings, The Humanistic Approach and The Existential Approach.

The humanistic approach is best represented by Abraham Maslow (1908–1970) and Carl Rogers (1902–1987). The existential perspective can be described in the formulation of Rollo May (born 1905). Both schools, humanism in America and existentialism in Europe, grew out of major social changes that seemed to dehumanize humankind (the technological society) and to devalue human life (the million-person slaughter of World War I). Both trends seemed to these theorists only to be growing in strength with Hitler, Stalin, World War II, and nuclear bombs. The emphasis of the humanistic perspective is to reestablish a belief in the basic strength of the human psyche, its goodness and great potential for growth; the concepts emphasized by existentialists are choice, the search for meaning, authenticity and social obligation. Existentialists identify, as a central anxiety-producing problem for humanity, the nothingness and non-being which death brings to everyone.

The Humanistic Perspective

The two outstanding proponents of a humanistic way of thinking about human adjustment efforts, Abraham Maslow and Carl Rogers, made the main focus of their perspective a principal concern not about pathology but about helping the average individual to move from being merely normal and mediocre toward full self-actualization.

ABRAHAM MASLOW

Maslow, working independently of Rogers, described in his hierarchy of human needs the aspirations humanistic psychology holds out for the developing individual. That hierarchy served, so to speak, as a map, providing guidance on the path to maturity.

The individual's life in Maslow's hierarchy is a progression from the lowest, yet fundamental, needs—physiological and safety—through the psychological needs of self-esteem and love/belongingness to the highest achievement of self-actualization. Each level of need must be met before the individual moves to the next highest. Environmental influences, especially within the family, that block this progress—for example, neglect, rejection, oversolicitousness or authoritarianism—are the negative forces that individuals must be helped to understand and to overcome in order for them to move toward self-actualization. That form of becoming is a continuing process through the life of the individual. Its strands are fulfillment of mission, a deeper understanding of capacities and personality, and a more fully integrated unity of personality.

CARL ROGERS

Rogers developed an almost revolutionary new form of psychotherapy, which he described in his book, *Client Centered Therapy,* published in 1951. The theory of personality development, which he later theorized, was fully described in his 1966 publication, *On Becoming a Person.* Rogers places the self concept at the center of personality. Through this concept, the individual organizes the world, decides what is good or bad for growth, and moves toward self-actualization in terms dictated by the self. Whether or not the individual accepts this valuing process is a result of the interaction of the organism (the sum total of the individual's perceptions of the world) and the self-awareness of one's own identity. When the two begin to come together, the individual moves toward self-actualization.

To have this happen requires that the individual, in the developing years, experience positive regard. Life sets conditions on what forms of behavior will be well regarded. In a happy environment, the child incorporates these into the self as conditions of worth. When those conditions are extreme or overdemanding, individuals redefine themselves to exclude any behavior or desire tabooed by the conditions set. The individual is thus prevented from being a fully-rounded, wholesome person. Taught by parents to be docile and sweet at all costs, a person may never be able to feel the anger that can be a normal human outlet. Anxiety is aroused by the unconscious tensions created by that abnormal inhibition. The individual resorts to defensive behavior, the process of self-actualization is stopped, and symptoms of abnormal behavior develop.

It is the nature of client-centered therapy to remove this blockage through the individual's own efforts by surrounding the client in therapy with warmth and unconditional expressions of regard, in the course of which the therapist reflects back acceptingly the feelings expressed by the client. In this way, the need for thwarting defensive behavior is reduced, and the person can move toward integrating the organism's perceptions and those of the self and thus be freed to move toward self-actualization.

The Existential Perspective

Although the vocabulary used by Rogers and that found among existentialists is notably different, the processes they describe leading to healthy growth instead of pathology and unhappiness have certain striking similarities. Rogers identified the organism and the self; the existentialists speak of "existence," which is the given, the world in which the individual finds himself or herself, and the "essence," what the individual makes of that world by the choices he or she makes. The latter point is succinctly made by Sartre: "I am my choices." Both schools place responsibility for fulfillment and happiness on the individual, but also credit him or her with the strength to assume that responsibility. In making choices, the individual is driven by the need to find meaning and value in life. Rollo May describes it as the person's effort to provide a stable foundation on which the center of existence can be preserved. Not inconsistent with Roger's understanding of maladjustment is May's contention that in the face of internal or external threats, essentially anxiety, individuals shrink the world that they admit into existence. May states: "That shrinking is a way of accepting non-being in order that some little being may be preserved." The goal in existential therapy is to help individuals to find a way of accepting a fuller world that is uniquely theirs, with the responsibility and loneliness that goes with it.

There is a pessimistic tone in the philosophy of existentialism: feelings of alienation or spiritual death, brought on by a vast amoral and technological society that seems to have no place for the individual. The point of living on, existentialists say, is to combat the anxiety of existence in such a world, with the feelings of nothingness it creates, by directing our choices to give significance to our lives. One way of doing so is to recognize our social obligations in an indifferent world.

Although they express their positions in differing words, adherence of the three perspectives described in this chapter—psychodynamic, humanistic and existential—agree on basic propositions: Human motivations have unconscious roots; a significant difference between unconscious motivations and what the individual believes motivates behavior will cause maladaptive behavior; the struggle between unconscious motives and controls that the individual imposes on behavior causes anxiety which the individual protests against through defensive behavior, which often constitutes the substance of the abnormal individual's disorder. Impulses and feelings that the individual cannot accept are repressed (in the psychodynamic perspective) or screened out (in the humanistic and existential perspectives). An overarching similarity among the three perspectives is recognition of the complexities produced in the individual's behavior by the dynamic interaction among opposing forces operating within the individual's psyche (the individual's functioning mind).

The psychodynamic perspective stemming from the early work of Freud, but much modified by those who came after him, has, as its central theme, the significance of unconscious conflicts originating in childhood. It sees abnormal behavior as the development of maladaptive symptoms unconsciously used by the individual as defense against the intolerable anxieties aroused by the childhood conflicts, the influence of which persists into later life. In orthodox Freudian theory, those conflicts grow out of a tension between biologically-based psychosexual impulses, the pleasurable expression of which are inhibited by limitations set by reality.

Adherents of psychodynamic deviations from Freud substantial enough to be thought of as a different perspective moved away from his biological orientation and gave less weight to the id and more significance to the ego or self. They all but dismissed the significance of early psychosexual development and focused on the broader concepts of interpersonal relations. They considered important not only interpersonal tensions of early life, but characteristics of the individual's present life. The anxiety at the root of abnormal behavior was considered traceable not only to psychosexual conflict but also to conflicts about aggressive behavior, feelings of inadequacy, and the difficulty of establishing satisfying interpersonal relations. Room is made for the pressures on the individual from the society itself.

The humanistic and existential perspectives developed separately and outside of mainstream psychoanalytic thinking. Both give heavy emphasis to the individual's own responsibility for self-fulfillment and assign, as a principal cause of abnormal behavior, the failure to accept oneself, which failure interferes in the humanistic perspective with self-actualizing efforts, and in the existential perspective with failure to develop authenticity, which is a way of living one's full personality.

Selected Readings

Becker, Ernest. 1969. *Angel in Armor; A Post-Freudian Perspective on the Nature of Man*. New York: G. Braziller.

Fromm, Erich. 1970. *The Crisis of Psychoanalysis* (1st ed.). New York: Holt, Reinhart, Winston.

Gay, Peter. 1986. *The Bourgeois Experience: Victoria to Freud*. Oxford University Press.

Martin, Jay. 1988. *Who Am I This Time: Uncovering the Fictive Personality*. New York: Norton.

Maslow, A.H. 1971. *Farther Reaches of Human Nature*. Escalem Institute Book Publishing Program, New York: Viking Press.

May, R., E. Angel, and H.S. Ellenberger. (Eds.). 1958. *Existence: A New Dimension in Psychiatry and Psychology*. New York: Basic Books.

Rogers, Carl R. 1989. *Carl Rogers: Dialogue, Conversations with Martin Buber, Paul Tillich, B.F. Skinner, Gregory Bateson, Michael Polanyi, Rollo May and Others*. Boston, MA: Houghton-Mifflin.

Van Herck, Judith. 1982. *Freudian Femininity and Faith*. Berkeley: University of California Press.

4

Behavioral, Cognitive, Biogenic, and Sociocultural Perspectives

A series of conditioning experiments by the Russian physiologist, Ivan Pavlov (1849–1936), provided John B. Watson (1878–1958) in the 1920s with the basis for the first major statement of behaviorism: Psychology is a purely objective, experimental science that needs introspection as little as do chemistry and physics. Watson was able to give scientific strength to his statement by demonstrating that a highly subjective human experience, fear, could be produced by the objective, measurable process of conditioning. Watson's campaign to establish behaviorism as the only scientific method of psychology was directed primarily against psychologists who were using introspection to identify mental states as a source of particular human reactions. Some of his criticisms brushed off on the methods of psychoanalysis.

Pavlov and Watson were interested in the causal effect of what preceded a response. Edward Lee Thorndike (1874–1949), in his animal studies, instead asked a reverse kind of question: What are the effects of what follows a response on the likelihood of its reoccurrence? He expressed his findings as the Law of Effect, which states simply that rewarded responses are strengthened, and unrewarded responses are weakened. B.F. Skinner (1940–1990), in years of carefully quantified research, refined Thorndike's Law of Effect and renamed it the Principle of Reinforcement.

In turn, the exclusively stimulus-response framework of behaviorism and reinforcement theory aroused the opposition of a group of psychologists, who contended that what effect a stimulus-response connection produced was dependent upon the mediation between stimulus and response of mental events or cognitions. They stated that, for example, thoughts or expectations, which themselves had been learned from past experiences, gave interpretation or meaning both to the stimulus and the response. For cognitive psychologists, it is the subjective meaning given to external events and their consequences that shape the influence of both the stimulus and the response.

Chapter 4 first describes respondent or classical conditioning and then operant conditioning, two of the principal ways through which behavior is changed or learned. Both respondent and operant conditioning function through the mediating influence of cognitive activities. The details of that mediating effect make up the cognitive perspective on human behavior. The chapter then goes on to discuss the two remaining perspectives: the biogenic perspective, which uses a medical model to examine abnormal behavior; and finally, the sociocultural perspective, the most recently developed perspective, drawn largely from sociology and anthropology.

THE BEHAVIORAL PERSPECTIVE

Behaviorists trace all human behavior to a limited number of biological drives (hunger is one) which are extended through subsequent conditioning experiences. Both respondent conditioning and operant conditioning are easiest understood through the experiments of Pavlov for respondent conditioning and Skinner for operant conditioning.

Respondent (Classical) Conditioning

In the latter part of the nineteenth century, Pavlov published the first account of respondent conditioning. His work earned him the Nobel prize. It was to have a dramatic effect on developments in the then-young science of psychology. As with many great scientific discoveries, Pavlov's work began with his scientific curiosity about a casual observation. He had noticed that when he merely walked into the room to feed a laboratory dog, the animal began to salivate. For Pavlov, this signaled that the animal had come to attach a reflex action, salivation, previously triggered only by taking food into its mouth, to a neurologically unrelated stimulus, his presence.

Fascinated by this observation, Pavlov then conducted a series of experiments that provided the first scientific basis for the behavioristic perspective.

PAVLOV'S EXPERIMENT

What Pavlov called the *conditioned stimulus (CS)*,—a tone—was sounded just prior to the animal's feeding. Food, the *unconditioned stimulus (US)*, elicited a flow of saliva, the *unconditioned response (UR)*. After several repetitions of that sequence, the animal had "learned" to connect the tone (the conditioned stimulus) to the now-*conditioned response (CR)*. Respondent conditioning can be diagrammed simply, as follows:

> Food (US) Saliva (UR)
>
> Tone (CS) Food (US) Saliva (UR)

repeated several times, which soon led to:

> Tone (CS) Saliva (CR)

SIGNIFICANCE OF PAVLOV'S EXPERIMENT

Such pairings as those illustrated by Pavlov's experiment are common human experiences. Responses, particularly autonomic responses, including those related to such emotional experiences as fear and anxiety (for example, rapid heartbeat and increased perspiration) can be readily conditioned. The behavioral perspective emphasizes the possibility that fears and anxiety may be initially brought about by such conditioning experiences. In the behavioral perspective, many disordered emotional responses, such as irrational fears (phobias), can be cured by reversing the process of respondent conditioning (see chapter 7).

The importance of respondent conditioning, in the view of the behaviorists, is that all emotions, preferences and even values in later life develop from conditioning of the Pavlovian type; that is, the associating of a neutral stimulus with an emotion being felt by the individual. In time, with a sufficient number of those couplings, or even with one coupling when the emotion, for example, is an intense one, the now-conditioned stimulus develops the power to elicit the emotional response. For example, if a person were mugged and physically assaulted on Avenue X, the next time he or she walked through that street the emotion experienced in the attack would again be experienced, perhaps less intensely. In this way, respondent conditioning produces a broad range of both pleasant and distressing emotional experiences. The latter, if intense, can be the source of phobias or anxiety attacks. With this possibility in mind, behaviorists have developed a number of treatment techniques to promote the extinction of abnormal emotional reactions.

BASIC PRINCIPLES OF RESPONDENT CONDITIONING

Two of the simplest principles operating in respondent conditioning were identified by Pavlov in his experiments.

Acquisitions. The first is acquisition of a response. Acquisition is the learning of a response based on the contingency (the timed togetherness) between a conditioned stimulus and an unconditioned stimulus; for example, the sequence of tone and food in Pavlov's experiment. Experience teaches that it usually takes from three to four pairings to acquire a conditioned response.

Extinction. A second principle is extinction, which is the loss of the conditioned stimulus's potential for eliciting the previously conditioned response. Extinction is produced by presenting the conditioned stimulus—in Pavlov's experiment, the tone—but no longer following it with the food, the unconditioned stimulus. The length of time required for extinction varies with the strength of the original conditioning experience.

Stimulus Generalization. There are two other principles operating in respondent conditioning, which were identified in work following Pavlov's original experiments. The first is stimulus generalization: Once an individual has been conditioned to one stimulus, the person may make the same response to other similar stimuli. For example, a child who, in a frightening experience, has learned to fear dogs, may come to fear other animals; or, in the behavioral perspective, a child who has been conditioned to respond with hostility to a parent may show less intense but nevertheless noticeable hostility to other people of the same sex.

Stimulus Discrimination. The remaining principle, stimulus discrimination, is almost the reverse of generalization; that is, through a proper sequence of stimuli, a person can be taught to discriminate, for example, between two quite similar tones. This will take place when a person experiences an electric shock following a high-pitched sound, but no shock when hearing a sound lower in pitch.

Operant Conditioning

Following the lead of Thorndike, Skinner initiated a lifelong research effort to study the principles governing the effect on future behavior of what follows a particular response. Those principles he named operant conditioning.

SIGNIFICANCE OF OPERANT CONDITIONING

Behaviorists hold that it is through operant conditioning, as a result of reinforcement following specific responses, that children acquire skills such as walking, reading and craft or athletic competencies and learn ways of behaving to satisfy their needs, both to gain what they consider desirable and to avoid what they consider undesirable.

It is the combination of respondent and operant conditioning that fleshes out the individual's efforts to adjust to life circumstances: respondent conditioning influencing preferences and creating needs; operant conditioning influencing the way an individual goes about satisfying them.

BASIC PRINCIPLES OF OPERANT CONDITIONING

The basic elements in the Skinnerian form of conditioning are operants (responses) that can be strengthened by positive reinforcement (a reward) or weakened by negative reinforcement. Negative reinforcement must be distinguished from punishment. A negative reinforcer is an aversive experience (in animal research, an electric shock is an example), the removal of which, by some action of the individual, increases the likelihood of that behavior's reoccurrence. Punishment is an aversive event (being sent to one's room) produced by an action of the individual; it may have an effect on the behavior that caused the punishment, but the effect is unpredictable. For example, the punished behavior may persist, but in covert fashion to escape punishment; or the punished behavior may be displaced by even more unacceptable behavior. A punishment may act as a negative reinforcer when the punishment is removed. For example, a child may be sent to his or her room for unruly behavior. Once in the room, the child picks up a book and reads quietly. When the mother comes upstairs to invite the child to rejoin the family, the act of reading is reinforced, and the probability of its reoccurrence is increased.

Acquisition and Extinction. Acquisition and extinction are produced differently in operant conditioning from the way they are in respondent conditioning. A response in operant conditioning is acquired when it is followed by a positive reinforcer a number of times. Extinction occurs when the response is unreinforced over a period of time. The time it takes to extinguish a response will vary with the schedule of reinforcement.

Schedules of Reinforcement. Skinner's research has revealed an extremely important (Skinner says it is the most important) aspect of operant conditioning, the scheduling of reinforcement. There are two types of reinforcement: continuous reinforcement, in which every response is reinforced, and partial reinforcement. Continuous reinforcement promotes rapid learning, but it allows rapid extinction once the response is no longer reinforced. In partial reinforcement, the aftereffect may be provided randomly or, for example, every fifth, sixth, tenth, etc., time.

Partial reinforcement causes two significant differences in the way learning occurs: it takes longer for a response to be learned, but once learned, it is more difficult to extinguish. Some troublesome symptoms of abnormal behavior—for example, addictive gambling—persist long after a partial pattern of reinforcement has ended.

Shaping. A significant process in operant conditioning, one that is especially valuable in treatment, is shaping. The shaping process can be compared with the children's game of "you're getting warmer," a comment which serves to guide the child to the hidden object. In operant conditioning, when the goal is to teach a complex response, any response the individual makes in the direction of the complex response, even though a meager one, is reinforced. An example is one of Skinner's early studies. His goal was to teach a pigeon to peck at the center of a target hung on an interior side of its cage. The sequence of reinforcement was as follows: any movement toward the correct side of the cage (in the children's game, equivalent to the comment, "You're getting warmer."), then any movement toward the target, then any pecking behavior in the direction of the target, then any pecking behavior directly on target. To encourage the pigeon to continue to move toward the goal, any approaching-response was reinforced only until a response more directly at the target occurred. That response was then reinforced. This process of shaping, which has been used to teach animals extremely complex skills, also is useful in teaching skills to human beings, especially children.

Modeling

A widely influential form of learning, modeling, is subsumed under the rubric of behavioristically viewed learning. Children soon learn to imitate the behavior of parents and, later in life, of other admired persons. Positive attitudes and emotional feelings toward parents develop, in the first instance, as a result of respondent conditioning. Early in the life of the infant, the image of Mother precedes the receiving of food, which is accompanied by the relief of hunger tensions. Repetition of that sequence soon allows only the image of Mother to produce a pleasant feeling. Once that loving attitude toward Mother (and later, toward Father) exists, operant conditioning takes over. As a parent expresses approval of a child's modeling efforts, those efforts are reinforced, and the probability of their reoccurrence is increased. In time, only a child's awareness that it has successfully modeled a parent's behavior or that of another admired person is reinforcement enough to cause the behavior to persist.

THE COGNITIVE PERSPECTIVE

Discontented with what they considered the simplistic SR stimulus-response explanation of human behavior, cognitive psychologists have done much to reestablish a place for the organism. Their research has indicated that memories, beliefs and expectations (characteristics of the organism, the individual) serve as a mediating influence between stimulus and response, and influence the kind of connection the individual will make to the stimulus. Cognitive psychologists write the old formula as follows: stimulus-organism-response (SOR).

In the cognitive perspective, there are four overlapping interpretations of how cognitive elements influence an individual's behavior. Categorized by the principal author of the concept, they are as follows.

Bandura: Expectations

For Albert Bandura (as he indicates in research published in 1977 and 1982), the important cognitive influence on behavior is the individual's expectations, which may be thought of as beliefs or hopes of what a particular response will bring. Bandura divides expectations into two types: outcome expectations, expectancies that a given response will lead to a certain outcome; and efficiency expectations, expectancies that one will be able to carry out the response effectively. Such expectations are, of course, the product of earlier experiences, including those of childhood.

Atkinson: Decision Theory

John W. Atkinson, a decision theorist, presents his point of view by asking how an individual will make a decision to do anything, to make any response. Faced with a situation requiring a decision, before taking action, Atkinson states, the individual will consider two elements. One he calls utility or subjective value to be gained by taking the action. The second is the probability of the individual's capacity to be successful in carrying out the action. Those are essentially the elements of Bandura's thesis, but Atkinson uses the language of decision theory.

The cognitive elements identified are no doubt shaped or at least influenced by the basic processes of conditioning, respondent and operant, which have occurred during the early childhood years and as a result of later experiences, especially those of an interpersonal nature, elements that are an important consideration in the psychodynamic perspective. To put it differently, the strict behavioristic and the cognitive perspective must be taken into account in understanding an individual's behavior. And both, some psychologists would say, have to be fitted into the psychodynamic perspective.

Mischel: Five Cognitive Variables

According to Walter Mischel, a cognitive psychologist, there are five variables that influence an individual's response to a stimulus: competencies, encodings, expectancies, values and plans. (Mischel, 1973, 1979)

COMPETENCIES

The individual acquires a number of skills through past learning, technical skills and social skills. The level of those skills will help determine the individual's response in a particular situation. Suppose a colleague, in a public situation, responds to one's statement by saying, "No, you're absolutely wrong there." If an individual has developed the trait of assertiveness, that individual will respond in one way; if not, in a quite different way.

ENCODINGS

All human beings perceive and categorize experiences in a particular way, perhaps even uniquely. The categories they create cause them to sort new experiences into one or another of those categories. An individual's response reflects the category into which he or she has sorted the situation. Political categories, for example, are an important source of encoding. How an individual responds to a Republican president's budget proposal will be significantly affected by that individual's party membership—Republican or Democratic—and also by the significance of political values in his or her thinking.

EXPECTANCIES

Here Mischel joins Bandura. Previous experience teaches us all to expect (hope, fear) certain outcomes from particular types of behavior. Those expectations influence significantly how an individual will respond.

VALUES

Very early in life, individuals learn to prize or value certain social, religious and artistic causes or points of view. Modernists in art would respond one way to a friend's invitation to visit a Rembrandt exhibition and quite a different way to an invitation to the Museum of Modern Art. On the other hand, the value they assign to friendship might cause them to accept either invitation.

PLANS

Most individuals start each day with some plan as to how they will spend it, detailed and formal or loose. The plan decided upon will influence their decision to enter into situation A or situation B. The decision will hinge, no doubt, on how much either will disrupt their plans. Plans can also be made as to how we intend to spend the next few years of our life; for example, to complete a law degree. Unless a proposed alternative is very attractive indeed, long-term plans will determine our response.

Attribution of Causality

The individual's thoughts about what causes the things that happen—that is, to what he attributes causality—will also influence behavior. Julius B. Rotter's theory of internal or external control (1973) provides a good example. People's beliefs in either can be measured on the Rotter Scale and be placed on a continuum that extends from beliefs that nothing they do counts (external control) to a conviction that they are master of their own fate, and that what they do counts a great deal (internal control). Given an opportunity to work hard for a promotion, it is easy to guess how those two different beliefs will influence behavior. Another major type of attribution is either the conviction that the world and its people are hostile, or that, in general, they are neutral or even benign. Behavior in a wide array of situations will vary accordingly. Early life experiences do much to shape the nature of one's beliefs about why things happen, good things and bad things.

THE BIOGENIC PERSPECTIVE

The most extreme form of the biogenic perspective expresses the belief that all, or at least most, abnormal behavior can be traced to organic (biophysical) factors, usually affecting the brain in one way or another. Some professionals in the medical field, physicians and medical researchers, accept this position. Most, however, accept a modified view of that position, believing that biochemical processes in the brain are at the root of some, but not all, mental illnesses. Biochemical balance, they would say, is disrupted (for whatever reason), and it is that imbalance that creates the necessary condition or predisposition for the development of psychopathology. An unanswered question is this: In which direction does the causality flow? Is abnormal behavior initiated by the prior occurrence of a biophysiological imbalance? Or do the emotions and tensions associated with abnormal behavior stir up the biochemical imbalance?

Aside from the broad implications of the biogenic perspective, it is certainly true that brain damage or malfunction can produce psychic changes and that a limited number of mental disorders and developmental aberrations directly result from biogenic causes, most of them very specific. Support is given for some version of the biogenic perspective by the increasingly successful use of a variety of pharmaceutical drugs in the treatment of certain mental disorders.

The Medical Model

An aspect of the biogenic perspective is the emphasis given to the medical model for studying mental illness. Possible causes of mental illness considered by those of the biogenic view are infection, genetics, chemical imbalance and neuroanatomy. Medical researchers, physicians and other scientists with a biogenic orientation approach the understanding of illness in a relatively standard fashion.

There is, first of all, the creation of a syndrome, a collection of diverse symptoms which seem to occur in the patient at the same time. Once the syndrome has been identified and its symptoms described in detail, the search for causes is begun, the etiological phase. Here, as has been previously indicated, four sources of hypotheses for the cause of the illness are considered: infection, genetics, chemical imbalance and neuroanatomy. Once etiology has been established, the next step is either to attempt to find ways of preventing the illness, which in modern medicine is a first priority, especially in illnesses deemed to be untreatable, or to search out methods of treatment for those who already suffer the illness. That approach, with appropriate adaptations for mental illnesses, is taken by those with the biogenic perspective. The medical model also sets a pattern for nonmedical professionals, principally psychologists, in their studies of mental illness, even though they may bring a different perspective to the problem.

INFECTION AS A CAUSE OF MENTAL ILLNESS

The first mental illness to be associated with infection was paresis, now recognized as the result of long-term infection by the syphilis spirochete. The syndrome-establishing phase was initiated in the latter part of the seventeenth century by Thomas Willis. He grouped together dullness of intellect and forgetfulness with the later development of stupidity and foolishness. Jean Esquirol added mental deterioration and paralysis, with death soon to follow. A.L.J. Boyle later brought the process to its conclusions by describing its symptoms in detail and identifying them as a separate disease, which he labeled "general paresis."

It was decades later before the specific cause of the illness was discovered, and still later before a reliable method of testing for syphilis was developed and a method of treating it was found.

INHERITED GENES AS A FACTOR IN MENTAL ILLNESS

"Bad seed" as a nineteenth-century derogatory term for defective genes has long been connected in the lay mind with certain kinds of abnormal behavior or unacceptable behavior: alcoholism, criminal behavior, and other forms of "immoral" behavior. In the twentieth century, science has vigorously pursued the nature of genetic influence, if any, on abnormal behavior. There are three principal methods of doing so: studying the families of those with pathological mental symptoms, twin studies, and adoptee studies. This section considers each briefly.

Family Studies. Science can now approximate the percentage of common genes in family members of varying degrees of closeness. It is, for example, estimated that siblings have in common 50 percent of their genes, aunts and uncles 25 percent, and cousins 12.5 percent. That knowledge provides one method of testing the influence of heredity on the development of mental disorders. Starting with a patient with a diagnosed mental disorder, a researcher can seek out relatives who vary in their closeness to that individual and count the number of family members of each degree of relationship showing signs of the same illness. A correlation between consanguinity and the illness, other factors being equal, suggests a hereditary influence.

Just that kind of research was undertaken with a group of schizophrenic patients. The results unquestionably indicated that the closer the relationship to the schizophrenic individual, the higher the incidence of the same disease. Such a study does not prove the certain influence of hereditary factors as a cause of schizophrenia, since common environmental conditions among the relatives could not be ruled out as a causative factor. It is nevertheless strongly suggestive of a relationship.

Twin Studies. The scientific reasoning in twin studies can be tighter than in family studies since monozygotic twins (identical twins developed from a single fertilized egg) have exactly the same genes and are said to be the same genotype. Their physical characteristics, and presumably their mental characteristics, are almost identical. They are to be contrasted with dizygotic, or fraternal, twins, developed from two separate eggs, fertilized at the same time. They are not more alike than any two siblings.

A twin study requires that a sufficient number of monozygotic and dizygotic twins with one or both twins suffering a particular mental disorder be identified. The concordance rate—that is, the percentage of times both twins have the same illness—is studied. Such studies of schizophrenics reveal, for example, that the identical twins show a concordance rate three to five times as high as nonidentical twins. The finding provides a very strong argument for a hereditary effect on the development of schizophrenia.

Adoptee Studies. When one schizophrenic identical twin has been adopted and raised apart from his or her co-twin, since the hereditary factor is identical but environmental influences can be assumed to be different, the situation provides a critical test of the possible hereditary influence on development of the disease. Since concordance rates, despite environmental differences, are high, such studies provide the strongest evidence for the hereditary transmission of a tendency toward schizophrenia, not as absolute as the inheritance of eye color, for example, but quite strong.

BIOCHEMICAL IMBALANCE AS A CAUSE OF MENTAL ILLNESS

An excess or deficiency in one or another chemical element in the body has also been studied as a possible cause of mental illness. It is again one of the psychoses that provides evidence to support the hypothesis. Research suggests, for example, that schizophrenics have excess dopamine (a chemical, known as a neurotransmitter) in the brain. Supporting evidence for its effect comes from one form of treatment used with schizophrenics. Drugs used in that treatment relieve some, but not all, of the symptoms of schizophrenia, and also reduce the amount of dopamine usable by the brain.

NEUROANATOMY AS A CAUSATIVE FACTOR IN MENTAL ILLNESS

It has long been known that mental symptoms associated with aging—particularly memory loss and difficulty in coping with new situations—results from changes in the cortical or higher levels of the brain, which tend to weaken before other parts of the brain. Basic biological functions are maintained long after memory is impaired.

Intensive studies of one family with a high incidence of manic-depressive psychosis provided a possible example of how genetic factors and chemical factors interact to effect mental illness. In the instance of the family studied, a genetic weakness seemed to produce biochemical changes in the brain, thus suggesting that it is the combination of defective genes producing a biochemical imbalance that tends to cause the development of manic-depressive psychosis.

THE SOCIOCULTURAL PERSPECTIVE

Study of the influence on personality and abnormal behavior of the surrounding social and cultural environment is a relatively recent development. Such a study has been largely influenced by the disciplines of sociology and anthropology, which emerged as independent fields only in the early twentieth century. The sociocultural perspective that developed as a result of the growth in importance of those two disciplines has two quite different aspects. One might be called cultural, largely having to do with differences in mores, family life, social pressures and religions that are prevalent in different regions of the world. The other has to do with the effect of differences in social, educational and economic levels existing among sectors of the same cultural area (intracultural factors); for example, in the United States or in large urban communities. This section will consider both aspects separately.

Cultural Influences

The field of study of social anthropologists is study of the ways in which people living in separated sections of the world carry on their daily routines, set up interpersonal structures, including sex and marriage, and develop ethical codes. Anthropologists compare one culture with another and attempt to draw conclusions about reasons for the different style of life and the effects of those different styles on the individuals affected. A principal interest is to contrast various world cultures with the Western/American culture. Anthropological studies are handicapped by weakness of scientific controls and difficulties in quantifying results of their efforts. Nevertheless, significant and widely influential conclusions have been drawn from their studies, which are usually conducted during a period of residence in the community under study.

Three principal conclusions about abnormal behavior can be drawn from their research, each of which is a facet of the sociocultural perspective.

CRITERIA OF MENTAL DISORDER

People who cannot control their own behavior, cannot assume basic roles in society and cannot even care for themselves in a prudent fashion are considered mentally disordered in all cultures. Interpretations of causality may vary, but acceptance of the fact of mental illness is universal.

CULTURE-BOUND PATTERNS OF MENTAL ILLNESS

Apart from universally recognized mental illnesses, some types of abnormal behavior seem to be tied to a particular culture; for example, anorexia nervosa, a disorder occurring mostly in women, in which there is such a preoccupation with staying thin that the individual loses all appetite for food, seems to occur only in Western societies, and most frequently in the United States.

PATTERNS OF CHILD-REARING PRACTICES

Americans tend to believe that their child-rearing practices are universal: how infants are nursed and toilet trained and when; who primarily takes care of the children; when children are considered adults. Anthropological studies suggest that quite the opposite conclusion is closer to the truth. Even among Western cultures, child-rearing practices vary. And as child-rearing practices differ in significant ways, one can expect different patterns of normal behavior in the adult population and different symptom patterns in abnormal behavior.

It should be noted that child-rearing practices can differ between social class levels in the same culture. British upper-class parents, for example, send children to private boarding schools at relatively young ages; lower-class members have neither the tradition nor the money to do so.

Intracultural Factors

URBAN VERSUS RURAL DIFFERENCES

There are correlational studies showing a covariance (two factors tending to vary together) between the presence or absence of psychosis and urban versus rural residence within the same large culture; for example, the United States. Three times as many psychoses are reported in urban society as in rural society, a result which may be due either to better medical facilities in urban areas (and therefore better reporting procedures) or greater willingness in rural areas to care for the mentally ill at home. A pinpointed study in support of the influence of sociocultural influences on abnormal behavior reports a greater number of mental illnesses among residents of cities undergoing rapid change than among those living in stable urban settings. The finding is only correlational and not necessarily demonstrative of a causal relationship.

INFLUENCE OF DEPRIVATION

Epidemiological studies (surveys) indicate higher incidences of mental illness in those areas where there is also a high incidence of impoverishment, discrimination and illiteracy. It is not difficult to understand that the misery of living under those conditions places a heavy burden on the individual's resources for healthy adjustment, and such conditions can be seen as a cause, but only a contributory cause, of mental illness. That analysis is supported by the fact that more impoverished individuals, for example, escape mental illness than suffer from it.

Mental Illness as the Product of Sociocultural Influences

A more strongly stated aspect of the sociocultural perspective describes mental illness as the product of social ills. Those who hold this belief might, for example, support their position with the finding that during the recession of the late seventies and early eighties, admissions to mental hospitals, suicides and stress-related deaths increased. That fact presents a strong argument, at the least, for the position that widespread economic setback, affecting many people, pushed some of them, perhaps only those with a preexisting predisposition or the presence of genetic weakness, into severe mental illness.

Mental Illness as a Social Institution

The most forthrightly stated position in the sociocultural perspective describes mental illness as a myth. One of its most ideologically convinced advocates (Thomas Szasz, 1961) holds that mental illness is a socially convenient myth used to explain away people who do not live according to society's norms. Such deviations from norms, it is said, are expressions of "problems in living" in society as it is now constituted. Adherents of this view ask the question, How does society decide which deviants from its norms are mentally ill? And why do individuals so labeled accept the label?

Adherents of this strong position along the sociocultural continuum might answer, "Deviant behavior is quite common, and for the most part, it is transitory; some deviant behavior, for a variety of unsatisfactory reasons, is labeled mental illness. Once so labeled, an individual has no choice but to behave in accordance with a socially prescribed role because society powerfully rewards such behavior. Although such a person is denied the reinforcements of the sane—a career, a respected position in the family— they are provided other rewards: the 'tender, loving care' of being a sick person."

There are seven perspectives or models that different psychologists use in defining human behavior as normal or abnormal. They are the psychodynamic view, which emphasizes the importance and interactive influences of childhood and later interpersonal experiences; the behavioral perspective, which stresses the role of learning, particularly conditioning experiences, both respondent conditioning, first demonstrated by Pavlov and seized upon by Watson to establish the school of behaviorism, and operant conditioning, which is the basis of reinforcement theory created by the research of Skinner; the cognitive perspective, which gives a central place to cognitions (expectations, beliefs, values, plans made) in determining what response an individual will make in confronting life situations; the humanistic perspective, which considers most important the individual's self-concept and his or her potential for growth; the existential perspective, which alone among the various perspectives focuses exclusively on the individual's present life and the difficulty of living authentically in the modern world. Becoming increasingly more important in abnormal psychology is the biogenic perspective, which attributes much abnormal behavior to biological anomalies—for example, defective heredity. Most recent to arrive among the more well-established perspectives is the sociocultural viewpoint with its emphasis on cultural and socioeconomic variables.

One helpful way to make use of the various perspectives is to take an eclectic point of view, which recognizes that no one perspective can explain all mental illness or provide effective therapy. Most mental illness results from or takes on characteristics influenced by causative elements featured by various of the perspectives. For example, biogenic factors may create a predisposition which is made worse by interpersonal problems, conditioning experiences, or ineptly learned coping mechanisms. The individual's self-concept will be an important variable in the prognosis of the illness, as will capacity to deal with problems presented by modern society.

Selected Readings

Bandura, A. and R. Walters. 1963. *Social Learning and Personality Development.* New York: Holt, Rinehart and Winston.

Harris, B. 1979. "Whatever Happened to Little Albert?" *American Psychologist,* 34: 151-160.

Hollingshead, A.B. and F.C. Redlich. 1958. *Social Class and Mental Illness: A Community Study.* New York: Wiley.

Mischel, W. 1979. "On the Interface of Cognition and Personality: Beyond the Person-Situation Debate." *American Psychologist,* 34: 740-754.

Kanfer, F.H. and P. Kavoly. 1972. "Self-Control. A Behavioristic Excursion into the Lion's Den." *Behavior Therapy,* 398-416.

Kazdin, A.E. and G.T. Wilson. 1978. *Evaluation of Behavior Therapy: Issues, Evidence, and Research Strategies.* Cambridge, MA: Ballinger.

5

Assessment and Classification

*I*n their initial contacts, clinicians set out to appraise the severity of the client's illness, strengths and weaknesses the individual brings to therapy, earlier life history, and the characteristics of the client's interpersonal life. That appraisal is formally labeled the assessment process. It may be a relatively informal procedure undertaken by the therapist in the early sessions of therapy; in many settings, particularly in hospitals or outpatient clinics, it may be an extensive process conducted by a team, including psychiatrist, psychologist, social worker, and often a physician to conduct a thorough physical examination. A variety of techniques are used, each related to the special competence of a team member.

The principal outcome of the assessment process in abnormal psychology is the development of what some psychologists refer to as the dynamic formulation of the client's problem. This may be formalized in a comprehensive case history which contains informative summaries of all material gathered in the assessment process. The case history describes the current situation and its history, also proposes hypotheses about the causes of the maladaptive behavior, and presents a diagnosis drawn from an officially approved classification system.

Assessment, then, is a scientific process that observes and describes significant aspects of a client's behavior. That description is used as a basis for predictions about future behavior of the client which, in turn, provides the information and hypotheses for making decisions about a program of treatment. In that regard, questions considered might be, what type of therapy is *indicated; what is likely to be the outcome; how long a term of treatment can be predicted; what should the characteristics of the therapist be?*

The assessment process is also used for making decisions other than those related to therapy. A variant of the assessment process is used in making personnel decisions; for example, is Ms. Jones likely to be an effective sales manager for product division A? In vocational guidance, the basis of recommendations to the client is data gathered in an assessment procedure that measures interests and aptitudes. A simple assessment procedure is used by universities in their admission procedures.

After considering the characteristics of a good assessment, the chapter considers four components of a comprehensive assessment: the physical examination, observation of the client's behavior, the interview, and the psychological test. The chapter concludes with a description and evaluation of the Diagnostic and Statistical Manual of Mental Disorders (DSM IIIR), which provides an official and widely accepted system for classifying psychological disorders.

THE CHARACTERISTICS OF A GOOD ASSESSMENT

There are two major characteristics of a good assessment: its reliability and its validity. Of lesser but notable importance are such practical considerations as the cumbersomeness of the procedure and the time it takes to complete.

Reliability

The degree to which an assessment consistently gives the same results is the measure of its reliability. The higher the reliability, the more likely is it that repeated assessments will arrive at the same conclusion, measure or diagnosis. Reliability says nothing about what is being measured; it speaks only to the dependability of the measure. The reliability of an assessment procedure or of a psychological test can be determined in three ways: internal consistency, test-retest consistency, and interjudge consistency.

INTERNAL CONSISTENCY

The method of internal consistency answers the question: Do different sections of the test appear to measure the same thing? For a psychological test, the method correlates one part of the test against scores earned on a different part of the test. If the correlation is high, the test is considered reliable. In the clinical assessment, a comparison might be made between conclusions drawn in the interview, from observations, and from the psychological test.

TEST-RETEST RELIABILITY

Will a second administration of the assessment device, conducted independently of the first, lead to the same judgments? If concordance is high, the assessment device would seem to be reliable. This method is most often used to test reliability of psychological tests; it is rarely used in the clinical assessment.

INTERJUDGE RELIABILITY

How likely is it that a test or assessment procedure, when scored or interpreted by different judges, will yield the same results? This mode of testing reliability has been used extensively in the work done to establish the *DSM IIIR*, which is the official classification system used in abnormal psychology. In that effort, the question asked was, when different clinicians use the diagnostic criteria set up in the manual, to what extent do their judgments correspond? Results in field testing of the most recent edition of the manual are reported later in this chapter.

Validity

The validity of a test or procedure is an indication of the degree to which it measures what it purports to measure. Does an intelligence test measure what is generally considered to be intelligence; does a personality test truly measure, for example, the trait of extraversion? Some psychologists would question whether or not traits, such as characteristic ways of responding in all situations, can indeed be demonstrated.

A test or procedure may be highly reliable without being valid. For example, the daily temperature can be measured with a high degree of reliability; it is not, however, a valid indicator of whether or not the sun is out. A test cannot be valid if it is not reliable. Validity may be evaluated in two ways: descriptive validity and predictive validity.

DESCRIPTIVE VALIDITY

Descriptive validity is a measure of how accurately a score, diagnosis or interpretation describes the current behavior of those who have been assessed. For example, a valid intelligence test should have a high degree of accuracy (not 100 percent) in indicating a child's academic performance in elementary school. With respect to psychiatric diagnoses, when it comes to descriptive validity, there is a problem. Individuals with different diagnoses may show identical current symptoms; for example, a manic depressive and those with certain types of anxiety-based disorders may exhibit both low self-esteem and depression. And those with an identical diagnosis may currently show quite different behavior. Of two individuals with a diagnosis of anxiety-based disorder, one may have somatic symptoms, and the other may not. The difficulty can be cleared up as the diagnosis is made more precise; one diagnosis might be somatoform disorder, the other phobic disorder.

A psychiatric diagnosis is not a statement of the individual's characteristics but a statement of the individual's typical pattern of behavior. There will always be an overlapping of individual symptoms among different diagnoses. If a diagnosis accurately describes the overall pattern of an individual's behavior, as it usually does, it meets the criterion of descriptive validity.

PREDICTIVE VALIDITY

When a test, assessment procedure or diagnosis accurately predicts future behavior, it meets the criterion of predictive validity. In abnormal psychology, the clinician is interested in predicting the course of the individual's illness, that is, its prognosis: the likelihood of recovery, in response to what form of treatment, in how long a period of time.

Failure to meet the criterion of predictive validity may result from low reliability of the test, assessment procedure or diagnosis. If three different clinicians arrive at three different diagnoses, their diagnostic procedures have low reliability and, therefore, also low validity. Recent modifications of the *Diagnostic and Statistical Manual* have increased reliability of its diagnoses. For example, one study indicates a 74 percent agreement on diagnosis among different diagnosticians. That percentage of agreement is considered a relatively high degree of reliability. Improving the reliability increases the likelihood of higher predictive validity.

PROBLEMS IN ASSESSMENT

There are three major types of influence that tend to bias the assessment process and negatively influence the end result, or diagnosis. They are characteristics of the clinician, especially the theoretical perspective he or she holds; the setting in which the diagnosis is made; and the purpose for which a diagnosis is made.

Characteristics of the Clinician

Such basic characteristics as the age, race and gender of the clinician may influence the rapport (warmth and sincerity of the relationship) between clinician and client, especially when there is a notable difference between the two. The result can be difficulty communicating on the part of the client, or even a selectivity in what the client will be willing to discuss. A formal and austere approach by the clinician may have the same effect.

A principal barrier to accuracy of diagnosis is the personal bias of the clinician and the clinician's theoretical perspective. Both will influence the weight clinicians assign to the components of the assessment process; for example, a particular clinician may be expert in one of the psychological tests and give more weight to it than to the total picture drawn by other components of the assessment. Clinicians may have a tendency to see psychological weaknesses more quickly than psychological strengths. A clinician with a strongly biogenic perspective may tend to favor diagnoses with a physiological or neurological basis.

Influence of the Setting

A clinician in a mental health setting may be quicker to pick up a mild anxiety-based disorder than a clinician working in a psychiatric hospital who is accustomed to seeing mostly seriously disturbed patients. The theoretical orientation of the chief of service may influence the interpretations and diagnoses made by staff members.

Purpose for Which a Diagnosis is Made

Psychiatric assessments are undertaken for a variety of purposes. The principal one is to plan a course of treatment. Such a purpose is least likely to bias judgments made. But assessments may be sought for other purposes: in criminal cases; for insurance, Medicare or Medicaid purposes; and the clinician may sensitively be influenced by what will most benefit the immediate circumstances of the client/patient.

THE COMPONENTS OF THE ASSESSMENT PROCESS

This section examines the four principal components of the assessment process: the physical examination, the interview, observation of behavior, and psychological tests.

The Physical Examination

The physical examination has as its purpose an evaluation of the individual's general health and the discovery of any physical/medical/neurological factors that may be influencing the individual's behavior. It is not always required as part of a psychological assessment.

THE MEDICAL CHECK-UP

Basic to the physical examination is a medical check-up, in which a physician takes a medical history from the patient and checks the major systems of the body. That examination will ordinarily include an electrocardiogram to test the heart, measurement of blood pressure, a blood chemistry test, palpation of various parts of the body, and a lung X–ray. The examination may have been done before the patient seeks psychotherapeutic help, especially by those suffering from somatoform disorders or hypochondriasis. It is especially important when addictive or organic disorders are suspected.

SPECIALIZED PROCEDURES

More advanced and highly technical procedures may be ordered for special purposes. Some of these are as follows:

1. The electroencephalogram (EEG), in which electrical activity in the brain cells is picked up by electrodes attached to the skull and recorded in oscillating patterns that are called *brain waves*. The EEG is used to help detect tumors or brain injuries that may be affecting the individual's behavior.

2. The computerized axial tomography (CAT) scan. The procedure uses a computer analysis of X–ray beams directed across areas of the patient's brain or other bodily parts. The CAT scan quickly and precisely provides information about brain injuries.

3. A more recently developed technique, the positron emission tomography (PET) scan adds to the data provided by a CAT scan, a measurement of the body's metabolic processes after a compound (such as glucose) is metabolized by the brain or other organs of the body. In this way, it pinpoints sites in the brain that produce epileptic seizures, brain damage or cancerous tissues.

Such medical procedures may be supplemented by the Halsted-Reitan Battery, which is an elaborate, six-hour psychological test that measures cognitive and psychomotor deficit resulting from any cerebral damage or disease. The test provides an index of cognitive impairment and information about functioning in various skill areas. Other tests assessing tactual or auditory functions may also be prescribed by the medical team.

The Assessment Interview

A face-to-face conversation, in which the clinician seeks information about the client/patient's complaint, typical behavior, life circumstances and early history, is the most commonly used assessment procedure. The interview with the client may be supplemented by interviews with family members, teachers, ward attendants, or others knowledgeable about the client. In many psychiatric situations, it is the only assessment made as the clinician uses the first few sessions to appraise the client. For relatively minor adjustments, emotional or interpersonal problems, such an approach is efficient and accurate enough to meet the client's needs. Nevertheless, such a relatively unstructured use of the interview has been criticized as too unreliable for arriving at a scientific diagnosis. Research suggests that there is basis for the criticism. There have been several attempts to improve the unstructured interview. Three are briefly reported here: the structured interview, the computer-assisted interview, and the self report.

THE STRUCTURED INTERVIEW

In the structured interview, a series of previously prepared questions, asked in a fixed order, and phrased so as to have the client describe what he or she did in a variety of life situations, assures full coverage, in the client's own language, of critical behavior patterns. Follow-up research using the interjudge method of testing reliability indicates a notable improvement in agreement on a diagnosis when this approach is used.

INTERVIEWING WITH THE HELP OF A COMPUTER

Computer-assisted interviewing, although not yet widely used, is a new approach to assessment. There are now a half-dozen programs that conduct psychiatric interviews for adults and children by presenting questions on a computer screen and recording answers on standard forms. The advantage claimed is that pertinent information is gathered more fully than would be the case in a less formally conducted interview. Some reports indicate a reduction in costs for conducting the assessment with the help of a computer. One criticism of the use of the computer is that it mechanizes a process that is and should be highly interpersonal. The absence of rapport between computer and client could limit the candor and completeness of the interview process.

THE SELF REPORT

The self report, in which the client writes answers about his or her own behavior to standardized questions or responds to a problem checklist, is less mechanized than the use of a computer, but it still minimizes the interpersonal aspect of the process. When the self report is followed by a personal interview, as it usually is, the danger of mechanizing the process is reduced.

Clinical Observation of Behavior

Observation of the client's behavior in natural and typical family and interpersonal situations is a rich and accurate source of information. The disadvantage, of course, is that it is expensive and time-consuming. It is usually more practical to observe children in the classroom— especially valuable when the problem is school related—and to observe psychiatric patients in a hospital setting.

To extend the process to other situations, the assessor can design role-playing situations among family members or with the partners in a marriage. The clinician sets the stage, usually around a communication problem or around a topic on which there is disagreement. While not as absolute as field observation, the role-playing approach does reveal nuances of the problem about which the client may not be conscious and therefore is unlikely to report in an interview. A rating scale can be used to standardize recordings of the observation. The rating scale usually allows the clinician to indicate not only the existence of the behavior, but also its frequency.

Added to those observations can be observations of behavior in the assessment process itself, especially during the psychological tests.

Psychological Tests

A principal means of assessing behavior, which is almost always administered and interpreted by a psychologist, is the psychological test. Tests are of two types: ability or performance tests, of which the principal type is the intelligence test; and personality tests. Among the ability tests are those that assess functioning in a variety of cognitive and psychomotor areas, a procedure that is useful in determining the presence of brain damage and locating it. The Halsted-Reitan is the most widely-used test of that type.

Intelligence tests may be entirely verbal, but most individually administered tests (the type used most frequently in clinical settings) combine verbal and performance items. Personality tests are of two types: projective tests, which offer the testee an unstructured way of responding, and objective tests, which limit the client's answers to yes or no or a choice from multiple choice items. Since the test is principally in the province of the psychologist, this section provides detailed descriptions of them.

INTELLIGENCE TESTS

The concept of the intelligence test and the first intelligence test was developed in 1905 by Alfred Binet, a French psychologist, who introduced it into the French schools to screen children for higher education. Although there are many intelligence tests, those used in the clinical setting in the United States are likely to be the Wechsler Scales, which have an adult version and two children's versions, or the revised Stanford-Binet, which can be used from two years of age to the superior adult.

The Stanford-Binet. The Stanford-Binet is the oldest American intelligence test, and until the Wechsler Scales were developed, it was the standard individual test for use with children. It now shares that distinction with the Wechsler Scale for children. Although there is an adult section of the Stanford-Binet, the Wechsler Scale is used commonly for testing adult intelligence. The Stanford-Binet and the Wechsler Scale for very young children are used for testing children less than five years of age.

The Stanford-Binet and the Wechsler Scales provide scores that can be directly converted into an intelligence quotient. Statistical procedures fix the mean IQ at 100. From an intelligence quotient, an individual's performance can be given a percentile rank in the general population. For example, an IQ of 130 places an individual in the upper 5 percent of the population.

The Stanford-Binet organizes such tasks as recognizing objects in a picture, remembering a series of digits, defining words, and completing sentences in a logical way, into age groups. In administering the test, which requires considerable training, the psychologist may begin testing at a level just below the child's chronological age. If the child passes all items (thus establishing a basal age), the test proceeds to older levels until a level is reached at which the child fails all items (the ceiling age). In scoring the test, the psychologist adds to the basal age the credits for all other passed items. It is that score that is converted into an IQ.

The Stanford-Binet requires a program of supervised training for anyone planning to use it and takes from two to three hours to administer, score and interpret. The latter requirement limits its usefulness in many clinical settings.

The Wechsler Scales. The Wechsler Adult Intelligence Scale (WAIS-R), used here to illustrate types of item content, consists of six verbal scales and five performance scales, which yield a verbal and a performance IQ. The subscale totals can be combined to provide a total IQ score.

Typical verbal items are word definition; identifying similarities in paired words, e.g., cat-dog versus tree-house; fund of general information; and mathematics. Performance items include assembling pieces of a jigsaw-like object, putting colored blocks together to match an exposed picture, and transcribing a code. Performance items are timed. Each type of item presents a scale of items from very easy to difficult. The score is the number of credits earned for each item, plus credit for speedy performance.

The other two Wechsler scales are the WISC-R—the Wechsler Intelligence Scale for Children—revised with a range from six years of age to superior adult, and the Wechsler Preschool and Primary Scale of Intelligence (WPPSI) for younger children.

EVALUATION OF INTELLIGENCE TESTING

There are four principal weaknesses or limitations of intelligence testing, and three significant strengths.

Weaknesses or Limitations. 1. They are time-consuming to administer. 2. In many clinical situations, the problem presented may not require a precise measure of intelligence. Frequently, indications from the client's job or educational level may provide an adequate indication of intellectual level. 3. Intelligence is not, as Wechsler himself has pointed out, an existing thing as is, for example, one's heart rate, which can be directly measured. It has to be inferred from the officially correct answers which the testee is able to report on an intelligence test. With this limitation in mind, some psychologists define intelligence as whatever intelligence tests measure. 4. The charge has been made that intelligence tests assume a common middle-class cultural background, and measure the individual's response to that background. Impoverished children and many ethnic minority children, for the most part, come out of a very different cultural background. Yet what happens to them, how they are classified for future educational opportunities, and what careers are recommended to them, all depend on a measuring device that might not be fair to them.

Strengths. 1. During the administration of an intelligence test, the psychologist has rich opportunities to observe clients' behavior as they respond to an unfamiliar and challenging situation. Such anxiety-producing situations are normally faced in everyday life. Does the client respond with apprehension and anxiety; does the client invest adequate effort and try hard enough; are there notable mannerisms; does the client try too hard, is success all-consuming; are there speech defects or idiosyncracies, or visual or hearing impairment? 2. Apart from the overall score, the intelligence test analysis details the client's cognitive functioning and lists strengths and weaknesses. In addition, the test may reveal the earliest indication of possible brain damage. 3. Finally, intelligence tests measure, fairly accurately, the likelihood of the individual's potential for success in the American educational system. Even though that may not be a full measure or definition of intelligence, it is a forecast of likely success in an arena in which a child or adolescent will spend a great deal of time, and in which success is a principal gate opener.

PERSONALITY TESTS

The two types of personality test, projective tests and objective tests, are a significant part of the assessment procedure and are typically administered and interpreted by the psychologist. This section will examine in detail the Rorschach and the Thematic Apperception Test (TAT), both of which rank among those most frequently used. The most widely used personality test in clinical practice, the Minnesota Multiphasic Personality Inventory (MMPI), an objective test, will also be described in detail.

The Rorschach. Herman Rorschach, a Swiss psychiatrist, created the test named for him in 1912. The test consists of ten cards, each having on it an ink blot such as might be made by folding in half a sheet of paper on which a blot of ink has been left. The ink blots, as a result, are all symmetrically balanced; they range in color from blacks and grays to bright, varicolored designs. There are three phases to the test: 1. A card is held up by the psychologist, who asks clients what they see there. After the clients respond, they are asked, can they find anything else? 2. After the ten cards have been exposed, the psychologist asks clients, what was it about the card that caused them to see what they reported? 3. The test is then scored in accordance with a manual of detailed instructions. Aspects of the test scored are: goodness of fit (form); content of response (e.g., animal, human figure); the use of the whole ink blot, a major detail, a small detail; the use of texture; attribution of movement.

It is that pattern of scoring that the psychologist uses to arrive at a description of the underlying personality characteristics, motivations, conflicts, level of intelligence, and possible psychoses or brain damage. When, for example, a client principally uses a small detail of a blot and avoids major parts of the card as a whole, a possible interpretation is that the client has difficulty in facing central issues and might tend to become bogged down in detail or trivia, a characteristic that might be related to such diagnoses as obsessive-compulsive personality disorder or one of the anxiety-based disorders.

A major criticism of the test is the low interjudge reliability reported for interpretations of the test and the paucity of information about its validity. Despite those criticisms, the test continues to be widely used, although psychologists have come to use it less often during the past twenty years. Still, many psychologists and psychiatrists continue to consider it a valuable tool for suggesting leads as to psychodynamic influences of unconscious materials.

New impetus may be given to the use of the Rorschach by the development of Exner's computer-generated interpretations for certain Rorschach scores. In using that approach, clinicians can count on interjudge reliability of interpretations, if there is initial agreement in scoring, about which there is little criticism.

Thematic Apperception Test (TAT). Like the Rorschach, the TAT offers the client a series of relatively ambiguous pictures to interpret. Developed by Henry Murray in 1935, the TAT uses up to 30 cards upon which there are pictures of one or more people whose activities are not entirely clear. Clients are asked to make up a story about the picture with three parts which answer these questions: What has occurred before the picture? What is happening in the picture? How will the story end? What are the people thinking, feeling, doing?

The stories are then scored subjectively and impressionistically, or in accordance with a formal scoring system. Despite the existence of a number of scoring and interpretation systems that assess client needs, perceptions of reality and typical fantasies, psychologists most frequently use their own method of qualitatively and quantitatively assessing the significance of the client's stories.

Among the factors considered to provide leads to the client's personality characteristics, unconscious motivations, and conscious concerns are: the style of the story—length and organization and any frequently occurring themes—for example, retribution, guilt, parental domination; who are the primary characters; and interpersonal and sexual concerns suggested by the stories.

Here, again, as with the Rorschach, there is caution in the clinical field about reliability and validity. Nevertheless, even though the test is time-consuming, it continues to be commonly used in the assessment process. The reason, no doubt, as with the Rorschach, is that it provides useful leads to be followed up in an assessment interview or in later psychotherapy.

Objective Personality Tests: the Minnesota Multiphasic Personality Inventory. Although, as has been indicated previously, there are hundreds of personality tests, the one upon which clinicians most commonly rely is the MMPI. That test is the most widely used personality test in clinical practice and for research in abnormal psychology. The test is essentially a self report, in which clients answer true or false, agree or disagree, to 550 statements.

Typical of the statements are the five listed below, taken from the test form published by Hathaway and McKinley in 1951:

1. I go to a party every week.

2. I forgive people easily.

3. I often feel as if things were not real.

4. Someone has it in for me.

5. I sometimes enjoy breaking the law.

The MMPI has been subject to more research scrutiny than any other personality test. That research foundation can be categorized as follows:

Original Validation Studies. The original questions were administered first to a large, representative sample of individuals and several groups of psychiatric patients. All statements were then subjected to an item analysis (with items clustered into identifiable groups). This enabled the authors to discover which items differentiate among the several groups; that is, which differentiated the normal population from psychiatric patients, and which differentiated one disorder from another in the psychiatric population.

The study enabled the authors to develop ten scales, each of which assesses tendencies to respond in deviant ways similar to the ways in which patients with known psychiatric disorders responded. In presenting its graphic summary to the clinician, the psychologist plots, on a graph, scores earned by the client on the ten scales, to be compared with a mean score on each scale for the normal population.

Thus, at a glance, the clinician can see, from the profile, in which areas the individual deviates significantly from normal. That evaluation does not necessarily establish a diagnosis, but it does suggest the characteristically deviant behavior of the individual under study.

Subsequent Validation. In the past, MMPI has been criticized for its dated language, circa 1950. Fourteen percent of the items have now been changed to bring them up to date. Additional scales have been validated and are now part of the test. Two forms of the test have been developed, one for adults and the other for adolescents.

Critique of the MMPI. Despite the endorsement suggested by its widespread use, criticisms of the test appear in the psychological literature. The most basic is that the test is a more valid indicator, not of an appropriate diagnosis, but of the degree of overall disturbance experienced by the individual; that is, whether or not the client is mildly disturbed or deeply disturbed. The more the individual's scores deviate in a negative direction from the normal profile, the more severe is the disturbance. It should be noted that even that finding, apart from any indication of diagnosis, is a significant contribution to the assessment process.

A second criticism is that response sets which a person brings to a personality testing situation may warp the accuracy of the answers. Clients, it is said, tend to give socially desirable answers, but they also have an acquiescence set, causing them to agree with statements proposed. These two sets would have opposite effects—for example, to the statement, I sometimes tell lies—a socially desirable set would motivate a no answer; an acquiescence set would stimulate a yes answer.

In answer to that criticism, it should be pointed out that three scales in the test tend to control response set. They are as follows:

1. The L scale, which assesses the tendency to claim excessive virtue; that is, a tendency to answer too often in a socially desirable way.

2. The F scale, which assesses a tendency to acquiesce too often and to report psychological problems inaccurately.

3. The K scale, in a reversal of the F scale, measures a tendency to see oneself in an unrealistically positive way; that is, for example, to acquiesce to the statement, "I have never had any nightmares."

DIAGNOSIS AND THE OFFICIAL CLASSIFICATION SYSTEM

One significant outcome of the assessment process is to provide a diagnosis that fits the individual into a category of psychiatric disorder that is recognized by an official classification system. In addition, the diagnosis also includes a rating on the severity of the disorder, the level of the individual's current functioning, an indication of acuteness or chronicity of the disorder, and a description of any current stressors the individual faces. All of these options are expressed in a way consistent with categories established by the official classification system.

The official American classification of psychiatric disorders is the *Diagnostic and Statistical Manual of Mental Disorders* (abbreviated to *DSM IIIR*). (See chapter 21 for detailed presentation of the *DSM IIIR*.)

Strengths and Weaknesses of the Diagnostic Process

There is psychological value in attaching a diagnosis to a client/patient, but there are also costs. Both are described below.

VALUE OF A DIAGNOSIS

A diagnosis places a client/patient into a group of other individuals with a known disorder. The diagnosis says that the symptoms and patterns of behavior of this client/patient are similar (not identical) to other individuals who have been diagnosed as suffering from the named disorder. The most immediate value of that decision is that, at this stage of development in abnormal psychology, we have learned much about the prognosis of the various disorders (its predicted future course, if untreated) and about which therapies are likely to interrupt that prognosis.

A second value is that, for a limited number of mental disorders, there is knowledge of specific causes of the disorder, in which case a diagnosis can be helpful in planning treatment. For other illnesses for which specific causes may not have been identified, certain other factors, sometimes (unfortunately) general, have been related to the illness. That knowledge can also be helpful.

Beyond the clinical focus, psychologists regularly conduct research that provides additional information about specific disorders, which information is also helpful to the clinician in planning treatment.

Finally, diagnoses help research psychologists to group people in accordance with some scientifically acceptable criterion, which adds scientific value to their studies.

CRITICISMS OF THE DIAGNOSTIC PROCESS

There are four principal criticisms of the diagnostic process: the problem caused by labeling; the suggestion in a diagnosis that the abnormal is qualitatively different from the normal; the illusory effect of believing that a diagnosis is an explanation; and the fact that a diagnosis accords with the medical school model of illness, an interpretation that some psychologists resist.

THE PROBLEM OF LABELING

A diagnostic label stereotypes clients/patients and tends to bias the way in which clinicians, and society in general, tend to regard them. It may, for example, blind the clinician to the individual's abilities and resources for growth and self-fulfillment, which could be of significance in a program of treatment. There is also danger that, to some extent, a diagnosis may become a self-fulfilling prophecy: once classified, the individual is expected (one fears that he or she is even encouraged) to behave in ways consistent with the diagnosis.

THE PROBLEM OF QUALITATIVE DIFFERENCE

Calling individuals phobic, obsessive-compulsive, histrionic or dependent personalities holds at least the suggestion that they are in a class by themselves; that is, that they are a different kind of human being. On the contrary, those with psychological disorders are not different in kind, but rather have carried certain kinds of behavior to such an extreme as to place them on the far end of a continuum, with many gradations along the way, from ideally adjusted to severely maladjusted.

THE PROBLEM OF BELIEVING A DIAGNOSIS IS AN EXPLANATION

A diagnosis, by itself, although helpful, without the support of a well-developed case history, does little to help explain what caused the illness or what treatment will cure it. As helpful as the diagnosis may be in the clinical process, its presence is open to the possibility that clinicians will tend to think about it in stereotyped ways, thus ignoring the fact that the person is a human being, different from other human beings, and entitled to be treated as such.

THE DIAGNOSTIC AND STATISTICAL MANUAL III REVISED (DSM IIIR)

Emil Kraeplin, a psychiatrist, developed the first useful classification system for mental disorders in the latter part of the nineteenth century. Although features of his classification system continue to influence recent developments, his approach to mental illness was based on a narrowly organic view of the field. Following the medical model, he tended to believe that similar groups of symptoms (a syndrome), labeled with the same diagnosis, would result from similar causes, respond to similar treatment, and would follow a similar course during treatment. Much of his ideology is questioned today.

In the earliest version of the *Diagnostic and Statistical Manual,* set out in 1952 by the American Psychiatric Association, many of the same assumptions were used. There have been revisions of that manual, the most recent in 1987. That revision, the *DSM IIIR,* has attempted to increase the reliability, validity and usefulness of its classification system. All syndromes (clusters of symptoms, which are the diagnostic categories) are presented descriptively, with no causative elements ascribed. Detailed and specific, and in some cases quantitative, criteria are listed to promote interjudge reliability. Most theoretical perspectives in abnormal psychology now find the manual acceptable and useful.

Characteristics of the DSM IIIR

Two aspects of the *DSM IIIR* are of concern to the student of abnormal psychology: the nature of the factors, or axes, considered by the manual for establishing a diagnosis; and the broad categories, or syndromes, which make up a list of the officially recognized psychological disorders.

As a guide to the assessment process, the *DSM IIIR* identifies five factors or dimensions of the client's/patient's behavior, including the individual's symptoms and other patterns of behavior. Those it calls Axes I through V.

THE DIAGNOSTIC DIMENSIONS OF AXES

Axis I lists and describes all mental disorders (called syndromes), except those listed under Axis II. (See chapter 21.) The clinician usually is able to select Axis I or Axis II syndromes as the diagnosis.

Axis II lists personality disorders—for example, antisocial personality disorder—which are usually manifest by adolescence, and other developmental disorders. (See chapter 21.)

Axis III lists any physical or medical disorders that may be present and complicating the mental disorder.

Axis IV briefly describes any stressors in the individual's life circumstances. The categories are rated on a seven-point scale affecting the individual, and range from catastrophic—for example, a recent airplane crash—to mild or moderate, such as a job change.

Axis V is headed, "Highest Level of Functioning." Here the clinician is asked to rate the individual's highest level of functioning (job, school, family, special interests) during the past year, as compared with the individual's present level of functioning.

*T*he assessment process seeks to evaluate and include in a case history the client's illness, strengths and limitations, life circumstances, early history, and current interpersonal relations.

The principal means of conducting the assessment process are as follows:

The physical examination, which may include such advanced medical procedures as the electroencephalogram, the computerized axial tomography (CAT scan), and the positron emission tomography (PET scan).

The interview, which may be largely informal and unstructured. Recent adaptations of the simple interview are a structured interview with a comprehensive list of questions for use by the interviewer, and a self report, completed by the client, for which a computer program has been developed.

Psychological tests, including intelligence tests. The most commonly used are the Wechsler Scales for use with adults and children, and the Stanford-Binet, with a range from age two to superior adult; and personality tests, which may be projective—ambiguous stimuli onto which the in-

dividual projects his or her own interpretations—or objective, which provide a list of statements with which the individual may agree or disagree. The most commonly used projective tests are the Rorschach ink blot test and the Thematic Apperception Test (a series of pictures about which the individual tells a story). The most widely used objective personality test is the Minnesota Multiphasic Personality Inventory, which, by means of 550 questions, provides a ten-scale personality profile.

The assessment process develops a dynamic formulation of the client's disorder and provides a diagnosis drawn from the Diagnostic and Statistical Manual (DSM IIIR), *which is the official American classification system for psychological disorders.*

Selected Readings

Cooper, W.H. 1981. "Ubiquitous Halo." *Psychological Bulletin*, 19: 218-244.

Erdberg, P. and J.E. Exner, Jr. 1984. "Rorschach Assessment." In G. Goldstein and M. Hersey (Eds.). *Handbook of Psychological Assessment*. New York: Pergamon.

Lopez, S. and J.A. Nunez. 1987. "Cultural Factors Considered in Selected Diagnostic Criteria and Interview Schedules." *Journal of Abnormal Psychology*, 96: 270-272.

Millon, T. and G. D. Klerman. 1986. *Contemporary Directions in Psychopathology: Toward the DSM-IV*. New York: Guilford.

Myers, J. K. and L. L. Bean. 1968. *A Decade Later: A Follow-up of Social Class and Mental Illness*. New York: Wiley.

Robins, L. N. and J. E. Helzer. 1986. "Diagnosis and Clinical Assessment: The Current State of Psychiatric Diagnosis." *Annual Review of Psychology*, 37: 409-432.

Sarason, I. G. and R. Stooks. 1978. "Test Anxiety and the Passage of Time." *Journal of Consulting and Clinical Psychology*, 46: 102-109.

Ward, C. H., A. T. Beck, M. Mendelson, E. Mock, and J. K. Erbough. 1962. "The Psychiatric Nomenclature: Reasons for Diagnostic Disagreement." *Archives of General Psychiatry*, 7: 198-205.

6

Psychodynamic Forms of Psychotherapy

In the United States, in any one year, one of every twenty Americans will visit a mental health clinic, a psychiatric hospital clinic or a clinician in private practice to seek help with an emotional or adjustment problem. Many of them will follow up and undertake a program of psychotherapy. Most of them will need only relatively short-term treatment, two or three months, occasionally only three or four visits; others will continue longer; some forms of psychotherapy continue for years.

What will they experience? There are so many different therapies as to make that a difficult question to answer. A 1976 survey estimated that there were, at that time, 130 or more specific therapies available. If anything, the number has increased since then. Unfortunately, research testing of the comparative effectiveness of the various therapies has not kept pace with the growth of therapies. All of those therapies can be grouped into one or another of the perspectives discussed in chapters 3 and 4. And many of them differ, one from another, in only slight ways.

Most clinicians will select a mode of treatment consistent with their perspective on human behavior. They will set therapeutic goals, follow procedures, and schedule and terminate treatment in ways consistent with that perspective. But increasingly, clinicians are adopting an eclectic point of view and, to some extent, adopting psychotherapeutic approaches from one or another of the ideologies in a way that best suits the needs of the client.

Psychotherapies may be classified in two major ways: 1. Therapies that set insight as a goal or those that set a change in behavior as a goal; and 2. therapies considered by the therapist as a precise science and those in which the therapist considers therapy a skilled but flexible art.

Another way of thinking about the differences in therapies is in terms of the behavior which the therapist believes needs changing, a decision reached only after several therapy sessions. Targets for change can be affective (emotional) reactions, such as irrational fears or depression; cognitive behavior, irrational or unrealistic thoughts, beliefs or expectations; or maladaptive ways in which the client is responding to environmental pressures. The seriousness of the abnormal behavior, measured by its disruptive effect on the client's life, is always a prime concern of the therapist.

The diversity of therapies can also be illustrated in the different ways therapists respond to the client. The behavior of therapists may vary from seemingly almost passive listening, with occasionally an interpretation or a question interjected, to active confrontation with the client about the irrationality of his or her beliefs; from active participation in activities with the client—for example, the client and therapist walking through the busy thoroughfares of New York City to desensitize the client to fears of open spaces— to intently listening to the client in order to really hear the client as he or she has, perhaps, never been heard or understood before.

No wonder choosing a therapist may be, for many people, a troubling question. Clinicians have developed guidelines to help a perplexed person make the right choice.

After dealing with those introductory but important questions, the chapter will describe the characteristic features of the principal psychodynamic therapeutic approaches, and the chapter will conclude with an evaluation of the effectiveness of psychotherapy in general.

THE DIVERSITY OF THERAPIES

Therapies differ in their goals, the attitude therapists hold toward the therapeutic process, their methodology, and in demands made upon patient and therapist.

Goals of Therapy

There are two principal and very different goals set by therapists with differing perspectives on human behavior: the development of insight into the causes of the client's abnormal behavior, or the direct modification of undesired or undesirable specific actions of the client.

INSIGHT AS A GOAL

The choice of insight as a goal, which is the preference of clinicians with a psychodynamic perspective, is based on their belief that certain critical previous experiences, some of them from early childhood, most of them long since repressed into the unconscious, are currently producing anxiety and its symptoms, as well as disturbed interpersonal relations, irrational thinking, and damaging affective behavior. The humanistic and existential clinicians also seek to develop insight, but they are more likely to focus on the present or the recent past than on early childhood.

The therapist will choose methods that make possible insight into unconscious material. He or she will encourage reexamination of current emotional patterns and existing interpersonal relations in the light of the insights developed. In developing insight, especially in psychoanalytically oriented therapy, care must be taken that the so-called insight is not a detached, cold intellectualization, which experience teaches will not have any real impact on the client's behavior. Once an emotionally felt and accepted insight is achieved and its relationship to current behavior is understood and accepted, the job of the therapist is to lead the client to behavioral change, a goal that brings the therapist close to action-oriented therapy.

ACTION THERAPY: BEHAVIORAL CHANGE

Behaviorists and their cognitive associates believe that faulty earlier learning is a principal cause of abnormal behavior. Their approach to therapy is to help the client unlearn abnormal patterns of behavior and to learn new, more adaptive patterns. That approach to therapy may involve the therapist and client together in real-life situations of the client. Their procedures heavily involve respondent and operant conditioning (see chapter 4). Little time is given to emotional experiences of the past, except if doing so helps to identify the faulty learning patterns that are producing the abnormal behavior. Whereas insight therapy might seem occasionally to have a meandering aspect to it, behavioral action-focused therapy is likely to be precise; it sometimes has technical aspects to it; for example, the use of measurement and instrumentation. (Behavioral and cognitive therapies are described more fully in the following chapter.)

The contrast between insight therapy and action-focused therapy is frequently one between a global approach to achieve a major change in personality and a specific approach to effect more efficient behavior directed toward the client's goals.

Attitude of Therapists Toward the Treatment Process

The most important attitude of therapists stems from their theoretical perspective. Related to perspective is the answer the therapist will make to the question: Is therapy a science or an art? Those therapists with a behavioral perspective are likely to consider it a science. The psychodynamic therapists, and also those with a humanistic or existential point of view, will tend to consider it an art form which uses intuition and empathy but nevertheless is based on scientific foundations.

THERAPY AS APPLIED SCIENCE

The clinician who considers himself or herself a scientist/therapist will enter into the therapeutic setting with the expectation that a predictable result will follow a carefully researched, step-by-step treatment process. Gordon Paul, in an overall review of behavioral therapy, puts it this way: The behaviorally oriented scientist/therapist, before beginning a treatment program, asks: "What treatment, and by whom, is most effective for this individual, with that specific problem, under which set of circumstances?" The questions are very close to those a brain surgeon might ask, except that the psychotherapist understands that the answers to such questions will not have the same precision as those to a brain surgeon's questions. The answers they identify as variables affecting therapy are nevertheless based on the solid evidence of careful research.

PSYCHOTHERAPY AS AN APPLIED ART FORM

Therapists within the psychodynamic, humanistic and existentialistic perspectives criticize the applied scientific approach as resembling too closely what might be done to an experimental animal. They would contend further that what must be done in psychotherapy can be learned as it gradually reveals itself in early sessions. How many sessions, they will probably not say, before treatment is well underway.

One must be careful not to conclude that, because intuition and empathy seem such subjective terms, the art form of therapy is a highly subjective process. The intuitive judgments and the empathic responses of the art-form therapists are the result of much prior training and experience under the supervision of experienced therapists.

Carl Rogers, in his humanistic approach, summarizes the point of view of the art form of therapy. He states that a soft, warm, empathic approach is necessary to gain the feedback from the client that will, as the sessions go on, enable the therapist to be helpful.

CHOOSING THE RIGHT THERAPIST

Given the diversity of therapies (a diversity that will be further elaborated upon later in this chapter), prospective clients face a puzzling decision. Fortunately, experienced clinicians with various perspectives agree on a set of suggestions which, when followed, are likely to increase the effectiveness of any of the various forms of therapy, even biologically based therapy, discussed in the following chapter.

Motivations and Expectations

Prospective clients should begin by examining their motivations for therapy and what they expect to get out of it. Unless they consider therapy a serious business at which they will be expected to work even more persistently than the therapist, psychotherapy can offer little help. To accept such a heavy burden requires that one's anxiety level or the painfulness of one's symptoms or the severity of life's problems provide strong motivation to learn more about the psychodynamics of one's behavior or to learn how to change undesired behavior.

Of almost equal importance is one's expectations—what one expects from therapy. Possibilities are elimination of a phobia, more satisfying interpersonal relations, a reduction in the level of anxiety, or recovery from depressing moods.

As early as 1905, Freud recognized the importance of expectations in these words: "Expectations . . . colored by hope and faith . . . is an effective force with which we have to reckon . . . in all our attempts at treatment and cure." Years of clinical experience since then have taught therapists how right he was.

The most important psychological assets a client can bring to therapy are strong motivations to use therapy effectively and to have realistic expectations.

Gathering Information about the Therapeutic Process

Few, if any, clinicians would want prospective clients to delay therapy until they had become technically knowledgeable about the treatment process. But knowledge gained by reading nontechnical but accurate books or pamphlets written just for prospective clients, supplemented by information gathered from "psychology-friendly" and knowledgeable family physicians or religious counselors, will be helpful. The knowledge gained will help shape realistic expectations about what will be required of the client and what behavior or procedures might reasonably be expected from the therapist.

Some Cautionary Rules for Prospective Clients

The client, once in therapy, might wisely keep in mind the following rules suggested by experienced clinicians: 1. Don't continue working with a therapist whose personality traits are unacceptable to you. 2. Be wary of therapists who urge you to behave in ways that go against your religious, moral or ethical standards. A therapist who makes sexual advances of any sort is behaving unprofessionally and destroying any possible effectiveness of the treatment. 3. Try not to hold back information from your therapist. 4. Don't hesitate to ask questions or to raise objections to what a therapist is doing or proposing.

THERAPIES OF THE PSYCHODYNAMIC PERSPECTIVE

Since the underlying philosophy of the psychodynamic perspective and the earliest techniques used were set by Freud, orthodox Freudian psychoanalysis will be described first. Then changes introduced following Freud, with an emphasis on modern psychoanalytic practice, will be set forth.

Basic Characteristics of the Psychodynamic Therapies

In general, all of the psychodynamic therapies are insight therapies and global in their expected outcome. Psychodynamic therapists are more inclined than others to see therapy as an art, in which the therapist's intuitions and theories are important ingredients.

The principal activity of the client is talking with the therapist. The therapist, through such techniques as free association and dream analysis, leads the client into verbalizations and emotional reactions that will reveal his or her early life history and uncover unconscious or less conscious feelings and attitudes toward principal family members and toward the client himself or herself. The therapist will be less active than the patient, suggesting broader or more significant meaning to what the client has reported and occasionally commenting on the client's behavior in therapy. Modern psychodynamic therapists are likely to be more active than orthodox Freudian analysts and are also likely to go beyond interpretations of what the client has reported in order to give direction and advice, particularly on current interpersonal difficulties. They are also more likely to accept supplementary assistance from the use of some biogenic methods, particularly the use of pharmaceutical drugs to lighten depression or anxiety.

Freudian Psychoanalysis

Orthodox Freudian analysis is now less frequently used than in the years following Freud's introduction of it to American psychologists, but it still remains a powerful influence on the practice of modern clinicians of the psychodynamic persuasion. Here we discuss the setting and principal techniques of orthodox Freudian psychoanalysis.

SETTING

In order to minimize any distractions to the client's efforts to explore unconscious material (Freud, as a medical doctor, might have referred to the individual in therapy as a patient), the individual reclines on a couch facing away from the therapist, who sits, for the most part, quietly in the background, occasionally providing an analytically oriented interpretation of what the client is saying. Aside from the infrequent interpretations, the client is expected to talk for most of the session, fifty minutes, on three or four days each week, a procedure that, in some cases, may continue for years.

TECHNIQUES USED

Since the goal is to explore the unconscious, the analyst depends principally on four techniques that efficiently help in that process: free association, dream analysis, analysis of resistance and analysis of transference.

Free Association. Here the therapist directs the client to say whatever comes into his or her consciousness, no matter how personal, embarrassing, painful, hostile to the therapist, or innocuous. These associations, to an untrained ear, or even (or especially) to the client, may seem random or unconnected. Analysts do not consider them so, but believe that they have connections which exist only in the individual's unconscious. With the analyst's background of training and experience (a condition of becoming a psychoanalyst is that the trainee undergo a personal analysis), he or she is, in time, able to see the connections. Bit by bit, the analyst interprets them to the client, gradually allowing him or her to form a meaningful explanation of long-repressed feelings, beliefs or attitudes. From these interpretations first comes beginning insight into significant unconscious motivations and, with the help of the analyst, later understanding of defense mechanisms the client is using. With that step taken, the client can begin to see that the maladaptive responses he or she is making in life are outgrowths or expressions of long-repressed material.

Dream Analysis. Long before Freud undertook dream analysis with his clients, Plato had described dreams (and fantasies) as substitute satisfaction for inhibited "passions." Freud, with his extensive knowledge of mythology and symbolism, was able, more fully than Plato, or others after him, to understand the rich contributions of dreams to an understanding of the unconscious, and made dream analysis a regular part of his treatment.

Freud recognized that in sleep, the individual's defenses were weakened and thus allowed unconscious material to surface. But since defenses are never completely given up, he also recognized that unconscious material would be expressed in dreams only in symbolic or masked fashion. The client's statement of the dream Freud called the manifest content, but he understood that there was a latent content—unconscious material that could be understood only by interpreting the symbolic message in the manifest content. A simple example might be the dreamed presence of a monster hovering over a small and frightened boy, which could symbolize the client's fears of an overbearing and punishing father. Free association of the dream's manifest content aids the therapist in unlocking the symbolic meaning of sometimes seemingly meaningless dreams.

Analysis of Resistance. Sometimes therapy bogs down. The flow of associations is sparse, there are no reported dreams, appointments are cancelled. Often that defensiveness occurs after a period of good progress. This suggests to the analyst the client's unwillingness to explore more profoundly certain unconscious material. This very unwillingness further suggests the probable importance of the content being protected. The job of the analyst is to point out what the client is doing and why, and perhaps even speculate on what the client is unconsciously trying to hide.

Analysis of Transference. As the analysis proceeds, the relationship between therapist and client increases in complexity and emotionality. Soon the relationship, for example, takes on the characteristics of childhood reactions to parents or other significant people; oversubmissiveness, dependence, hostility, childlike love's attempt at gift giving. Analysts consider this an important step in therapy and use the behavior as examples of unconscious material affecting the client's present interpersonal relations; that is, long-forgotten (repressed) mechanisms for relating to parents or others now being utilized in relating to the therapist. This process of transferring to the therapist feelings characteristic of early life is described by some psychoanalytic therapists as a transference neurosis, which then has to be worked through before the client can face up to the shadowy presence of childhood conflicts and longings in his or her real life disorder.

Post-Freudian Psychodynamic Therapies

Relatively few clinicians now closely follow the therapeutic practices of Freud. Yet notable traces of his thinking still color the theoretical orientation and technical practices of present-day psychodynamic therapists. They depart from some of his basic concepts about human development and personality formation. For example, they tend to ignore Freud's strongly biological emphasis, downgrade his stress on id and libido, and pay little attention to the early psychosexual stages so prominent in Freudian theory. As they have moved away from his theories, they have also modified and, in some cases, eliminated, the techniques he used to explore the unconscious.

FREUDIAN INFLUENCES ON CURRENT PSYCHODYNAMIC THEORY

Nevertheless, in a broader sense, psychodynamic therapy still shows the influence of Freudian thinking and practice. A central theme is the influence of the unconscious motivations on the development of anxiety and symptom formation. There still remains the Freudian goal of providing clients with insight into the sources of their unhappiness and maladaptive behavior. And although methods of conducting psychotherapy have changed radically, techniques developed by Freud—for example, dream analysis, examination of resistance and transference—are still found useful, although not as heavily depended upon.

POST-FREUDIAN CHANGES

Departures from Freudian thinking and practices fall into two major categories: changes in the theoretical framework within which therapy is conducted, and the techniques used by therapists.

Changes in Theoretical Perspectives. Today, modifications of Freudian theory introduced by post-Freudian analysts dominate the content of therapy sessions. And so analysts now talk of a Jungian analysis, bringing into the sessions Jung's archetypes and unconscious material and psychodynamics quite different from those of Freud; an Adlerian analysis, with much emphasis on the drive for power; or a Sullivanian analysis, in which the focus is on current interpersonal relationships; or an analysis stressing the object relations of Mahler or the societal pressures pointed up by Horney (see chapter 3). All of these changes are in sharp contrast to the Freudian accent on sexual and aggressive impulses.

Perhaps the most striking theoretical change in modern psychodynamic theory is a shift from id dominance to a recognition of the importance of the ego, which, in its conscious and rational functioning, can serve constructive purposes in leading the client back to normal adjustment. With that shift has come an increasing interest in the client's interpersonal relations, especially those within the family.

Changes in Therapeutic Practice. There are three principal ways in which modern psychodynamic therapy differs from traditional analytical practices. They are as follows: 1. Today's therapist is more active—more direct in providing interpretation, giving advice and elaborating options available to the client. 2. Therapy is briefer and, in a sense, more to the point. The couch is rarely used. Sessions are held once or, at most, twice a week. Therapy is of shorter duration. For example, one approach is to set time limits on the duration of therapy. One that focuses on symptom relief limits the number of sessions to twelve. Even where the therapy is more global with a goal of changing the client's personality, another time-related approach offers only up to thirty sessions. 3. The therapy is more likely to explore the client's current life and interpersonal relations, going back to earlier life experiences to give perspective and understanding to the present.

OVERVIEW OF PSYCHODYNAMIC THERAPY

Surveys indicate that short-term psychodynamic therapy is probably the most widely practiced of any of the psychotherapies, yet there is controversy about its theoretical foundations and its effectiveness. There are three principal criticisms leveled against the psychodynamic approach. They are as follows:

1. The theoretical propositions of psychodynamic therapy, it is said, are difficult to prove scientifically. Those outside the psychodynamic perspective charge that most writings of psychodynamic therapists, including reports on successful treatment, are influenced more by intuition and subjective judgment than by scientific investigation.

2. The number of psychodynamic theories and the differences among them are also seen as weaknesses. The question is asked: How can such different perspectives about the causes of abnormal behavior provide, in any consistent fashion, useful insights to the client? Do the insights vary with the therapist rather than the dynamics in the client's life? Is it, for example, more a matter of the therapist persuading the client to his or her point of view, and is the success of therapy more dependent on the therapist's persuasive powers than on the accuracy of the insight? Can it be that the helpful nature of the relationship between therapist and client is the source of the healing, rather than the content discussed? That question cannot be answered yet. Clients do get better, and they often attribute their improvement to new ways of looking at themselves.

3. A third criticism is that psychodynamic therapy is for a relatively narrow slice of the population needing psychological help. Costs are high. And although some health insurance programs help in meeting those costs, not everyone who might benefit from psychological help has access to such insurance. Without it, only the comparatively affluent can afford therapy. In addition to the financial barrier, there is a psychological barrier. Psychodynamic therapy is a highly verbal procedure that requires the client to be intelligent and articulate. The statement is made in criticism that only "YAVIS" clients can benefit; that is, only the young, attractive, verbal, intelligent and successful client can be helped. It can be defended by noting that, at least, it does benefit some part, if not a large one, of the mentally disturbed population. Not all medical cures work for everyone, either.

Despite criticisms of psychodynamic therapy, there are positive statements to be made about it. Large numbers of clients who have experienced psychodynamic therapy report deeper understanding of themselves, a reduction in anxiety and maladaptive behavior, and better interpersonal relations. Those word-of-mouth testimonials have, no doubt, something to do with the large number of troubled people who undertake psychodynamic therapy. Beyond that, there are carefully conducted studies which report positive results with a substantial majority of those who have completed therapy.

CLIENT-CENTERED, EXISTENTIAL AND GESTALT THERAPIES

There are three therapeutic approaches that stand apart from mainstream psychotherapeutic effort, whether psychodynamic or behavioral. They draw neither on the Freudian-toned concepts of the first or the learning concepts of the second. Although even when combined, the number of clients they treat make up a very small minority of all clients in other forms of therapy, they are discussed here because of the contrast they provide with major forms of therapy and the range of therapeutic approaches they suggest. They are client-centered therapy (based on the humanistic perspective), existential therapy, and Gestalt therapy.

All three have as their primary goal increasing the clients' insights into the causes of their behavior by bringing into awareness repressed and unconscious material and are global in their hoped-for outcomes. Beyond those commonalities with psychodynamic therapy, their conceptual underpinnings and the therapeutic techniques they employ are notably different. (For a discussion of the humanistic and existential perspectives, see chapter 3.) The client-centered and existential therapies particularly have in common the goal of maximizing the client's sense of freedom to choose, reducing any feelings of being bound or determined by circumstances, and encouraging clients to choose their own destiny.

Client-Centered Therapy: The Humanistic Approach

Client-centered therapy has evolved from an original treatment described by Carl Rogers in 1950. He initially called it nondirective therapy. In subsequent publications, he has developed parallel developments to his therapeutic approach, a conceptual framework for it, the humanistic perspective. Rogers now prefers to call his approach person-centered therapy, thereby suggesting the equal standing of the two individuals involved in the therapeutic endeavor. A principal emphasis in the therapy is to create a profound and intensely personal relationship between therapist and client. To accomplish this, there are two principal thrusts made in the therapeutic effort: helping the client to experience the therapist's unconditional regard, and the therapist's efforts to achieve empathy with the client in order to see the world as he or she does.

UNCONDITIONAL POSITIVE REGARD

The most fundamental conviction giving direction to client-centered therapy is the belief that people are basically good even when they are doing "bad" things. It is, Rogers would say, because they have not received unconditional positive regard from significant people in their lives that they do "bad" things. Unless the therapist first attempts to meet the client's need for positive regard, the client remains defensive and will not let down his or her psychological guard to relate honestly to the therapist. Unconditional acceptance of the client is the most important message a Rogerian therapist initially attempts to deliver.

EMPATHY WITH THE CLIENT

Once the therapist feels that the message of unconditional positive regard has been felt by the client, the therapist uses his or her trained skills to relate to the client so empathically as to share the client's world as the client, in the security of the therapist's positive regard, reveals it. To move the client toward insight, client-centered therapists listen intently to what the clients are saying, and then reflect back their understanding of feelings expressed, conflicts and frustrations experienced, and goals envisioned. In that way, the therapist helps the client to clarify and know life experiences for what they are, and eventually to accept and deal with them.

Existential Psychotherapy

The treatment practices of this school can best be described by stating the two major conceptual propositions of the existential perspective (discussed more fully in chapter 3). The first is that human beings are free to make their own choices, but they must assume responsibility for the consequences of those choices. Their problems are of their own making, and only they can undo them. The second proposition has been labeled "the ontological context," the "here and now," the individual's "lived world." The therapists's goal in promoting insight is to focus on that world, to clarify it, and to confront the client with the problems of dealing with it. Existential therapeutic practices are whatever will bring into focus and clarify for the client those two determinants of the individual's problems.

The approaches of existential therapists and the techniques used vary from therapist to therapist. Two techniques used by Viktor Frank (1905–), a founder of the existential mode of therapy, illustrate the wide range of existential therapeutic practice that characterize existential therapy.

PARADOXICAL INTERVENTION

Here clients are encouraged to act out, even to exaggerate their symptoms—for example, to eat a gluttonous meal when overeating is the problem. The point is to drive home the individual's freedom of choice, even to choosing that very behavior he or she considers the most undesirable.

DEREFLECTION

That odd term refers to the second of Frank's therapeutic techniques, in which the client's attention is directed away from his or her symptoms, and then the therapist helps the client to visualize how much richer life could be, how much more enjoyment there could be, if the client was not so preoccupied with his or her symptoms.

To the extent that those exercises lead clients to take responsibility for what they do, they become conscious of what they are doing with their lives, more aware of their choices and values, with the possibility that their lives will then become more open, honest and meaningful; or, in existential terminology, more authentic.

Gestalt Therapy

Drawn from a major German school of psychology, Gestalt therapy emphasizes the wholeness of the human being. It combines insight and behavioral change components. It requires, to begin with, that the client identify significant emotional conflicts of the past and then that the client act those out in a role-playing way. Clients are encouraged to be as vivid, even violent, as possible, stopping only at physical attack, except, for example, such minor assaults as kicking over a chair or banging on a table.

Frederick (Fritz) Perls (1893–1970), the founder of Gestalt therapy, maintained that in identifying an early emotional crisis and acting it out with strong feeling, clients will confront their feelings, assume responsibility for them, and gradually control them. The ultimate goal of Gestalt therapy is to integrate past disruptive feelings into a wholeness of personality—healthier, more spontaneous, open and honest—and, in that way, less maladaptive.

Overview of the Humanistic, Existential and Gestalt Therapies

Two principal criticisms have been levelled against those therapies: their failure to base therapeutic approaches on a fully developed and integrated view of the human personality, and a certain airiness about what their goals in therapy are. They have also been criticized for the great variability in the approaches they take to therapy; but since clients range so widely in the nature of their problems, their motivations and the circumstances of their lives, that diversity in treatment techniques might be considered more strength than weakness.

The humanistic approach is less subject to those criticisms since Rogers has systematically developed a theory of personality that is widely respected. In order to submit his approach to outside evaluation, he has been one of the first to tape his therapy sessions for discussion and evaluation by peer groups.

Despite critical comment, there is no doubt that these newer therapies have influenced the thinking and practices of psychodynamic therapists. Their hopeful view of the client's basic psychological strengths and uniqueness, their emphasis on personal responsibility and self-determined choice, have constructively influenced those therapies and introduced a broad eclecticism in their methods of treatment, so much so that it may be said that an eclectic form of psychotherapy is today the most widely practiced.

One of every twenty Americans seeks psychological treatment in any one year, visiting a mental health clinic, a psychiatric hospital, or a clinician in private practice. Therapies offered are remarkably diverse. Estimates indicate that there may be more than 130 different specific therapies available today. Although most clinicians will select an appropriate mode of therapy consistent with their psychological perspective, more and more therapists take an eclectic approach (one that draws on a number of points of view) and uses a flexible set of techniques.

Therapists differ in the goals they set, the attitudes they hold, and in the demands they make of their patients. There are two different types of goals set in therapy. One is providing the individual with increased insight into motivational elements; the other is producing a change in behavior, a goal set principally in behavioral and cognitive therapies. Therapists consider therapy either a precise science (behavioral therapists) or an applied art form (Rogerian therapists, for example). Their methodologies will follow their perspective on those two matters. All therapists count on the individual's strong motivation to get well.

Choosing a therapist is an important decision and should be carefully considered after consultation with knowledgeable others. Once in therapy, the individual should consider such issues as the congeniality of the relationship; behavior or suggestions that contravene his or her ethical standards; candor in revealing problems; and freedom to ask questions and to challenge the therapist.

The principal psychodynamically oriented therapies are psychoanalysis, person-centered therapy, existential therapy, and Gestalt therapy.

Psychodynamically oriented therapy involves principally talking to the therapist, particularly about early life experiences. The therapist will employ such therapeutic approaches as free association, dream analysis, analysis of the client's resistance to therapy, and an analysis of transference relationships. It is often a long-term, intense commitment. More recently developed psychoanalytic therapies, sometimes called neo-Freudian, have shortened the process, moved away from the biological emphasis of or-

thodox Freudian therapy, given more attention to current problems than to early childhood relationships, and are more willing to give advice and direction.

Client-centered, existential, and Gestalt therapy stand apart from both orthodox psychoanalytic and behavioral theory. In client-centered therapy, also referred to as the humanistic approach, the therapy is totally influenced by the goal of providing a sense of unconditional self-regard by empathizing with the patient; that is, demonstrating an understanding and acceptance of the client's feelings.

The existential therapist emphasizes the client's freedom for making his or her own choices and the need to accept responsibility for them. The essence of Gestalt therapy is a process of reenacting, in vivid, emotional fashion, early emotional conflicts and, in this way, reintegrating them more fully into one's personality.

Selected Readings

Devine, P.A. and P.S. Fernald. 1973. "Outcome Effects of Receiving a Preferred Randomly Assigned or Nonpreferred Therapy." *Journal of Consulting and Clinical Psychology*, 41(1): 104-107.

Jourard, S.M. 1974. *Healthy Personality: An approach from the Viewpoint of Humanistic Psychology*. New York: Macmillan.

London, P. 1964. *The Modes and Morals of Psychotherapy*. New York: Holt, Rinehart and Winston.

Lubovsky, L. and D.P. Spence. 1978. "Quantitative Research on Psychoanalytic Therapy." In S.L. Garfield and A.E. Bergin, eds. *Handbook of Psychotherapy and Behavior Change: An Empirical Analysis*, 2nd ed. New York: Wiley.

May, R. 1961. "Existential Bases of Psychotherapy." In R. May, ed. *Existential Psychology*. New York: Random House.

Menininger, K. 1938. *Man Against Himself*. New York: Harcourt.

Rogers, C.R. 1980. *A Way of Being*. Boston, MA: Houghton Mifflin, 1980.

Strean, Herbert S. 1988. *Behind the Couch: Revelations of a Psychoanalyst*. New York: Wiley.

7

Behavioral, Cognitive-Behavioral, and Biogenic Therapies

*H*istorically, and up through modern times, one or another variant of the psychodynamic approach to therapy has dominated psychotherapeutic practice. In this chapter we examine three rapidly growing forms of therapy, radically different in their methodology from the psychodynamic approach, developed largely in the post-Freudian era, with little, if any, traces of psychoanalytical influence.

These new therapies are as follows: 1. behavioral therapy, with its foundations in learning theory, principally classical and operant conditioning; 2. cognitive-behavioral therapy, which combines the behavioral perspective with developments in cognitive psychology and traces its beginning less to Freud than to John Dollard (1900–1967) and Neal Miller (b. 1909), who theorized in 1950 that cognitive activities are as much events (and, therefore, proper subjects for psychological study and use) as are overt activities, and translated psychoanalytic theory into the terminology of classical and operant conditioning; and 3. biogenic therapy, which treats mental illness through medical/physical intervention. The chapter examines them in that order and concludes with a brief discussion of several forms of multiple person therapy.

BEHAVIORAL THERAPIES

Of all the perspectives described in this book, the cognitive-behavioral model is the one that has, in the past quarter century, most increased its influence on therapeutic practice in the United States. It is, to a notable extent, drawing clinicians away from an exclusively psychodynamic practice, especially for certain types of emotional disorders. For example, behavioral therapy is now recognized as the treatment of choice for phobias; it has also been called the backbone of modern psychotherapeutic practice for sexual disorders.

Behavioral therapy is an action-oriented therapy; specific, not global, in its focus; and is conducted as an applied science using precise technical approaches.

As described in chapter 4, behaviorists believe that maladaptive behavior is the result of faulty learning that prevents the individual from developing effective coping mechanisms for adjusting to life's stresses. The behavioral perspective further states that much, if not all, learning results from either respondent or operant conditioning. Although behavioral therapy takes a variety of forms, all, in one way or another, make use of the basic principles of conditioning. Since the behavioral therapies are embraced by the conditioning framework which has already been discussed in detail in chapter 4, it will be possible here to consider the most frequently used of them only briefly.

Basic Principles of Behavioral Therapy

The basic principles of conditioning used most frequently in behavioral therapy are the following: 1. Reinforced behavior is strengthened and likely to reoccur. 2. A stimulus regularly paired with a second stimulus that elicits a response will come to elicit the same response. 3. Behavior that is not reinforced will tend to disappear from the individual's behavioral repertory. 4. Any response that removes an unpleasant or hurtful condition will be strengthened. 5. Reinforcement of the components of a desired response in a way to move the individual toward that response will eventually make that response a part of the individual's way of behaving. 6. Although infrequently and warily used, punishment following a response will cause an undesired response to disappear, but may produce other undesired consequences.

The therapeutic application of those principles essentially involves an unlearning of the faulty and maladaptive learning. That initial step is best followed by other learning sessions in which effective coping behavior can be learned.

Specific Types of Behavioral Therapy

There follows brief descriptions of widely used behavioral therapeutic techniques with examples of behavior they seek to modify.

EXTINCTION BY REMOVAL OF REINFORCERS

Undesirable behavior is sometimes taught by situations in the environment that, in an unplanned way, reinforce the behavior. A common example in many homes is that of the child throwing a temper tantrum, which is unwittingly reinforced by the child becoming the center of everyone's attention, especially that of the parents. Once the parents leave the room or totally ignore the tantrum, thereby no longer reinforcing it, the temper tantrum subsides. If that practice is followed regularly, temper tantrums disappear or, at least, become less frequent.

Dependency or helplessness in adults can be reinforced by giving in to it; and contrariwise, can be reduced if the person appealed to—a spouse, an older child or a friend—can be taught to refuse to comply with the plea for help in a compassionate way.

A particular form of the technique of extinction has been labeled "time out." Principally used with children, the behavioral technique is to place the child in a completely neutral setting, where there are no reinforcements to be found, when the undesired behavior occurs. Compassion for the child demands that the isolation be relatively brief and that the place of removal is not frightening to the child.

EXTINCTION BY SYSTEMATIC DESENSITIZATION, FLOODING, AND IMPLOSION

There are three specialized techniques for extinguishing undesired avoidance responses (an example of which would be agoraphobia, a disorder causing people to avoid crowds or open places). These techniques have in common the goal of making the client less sensitive to the stimulus that causes the avoidance response. They are systematic desensitization, flooding, and implosion. In each of them, there is exposure to the very stimulus producing the avoidance response for which treatment has been sought. The exposure may be to the actual situation, to a vivid representation of it, or to the client's imagining of it.

Systematic Desensitization. Joseph Wolpe created a three-step procedure for reducing anxiety produced by specific tension-causing situations; for example, open spaces for the agoraphobic.

Wolpe first trains the client in relaxation. He uses any of several methods, including the occasional use of hypnosis and drugs. Once the client has learned to relax, the therapist encourages the client to describe a number of anxiety-producing situations, ranging from those that cause mild anxiety to those producing extreme anxiety. With the client fully relaxed, the third step is to have the client imagine the previously identified anxiety-producing situations, beginning with the least disturbing and gradually working up to the most disturbing. Because of the incompatibility of feeling safely relaxed and anxious at the same time, the client is gradually desensitized to the unpleasant anxiety, and the maladaptive response is extinguished.

Flooding and Implosion. Here the principle of extinction by the non-reinforcement of a negative, undesired response is used. But no gradual approach is allowed. Instead, the client is exposed to the prolonged presence of the feared stimulus or to a vivid representation of it. Implosion is similar to flooding, except that feared stimuli are vividly imagined by the client at the direction and encouragement of the therapist. The process is continued as the client is encouraged to seek out the symbolic meaning of the anxiety-causing stimuli. The stimulus is maintained at a high level until the response is extinguished. One advantage of having the client imagine the feared stimulus is that the client can "practice" the technique between therapy sessions, thus increasing the likelihood that the client would actually confront the anxiety-producing situation in real life. Repeated many times in a calming situation, the techniques reduce the anxiety attack and the maladaptive response of avoiding the previously feared situation.

Flooding has been particularly effective in controlling obsessive-compulsive behavior. For example, if the compulsion is hand washing to avoid contamination, the client is actually "contaminated" and prevented from washing, an activity which, in the past, had been reinforced by a reduction in anxiety. The client, in time, comes to discover that there is really nothing to fear and therefore no compulsive behavior is required to remove it.

Flooding and implosion, because of their simpler but just as effective procedures, have, to some extent, replaced systematic desensitization as a treatment of choice for some forms of anxiety disorder. One significant disadvantage is the intensity of anxiety experienced early in treatment. For that reason, some therapists are reluctant to use either flooding or implosion.

AVERSION THERAPY

Instead of using removal of reinforcement as a means of modifying behavior, aversion therapy pairs undesirable behavior with an aversive aftereffect. It has been found useful in problems of impulse control; for example, alcohol abuse or cigarette smoking. Here, the undesired activity is paired with a nausea-inducing drug, or one that produces a severely unpleasant taste. Some sexually deviant behavior has also been controlled by using a comparable technique. It can be easily understood that full cooperation from the client is required for the use of aversive therapy.

COVERT SENSITIZATION

An occasional substitute for aversive therapy is to have the client imagine, rather than experience, the unpleasant consequences of maladaptive impulsive behavior. The client is directed to pair the image of the undesired behavior with vivid images of unpleasant consequences; for example, imagining the revolting and possibly dangerous consequences of getting drunk.

POSITIVE REINFORCEMENT

The most satisfactory method of modifying behavior is reinforcement of desired behavior. But since therapy is principally sought to eliminate undesired behavior, the primary challenge to using that method is eliciting the desired behavior. There are four well-tested techniques for successfully meeting that challenge: shaping, modeling, assertiveness training, and biofeedback.

Shaping. When an individual seems unable to make a desired response instead of a maladaptive one, or when the desired response is a complex one, the client can be gradually led in the right direction by shaping his or her behavior; that is, reinforcing any response, no matter how slight, that moves the client toward the targeted goal, which is any behavior that approximates the desired response. For example, where an autistic child (see chapter 18) avoids any interaction with other children, behavior as simple as turning in the direction of another child sitting in the room would be reinforced every time the child does so; a step toward the other child, as it occurs, would next be rewarded, until finally, the child has reached the point of standing in front of the other child and making eye contact with him or her. The procedure would be repeated at subsequent sessions, taking care not to reinforce a previous response once the child has made a promising one, which is, of course, reinforced. The procedure does work to produce rudimentary social behavior, which, once engaged in, can produce its own reinforcing effects.

Modeling. Observing the successful efforts of others and then modeling one's behavior on theirs is a very common human learning experience. It begins early—for example, the success of the one-year-old imitating behavior of an older sibling or a parent—and continues on throughout life; for example, the middle-aged golf duffer imitating the stance of the golf professional. We all model our behavior on that of parents, teachers, friends, and, particularly in adolescence, on movie and television stars.

It is just as easy to imitate good behavior as bad behavior, adaptive behavior as maladaptive behavior. That fact has turned the attention of psychologists to modeling as a form of treatment. The positive reinforcement that motivates modeling is two-fold: anticipated success in enjoying what another person seems to be enjoying, and the self-satisfaction of modeling the behavior of an admired person.

Its use in therapy is ordinarily easy to arrange: the admired therapist demonstrating his or her lack of fear of snakes; allowing the client to watch a group of children enjoying the antics of a dog; in a controlled setting, surrounding a child with children who are modeling desired behavior. Assertiveness training (to be discussed below) offers positive modeling experiences for adults.

Assertiveness Training. A well-known and widely used technique for encouraging shy or submissive people to assert themselves, assertiveness training can be viewed both as a desensitizing technique and a shaping procedure. The trainer, or group leader, might begin by stating the goal of the training, describing nonassertiveness as a common but handicapping trait, and assuring the group that active participation was voluntary. A next step is to get someone to volunteer to act out a very mild expression of assertiveness. The trainer might suggest a possible situation. After the performance, the encouraging comments of the trainer serve as reinforcement. Other volunteers are drawn into role-playing assertiveness in a variety of situations. The participants are then directed to attempt a real life demonstration of an assertive position.

Three positive influences are operative in assertiveness training: positive reinforcement, the desensitizing effect of engaging in behavior that is gradually made more assertive, and the modeling effect of peer behavior. Assertiveness training is a useful therapy when maladaptive anxiety is due to a lack of self-assertiveness; however, the treatment has little relevance for phobias involving nonpersonal situations.

Biofeedback. The essential element in biofeedback is immediately reporting back to a person any changes in autonomic activity, such as heart rate, blood pressure, changes in skin temperature, or galvanic skin response. Those are all associated with emotional responses and are involved in anxiety attacks and phobic reactions.

Until the early sixties, voluntary control of autonomic responses was not thought to be possible. With the development of sensitive electronic devices that could accurately measure such physiological responses, it was soon discovered that they could be modified by such learning procedures as respondent and operant conditioning. With that discovery came the possibility that the unpleasant subjective experiences associated with heightened autonomic response could be controlled by the process of what has been called biofeedback. The procedure is itself a rather simple one, although it requires the use of elaborate and expensive equipment. Autonomic responses are carefully measured, and the measurements are converted into visual or auditory signals which are quickly fed back to the client, who is then encouraged to use the signals in an effort to reduce the undesired autonomic response. The goal of treatment is to teach the client to control internal responses that may intensify the emotional responses associated with anxiety or panic reactions.

In the short term, it is now known that that goal can be achieved to some extent, but the effect is not a lasting one outside the therapy setting. With that finding, many clinicians have drawn the conclusion that a more efficient and longer-lasting treatment is relaxation training. Today, biofeedback is more likely to be used as a research tool than in therapy.

OVERVIEW OF BEHAVIORAL THERAPY

Behavioral therapy is here to stay, at least for the treatment of specific symptoms; for example, phobias, certain types of anxiety attacks, and impulse control. It has two strong advantages: sound, widely accepted theoretical underpinnings (the behavioristic principles of learning on which it is based) and the precision and relative ease with which it can be used.

Its disadvantages are that as an action-oriented therapy, it leaves the client with little insight as to underlying causes of the symptom or its associated psychological disorder. A possible, although not frequent, unfortunate result can be that the treated symptom is replaced by a different one, which may be even more disruptive than the original symptom. One other possible limitation (at least for scientific purposes) is that subtle and unreported behavior of the therapist—for example, powerful suggestion—may be as influential as the behavioral procedures themselves.

COGNITIVE THERAPY

As early as 1950, Dollard and Miller, themselves both possessing strong behavioristic leanings, had proposed that cognitions (previously excluded from psychological research by behaviorists) were as much events subject to psychological study and modification as were actions. They, in effect, proposed changing the stimulus response formula to one including the organism with all its idiosyncratic cognitions in the formula, making it an S-O-R arrangement.

Not until 1965 was this followed up in any systematic way. At that time, other behaviorists argued that S - R connections were not automatic, that what cognitions the individual brought to the situation influenced interpretations given to a stimulus and placed particular values on one response as compared with another response. Chapter 4 discussed those in detail. Examples of important cognitions that might influence what response an individual makes to a given stimulus are expectations, plans and competencies.

The new approach drew from both behaviorism and cognitive psychology to establish new therapies and is frequently labeled cognitive-behavioral therapy. There is no one accepted mode of the therapy. Here we exemplify it in the practices of three clinicians: Albert Ellis, Aaron Beck, and Donald Meichenbaum and associates. Each is described briefly.

Albert Ellis: Rational-Emotive Therapy

Ellis bases his therapeutic approach on what he calls the irrational beliefs individuals bring to situations that cause them to respond maladaptively. An example is the belief that one should be competent, intelligent and achieving in all situations. The client with such a belief sees depression-causing failure in many situations in which success should never have been expected; expectations of successful performance were irrational.

Ellis's treatment is aggressively confrontational. After discovery of the client's principal irrational beliefs, Ellis bluntly spells out the irrationality of the belief and directs the client to monitor behavior dictated by such beliefs and correct it. Between therapy sessions, the therapist encourages the client to behave in ways contrary to one or another of his or her irrational beliefs.

Ellis's proposed theory was so radical a departure from the well-established therapies that it was first looked upon scornfully by many clinicians. However, despite the discouraging start, one 1976 survey reported rational-emotive therapy to be one of the more widely used therapies.

Aaron Beck: Cognitive-Behavior Therapy

Close in theory to rational-emotive therapy, Beck's therapeutic methods are notably different. His methods are based initially on Beck's theory of depression, which he thought to be the result of irrational self-devaluation, an irrationally pessimistic view of one's life expectancies, and an irrationally gloomy view of the future.

The job of the therapist in Beck's approach is to draw out the client's defenses of the unidentified irrational beliefs by Socratic questioning and, in that way, help the client perceive their irrationality. Beck's soft approach gradually allows clients to reach their own conclusions about the irrational nature of their beliefs. Beck has reported success in using his method for treatment of depression, anxiety and phobias.

Donald Meichenbaum: Self-Instructional Therapy

The unique feature of Meichenbaum's therapy is self-talk. Behavior, he believes, is influenced by what people say to themselves before, during and after their actions. For example, a nail biter, unhappy with the habit and unable to break it, might habitually self-talk in these words: "There I go again. I'll never be able to stop." Once the therapist is able to discover self-talk patterns such as that one, he or she attempts to change it from a self-defeating to a coping way of talking. Meichenbaum gives this example:

"There I go again. Just this one nail. Then I'll stop . . . I knew the treatment wouldn't help me. I just can't control myself. Cut it out! You always make excuses for yourself. Take a slow, deep breath. Relax. Just think of sucking my finger in front of everybody. What a picture!" Clients are trained to practice encouraging self-talk on their own. The technique is useful not only in therapy but in everyday use to build confidence. Today, star tennis and baseball players can be seen on television engaging in self-talk at critical moments in their games.

OVERVIEW OF COGNITIVE-BEHAVIORAL THERAPY

Within the limits set by its goal, a change in specific behavior, research reports indicate positive outcomes for all three therapies described here. Control of depression has been particularly promising. The technique offers the client little insight into broader personality characteristics and has not yet developed a significant theoretical framework for its successes. Nevertheless, its positive outcomes are likely to encourage its growth in both therapeutic practice and theory development.

BIOGENIC THERAPIES

Treatment of mental illness by direct alteration of bodily states has a long history. Even prehistoric people drilled holes into the skulls of those judged abnormal to allow evil spirits to escape. Long after that, primitive practices continued: purging the body of substances thought to cause mental disorder by laxatives; bleeding, which continued through the eighteenth century as a common medical practice for physical and mental illnesses.

Successful treatment of mental disorders has trailed far behind effective treatment of physical illness. But as bodily functions have become better understood, and as science has learned the effect of surgery, drugs, and even electricity on those functions, progress in treating physical disease has led, in the twentieth century, to increased physical treatment of mental disorders.

Some of those early efforts now seem as primitive and, in fact, were at least as dangerous, as the primitive efforts of earlier centuries. Two of them, insulin coma shock and psychosurgery, have all but disappeared. Today's biogenic therapies for mental illness are relatively safe and easily administered. But as with all treatment, in the hands of hasty and careless therapists or as used by careless, severely anxious or depressed patients, they can have uncertain consequences.

One form of convulsive therapy—electroshock, as distinguished from insulin coma shock—is an effective form of therapy for severe depression. But the most progress in biogenic forms of treatment has come from developments in the field of pharmacology (the study of drugs and their effects on the body). Pharmaceutical drugs in current use aim at producing physiological changes that affect specific symptoms of mental illness. They have proven strikingly effective in the treatment of anxiety-based disorders, mood disorders, and for some symptoms of schizophrenia.

This section describes briefly electroconvulsive therapy, psychosurgery, and four types of drug treatment: antianxiety drugs, drugs for psychotic symptoms, antidepressant and antimanic drugs. All the described treatments are administered in a medical setting.

Electro-convulsive Therapy

Coma, induced by the administration of increasing dosages of insulin, a procedure that brings on shock and coma from an acute shortage of glucose (sugar) in the blood, was introduced in 1932. It was a drastic form of biogenic treatment with significant physiological complications, some fatal, but was nevertheless used widely in the treatment of schizophrenia until the end of the thirties, when it gradually faded out as a treatment because of a high rate of relapse and a relatively high fatality rate.

Beginning in 1938, electrically induced convulsions gradually became the preferred form of convulsive type therapy. Following a short period when electroshock was used to induce convulsions in schizophrenics, its use was shifted to the severely depressed. Although surrounded by controversy because of its side effects, including memory loss, electroconvulsive shock treatment is now an established mode of treatment for severe depression and some forms of manic behavior. But the selective use of drugs for depression and other forms of mental disorders has narrowed its use to that of a treatment of last resort.

Psychosurgery

For a twenty-year period (1935 to 1955), prefrontal lobotomy, which involved the destruction of precisely defined and minute parts of the brain, was a frequently used treatment for severe psychoses. While the operation did eliminate or reduce the most disturbing symptoms of the patients and thus made them more manageable, it also brought many of them to mere vegetative existence. Since the development of effective antipsychotic drug therapies with only relatively mild side effects, psychosurgery is used only in extreme situations; for example, to reduce intolerable pain in the terminally ill.

Drug Therapies

Among biogenic therapies, drug treatment is far and away the most commonly used treatment for mental disturbances. It is easily administered and relatively effective for a variety of mental disturbances. Valium, one of the minor tranquilizers, is the second most frequently prescribed drug in the United States. Drug therapies have been found effective in the treatment of anxiety, depression and schizophrenia. We will describe four types of drug treatment: antianxiety, antipsychotic, antidepression and antimanic drugs.

ANTIANXIETY DRUGS

Drugs used to reduce the symptoms of anxiety are the most frequently used of biogenic therapies. One of every ten Americans, at least once a year, uses one of the antianxiety drugs. The most commonly prescribed are Valium, Librium and Traxene. Their widespread use suggests that they are an effective means of reducing tension. When followed up with psychotherapy, they can help the patient to deal with problem-causing anxiety. However, too often, both doctor and the troubled individual settle for regularly renewed prescriptions, with no attempt at insight therapy. When that happens, both doctor and patient are inviting troublesome secondary problems: overdependence on the drug and the likely need to increase the dosage or to experiment with other, perhaps dangerous, drugs; failure to confront important psychic problems; and, in extreme cases, the temptation to take overdoses or to mix one drug with another, a step that has resulted in serious illness or death.

Perhaps the best that can be said for anxiety-reducing drugs is that they are useful in the short term to help an individual gather psychological strength to undertake a proper course of psychotherapy or to deal with an immediate crisis.

ANTIPSYCHOTIC DRUGS

The major tranquilizers, as these drugs are called, often reduce major symptoms of schizophrenia. The most commonly prescribed of the antipsychotic drugs is the group of phenothiazines, which are available under the names Thorazine, Mellaril and Stelazine. Clozapine, which requires an expensive blood-monitoring program to prevent negative and possibly fatal side effects on the white blood cells, is, nevertheless, increasingly being prescribed, with beneficial results, for schizophrenic patients. The principal result of the drug treatment is to calm the schizophrenic, sometimes into a state of harmless drowsiness.

Many patients, while still on the drug, are able to return home, where they seem to function adequately; those who are required to stay in the hospital are, unfortunately, often overmanaged by heavier and heavier doses of the drug, soon reducing them to almost complete impassivity.

These drugs are not a cure for schizophrenia, only a means of controlling the illness's most disturbing symptoms. A major social problem created by the therapeutic use of the drugs is the early release into the community of still-schizophrenic patients, with no family support and no community program of aftercare. Many such individuals have become part of America's population of the homeless.

ANTIDEPRESSANT DRUGS

Commonly used antidepressant drugs are Tofranil and Sinequam, part of a group named the tricyclics. Although the drug is slow to take effect, it has become a major source of relief for depressed individuals. As is true for all drug therapies, full treatment is best effected when it is combined with a program of psychotherapy.

ANTIMANIC DRUGS

The principal antimanic drug is Lithium, a natural mineral salt that has proved effective in ending 70 percent of all manic episodes. The principal problem in its use is establishing the proper dosage. The difficulty is that raising the dosage too close to the margin of toxicity in an attempt to increase its effectiveness can produce serious illness. Fortunately, the patient on a self-maintenance regimen is usually troubled by minor physical symptoms which should signal the need to reduce the medication. In any case, Lithium levels have to be monitored regularly.

MULTIPLE-PERSON THERAPIES

One of the most distinctive developments in psychological treatment is multiple-person therapy. It takes a variety of forms. The most common of them are group therapy, peer group therapy, family therapy and marital counseling.

Group Therapy

Simply defined, group therapy is the assembling of a group of people with psychological problems for the purpose of discussing their problems under the guidance of a professionally trained leader, usually a psychologist. Within that framework, group therapy can take a variety of specific forms determined principally by the theoretical perspective of the leader and the kinds of problems the participants bring.

The most precise way of describing possible therapeutic values to be found in group therapy is to describe, from Irwin Yalom's book, *The Theory and Practice of Group Psychotherapy,* (1975), nine benefits that group therapy offers. They are as follows: 1. Information about a problem, its possible causes, and remedies that might be helpful. 2. Hope. Knowing something about a problem generates a feeling that something can be done. 3. Commonality. Other people have similar problems. "I am not alone." 4. Altruism. Since group members soon try to help each other, they come to feel better about themselves. 5. Family membership. A group can soon establish familylike relationships. This new family can teach new ways of relating to parents, spouses, children and friends. 6. Development of social skills. Listening, talking and interacting with others are all likely to improve social skills. Particularly helpful is the feedback one gets to one's own behavior from other members of the family. 7. Modeling. An individual may find it helpful to emulate the behavior of other participants or of the group leader. 8. Catharsis. The open exchange of feelings among members may encourage the venting of hostile or embarrassing feelings that, when previously bottled up, caused tensions. 9. Belongingness. A well-run group soon establishes a sense of cohesiveness, which, one hopes, creates in the participants a sense of belonging.

Peer Group Therapy

Some of the benefits of professionally led groups can be found in peer groups, a group of individuals with similar problems—substance abusers, for example—who come together to give each other social support and possible guidance in solving problems. One widely known and well-thought-of peer group is Alcoholics Anonymous. The group is distinctive, since its operation is based on a number of strongly held beliefs: once an alcoholic, always an alcoholic; no one can stop drinking without help; in offering that help to others when called upon, one helps oneself. The program is widely supported by former alcoholics who have benefited from it and by many clergy of all faiths. Since hard research evidence has not been developed about the benefits of AA, most psychotherapists prefer to see it used as a supplement to other treatment modes.

Family and Marital Therapy

A family with children or a childless couple can be thought of as a group with a structure, roles that are enacted, and communication among members, good or bad. Where any of those elements are warped—for example, a family structure with a domineering head, a scapegoat role for one of the children, or contradictory messages from parents or sometimes from the same parent—problems will develop. Both family and marital therapy, with the help of a neutral outside person, attempt to bring maladaptive practices out into the open and effect changes in them.

A variety of techniques has been found useful in family and marital counseling. Two examples are: the communication approach, in which an effort is made to identify and discuss covertly contradictory messages used by one or more members of the family or marital groups; and paradoxical intention, in which a family member will be encouraged to role-play offensive behavior that has been identified and to learn how it affects other members, who are encouraged to react to it. An emphasis in marital therapy is dialogue between the two members, with an attempt to motivate each to express their feelings about what is wrong with their ways of talking to each other.

*B*ehavioral therapy is an action-oriented therapy with the goal of effecting specific behavioral change; it is therefore considered specific, not global, in its focus, and is looked upon as an applied science in its methodology. There are seven strictly behavioral therapies, and three which are considered cognitive-behavioral.

EXTINCTION OF UNDESIRABLE BEHAVIOR. Here is a form of behavioral therapy in which any reinforcement of the undesired response, no matter how subtle or indirect—for example, merely paying attention to it—is eliminated. A common form is "time out" in which, for example, a misbehaving child is placed in a neutral situation and isolated from all social reinforcements of the undesired behavior.

EXTINCTION BY SYSTEMATIC DESENSITIZATION. Used principally to reduce anxiety or phobias, the goal is to gradually allow the individual to experience graded levels of tension-producing stimuli under highly relaxed and protected circumstances until the individual becomes desensitized to the stimuli. Flooding and implosion are variants of this therapy.

SHAPING. To encourage an individual to move toward more complex but desirable social skills, for example, the therapist reinforces any behavior that moves the individual in the desired direction.

MODELING. This is a simple therapy in which a situation is created to allow the client to observe examples of the desired behavior and to imitate them.

ASSERTIVENESS TRAINING. This is a group form of therapy in which an overly-inhibited individual is taught to be more assertive, that is, to be more demanding and expressive, by verbal instruction, protected trials, and then, relatively safe real life trials, which are later reported to the group.

BIOFEEDBACK. To learn to control various physiological responses that support undesired symptoms—for example, anxiety—the therapist arranges equipment so that the client can immediately get feedback on such physiological responses as pulse rate and blood pressure and then, while watching the feedback data, the client is directed to lower the physiological response.

In cognitive-oriented therapy, faulty ways of thinking, such as "everyone must like me," that would lead to maladaptive submissive behavior, are first identified and then corrected. Such thinking includes unrealistic expectations, impossible plans, and feelings of inferiority about one's competence. There are three principal cognitive therapies.

RATIONAL-EMOTIVE THERAPY. Developed by Albert Ellis, the therapy first identifies irrational beliefs. The therapist, in a confrontational fashion, then points out in multiple ways how irrational the belief is.

Aaron Beck, instead, uses a soft and gentle form of changing irrational beliefs. He employs a Socratic questioning method to reduce the grip of the irrational belief on the individual's behavior.

Donald Meichenbaum encourages clients to take a self-instructional approach. He directs them to talk to themselves in ways that attack the false beliefs or encourage desired behavior.

There are two principal forms of biogenic therapy. The most widely used is drug therapy. Drugs are now available to reduce anxiety, psychotic symptoms, depression and manic behavior. All have at least a short-term effect on the undesired symptoms, but are most effectively used when accompanied or followed by psychotherapy. A second form of biogenic therapy, convulsive therapy, is occasionally used to treat severe and persistent depression.

Much therapy takes place in a one-to-one relationship between client and therapist. In recent years, a variety of multiple-person therapies have been developed. The two principal types are peer group therapy, which may be led by a professionally trained leader or carried on by the clients themselves as in Alcoholics Anonymous, and family/marital therapy, in which all members of a family group are seen in therapy, both as a group and individually.

Selected Readings

Bandura, A. 1969. *Principles of Behavior Modification*. New York: Holt, Rinehart and Winston.

Beck, A.T. 1976. *Cognitive Therapy and the Emotional Disorders*. New York: International University Press.

Ellis, A. and R.A. Harper. 1975. *A New Guide to Rational Living*. Englewood Cliffs: Prentice Hall.

Meichenbaum, D. 1977. *Cognitive-behavior Modification*. New York: Plenum.

Mowner, O.H. 1948. "Learning Theory and the Neurotic Paradox." *American Journal of Orthopsychiatry*, 18: 571-610.

Panloff, M.B. 1976. "Shopping for the Right Therapist." *Saturday Review*. February 21, 1976, pp. 14-20.

Skinner, B.F. 1965. *Science and Human Behavior*. New York: Free Press.

8

The Anxiety Disorders: (Anxiety Neuroses) Anxiety Observed

The most prevalent of all the clinical syndromes studied in Abnormal Psychology are the anxiety disorders. The National Institute of Mental Health estimates that nearly fifteen million people in this country suffer from one or another of the disorders.

Because of their prevalence and the suffering caused by them, much effort has been expended in attempting to understand the nature of these psychiatric illnesses. That understanding is not only necessary for the work of psychologists and psychiatrists, but is also of practical value in such other professional fields as medicine, social work, teaching, the ministry, and police work. Those professions are often asked to help those who suffer the disorder. It is also of usefulness in giving the healthy person insight into his or her own fears and occasional attacks of anxiety.

Beginning with a discussion of fear and anxiety which are complexly involved in certain of the anxiety disorders, the chapter continues with a statement on the DSM IIIR classification of the anxiety disorders. It then describes four types of anxiety disorder: phobic disorder, post-traumatic stress disorder, generalized anxiety disorder, and obsessive-compulsive disorder, their symptoms and how widespread they are. Causal factors and therapeutic approaches are examined in chapter 9 after all the anxiety-related disorders have been described.

FEAR AND ANXIETY

Fear and anxiety are disturbing emotional states that occasionally beset the normal individual but appear more prominently and with more disruptive effect in the lives of those with anxiety disorders. Although they are intertwined in the symptomatology of the anxiety disorders and tend to reinforce each other in harmful ways, they are distinguishable, and their differences are a concern of the student of Abnormal Psychology.

Fear

Fear occurs more frequently than anxiety. It is an emotional and apprehensive response to a specific thing or situation. People fear heights, dogs, snakes, crowds or disease. Anxiety is a diffuse response focused on no specific object.

THE ELEMENTS OF FEAR

Psychologists have identified four elements in the fearful response: *the cognitive element,* in which there is a preoccupying dread of possible danger or harm from a physical injury, an embarrassing situation or a discovered incompetency; *the somatic reaction,* which ranges from pupillary and respiratory changes through digestive disorders, and bladder tension or release; *the emotional element,* which includes feelings of apprehension, queasiness, and trembling; and finally, there is *the behavioral element,* the classical fight-or-flight reaction, in which the individual is motivated to attack and destroy the cause of the fear or to flee the situation and thus escape harm.

NORMAL FEARS

The experience of fear in the face of real or threatened danger is a normal and healthy experience. Walking through a dangerous neighborhood late at night will arouse some fearfulness in almost everyone. A construction worker atop a skyscraper may experience fright in the face of a strong wind. Few men in combat have escaped fear.

ABNORMAL FEARS

Fear is an abnormal response when there is no real or possible danger, and when most people would not be frightened; that is, when the fear is irrational. Examples of such fears are fright at the approach of a leashed dog or the presence of a cat rummaging in the garbage. The abnormality of the fear is more certain when the fearful response takes extreme form and severely limits the individual's life activities. Such fears are called phobias and are known to the phobic individual to be irrational.

Anxiety

Although anxiety has the same four elements as fear, it is to be distinguished from it. In anxiety, the cognitive element is vague and intellectually unfocused. Instead of awareness of a clear and known danger, the individual feels a generalized apprehensiveness. The predominating thought is that "something terrible is going to happen to me." The sufferer cannot attack or destroy the cause of anxiety because it has no specific existence, nor can he flee from it. The emotional and somatic elements of anxiety are similar to those of fear but usually more intense.

An anxious response is maladaptive; yet, short periods of anxiety can occur to the normal person. When anxiety is severe, persistent and disruptive of normal life activities, it signals an anxiety disorder.

DSM IIIR *RECLASSIFICATION OF ANXIETY DISORDERS*

All of the anxiety disorders to be described in this chapter were formerly labeled neuroses (occasionally psychoneuroses). *DSM IIIR* has eliminated that diagnostic classification, except parenthetically. The change has discouraged psychologists from using the term. (Chapter 9 presents a fuller discussion of controversy in Abnormal Psychology arising from that decision.)

Basis of DSM IIIR Classification System

The decision to declassify the diagnosis, neurosis, arose from a rejection by the American Psychiatric Association of the concept of anxiety as a unifying construct underlying the so-called neuroses. Its reason was the undetectability and, therefore, the unmeasurability of anxiety in certain types of neuroses (principally, those to be discussed in chapter 9). The classification now used substitutes dividing the clinical syndromes formerly called neuroses into categories delineated by the symptoms observed in the behavior of the individual and the severity of those symptoms. The change, it is argued, provides a more objective, and therefore more reliable, means of classifying the disorders.

The DSM IIIR Classification

The new classification system organizes all disorders formerly labeled neuroses into three separate categories or clinical syndromes: anxiety disorders, somatoform disorders, and dissociative disorders. (Chapter 9 discusses the latter two categories.)

Table 8-1
DSM IIIR Classification of Anxiety Disorders

Panic disorder
    with agoraphobia
    without agoraphobia
Agoraphobia
Social phobia
Simple phobia
Obsessive-compulsive disorder
Post-traumatic stress disorder
Generalized anxiety disorder

(Discussion in this chapter deviates from the ordering of the *DSM IIIR* classification for clarity of presentation.)

PHOBIC DISORDER

A phobia is a persistent fear reaction to some specific object or situation. The fear is disproportionate to the likelihood of danger. Some phobias, even though maladaptive, may have minimal influence on a person's activities; for example, a snake phobia will not much trouble a city dweller and hardly needs treatment. Other phobias may completely disrupt a person's life.

Types of Phobia

There are three types of phobia: agoraphobia, social phobia and simple phobia. A study of the National Institute of Mental Health indicates phobic disorders to be the most common psychiatric disorder for women and the second-most common disorder for men (exceeded only by alcohol abuse).

AGORAPHOBIA AND PANIC DISORDER

These two anxiety disorders, although listed separately in *DSM IIIR*, feed on each other and are frequently intertwined. Each can exist separately from the other and would be so classified.

Agoraphobia. Far and away the most common phobia is agoraphobia (fear of the marketplace). The principal symptom is a fear that a panic attack will occur when the individual is in a crowd, in an open space, when traveling, or even on the street. The fear may be present without such an attack ever having materialized. A common concern is that away from home, there will be no one to help should the feared attack occur.

Agoraphobia is the most disabling of all the phobias; in many cases, the individual is unwilling to leave home, even to go out on the street. Agoraphobics have more other psychological problems than other phobics: panic-proneness although in a "safe" situation, depression, and anxiety. The phobia, in extreme cases, may be a lifelong illness, may occur intermittently, or may remit spontaneously.

Panic Disorder. This anxiety disorder is defined as an unexpected panic attack which is not provoked by the individual's being the center of attention (which would classify it as a social phobia). The symptoms are multiple and terrifying, although usually lasting only a few minutes. Typical symptoms during the attack are shortness of breath, heart palpitations, profuse sweating, dizziness, and wild fear of dying or going crazy. Often such an attack seems to follow a disturbing life experience such as an enforced job change.

There is some evidence that agoraphobia and panic disorder may be genetically linked.

SOCIAL PHOBIAS

The exclusive concern of the social phobic is being seen or watched. Thus, they would avoid or worry about eating in restaurants, performing a job chore while being watched, speaking or performing in public. They avoid crowds because they may be watched critically. All of these experiences produce an acute sense of embarrassment and the urge to escape.

Social phobias most frequently develop in adolescence. Onset is gradual; later on, the disorder may produce serious disruption in the life of the individual, causing him, for example, to give up job after job for fear of being watched. In social phobias, unlike agoraphobia, the individual usually experiences no other psychological disorder.

SIMPLE PHOBIAS

The simple phobia most closely approximates the formal definition of phobia. It is a fear of a specific object or situation. Frequently it is a fear many normal people also feel, such as fear of darkness, heights, spiders, snakes or disease. The phobic's response, however, is extreme. In the case of dog or cat phobias, for example, the fear response can make a normal life difficult or impossible.

Simple phobias fall into three categories: *animal phobias,* particularly, dogs, cats and snakes, but also occasionally birds and insects; *injury or disease phobias,* also called nosophobia; and *inanimate-object phobias,* such as heights, closed-in spaces (claustrophobia), airplane flights, storms or darkness.

In all the simple phobias, the individual goes to extreme lengths to avoid the source of fear. In nosophobia, for example, the phobic, although in apparent good health, worries constantly about contracting the feared disease. As a result, his or her behavior is irrationally defensive as the individual constantly looks for symptoms and scrupulously avoids contacts that he or she imagines may cause the disease.

Prevalence of Phobias

Agoraphobia, which accounts for half of the phobias, afflicts 3 to 6 percent of the population. Panic disorder, with or without agoraphobia, affects 1 percent of the population. Social phobias constitute about 10 percent of all phobic reactions, occurring more frequently among women than men. Mild and unreported cases of stage fright, a form of social phobia, are probably much more prevalent. Simple phobias are the rarest seen in clinical practice. Estimates suggest that simple phobias account for only 3 percent of all phobic disorders. The majority of them occur in women, and they often begin early in childhood.

REACTIONS TO STRESS: ADJUSTMENT DISORDERS AND POST-TRAUMATIC STRESS DISORDER

What distinguishes adjustment disorders and post-traumatic stress disorders from the phobic disorders is that the former are reactions to an actual undesirable and usually recent or ongoing event; the latter are fearful anticipations of an undesirable and unlikely event. Phobias grow out of fear, an anticipatory emotion; adjustment disorders and post-traumatic disorders grow out of stress, the consequence of a trying situation to which the individual is attempting to adjust. The phobic says something will happen to me; the individual with a stress disorder says something has happened to me.

Stressors and Stress

Stressors are adjustive demands made on the individual by such events as missing an important engagement or an argument with a spouse. But life also requires adjustive demands to very serious events: divorce, death of a loved one, and even such catastrophic events as military combat or natural disasters.

Adjustive Demands Imposed by Stressors

Stressors impose one or another of three types of unpleasant psychological states to which the individual must adjust: frustration, conflict and pressure.

FRUSTRATION

When an obstacle, either external or internal, stands in the way of an individual's goal-striving, or when the individual can find no suitable goal to focus on, frustration results. External obstacles are unavailability of satisfying employment or rejection in a romantic pursuit; internal obstacles (characteristics of the individual) may be incompetence, physical handicap or handicapping personality traits.

Frustration causes anger, feelings of inadequacy, and self-deprecation. When prolonged, it can elicit the fight-or-flight reaction.

CONFLICT

Everyone's life is occasionally beset by conflict, minor or major. There are three patterns of conflict: *approach-avoidance conflict,* a situation in which the individual has reason both to approach a goal and to avoid it—a desirable goal has an undesirable consequence, such as an early marriage, which might necessitate giving up a college education; *double approach conflict,* in which an individual seems doubly blessed having to choose between two equally desirable goals—two attractive job offers, for example, although a happy type of problem, the stress in making a decision can be trying; and *double avoidance conflict,* a problem of choosing between the devil and the deep blue sea. A poignant example is that of the elderly individual who must choose between a painful and risky operation or continuing to live with a painful and debilitating medical condition.

The stress of conflict causes troubling thoughts, fits and starts of activity, and, if prolonged, emotional exhaustion.

PRESSURE

Life, especially for young people, can be full of pressure; to do well at school, to get a job, to "shape up." Sometimes the pressure is from parents; at other times it may be self-imposed; surprisingly, the latter may be the more stressful. Later on, life may bring other pressure; from a spouse, from the demands of a job, pressure to care for elderly parents.

Factors Affecting the Severity of the Stress

Severity of the stress is judged by its disruptive effects on the individual's behavior. Disruptive effects are determined by characteristics of the stressor, the psychic make-up of the individual, and by the social supports available to him or her.

CHARACTERISTICS OF THE STRESSOR

Duration, cumulative effect, and multiple stressors all increase the extent of the disruption. A second day of a nagging headache is disruptive indeed. Mounting stress can lead to a breakdown. One stressor after another is bound to weaken the individual's capacity to adjust. Some values in life are especially meaningful; an attack on them can be extremely stressful.

THE INDIVIDUAL'S PSYCHIC MAKEUP

Vulnerability and the presence of positive coping mechanisms are key to understanding the likely disruptive effects of stress. A lifetime of un-rewarding experiences, negative interpersonal relations or frail health can make an individual especially vulnerable even to relatively minor stress. The coping techniques life has taught an individual are critical. A problem-solving approach reduces the negative impact of stress; the very effort of doing something helps. Defense-oriented behavior, which is essentially a protective effort to reduce the painfulness of the symptoms, helps only in the short term.

SOCIAL SUPPORTS

Never are helpful relatives or friends more appreciated than in times of stress; to talk with, to suggest options, and to provide tension-relieving social activities. Group support, although less personal, can provide helpful resources. Support can be found in religious or fraternal groups, and profes-sional help from social or governmental agencies.

Reactions to Stress

There are three principal reactions to stress: task-oriented behavior, defensive behavior, and, ultimately, decompensation.

TASK-ORIENTED BEHAVIOR

The secure and confident individual, taught by earlier life experiences to be resourceful, will direct efforts toward a goal in a task-oriented way, meeting the adjustive demands of the stressor, yet protecting himself or herself from psychic damage or behavioral disorganization.

Typical task-oriented responses include objectively appraising the situation, developing possible options, selecting one and observing its impact on the stress. The more secure the individual, the more flexible the individual, the more willingness there will be to change behavior in response to feedback obtained from its effect. If attempting to change the situation won't work, a person may shift to making personal changes. Examples are lowering one's expectations or changing goals, changing the nature of one's emotional responses in interpersonal situations, becoming less demanding or critical, or leaving the situation altogether to seek other satisfactions, e.g., divorce in an impossible marriage.

DEFENSE-ORIENTED BEHAVIOR

Defensive behavior has both short-term positive effects and long-term maladaptive effects. Expressive defensive behavior, such as crying, repetitive talking, mourning behavior, has the short-term effect of releasing tension, and also, perhaps, gaining sympathy. But as time goes on and no effort is made to attack the problem, the individual seeks escape in one or another of the defense mechanisms. Principal mechanisms are denial of unacceptable reality—"things are not really that bad"; repression, in which painful thoughts or feelings are excluded from consciousness, sometimes only temporarily, by resorting to a frenzy of unimportant but distracting activities; or regression to earlier, less mature and less demanding forms of behavior—for example, setting up babyish or at least childish forms of dependency, and in that way escaping responsibility for solving the problem.

Defense mechanisms do offer protection from the most extreme demands of the stressor; but they are, in the long run, maladaptive because they are self-deceptive, distort reality, and deflect problem-solving effort.

DECOMPENSATION

The most seriously disruptive reaction to stress is decompensation. When the stressor situation is extremely demanding or prolonged—a siege of combat duty or being held captive as a hostage or in a concentration camp, for example—any adaptive capacities of the individual may be overwhelmed. Efficiency is lost, vulnerability to other stressors is increased, somatic disorders develop, and complete exhaustion makes any self-sustaining effort impossible. Decompensation usually is both biological and psychological.

Biological Decompensation. The general adaptation syndrome of Hans Selye is a widely used model to picture the course of biological decompensation under extreme stress. He pictures three phases of that reaction: the *alarm phase,* during which the body's resources are called into action and all the body's physiological defenses against assault are alerted; the *stage of resistance,* a prolonged period when the biological resources of the individual work at maximal level to reduce the stress; *collapse* results when the body's resources are exhausted. The consequence is disintegration, and if outside help is not provided, death.

Psychological Decompensation. The psychological analogue follows exactly the stages of biological decompensation except that psychological, not biological, resources are utilized. In the alarm stage, the individual is alert and mobilizes psychic energies. Emotional arousal, tension and sharpened sensory power lead to the initiation of coping responses. The stage of resistance intensifies task-related or defensive behavior. If stress continues unabated, the individual's psychic resources are expended. Individuals vary in the length of time that that process will take. When decompensation does take place, psychological collapse matches biological collapse.

ADJUSTMENT DISORDERS AND POST-TRAUMATIC STRESS DISORDER

DSM IIIR gives formal recognition to two types of stress-related disorder: *adjustment disorder,* a response within three months of the occurrence of a stressor within the range of common experience (death of a loved one, divorce), and *post-traumatic stress disorder,* the development of severe symptoms following a traumatic event outside the range of human experience (an earthquake, military combat, being held hostage).

Adjustment Disorder

The essential feature of the adjustment disorder is a maladaptive response to an identifiable psychosocial stressor. Critical diagnostic signs are notable impairment in social, occupational (academic) functioning, or symptoms that exceed normal or expected response to the stressor.

ONSET

The disorder may occur at any age but may be associated with critical developmental stages, such as going off to school, leaving the parental home, marriage, becoming a parent, or retirement. The disorder is expected to remit after the stress eases or when a new, more adaptive level of adjustment is achieved, with or without therapy.

SYMPTOMATOLOGY

The severity of the symptoms varies with the duration of the stressor, the presence of secondary stressors, timing in the individual's life cycle and the importance of the value threatened by the stressor. The same stressor does not affect all people in the same way. In a vulnerable individual, a mild or moderate stressor can produce severe symptoms; a strong or continuing stressor may produce only minor symptoms in a nonvulnerable person. Aside from disruption in work or ordinary routines, adjustment disorder may cause depression, with feelings of hopelessness, crying, apprehensiveness, jitteriness, and restless behavior. Erratic behavior may also be present during which the individual ignores the rights of others, is combative, reckless or irresponsible in meeting legal or financial obligations.

PREVALENCE

There are no reliable figures on the prevalence of adjustment disorders. The diagnostic manual states simply, "apparently common."

Post-traumatic Stress Disorder

Diagnosing PTSD rests on two essential elements: the occurrence of a catastrophic stressor in the past history of the individual and a characteristic pattern of symptoms.

STRESSORS ASSOCIATED WITH PTSD

These are always experiences that do not occur to the average individual: military combat, rape, being held hostage, captivity in a concentration camp or natural disasters such as flooding or earthquakes. Almost everyone would show significant signs of distress following any of those experiences. The condition is PTSD if three highly specific symptoms occur.

CHARACTERISTIC SYMPTOMS

The three symptom patterns are as follows:

Reliving the event, which may take the form of recurrent nightmares, sharp periodic recollections of the event or feeling as though the event was reoccurring.

Numbness to outside events or withdrawal from such events.

Cognitive and emotional symptoms, such as memory impairment, inability to concentrate, feelings of guilt about those who did not survive, exaggerated startle response, and avoidance of activities that stir up memories of the trauma.

PREVALENCE

The *DSM IIIR* states only "no information." Since that statement, a number of studies clearly suggest that few if any victims of catastrophic events come away symptom-free. The reports vary depending on the nature of the catastrophe (human-made catastrophes cause a more severe response), its duration, and the criteria used in the determination of the presence of symptoms.

Here follows some representative figures on prevalence: in a nightclub fire in which 500 persons died, more than 50 percent of the survivors required treatment for severe shock; one study reports that about 70 percent of those with prolonged combat experience in the Vietnam War experienced PTSD. Among survivors of concentration camp captivity, 90 percent still experienced disturbing symptoms twenty years later.

REACTIONS TO THREE SPECIFIC TYPES OF CATASTROPHE

Natural disasters, rape and military combat tend to produce somewhat different patterns of response.

Natural Disasters. Psychological reports of reactions to earthquakes, tornadoes and similar disasters outline three phases through which victims move, in what they have called the disaster syndrome. The stages are these: *the shock phase,* which is characterized by numbness and immobility (in extreme cases, there may also be memory loss and disorientation); *the stage of suggestibility,* in which victims are passive and submissive to the directions of rescuers; *the recovery phase,* in which most victims begin to function more efficiently and to be more rational about their plight.

Among those who do not recover in this way, early symptoms of a more lasting PTSD develop, perhaps because of vulnerability created by earlier life experiences. A striking and lingering symptom among many victims of natural disaster is a sense of guilt about their own behavior and their survival, and the deaths of others, especially loved ones.

Military Combat and Concentration Camp Captivity. Although these experiences are equally grueling, except for duration, typical reactions differ. In military combat breakdown, the prime symptom is depression and apparent physical exhaustion. Among concentration camp victims, there are marked personality changes: heightened irritability, stealing food and other comforts from other victims, and pandering to the enemy. One study characterizes the reactions as debility, dependence and dread. Guilt reactions are prominent in both types of catastrophe.

Rape. The reactions of victims of rape, although the experience is an individual one and not a mass experience, is increasingly being categorized as PTSD, with the addition of the special label, rape trauma syndrome. Reactions fall into two quite different patterns. About half the victims respond expressively with crying, sobbing, fear and anxiety; the other half show a first response that is highly controlled, with a calm exterior masking the underlying turmoil. The calm is soon followed by periods of terror in which the victim relives the dreadful experience and experiences symptoms typical of PTSD. One-quarter of the women victims continue to show stress symptoms years after the rape. Sexual dysfunction, as might be expected, is a long-term problem. A beneficial activity in relieving symptoms seems to be involvement in the women's movement or in rape crisis centers.

OBSESSIVE-COMPULSIVE DISORDER

The primary symptoms characterizing obsessive-compulsive disorder are preoccupying yet unwanted thoughts (obsessions) and repetitive, irresistible and undesired behavior (compulsions). Both types of behavior in mild form commonly appear in the general population. Though maladaptive, they do little harm.

In severe form, they are disruptive of ordinary life activities and are often associated with depression.

Normal Obsessions	Examples are persistent thoughts, sometimes unpleasant, about an upcoming event, a longed-for experience, a repeated melody that cannot be cleared from consciousness or a persistent thought that harm will come to a loved one. They are irritating and maladaptive but not pathological.
Normal Compulsions	Examples are repeatedly checking to see that a door has been locked or a stove turned off, or that the baby is safely asleep. The superstitious and repetitive behavior of batters and pitchers in baseball is a good example of a compulsion that results from the past reinforcement of the repetitive behavior. Normal compulsions, for the most part, occur only sporadically. Although they are bothersome, they cause no major disruption in the individual's life.
Pathological Obsessions	Pathological obsessions do not easily pass away, they are not easily controlled, and they significantly disrupt the individual's life. Their content is often unacceptably sexual or hostile and violent.
Pathological Compulsions	These are most often of one or two types: *a checking ritual* or *a cleansing ritual.* They are not the occasional rituals of many normal people but use up hours of the day in compulsive behavior. In the checking ritual, the individual may go from checking all the doors to checking all the windows, repeating the process again and again in fear that he or she may have missed one. In the cleansing compulsion, the sufferer seems driven to engage in some cleansing activity to get rid of contamination or to prevent it. It most often takes the form of hand washing, which may, in extreme cases, take place a hundred or more times a day, every time an object has been touched.
Other Symptoms of Obsessive-compulsive Neurosis	With both obsessions and compulsions, the individual finds no satisfaction in either the thoughts or the actions. In the former case, the person's helplessness in driving the thoughts out of his or her mind is depressing; with compulsions, the individual is continuously fearful about the result of not carrying them out.

In the most extreme cases of obsessive thinking, the individual does not listen to what other people are saying; their words are lost in the obsession. With compulsions, the individual can do little else during the day except to carry out the compulsion and is thus prevented from living a normal life in the family or on the job.

The compulsions of this disorder should be distinguished from "compulsive eating" or "compulsive gambling." In those activities, the individual finds satisfaction (even though of an abnormal sort) from the activity itself. In the obsessive-compulsive disorder, the compulsion is forced on the individual to avoid the tension of not carrying it out.

Prevalence   The obsessive-compulsive disorder, as compared with other neurotic disorders, is reported by the American Psychiatric Association to be a relatively uncommon one, occurring in 1 to 2 percent of the general population. Still, a substantial number of people suffer these symptoms.

It is more common among women. Onset is usually in adolescence or early adulthood, although it may develop in childhood.

GENERALIZED ANXIETY DISORDER

In all the neurotic disorders described thus far, there is a central core of anxiety. In all but this one, the individual uses defensive mechanisms, some of them severely disabling, to reduce the pain of anxiety. In generalized anxiety, the central symptom is the anxiety itself, persistent (for at least a month) and unfocused. It is sometimes labeled "free-floating anxiety." It may be centered in one or two aspects of the individual's life—for example, school grades or career prospects—but it usually cuts across all the individual's life adjustments.

Symptomatology   There are four sets of specific symptoms: motor, physiological, apprehensiveness, and hypervigilance with scanning behavior.

MOTOR SYMPTOMS

Here the muscles of the body adopt a posture of timidity. The brow is furrowed, muscles are tense and achy, the face is strained. There is a pronounced startle reaction, jumpiness and fidgeting.

PHYSIOLOGICAL SYMPTOMS

Accompanying the external motor symptoms are internal bodily changes, such as dizziness, heart pounding, frequent urination, hot flashes, and cold and clammy hands or feet.

APPREHENSIVENESS

The individual ruminates and worries about possible impending calamities: a school exam will be failed, a parent will become ill or die, something dreadful will happen.

VIGILANCE AND SCANNING

The individual seems always to be on edge, looking for trouble that rarely, if ever, comes. As a result, there is distractibility, loss of capacity to concentrate, and difficulty in falling asleep.

A secondary problem that frequently develops is overuse of alcohol or anxiety-reducing drugs. These are activities which, in the long run, can be more damaging than the anxiety.

Prevalence

Possibly because many individuals somehow manage to live with this disorder without seeking psychological help, except in occasional conversations with the family doctor or a clergyperson, little is known about its prevalence, age of onset or sex differences in the occurrence of the illness.

The anxiety-based disorders (those described in this and the following chapter), estimates indicate, together constitute the most prevalent form of psychiatric illness. Studies suggest that some 20 million people, between 8 and 15 percent of the adult population of the United States, suffer from one or another of these disorders. Since the time of Freud, psychologists have referred to them as neuroses. The DSM IIIR now lists them separately and downgrades the label "neurosis" to parenthetical status. Nevertheless, because of the explanatory value of the concept of neurosis and its broad familiarity, most psychologists continue to use the term.

This chapter has described the disorders categorized in the diagnostic manual under the heading, anxiety disorders: phobic disorder (including panic disorder), in which the central anxiety characterizing all of those disorders is expressed in an irrational fear; post-traumatic stress disorder, in which a variety of debilitating symptoms develops as the direct result of a catastrophic event; obsessive-compulsive disorder, in which the core anxiety is masked by tensions associated with the individual's obsessions and compulsions; and generalized anxiety, in which a disruptive, unfocused apprehensiveness is the predominating symptom.

Selected Readings

Bettelheim, B. 1943. "Individuals and Mass Behavior in Extreme Situations." *Journal of Abnormal and Social Psychology*, 38: 417-452.

Grant, L., H.L. Sweetland, J. Yager and M. Gest. 1981. "Quality of Life Events in Relation to Psychiatric Symptoms." *Archives of General Psychiatry*, 38(3): 335-339.

Janis, I.L. and H. Leventhal. 1965. "Psychological Aspects of Physical Illness and Hospital Care." In B.B. Wolman (Ed.). *Handbook of Clinical Psychology*. New York: McGraw-Hill.

Medianic, D. 1962. *Students Under Stress*. New York: Free Press.

Meyer, C.B. and S.E. Taylor. 1986. "Adjustment to Rape." *Journal of Personality and Social Psychology*, 50: 1226-1234.

Rachman, S.J. and R.J. Hodgson. 1980. *Obsessions and Compulsions*. Englewood Cliffs, N.J.: Prentice-Hall.

9

Somatoform and Dissociative Disorders: Anxiety Inferred

*T*his chapter continues a discussion of the anxiety-based disorders that, in the past, have been grouped under the generic heading of neurosis. It follows the classification system established by the DSM IIIR, which organizes the eight disorders described here under two different categories of Axis I of the manual: Somatoform Disorders and Dissociative Disorders, each of which is justified more on the basis of symptomatology than on distinctiveness of etiology (causation).

The disorders described in this chapter show few, if any, signs of the anxiety characteristic of the other anxiety-based disorders; it therefore must be inferred. The psychodynamic school considers the symptomatology a defense against an underlying and unconscious core of anxiety.

The chapter concludes by considering an important but as yet unsettled question: Is there a neurotic way of behaving, a neurotic personality which precedes and underlies the anxiety-based disorders?

SOMATOFORM DISORDERS

A sharpened focus on some bodily function, with the development of physical symptoms or complaints without an organic basis, is the common characteristic of the somatoform disorder. Dysfunction produced by the symptoms ranges from specialized sensory or motor disability through preoccupation with and symptom formation in any bodily function to hypersensitivity to pain. There are four principal somatoform disorders: conversion disorder (also known as hysteria), hypochondriasis, somatization disorder, and somatoform pain disorder.

Conversion Disorder

This disorder almost always develops in a setting of extreme stress, i.e., military combat or the death of a loved one. Its course is usually dramatic and short-lived. While symptoms are present, the individual may be severely handicapped; and in unusual circumstances, the primary symptom may persist for a prolonged period, causing atrophy or contracture of the muscle groups involved.

SYMPTOMATOLOGY

The primary symptom is a loss or alteration in physical functioning without a detectable organic basis. Despite the seriousness of the physical disability, the individual commonly reacts with a relative lack of concern, an attitude which has been named, "la belle indifference."

Common forms of the primary symptoms are paralysis, fits or seizures, aphonia (loss of speech), blindness, or amnesia. Of significance in the conversion disorder is the secondary gain (side benefits) that results from the disability: the primary symptom is a defensive reaction enabling the individual to escape from or avoid a psychologically stressful situation without the need to admit to responsibility for doing so.

The primary symptom is beyond the individual's control and is not seen by the person as related to the stressful situation which is being avoided. There may be a gray area in which awareness of the secondary gain (including insurance payments or court settlements) tends to worsen or prolong the symptoms.

For convenience, the primary symptoms are grouped into three categories: sensory symptoms, motor symptoms and visceral symptoms.

Sensory Symptoms. These include anesthesia, excessive sensitivity to strong stimulation (hyperesthesia), loss of sense of pain (analgesia), and unusual symptoms such as tingling or crawling sensations.

Motor Symptoms. In motor symptoms, any of the body's muscle groups may be involved: arms, legs, vocal chords. Included are tremors, tics (involuntary twitches), and disorganized mobility or paralysis.

Visceral Symptoms. Examples are trouble swallowing, frequent belching, spells of coughing or vomiting, all carried to an uncommon extreme.

In both sensory and motor symptoms, the areas affected may not correspond at all to the nerve distribution in the area.

CAUTION IN DIAGNOSIS

Because conversion hysteria can simulate almost every known physical ailment, care must be taken to exclude any organic basis for the disorder. Support for the psychological basis of the disorder can be found in such criteria as these: an attitude of indifference to the symptom; a lack of correspondence between the known symptoms of a particular disease and the individual's complaints; the disappearance of the symptom under hypnosis or narcosis (drug-produced sleep); or suggestibility of the individual in responding to the therapist's efforts to control or change the symptom.

PREVALENCE

Although conversion disorder, along with hypochondriasis and the dissociative disorders of amnesia and multiple personality, are given much notoriety in news stories, on television and in motion pictures, they are, as a group, much less prevalent than other anxiety disorders and seem to have been more prevalent in past years than they are today. Only about 5 percent of all the neurotic disorders fall into this category today. Onset is usually early in life, but may occur at any time. It is usually triggered by a severely stressful event.

Hypochon-driasis

In conversion disorder, the individual develops a functional disorder (psychologically caused) and is indifferent to it; contrariwise, in hypochondriasis, the hypochondriac has no real physical disability or illness but is nevertheless preoccupied with and worried about ordinary bodily functions, e.g., heartbeat, bowel movements, or minor sores, blemishes or coughs. The individual reads into the sensations of normal bodily functions the presence of a feared disease.

SYMPTOMATOLOGY

The individual magnifies small irregularities in bodily functions and expresses concern about the general state of his or her health. He or she may shift from one bodily system to another or focus on one major system, e.g., persistent concern about a heart condition. There is much doctoring as the individual goes from one doctor to another after being told that there is nothing wrong. Hypochondriacs find pleasure in criticizing doctors and explaining to family and friends why the doctors are wrong.

Those with hypochondriasis experience some impairment in interpersonal relationships and in job performance. But often, except for frequent job changes, the illness is limited to years of doctoring and endless descriptions of symptoms with no other impact on functioning. In extreme cases, however, the individual may become a lifetime invalid and take to bed with a complete collapse in independent activity.

PREVALENCE

The ailment is frequently seen by family doctors, but because of the individual's resistance to accepting a psychological interpretation of the illness, the disorder carries over to rejecting any referral to a mental health facility. Onset is any time from adolescence through the forties. Hypochondriasis affects men and women equally.

Somatization Disorder

Although listed as a separate disorder in the *DSM IIIR*, somatization disorder very much resembles hypochondriasis, with only nuances distinguishing the two.

SYMPTOMATOLOGY

The primary symptom in somatization disorder is multiple complaints of physical ailments over a long period of time, beginning before the age of 30. One strong difference between hypochondriasis and this disorder is in the attitude the individual has to the physical disorder. The hypochondriac fears there might be a physical disorder, yet seems to hope that the doctor will find it upon examination. In somatization disorder, the symptoms of physical disorder are believed to be real, and the individual is convinced of its existence and worried about it. There may also be dramatic reactions to this strongly-held belief: submission to unnecessary surgery, threats of suicide, or seeking release in substance abuse.

Perhaps understandably, given his or her belief in the presence of serious illness, the individual is frequently depressed and finds difficulty in living an orderly existence.

PREVALENCE

The *DSM IIIR* reports that 1 percent of females have this disorder. It is not usually found in males.

Somatoform Pain Disorder

The primary—indeed, the only—symptom in somatoform pain disorder (except when other psychiatric disorders are also present) is severe and prolonged pain in the absence of a physical basis for it. Diagnosis may be difficult, since extensive medical testing may be necessary to rule out an organic basis.

Certain psychological cues may be helpful in clarifying the functional (psychological) nature of the illness: a conflictful or stressful event preceding the experience of pain, the existence of secondary gain if pain is present, or the individual's persistent need of attention. A history of past physical injury or illness, which no longer accounts for the pain, may nevertheless provide the patient with justification for complaining.

No reliable figures on prevalence are available, although reports from family doctors suggest that it is a frequently seen disorder. It is more common among women than men.

DISSOCIATIVE DISORDERS

The *DSM IIIR* lists four varieties of dissociative disorder: psychogenic amnesia, psychogenic fugue, multiple personality, and depersonalization disorder. As a group, although much notoriety is given to them by the media, they are relatively uncommon disorders.

They have in common an attempt by the individual to escape from a significant personal problem or responsibility by severing, forgetting or distancing himself or herself from the core personality.

Psychogenic Amnesia

Amnesia is inability to recall or identify one's past experience or identity. It may result from a variety of pathological brain conditions. When it develops as a response to extreme psychosocial stress, it is labeled psychogenic amnesia. Common examples of such stressful situations are living through a catastrophic event such as an earthquake, a personally experienced threat of death or major injury, the need to escape an unacceptable impulse or an unbearable life situation; for example, facing a bankruptcy or other financial calamity.

SYMPTOMATOLOGY

Symptom formation in psychogenic amnesia may follow any one of four different patterns: localized amnesia, selective amnesia, generalized amnesia, and continuous amnesia.

Localized Amnesia. In this pattern of psychogenic amnesia, the individual fails to recall all details of a particular event, usually one that is traumatic. An example would be failing to recall all the circumstances of an atrocious rape. Localized amnesia is the most common form of psychogenic amnesia.

Selective Amnesia. Following closely behind localized amnesia in prevalence is selective amnesia. Here the individual blanks out certain details of a traumatizing experience. The *DSM IIIR* gives the example of an uninjured survivor of a car accident that killed all of his or her immediate family, who can remember making the funeral arrangements but not discussions held with other family members.

Generalized and Continuous Amnesia. The least common forms of psychogenic amnesia are generalized amnesia, in which the individual may be unable to recall the details of an entire lifetime, and continuous amnesia, in which the person "forgets" everything subsequent to a specific time or event, including the present.

PREVALENCE

Psychogenic amnesia of the first or second type is a fairly common initial response to catastrophic events. When it results from more common stressful experiences which most people are able to overcome, it is an example of disordered functioning.

Psychogenic Fugue

Although listed in the *DSM IIIR* as an independent clinical syndrome, a fugue is simply a type of generalized amnesia in which the added feature is a flight from family, problem and location, and the creation of a new identity which may be maintained for days, weeks or months, and even for years. The individual's behavior during fugue states of limited duration may be very casual, such as going from one movie theater to another without being able to recall where he has been. An uncommon pattern is for the person to create a whole new life.

Multiple Personality

The most dramatic of all the dissociative disorders is multiple personality, in which there is the occurrence in the same individual of two or more personalities, each of which is able, for an interval in the person's life, to live a stable life and to take control of the person's life, although not necessarily in a mentally healthy way.

SYMPTOMATOLOGY

In multiple personality, the individual acts out one or another of coexisting personalities. In a famous case of Dr. Prince, there were seventeen different personalities, each quite different from the other. One personality may be the governing or good personality, and the other full of unacceptable and immoral impulses. There may be complete or partial amnesia during the existence of other personalities or a pattern in which whatever becomes known to the principal personality (but to that person only) is known to all other personalities (asymmetrical amnesia). There have been a number of notorious cases of feigned multiple personality, with the purpose in mind to evade criminal culpability. One means of detecting the feigned disorder is the likelihood in such cases that the amnesia is symmetrical, i.e., what is known by any of the individuals is known by all.

Impaired functioning or illegal behavior may occur in a form that depends on the number and characteristics of the personalities assumed.

PREVALENCE

Much has yet to be learned about multiple personality. There is no certainty about even its prevalence. In past decades, only two hundred known cases were listed—not a very significant number among the millions afflicted with other neurotic disorders. During the late eighties, several psychologists have reported larger numbers. These reports come only from the United States and are thought by some psychologists to be the result of suggestion under hypnosis or therapy. Onset is frequently reported in late adolescence and among young adults females.

Depersonalization Disorder

Mild feelings of depersonalization or feelings of being someone other than oneself or of not being able to control one's movements are common human experiences, occurring to more than 30 percent of young adults. When the symptom is recurrent and impairs social or occupational adjustment, the person is said to be suffering from depersonalization disorder.

SYMPTOMATOLOGY

The disorder is characterized by a change in the person's perception of self and in the way self-identity is experienced. Strange feelings about the size of arms and legs abound, and the individual has a sense of looking at his or her body from a distance, sometimes described as floating above the body and looking down at it. Despite the extreme distortion of self-awareness, the individual's reality-testing function remains intact, and there are no delusions or hallucinations. The sufferer may experience difficulty of recall and a loss of awareness of time going by.

Other people may be seen as mechanical or dead. Others, or the self, may be described as existing only in a dream. The individual often worries about going insane.

Feelings of depersonalization are frequently accompanied by spells of dizziness, depression and obsessive thoughts.

PREVALENCE

Onset is sudden, rarely occurring after midlife, but symptoms linger, disappearing only gradually. The disorder is extremely rare; no sex differences are reported.

CAUSAL FACTORS IN ANXIETY-BASED DISORDERS

Anxiety is the central and immediate cause of what, in the past, has been called neurotic behavior. Early life experiences have prevented the development of effective coping responses and, as a result, the individual is made vulnerable to the development of maladaptive and neurotic ways of behaving and ultimately to the development of symptoms of the disorders described in this and the previous chapter.

The Principal Causes of Neurotic Behavior

There are three principal sets of life experiences that interfere with the development of healthy coping mechanisms: those emphasized in the psychodynamic point of view, which are negative interpersonal experiences (especially within the family) and the consequent development of maladaptive defense mechanisms; faulty learning experiences, which are the emphasis of the behavioral perspective; and blocked personal growth, which is central to the humanistic-existential perspective. Of lesser causative impact in these disorders are sociocultural and biogenic factors.

Where vulnerability exists, the neurotic disorder is frequently triggered by a stressful event.

THE PSYCHODYNAMIC PERSPECTIVE: DAMAGED INTERPERSONAL RELATIONS

Stemming from the early work of Freud but going beyond it, the psychodynamic perspective gives great weight to the causal effect of such early life experiences as deprivation, parental oversolicitude and seductiveness, and paternal authoritarianism. It explains the development of neurotic symptoms as a defense against the anxiety produced by the later effects of such paternal treatment.

Early Deprivation. Emotional or physical neglect by parents can cause a child to feel unwanted and unworthy. Those feelings generate anxiety in the face of normal exigencies in life. Sometimes such deprivation takes the form of coldness and intellectualization in paternal attitudes which lack any nurturing warmth, even though perfunctory care is provided.

Oversolicitude and Seductiveness. When a parent blocks the development of independence and self-confidence through overbearing supervision and control, worries fretfully about the child, or disturbs the child by seductive physical or emotional behavior, the child falters in developing adequate coping behavior required for adjusting to life's ups and downs, with resultant anxiety when those trials appear.

Authoritarianism and Dictatorial Parental Behavior. Dogmatic behavior in setting absolute and detailed rules or rigid standards and demands for submissiveness and total compliance can cause one of two reactions: rebellion, which brings its own problems, or anxiety aroused by the hostile thoughts and aggressiveness, covertly felt, in an overly submissive child. Unable to contain the anxiety, the child's reaction may take the form of inhibitory tensions which forbid involvement in ordinary life activities. With those satisfactions lost, the next step might very well be the development of an anxiety disorder.

THE BEHAVIORAL/LEARNING PERSPECTIVE: FAULTY LEARNING

This perspective considers three possible paths to the development of neurotic behavior: failure to learn adaptive coping mechanisms; learning anxiety through conditioning experiences; or learning neurotic patterns by observation or modeling.

Failure to Learn Adaptive Coping Mechanisms. Faced with parents such as those described earlier and the consequent feelings of inadequacy and insecurity that they elicit, a child judges himself or herself to be incompetent and fails to make an effort to learn adequate coping mechanisms. Failure or the expectation of failure leads to mounting anxiety and the possibility of disordered behavior as a defense.

Learning Anxiety Through Conditioning. A two-stage set of conditioning experiences illustrates another way in which anxiety may be learned. An example best illustrates the two stages. The first is *respondent conditioning*. A father, who previously has been considerate, makes an impossible demand on his daughter. The daughter grows anxious at her inability to comply. If the demand is pressed, the father himself becomes a source of anxiety.

In stage two, the daughter comes to avoid her father, and her previous anxiety is not felt. In this fashion, the *avoidant response,* in accordance with *operant conditioning,* is reinforced. Later on, through *generalization,* the daughter tends to avoid all men and become inhibited, shy and withdrawn.

Observation and Modeling. A criticism of avoidance learning is its failure to take account of cognitive activity, such as images and verbal self-statements, which may operate in the absence of concrete stimuli for anxiety. It leaves no room for learning anxiety by observation of others or modeling behavior of parents. Observation of a horrifying experience involving someone else or the model of a worrying, fretful parent can be carried over into a child's life and serve as the basis for anxiety.

THE HUMANISTIC-EXISTENTIAL PERSPECTIVE: BLOCKED PERSONAL GROWTH

The humanistic perspective shares with the psychodynamic view a concern about the individual's early interpersonal experiences which, it states, may limit the individual's capacity for self-actualization and growth. It is, according to this school, that discrepancy between the individual's damaged self image and the ideal self envisioned by the person that causes anxiety and the move toward neurotic behavior.

The emphasis in the existential perspective is on the concept of authenticity. Individuals suffering an anxiety disorder, it is stated, are uncomfortable living with the gap that exists between the true self and the self which the adjustment to society demands. It is this conflict, no doubt stemming back to vulnerability produced by early life experiences, which produces the anxiety and ultimately the psychological disorder. Others accept the personality mask imposed by society, forgetting their real selves. In so doing, they avoid the troubling anxiety.

THE SOCIOCULTURAL PERSPECTIVE

The culture in which a person lives is more likely to influence the type of neurosis the individual develops than cause the occurrence of the neurosis. Several examples illustrate a seeming relation between cultural influences and type of psychological ailment. Conversion disorders, studies show, were more prevalent in the American culture of the early part of this century than they are today. They are also more prevalent in underdeveloped countries; in more industrialized countries, anxiety and obsessive disorders are more common. Although anxiety-related disorders occur among all segments of the population, in lower economic and educational groups, somatic symptoms prevail (unexplained aches and pains); while in the middle and upper classes, the more frequent disorders are anxiety and obsessive-compulsive disorders.

Despite this emphasis, psychologists agree, when describing the causal effects of sociocultural elements, that as a culture tends to put pressure on its members to strive for money and success, so-called neurotic behavior is likely to increase.

THE BIOGENIC PERSPECTIVE

Biogenic factors seem the least important in causing anxiety disorders. There are studies suggesting that genetic influences may cause vulnerability to generalized anxiety disorder and to panic disorder (including agoraphobia). Beyond these findings, genetic factors can be assigned only remote and indirect influence on the anxiety-based disorder; for example, a genetically caused frail constitution or congenital skin blemishes can lead to feelings of inadequacy which may, if intensified by environmental elements, lead to neurotic symptoms.

THE CONCEPT OF NEUROTIC STYLE

In addition to the specific causes described above, of value in understanding the long-term development of neurotic disorders is the concept of neurotic style postulated by Carson, Butcher and Coleman (1988). They favor the concept as a way of describing a variety of maladaptive patterns of behavior which nevertheless may be free of the more disabling symptoms of the disorders described in this chapter and in chapter 8. Clinical psychologists have long reported these patterns in the case histories of their clients, and an abundance of research supports their reports.

Causative Aspects of Neurotic Style

Although sometimes maintained as a symptom-free but maladaptive pattern of behavior, neurotic style is regularly associated with the later development of the pathological symptoms of the anxiety-related disorders. In fact, it seems to be a matrix in which the roots of the disorder can be formed. Which of the disorders will develop is determined by the nature of the individual's early life experiences (particularly learning experiences) and specific traumatic or stressful events the individual faces.

The Characteristics of Neurotic Style

With a neurotic style, in ordinary interpersonal situations, the individual tends to behave in any one of five maladaptive ways: extreme avoidance of aggressive or assertive behavior, even when it might be justified; unwillingness to comply or to submit to authority, although the average individual would do so; lack of capacity to develop intimate or trusting relationships; aversion to acting independently or to accepting responsibility; and impaired interpersonal relations, in which the individual develops a life pattern of outraging friends and relatives by the quirkiness of his or her neurotic style.

The major cause of these varied reactions seems to be the development of inhibitory tensions restricting the person's capacity (willingness) to respond in a normal way in ordinary social situations. Through early life experiences of the types described earlier, the person has come to sense the threat of anxiety should he or she not inhibit certain types of behavior considered quite ordinary by the average individual.

These inhibitory tensions often produce reaction formation (see chapter 8), in which extreme behavior of a type opposite to that being inhibited shows itself. Examples are these: with the inhibition of aggressiveness and assertiveness, there may be extreme submissiveness and overweening agreeableness; in the absence of normal compliant behavior, there may develop a rebelling personality or zealotry against established authority. As a result, the individual maintains a low-grade but persistent sense of apprehensiveness.

THERAPEUTIC APPROACHES TO THE NEUROTIC DISORDERS

Chapters 6 and 7 provide a detailed description of the various treatment approaches to psychiatric illness. Here only brief reference is made to those thought to be helpful in treating neurotic behavior.

Therapeutic Effectiveness in Treating Neurotic Behavior

Examining and statistically analyzing eighty-one controlled studies of the results in treating neurotic individuals, one major research study reports that the treated individuals were more functional (met their responsibilities) than 80 percent of untreated individuals with the same level of illness. The relapse rate after treatment was slight.

Basic Considerations and Goals of Therapy for Neurotic Disorders

The choice of a particular therapy is dictated by the specific diagnosis established, the psychic resources and level of functioning of the individual, and the hypothesis developed by the therapist as to possible causes.

Increasingly, an eclectic approach to therapy is being used, in which methods from any of the major perspectives are adopted by the therapist to suit the individual's needs; for example, an interpersonal, psychodynamic approach may be supplemented by one of the behavioral/learning techniques. In the eclectic approach, the goals of therapy, which are insight, elimination of symptoms, and improved functioning, are more influential in selecting a treatment approach than theoretical perspectives.

Specific Treatment Approaches to Neurotic Disorders

Specifically and briefly: each of the four theoretical perspectives offers particular treatment techniques.

THE PSYCHODYNAMIC PERSPECTIVE

The psychodynamic perspective offers insight development, which may take the form of orthodox psychoanalysis or one or another of the modified procedures developed since Freud.

BEHAVIORAL/LEARNING PERSPECTIVE

From the behavioral/learning perspective comes relearning strategies, the principal one of which is desensitization to the anxiety-causing object or situation.

HUMANISTIC-EXISTENTIAL PERSPECTIVES

Carl Rogers, the chief exponent of the humanistic school, has developed person-centered therapy, the goal of which is to expand and strengthen the individual's self-concept. In it, the therapist's role is to listen empathetically and reflect back the meanings and feelings the client is expressing. The therapist's role is to give the client the conviction of really being heard, perhaps for the first time in his or her life.

The existential therapist is even more extreme in holding back any of his or her own thoughts and, in this way, participates empathetically in the client's own world.

The DSM IIIR no longer classifies the psychological disorders described in the preceding two chapters as neuroses. Instead, it groups them into three major syndromes (clusters of syndromes). They are the anxiety disorders (which have been described in chapter 8), somatoform disorders, and dissociative disorders.

The primary symptom of conversion disorder is a loss or alteration in physical functioning—for example, blindness or paralysis—without a detectable organic basis. In hypochondriasis, the individual has no real physical disability, but nevertheless is preoccupied with and worried about ordinary bodily processes. The primary symptom of somatization disorder (which may be easily confused with hypochondriasis) is multiple complaints of physical ailments over a long period of time, a set of symptoms that cause the individual to go from doctor to doctor, seeking confirmation of his or her complaints. Somatoform pain disorder causes severe and prolonged pain in the absence of any physical basis for it.

The dissociative disorder includes psychogenic amnesia, psychogenic fugue, multiple personality, and depersonalization disorder. All those disorders have in common an attempt by the individual to escape from an unpleasant life situation by forgetting or distancing himself or herself from the core personality. In psychogenic amnesia, the individual loses memory for some aspect of a previous existence. The amnesia may be selective or general. In fugue, the individual not only "forgets," but also creates a new life, escaping from the old life. In multiple personality, there is the occurrence in the same individual of two ore more personalities, each of which controls the individual's behavior for some period of time. Depersonalization disorder causes a loss of self-identity and strange feelings about the victim's body and his or her relation to other people. The suffering individual may feel as though existence is a dream.

Selected Readings

Brady, J.P. and D.L. Lind. 1968. "Experimental Analysis of Hysterical Blindness." in L.P. Ullman and L. Krasuer, (Eds.). *Case Studies in Behavior Modification.* New York: Holt, Rinehart and Winston.

Freud, S. 1894. 1976. The Neuro-psychoses of Defense. in J. Strachey (ed. and Trans.). *The Complete Psychological Work,* (Vol. 3). New York: Norton.

Kellner, R. 1985. "Functional Somatic Symptoms and Hypochondriasis: A Survey of Empirical Studies." *Archives of General Psychiatry,* 42: 821-833.

Keyer, D. 1981. *The Minds of Billy Mulligan.* New York: Random House.

Thigpen, C.H. and H. Cleckley. 1957. *The Three Faces of Eve.* New York: McGraw-Hill.

Watson, C.G. and C. Buranen. 1979. "The Frequency and Identification of False Positive Conversion Reactions." *Journal of Nervous and Mental Disease,* 167: 243-247.

10

Psychological Factors Affecting Physical Condition

*T*he topic of our chapter, the effect of the psychological on the physical, prior to the arrival on the philosophical front of scientific rationalism, would have been labeled a mind/body problem. Prescientific humanity, led by their philosophers and religious leaders, considered mind and body to be independent entities.

The dichotomy of the two was an easy concept for primitive humans. It provided an explanation of death. There was the body, but it was lifeless. Its spirit, or soul, had left it. It was dead. That way of thinking about body and mind became a part of the Judeo-Christian religious beliefs. The concept dominated religious thinking throughout the Middle Ages and was formally elaborated in the thirteenth century in the scholastic philosophy of Thomas Aquinas, who was an influential interpreter of Christian thought in medieval Europe.

In philosophical, apart from religious, thought, Plato created a complete dichotomy between body and mind. The "rabble of the senses," which he equated to bodily processes, was a different order of being and knowing from the world of ideas, created out of the thought processes, and unchanging.

Other philosophers were even more extreme in their thinking: for example, Berkeley, the eighteenth-century Irish philosopher and idealist, maintained that everything was mind. Whatever existed, existed in the mind only.

René Descartes removed the mind/body problem from religious thinking and constructed a dual way of thinking about the two. Early scientists Galileo and Newton provided the kind of early scientific thinking that brought medicine and psychology to their modern interpretation of mind/body relationships. The two put philosophical and religious thinking aside as not within their province. Their thinking blazed the way for modern theory, which considers that body and mind function as a unit.

INTERACTIONS BETWEEN PSYCHOLOGICAL AND PHYSICAL FUNCTIONING

We have seen, in the history of abnormal psychology, that at least by 1883, with the publication of Emil Kraeplin's textbook on psychiatry, recognition of the influence of somatic (bodily) changes on mental activities was commonplace. The important effect of organic conditions on particular mental disorders had been recognized well before Kraeplin; but his broadened interpretation of those influences gave additional emphasis to their presence.

The acceptance of influence in the opposite direction, that is, the mind influencing physical disease, was a much later concept. There were exceptions: For years, observant physicians had noted the cause-and-effect relationship, for example, between physical ailments, such as high blood pressure and ulcers, and worrying and chronic emotional tension. Conditions known as psychosomatic disorders had been introduced gradually into classifications of medical diagnoses.

But it was not until the 1960s that a much-broadened way of thinking developed about the influence of psychic factors on bodily processes. During that period, physiological psychologists, aided by the development of sensitive electronic instruments that could precisely measure physiological responses such as blood pressure, pulse rate and bodily temperature, demonstrated that those responses, once thought to be involuntary, could be brought under voluntary control. Their work was a very persuasive demonstration that psychic forces—for example, the decision to lower one's heart rate—could affect autonomic system responses.

That research generated speculation that perhaps psychological influences also operated, even in cancer and infectious disease. There are reports in the psychological and medical literature that make it unwise to dismiss those speculations out of hand. In 1991, for example, carefully controlled, parallel studies conducted in Pittsburgh and in Salisbury, England, lead to the conclusion that high levels of psychological stress could almost double a person's chances of catching a cold. Apparently the stress lowers bodily resistance to viral infection. While much more work needs to be done with those particular physical disorders, in recent years, a dozen or more illnesses—for example, coronary heart disorders, ulcer, asthma and migraine headaches— have been related to psychological causation. They were first labeled as psychosomatic illnesses; then the *Diagnostic and Statistical Manual* listed them separately as psychophysiological disorders. Currently, the *DSM IIIR,* on Axis I, provides the heading, "Psychological Factors Affecting Physical Condition." The manual asks the diagnostician to list on Axis III the specific physical condition related to the psychological factors specified in Axis I; for example, ulcer, asthma, headaches, obesity, hypertension, and certain cardiac conditions.

MODELS OF PSYCHOLOGICAL-PHYSICAL INTERACTION

Science today knows that the brain is the bodily organ that controls both bodily activities and subjective events, such as cognitions and feelings; but what biological processes does the brain command to produce the interaction between mind and body? We examine two models that suggest how that interaction takes place: the diathesis-stress model and the general adaptation syndrome.

Diathesis-Stress Model

The diathesis-stress model states that human disorders, both physical and mental, result from the presence of a diathesis, or predisposition for developing a particular disease; for example, tuberculosis or schizophrenia. The diathesis, or vulnerability, may result from genetic deficiencies or from earlier physical disease; for example, whooping cough in infancy. That predisposition is provoked by a stressor, that is, a disturbing bodily invader, in the case of a physical disorder, or a disturbing early life emotional experience, in the case of a psychological disorder. Here we will be applying the model to psychophysiological disorders, which may be defined as disorders in which psychological events, such as cognitions and feelings, contribute to the development of physical disorders or diseases. The stressors on which we focus in this discussion are distressing emotional experiences.

The damage caused by a stressor acting on a vulnerability is dependent upon the coping mechanisms available to the individual. Those mechanisms are outcomes of positive earlier experiences: for example, favorable parent/child relationships or positive learning experiences when facing earlier stressful situations. To put it more succinctly, psychologically healthy individuals ordinarily deal with stress in ways that do not trigger physical vulnerabilities to produce a psychophysiological disorder.

The General Adaptation Syndrome

Selye's adaptation model does not deal with causal factors, but rather describes the sequential way in which the individual psychologically and physically responds to stressful events. He identifies three stages of the organism's response to a stressor event. The first stage is the alarm phase, which arouses the individual's defenses, either psychological defenses or the defensive reactions of the autonomic system, which in general prepare the body for action. The second stage is the stage of resistance, in which all the resources of the individual are employed defensively. If they succeed, there is no third stage; but if they are inadequate, a third stage of collapse is reached, called decompensation, in which the tensions produced by the stressor cannot be reduced, and there is the likelihood that those tensions will now combine with a vulnerability in the body, and a psychophysiological disorder will develop. Once developed, the disorder may remain as a lifetime weakness of the individual that flares up whenever stressor events threaten.

By integrating those two models, we can, at least hypothetically, outline the development of a psychophysiological disorder. Examining the specific ways in which stressors affect the individual will further clarify the etiology of those disorders.

THE ROLE OF STRESS IN PSYCHOPHYSIOLOGICAL DISORDERS

In chapter 8, we examined the influence of stressors on human behavior. Stressors can range from catastrophic events to highly personal events—divorce, for instance—which arouse the body's autonomic system and, in turn, its immune system.

Autonomic Reactions to Stress

Walter Cannon, very early in the history of what was then called psychosomatic illness (1936), postulated that in order to survive, our primitive ancestors had need of bodily reactions that would respond to the life-and-death struggle of their daily lives. Cannon called that process "the fight-or-flight" pattern, and he identified the autonomic nervous system as the mechanism that prepared the individual to make either of those responses.

The autonomic system responds to external events that threaten the individual by initiating a whole series of physiological changes, Selye's "alarm reaction." Those changes increase the individual's capacity to respond to external danger, either to fight or to flee. The autonomic nervous system increases breathing and heart pumping in order to increase the body's oxygen supply, causes flushing, which brings a supply of blood to the musculature, increases the blood sugar for increased energy, causes pupillary dilation for increased acuity in seeing, and increases the flow of neurotransmitter secretions to increase the speed of reactions.

All of those physiological changes aided primitive humans in their "fight" to survive. The effects of those changes were consumed in the battle or race that ensued; but for civilized humans, most of whose threats are not physical but the emotional tensions of intangible psychological situations, those autonomic changes are not helpful or even relevant, and only intensify apprehensiveness and anxiety. There is no way to discharge the energy and power built up in the alarm reaction. Undischarged and pent up, with no opportunity to subside, especially when the disturbing conditions are repetitive or long-lasting, they negatively affect one or several organs of the body. They affect most often those that are vulnerable, possibly for genetic reasons. With the body weakened in that way, the individual's immune system may be called into action.

The Immune System

The body's alarm reaction, in itself, does not cause infection or disease, but may, over time, reduce the body's defenses by impairing the functioning of the immune system. The components of the immune system are the blood, thymus, bone marrow, spleen, and lymph glands. The system is a complex one, and there is much yet that medical science has to learn about its functioning. We focus here on a critical element, the white blood cells.

The white blood cells of the immune system recognize and destroy pathogens that have invaded the body, such as bacteria, viruses, fungi and tumors. Their massive presence in the lymph system and the bloodstream is an indication of the importance and complexity of the work done by the white cells. In the healthy individual, there are over one thousand billion cells.

We do know that there are two types of white blood cells, lymphocytes and phagocytes. Their composition and function are somewhat different, but their combined functions are to detect and destroy antigens (invasive agents in the body) or foreign cells. Any impairment on the functioning of the immune system will reduce its ability to protect the body against disease-causing elements or damaging tissue growth. For example, the cancerous disease leukemia reduces the white cell count and therefore weakens the body's resistance to other diseases. The frightening effect of AIDS is basically its attack on the body's immune system, which leaves the body defenseless against a multitude of antigens, some of which can prove fatal.

Physical Effects of Psychological Stressors

One explanation of the way in which psychological tensions cause or contribute to the development of physical disease is that some physiological changes of the psychologically intense alarm reaction may impair the effective working of the immune system. It is known, for example, that in the alarm reaction, there is a release into the bloodstream of such neurohormones as catecholamine, cortical steroids, and dorphins, each of which, in different ways, lowers the efficiency of the white blood cells in their defensive work. The effect is a vulnerability to what are now called psychophysiological disorders.

There is abundant evidence that stressors, some of them present sooner or later in the lives of all of us, will reduce the effectiveness of the immune system and create a vulnerability to physical illness. The research literature cites the following examples: for husbands and wives, the intense grief at the death of their spouses seems to produce a measurable lowering in the activity of the immune system; and development of a chronic active stage of tuberculosis seems to be more likely when the individual is an unhappy person.

The influence of psychological factors on physical health is also demonstrated in "positive" ways. People who are happy in their interpersonal relationships and content with the work they do seem to develop an immunity to certain physical disease; for example, respiratory infections such as colds. If they are not totally immune, they at least recover more quickly.

Mediating Influences on the Effects of Stressors

Distressing events are part and parcel of the human condition. They occur more frequently to some than to others; their severity varies, and some stages of the life cycle seem more vulnerable than others. But regardless of those variables, there is abundant evidence, from research on the problem, and even from casual observations of the resilience of some people we know, that stressful events need not lead to physical disorders. What are the critical factors that control that effect?

To illustrate that range of possibilities, we examine three influencing factors of many that have been suggested in the research. They are life-style, what has been called "explanatory style," and certain personality traits.

LIFE-STYLE

Aspects of how one chooses to live one's life have been related to the development of psychophysiological illness. People differ in what they eat, how much they eat, and in their manner of eating. Powerfully persuasive evidence points to the damaging effect of smoking; lung cancer is only one of the fatal diseases it causes. On the other hand, physical exercise is suggested as a healthful aspect of life-style by all health experts.

More subtle factors are also part of life-style: one's impatience to get things done, temper flare-ups, strongly conflicting attitudes or needs. Those traits have been identified with the "Type A" personality, which is also associated with coronary illness.

J. H. Knowles, in an editorial in *Science* (1977), describes a healthy life-style: If no one smoked cigarettes or consumed alcohol, and everyone exercised regularly, maintained optimal weight on a low-fat, low-refined carbohydrate, high-fiber diet, reduced stress by simplifying their lives, obtained adequate rest and recreation, drank fluoridated water, followed the doctor's orders for medication and self care if disease was detected, and used available health resources, we would all live healthier and happier lives.

Sadly, it will take more than reading that paragraph to produce any converts.

EXPLANATORY STYLE

People differ in the way in which they explain life's events; consequently, they also differ in what they expect from life. Explanatory styles have been sorted into two principal types: the pessimistic and the optimistic. Individuals who have developed a pessimistic outlook see events as a part of the way things are, or as the result of what they seemingly are always doing. We are, they conclude, surrounded by bad happenings.

Individuals with a pessimistic explanatory style unfortunately are creating their own fate in that attitude. For example, they are, as a group, at greater risk of illness, infectious disorders as well as those that are more apparently related to emotional tensions, such as ulcers.

The physiological team of Peterson and Seligman (1988), who have been pursuing the effects of varying explanatory styles, identified explanatory style as a mediating influence on the effect of stressors.

In what has been called the Harvard study, 5 percent of the Harvard classes of 1939–44 have been followed since leaving college. At the age of 25, their explanatory style, one axis of which is important here, pessimism-optimism, was assessed. Peterson and Seligman report that pessimists at age 25 were in poorer health at age 45 than were those at the optimistic end of the scale.

In an earlier study (1987), they report that similar results were obtained in a group of undergraduates whose health was monitored for a year after explanatory style was measured. Pessimists reported twice as many infectious disorders and visits to the doctor as did optimists.

One other study, reported by researchers at the National Cancer Institute, suggests that even the effects of breast cancer reflect the level of pessimism of the patient. In a group of 34 patients with a recurrence of breast cancer, pessimists died sooner than optimists.

PERSONALITY TRAITS

One group of psychologists, focusing on a trait they called "hardiness," studied a group of executives in high-stress jobs. They found that three aspects of the trait identified stress-resistance individuals, those in whom stress produced minimal health changes: openness to change (the most powerful variable), a sense of involvement or commitment to their jobs, and feelings of being in control of their lives.

Hopelessness, a trait very different from hardiness, has been studied extensively as a factor in vulnerability to illness. The persistence and severity of diseases as different as cancer and influenza have been related to depression or feelings of hopelessness. Studies of residents of nursing homes suggest that survival rate after placement in a nursing home is related to the amount of control the individuals felt they had over what happened to them. That feeling of control enhances the attitude of hopefulness which the individual develops about future events.

PSYCHOLOGICAL FACTORS IN SPECIFIC PHYSICAL DISORDERS

Mounting evidence such as that which we have reported indicates that mind and body act as a unit. Here we examine the effect of psychological facts in triggering or in contributing to specific disorders. Although there are many specific psychophysiological disorders, this section reports on those that have been researched most extensively.

Coronary Disease

An exciting event on the psychosomatic front was the arrival of the concept of the "Type A" personality. In 1974, in a book of that title, Friedman and Rosenman described the concept, and they were able to relate that personality type to heart disorders. The concept caught on with many health-conscious people and also elicited research activities among medical and psychological professionals.

Friedman and Rosenman described Type A personalities as aggressive, competitive, hostile (at least unconsciously), feeling pressured by time, and always striving to succeed. They also described Type B individuals as relaxed, and opposite in many ways to Type A personalities. Diagnoses of the personality types are made either on the basis of a stress-type interview or by a self-administered questionnaire.

On either type of assessment, Type A personalities are likely to admit such things as eating too fast, being too active, needing to slow down, setting work deadlines or quotas, and being irritated at interruptions in their work. Type B answers are at the opposite pole to those responses.

Two levels of research have been directed at the Type A concept: 1. prospective studies predicting risk of heart attack from a personality assessment; and 2. research attempting to pinpoint what it is in a Type A personality that increases risk of cardiac disease.

PREDICTING CORONARY HEART DISEASE FROM PERSONALITY ASSESSMENTS

This section describes the three best-known and carefully-researched studies of the relationship between a heart attack and personality type.

The Western Collaborative Study. (Rosenman 1975) The researchers tested first for personality type, then followed 3,200 males and monitored their medical status for the next eight years. They found that Type A personality types had more than twice as many heart attacks as did those men who had been judged to be Type B.

The Framingham-Massachusetts Study. (Haynes 1980) In a population of 1,600 male and female white-collar workers, who had been classified as Types A or B, the researchers found three times as many cases of coronary heart disease among Type A men and two times as many among Type A women than among Type B men and women.

The Belgian Heart Disease Preventive Program. (Shekelle 1985) Two thousand men in good health, as determined by a physical stress test, were rated on a Type A/Type B scale and followed for five years. The results were similar to the earlier studies. The men on the Type A side of the scale had almost twice as many cardiac symptoms as did those on the Type B end of the scale.

CHARACTERISTICS OF THE TYPE A PERSONALITY THAT CAUSE CORONARY HEART DISEASE

Findings such as those just summarized have challenged research psychologists to find precisely what it is about Type A personalities that makes them high risks for heart disease. They have pursued most vigorously two characteristics: hostility and response to being helpless in an apparently hopeless situation.

Hostility. Several researchers have followed a lead provided in the writings of the psychoanalytically oriented Franz Alexander, who related high blood pressure to the way in which individuals dealt with their aggressions. They found that when hostility was felt but not expressed overtly, the frequent result was high blood pressure, inhibited hostility and a Type A personality, and it is now thought that those relationships play a significant role in causing the coronary reactions in the Type A personalities.

Helplessness. Later research seems to suggest that the significant element producing the pathology is not the hostility itself but a sense of helplessness that is felt when hostile individuals cannot express their feelings. It is not the helplessness of the depressed individual that researchers associate with Type A personalities; it is a much more covert helplessness than that.

David Glass, in his 1977 publication, *Behavior Pattern Stress in Coronary Disease,* describes what he believes to be the underlying principle of the Type A personality: a lifelong struggle to control a world that is threatening. Many of the traits most often assigned to Type A—competition to be the best, time pressure to get things done, hostility at interference with work—seem to be expressions of that unconscious struggle.

Glass's research design to test his hypothesis is both interesting and convincing. His subjects were first sorted into two groups, Type A and Type B. Glass confronted both groups with a set of unsolvable problems to guarantee that each group would have a failure experience. Later in the experimental situation, he asked both groups to work on another set of problems with easier solutions. He then observed the reactions of both groups to each set of problems. The Type A personalities could be identified in the way in which they responded to his experimental design. In response to a task that had been made highly salient for subjects, they 1. responded with initial vigor to the challenge. That response changed to desperation when they found that they could not control the situation, that is, solve the unsolvable problems; and 2. faced with that sense of helplessness, they totally gave up. That despair interfered with their attempts to solve the easier problems, confronting them once again with failure. Type B subjects were disappointed but did not surrender in such a complete way. They proceeded to solve the second set of problems easily and with less emotional stress. Glass concluded that the sequence of attempting to control, then giving up, then trying again, tends to produce in Type A individuals the physiological changes—for example, heightened blood pressure—that put them at high risk for a heart attack. His findings have been supported by research of quite a different design, in which there were definite indications that when an individual's need for power — that is, desire for control—was inhibited, this factor often was predictive of hypertension later in life.

Reported by David McClelland (1979) in one of a series of his studies on human motivation, the research study used projective testing to measure need for power (need to control others), need for affiliation or friendship, and the inhibition of need for power, in a group of 94 students. Of the initial group, 23 students fell into the group with high need for power (higher than their need for affiliation), but with inhibitions on their expressions of power which left them helpless to control their environments. Years later, when the former students were in their fifties, 61 percent of the "helpless" had developed symptoms of hypertension, compared with only 23 percent among the other subjects of the study.

THE EMERGENCY REACTION AND TYPE A PERSONALITY

Pulling together all of the evidence that relates coronary heart disease to psychological influences, psychologists now point to what has been described as an "emergency" reaction which, in the face of threat, raises heart rate and increases blood pressure. We have described already the sense of helplessness which Type A individuals feel more frequently than others; and because they feel helpless, they also feel more threatened than others. It is this relatively continuous emergency reaction, with persistently rapid heart rate and high blood pressure, that wears out their heart muscles and causes the coronary disease.

That hypothesis also suggests a prescription for Type A patients (and for others): regular exercise. Reasonably taxing exercise does indeed raise pulse rate and blood pressure, but only while exercising. However, it also strengthens the heart and the vascular system so that the individual's heart rate and blood pressure are lowered, which is just what Type A people need most!

Peptic Ulcer

Acid indigestion is a frequent complaint of American adults; the druggist's shelves have tens of nonprescriptive medications for its amelioration. None of them, however, remove the cause of stomach acidity; they merely alkalize the acidity of the stomach's content, treating the symptoms only. But what causes the excessive flow of acid into the stomach that, in time, erodes the lining of the stomach or duodenum (the first part of the small intestine), creating a craterlike, open and painful sore.

First reported in the early part of the nineteenth century, when it was more prevalent in women than in men, ulcers now affect more than twice as many men as women. Estimates suggest that up to 25 million Americans will, at some time in their lives, develop ulcers. It is treatable, yet ten thousand ulcer patients die every year.

CAUSES OF AN ULCER

A variety of possible causes has been identified. On the biogenic side, these are principally dietary; heavily acidic foods, alcohol consumption, and possibly smoking, are forbidden. There may be a vulnerability factor that makes some individuals more susceptible than others to those substances; but the consensus of medical and psychological opinion is that psychological factors, among them such negative emotions as strong dependency needs, repressed anger, and resentment, are at the root of the difficulty. A high activity level has also been associated with peptic ulcers, perhaps driven by those negative emotions.

CONFLICTING DEPENDENCY NEEDS

Traceable to Freud's concept of frustrated oral needs, one psychological factor that has been described most often as a cause of ulcers is conflicted dependency needs. Franz Alexander has offered a psychoanalytically oriented interpretation of this concept.

The Alexander Hypothesis. Alexander's description of the ulcer-prone personality portrays an individual in whom early life experiences have developed a conflict between deeply felt dependency yearnings and the guilt and shame accompanying those feelings. That conflict causes the repression of dependency needs.

Perhaps because of early frustration of oral needs, the individual develops infantile needs to be loved and nurtured. As an adult, he (Alexander's practice was mostly a male group) cannot express those needs and represses them by developing a "pseudoindependent personality." With that externally expressed but false manner, he hides behind the appearance of self-sufficiency, his relentless ambition, and his pronounced masculine forcefulness. In Alexander's formulation of the ulcer-prone individual, rearousal of this conflict by external events increases the flow of acid-carrying digestive juices. When such rearousals are frequent (as they are likely to be in an individual with such a false pose), an ulcer results.

Alexander states that there are three conditions to be met for an ulcer to develop: 1. a predisposing vulnerability to depend on the defense of reaction formation, which causes the conversion of dependency to pseudoindependence; 2. an event or situation that rearouses the dependency/independence conflict, thereby threatening the individual; and 3. a physical response to that threat that results in the generation of excess gastric secretions.

Alexander's formulation of the ulcer-prone personality has captivated the scientific imagination of many clinicians and spurred some to seek support for it. In 1968, Alexander and colleagues tested the ability of a group of internists and psychoanalysts (all of whom were presumably familiar with the Alexander formulation) to identify the ulcer patients in a total group of 83 patients who had one or another psychosomatic illness, including, of course, ulcers.

The judges were given a summary of the interview with the patient, which excluded all references to physical symptoms. The psychoanalysts accurately diagnosed 50 percent of the male ulcer patients; the internists accurately diagnosed 40 percent. In the female group, predictions were higher than chance levels. The difference in accuracy of diagnosis between internists and analysts can be interpreted as a result of the analysts' increased knowledge of and sensitivity to the Alexander formulation.

The study, by no means definitive, did nevertheless show the usefulness of the formulation in differentiating ulcer-prone patients from those with other disorders, even though those disorders also involved psychological elements.

More Evidence on Dependency as a Factor in Ulcers. Approaching the problem of the identification of psychological factors leading to ulcers from a different perspective, and using large-group data, Weiner and associates add even more convincing evidence to the causative presence of dependency needs in the development of peptic ulcers.

Their design was a prospective research (one intended to predict) in which the objective was the prediction of later measurements (ulcer-related physiological changes) from earlier measurements (personality traits indicating conflicted dependency needs). Such studies are more convincing than correlational research.

Starting from the proposition (established in prior research) that ulcer-prone individuals experienced high rates of gastric secretions, as measured by pepsinogen in the blood serum, they tested 2,073 army draftees in basic training for that substance. From those measurements, they selected for further study individuals who were very high in pepsinogen and another control group of soldiers who were very low in that substance.

They now had a group of individuals at high risk of ulcers and another who were not. Membership in one or another of those groups reliably predicted the incidence of ulcer development during the stress of basic training; but for psychologists, a more significant finding was that personality test scores assessing conflicted dependency needs distinguished predictively between the high pepsinogen and the low pepsinogen groups. Beyond that, the measured presence of conflicted dependency needs predicted (in a statistically significant way) which of the high pepsinogen group were most likely to develop ulcers.

Because of the presence of pseudoindependent behavior among many or all dependent individuals, it is not easy to detect the relationship between dependency and ulcers from the behavior of the individuals. Nevertheless, the Weiner study clearly indicates that inhibited dependency is one of the psychological factors leading to an ulcer-prone personality.

There are, of course, other contributing agents, both psychological and biogenic. Other psychological factors are job experiences that create emotional tensions; persistently threatening life situations, in which the individual gets disappointing results from his or her efforts to change things; or chronic states of tension from any cause. The tensions produced in air traffic controllers, a group that shows a high incidence of ulcers, is an example of the effect of long-term emotional tension.

THE DIATHESIS MODEL AND PEPTIC ULCERS

Ulcers, which we know to be a psychophysiological disorder, illustrates effectively the application of the diathesis-stress model in the understanding of such illnesses. To see its relevance, start with the survey findings of McConnell in 1966, which show that peptic ulcers run in families. For example, among relatives of ulcer patients, there is three times the incidence of ulcers than in the general population. In the ulcer-prone individual, there is the strong possibility of a diathesis, or vulnerability. That vulnerability may express itself in a tendency toward the excessive secretion of gastric juices, or weakness in the individual's mucous membranes, or even to a weakened stomach lining. The psychological tensions that have been described complete the model by adding stress, which, acting upon the weakness, causes the ulcer.

Essential Hypertension

Medical findings indicate that in 90 to 95 percent of hypertensive patients, there is no preexisting physical cause. Thus, almost all patients with high blood pressure are diagnosed as essential hypertension. In medical terms, "essential" means the absence of known physical causes. This is not to say that there is an absence of physical correlates of high blood pressure. The first advice of a doctor to an overweight patient with high blood pressure is, "Lose some weight" or "Let me suggest a diet."

Even granted the presence of potentially dangerous dietary practices, the consensus of psychomedical opinion emphasizes the large role played by psychological elements in high blood pressure. A variety of psychological causes have been suggested. Two important ones come with research support: 1. a psychoanalytically oriented hypothesis that high blood pressure is associated with suppressed rage; and 2. research indicating the importance of an inhibited power drive.

SUPPRESSED RAGE

Anger is a strong emotion. Its immediate effects on the body are, in time, usually reduced by its open expression, that is, assuming no physical violence against others which may produce other negative results. When, in the life situation of the individual, there is, for example, a strongly authoritarian and punitive father, or a life role that requires obsequiousness and containment of emotional expression, the result may be that the tensions present can be internalized and inflicted upon the body's vascular system by raised blood pressure. A 1977 study by Esler and others reports that individuals with hypertension who also exhibit signs of repressed hostility frequently have personalities that are overly submissive, overly controlled, and guilt-ridden. It is that pattern that would seem to provide the background for high blood pressure.

What is needed beyond such findings, in order to substantiate the causative role of suppressed hostility, is a prospective study that predicts, from early childhood parenting practices, which children will develop hypertension. Unfortunately, practical problems and the time period required for such an effort, make that research difficult, if not impossible.

INHIBITED POWER NEEDS

From what most of us think about high blood pressure, it would seem reasonable that an individual who has developed a strong drive for power, which drive is inhibited by life circumstances, is likely, over a period of time, to show elevated blood pressure. McClelland, in a study (1977) described earlier in our discussion of coronary heart disorders, provides research for just that relationship. Therefore, essential hypertension is considered an indication of high risk for the development of coronary heart disease. In conclusion, it must be suggested that the close correlation between high blood pressure and the likelihood of cardiac disorder, putting aside physical correlates, would point to similarities in the psychologically causative factors for both disorders.

Other Physical Disorders Affected by Psychological Factors

A significant number of physical disorders, in addition to the two already described here, have been characterized as psychosomatic, including asthma, eating problems (anorexia nervosa, or not eating enough, and bulimia, excessive eating binges), and recurrent headaches, including migraine. In the following section, psychological correlates of these disorders, where they exist, are described briefly.

ASTHMA

Asthma attacks occur when there is a narrowing in the bodily passages that allow oxygen to enter the lungs and carbon dioxide to be exhaled. This disorder of the respiratory process causes coughing, wheezing, and often a degree of breathlessness that leads to gasping for air and extreme apprehensiveness. The attacks may last from under an hour to one or two days. Three percent of the general population suffer from some level of severity of the disease. It develops often in childhood, and one-third of all asthmatics are under the age of sixteen. Since death rates from asthma are not high, that is a happy statistic, suggesting that there is a high rate of recovery.

There is evidence that the earlier the disorder occurs, the longer it lasts. For example, it was found that when the disease developed before the age of one year, 80 percent of the children were found to still have the disease five years later; when the age of onset was five years, that percent dropped to 20. Two-thirds of asthmatics are male.

Incidence of Biogenic and Psychological Types of Asthma. In those cases of asthma in which the allergies are to specific irritants, such as pollen, mold or dandrufflike sheddings of animals, or when the attacks follow such serious respiratory illnesses as pneumonia or whooping cough, psychogenic factors cannot be considered to be primary causes, although they may be contributory. In other cases of asthma attacks, no biogenic factors can be identified. It is in those cases that psychological factors may be considered to be primary causes.

One of the most extensive studies of asthma was conducted in a hospital in Wales by Rees in 1964. He divided asthma into three categories, according to its etiology: allergic, infective, and psychological. Careful medical examinations established the first two categories. For "psychological" asthma, possible factors identified in case histories were anxiety, tension produced by frustration, anger, depression, and anticipated pleasurable excitement. Those psychological conditions seem to be more emotional states that trigger an asthmatic attack than the primary cause, such as were the allergies and infections identified in the other two categories of asthma.

Putting that criterion aside for the moment, Rees concluded that psychological factors were dominant in 37 percent of his cases, and unimportant or subsidiary in 63 percent. Biogenic factors, either infective or allergic, were important in 61 percent.

In other efforts to find a specific cause of asthma, scattered studies have suggested childhood depression or family conflict as important etiological elements in some cases. Studies have reported such psychological findings as 1. once the disease has occurred, asthmatic children can be highly suggestible to elements in the environment that are proposed as causes of asthmatic attacks; 2. asthmatic children are sometimes capable of using their asthmatic condition in an attempt to control parental behavior; and 3. asthmatic children are no more "neurotic" than are other sickly children; for example, cardiac children.

Overview of Psychological Effects on Development of Asthma.
Summarizing the research evidence, we can conclude that it hardly supports the widespread notion that asthma is always psychosomatic in origin; nor is there much evidence, such as has been found in other psychophysiological ailments, that there is a personality type that predisposes a child to the illness. Stress or emotional tensions trigger an emotional attack when the disease is already present. No convincing evidence exists that personality traits play a significant etiological part in asthma.

ANOREXIA NERVOSA AND BULIMIA

These two troubling eating disorders, with symptom patterns that are the very opposite of each other, are nevertheless linked, by specialists in the field, as cyclical reactions which are caused by the same underlying psychological disorder.

Anorexia. In anorexia, the individual eats too little and borders on a starvation diet.

Onset of the principal symptoms often occurs at the time of a critical life change, such as going to college, becoming engaged, or beginning a new job. Those experiences are hardly limited to anorexic females; and for that group, no especially anxiety-producing features of their life "crisis" have been identified. The reaction sometimes is an extreme continuation of early dieting efforts; but here, again, ordinary dieting is no basis for the extreme reactions of the anorexic individual.

In studies of the interpersonal relations of anorexic women, it is reported that they are frequently perfectionists in their standards and tend to be hypercritical of their mothers, using such adjectives as "intrusive" and "domineering" to describe them; but no control groups are available to assure us that those views are not common in normal young women of that age group. Carson et al. (1988), in their analysis of the illness, caution about giving credence to those criticisms since, as they say, "Mothers frequently respond in that way to the self-starvation of their children."

The fact that the phenomenon occurs only in the United States and in a few European societies suggests that there may be significant cultural influences that operate on psychological or even physical vulnerabilities that have not yet been identified. Since anorexia is not a newly recognized disorder (it has been diagnosed for almost a century), it cannot be considered a dieting-related fad among certain socioeconomic levels in our society. It is not commonly found among the poor. There are no answers to explain a very unfortunate problem in a relatively small fraction of today's young women.

Prevalence of anorexia is one in 250,000 (all will develop the disorder between the ages of twelve to eighteen, which is the period of high risk). The mortality rate is estimated to be between 15 and 21 percent. Ninety-five percent of anorexics are women. Anorexics typically refuse therapy, and frequently deny any illness.

Bulimia. In bulimia, the principal symptom is episodes of binge eating. These may be planned ahead of time, but are usually engaged in covertly, when the individual is alone. Bulimics gulp down their food as if emerging from a period of starvation. The binge-eating generates self-deprecating thoughts, guilt, and even depression. Binges usually end with the individual in pain from a distended stomach, and are frequently followed by self-induced vomiting. Weight fluctuations are common because the individual alternates between binges and fasting. Despite binge-eating and perhaps because of it, there is a continuing preoccupation with weight.

Although appearing to be the very opposite of anorexia, bulimia is considered by some psychologists as the off-phase of anorexia. No data on prevalence are available for bulimia.

Among those who have studied these eating problems, anorexia and bulimia are believed to stem from an identity crisis which can be traced back to early family relationships. Simply put, those who suffer from the disorder have either not answered the question, "Who am I?", or are dissatisfied with the answer.

RECURRENT HEADACHES

It is the rare person who has never experienced the unpleasantness of a headache. No one knows, with exactitude, the number of people who suffer recurrent headaches during some period in their lives. One estimate, reported in *Newsweek* on health (1988), offers the statement, "Forty-five million Americans suffer chronic or recurrent headaches that vary in intensity from dull to excruciating." How exact that statement is is uncertain.

Headaches usually first appear during adolescence. A 1959 survey of college students found 52 percent of them reporting headaches at least once or twice a week. Recurring headaches may be a lifetime pattern, or may disappear as a regular problem later in life. Their occurrence is almost always related to the presence of some stressor, major or minor.

Although one survey of headache research (1982) states that there is little support for believing that one type of headache can be distinguished from another, three types of headache are discussed in the literature: migraine, tension, and cluster headache.

Migraine Headaches. Of the three types of headache, migraine has been studied most extensively. We have descriptions of migraine headaches going back to antiquity, but it was only in the 1940s that medical science was able to identify the physiological changes associated with migraine. Sudden dilation of certain cerebral and cranial arteries and the irritation of attached nerve endings causes the migraine pain. The actual dilation is preceded by a nonpainful, reduced flow of blood to the affected parts of the brain. That event is experienced as an aura announcing the arrival of the migraine attack. Migraine is the most severe of all headaches, and attacks can last from a few hours to three or four days.

Migraine headaches are subdivided into two types, principally on the basis of the severity of the attack: classic and common.

Classic Migraine. Characterized by pain that is described as excruciating, the classic migraine headache begins with a pulsating pain on one side of the head, coinciding with each heart beat. Soon thereafter, the pain stabilizes and becomes continuous. Classic migraine brings with it nausea and vomiting and such neurological symptoms as visual distortion, numbness, and speech and coordination problems.

Common Migraine Headaches. These headaches, although resulting from the same physiological pattern as classic migraine, differ from it in that they are less severe at each stage of the attack. The aura is less pronounced, the pain is less severe, and the neurological symptoms are likely to be absent.

Causative Factors in Migraine. Historically, migraine sufferers were stereotyped as rigidly moral, ambitious, perfectionistic, of better-than-average intelligence, and suffering from suppressed emotional expression. More recent research has not confirmed that description, nor have migraine victims been found to lead more stressful lives than do others. Contemporary thinking attributes migraine to genetic factors, possibly causing hypersensitivity in the cranial blood vessels. That conclusion does not rule out a diathesis-stress interpretation of the illness.

Tension Headaches. Despite the apparent prevalence of these headaches, which are much less severe than migraine and without neurological or gastric symptoms, no certain interpretation exists telling us why some people respond to tension with headaches and others do not. In Friedman's (1979) survey of 1,420 people with tension headaches, he reports that 77 percent of them identified psychologically precipitating factors, which were wide-ranging in their nature. In the absence of a control group, it is difficult to draw any conclusions from that finding.

The problem of tension headaches only occasionally provokes a visit to the doctor.

Cluster Headaches. These headaches occur less frequently than either migraine or tension headaches. The pain is extremely severe and often causes violent reactions in the affected individual, such as head-banging or wall-pounding. Psychological factors are thought to be involved, but no pattern has been established.

The Possibility of Psychological Factors in Cancer

Most people find it understandable that certain physical disorders can be caused by emotional strain. Among those disorders are those we have discussed. On the other hand, the possibility of such a relationship in cancer is most often greeted with skepticism. It is not the severity of the disorder that causes that skepticism. Both cancer and coronary arterial disease have a high death rate. In this country, six hundred thousand people die of cardiac failure each year; cancer causes death in 514,000 people each year.

Perhaps the skepticism results from the appallingly imaginable physical nature of cancer's physical growth, increasing in size each day, or spreading in minute cells that travel throughout the body. Other diseases do not seem to be so vividly imaginable. Another factor in causing the skepticism may be the well-known emphasis medical science gives to biological treatment and its effectiveness in many cases. When we think of cancer, we think immediately of radiation, chemotherapy, or even surgery. We do not often consider the calming influence of psychotherapy, although it can indeed be helpful in dealing with the knowledge that one has cancer.

EMOTIONAL INHIBITION

One researcher (Caroline Bedell Thomas) had her own thoughts about that skepticism. She and other researchers, in the early 1940s, had noticed the coincidence of cancer and particular personality characteristics. In 1946, she administered a series of personality tests to a group of medical students who were conveniently available to her. Each year thereafter, with admirable persistence, she contacted them to inquire about their health. Since most of them were medical doctors, they were reasonably cooperative in replying. By 1977, forty-eight of her subjects had developed cancer. Comparing their personality profiles with those of her subjects who had not developed cancer, she noted strong tendencies to repress strong emotions in the cancer patients. These subjects, she felt, might be described as emotionally inhibited personalities.

Other researchers have confirmed her original findings of relationships between cancer and psychological characteristics, but in a somewhat different way. Rogentine and others, for example, reported in 1979 that those cancer patients who freely expressed negative emotions about the illness were more likely to survive than those who were more emotionally restrained.

HOPELESSNESS IN CANCER

Subsequent research has focused on hopelessness as a factor in development of cancer. One illustration of this is what might be called a serendipitous opportunity for research: fifty-one women who entered a clinic for a cancer test were interviewed after medical examinations had revealed suspicious cells in the cervix which had to be investigated further before a definite diagnosis of cancer could be made.

The interview revealed that eighteen of the fifty-one had suffered significant losses in the preceding six months to which, the interview further revealed, they had responded with feelings of hopelessness and a resultant sense of helplessness. Of the eighteen, eleven had a cancer diagnosis. Among the other thirty-three, with no such preceding life experiences reported, only eight had cancer. Although the difference seems small, statistical tests revealed those differences to be significant; that is, the likelihood was that they were more than chance happenings. Other research with different types of cancer (lung cancer and breast cancer) has confirmed those earlier findings. One study reported that upon the news of a cancer diagnosis, a "fighting" spirit was associated with a better rate of survival five years later. Those studies by no means designate hopelessness as a primary cause of cancer; they suggest rather that personality variables play a part, at least, in affecting survival rates once cancer is diagnosed.

Overview on Causative Factors in Psychologically Affected Physical Disorders

We have considered in this chapter eight of the principal so-called psychosomatic ailments. There are others: allergies, skin eruptions, chronic diarrhea and ulcerative colitis, rheumatoid arthritis, diabetes, menstrual irregularities, and Raynaud's disease; and medical research is opening the door to the labeling of other physical disorders as psychosomatic.

With that number of psychosomatic ailments, and with so extensive a body of research on them, there is a place for each of the major perspectives on human behavior to provide interpretations of their etiology.

THE BIOGENIC PERSPECTIVE

There are two principal emphases in the biogenic perspective on psychosomatic disorders. They are genetic influences and involvement of the body's immune system.

A Genetic Factor. Family studies, twin studies, and animal breeding research lend strong support to the presence of genetic factors, at least in certain of the psychosomatic disorders.

Extensive research of the development of ulcers supports the proposition that a vulnerability to ulcers is genetically based. Both family studies and twin studies indicate a genetic basis for hypertension.

Genetic hypothesizing has suggested the somatic weakness theory. In that theory, it is speculated that genetic factors (but also prior illness or trauma) may create a vulnerability in some organ systems of the body, which makes them the weakest links in the body and thus especially sensitive to psychological tensions. A study (Rees 1964) of asthmatics reveals that 80 percent of an asthmatic group had a history of earlier respiratory infections, but only 30 percent of a nonasthmatic group did likewise. The suggestion is therefore present that the respiratory system is a genetically weakened organ.

There is also evidence that each of us has a unique physiological reaction to all types of stressful situations. That this pattern is an inherited one is implied by research indicating that the infant's distinctive autonomic response persists throughout life. Given such a predisposition, it can be argued that any triggering emotional stress will produce a specific psychosomatic ailment.

The Immune System. The body's immune system, as we have described earlier in this chapter, defends the body against disease-causing foreign agents. Much evidence from the animal laboratories demonstrates that in animals such psychological tensions as, for example, those created by a condition of helplessness, reduce the effectiveness of the immune system. In that way, the body's vulnerability to physical disease is increased.

A question that is now the target of a new and fast-growing branch of medicine, psychoneuroimmunology, is, are there other diseases not now considered psychosomatic which are triggered by emotional tension that consequently reduces the functioning of the immune system? A prime suspect is infectious disease. The role of that relationship in cancer is also the subject of study.

Current focus of the biogenic perspective is the diathesis-stress model as a way of thinking about the interaction between physical and psychological factors.

THE PSYCHODYNAMIC PERSPECTIVE

The oldest, but not now the most vigorously researched, interpretation of psychosomatic illness is the psychodynamic perspective. Two elements of Freudian thinking provided the basis for early interpretations of psychosomatic ailments. The first suggests that unconscious motivations left over from unresolved aspects of the individual's early-life psychosexual development create organ neuroses. As with all neuroses in the Freudian conceptualization, the individual's reaction is to set up a defense against underlying anxieties and conflicts. For individuals with psychosomatic disorders, the defense is a disorder in one of the body's organ systems. Ulcer patients, in a way that current thinking considers too glib, are considered to be "orally conflicted," and colitis patients are "anally conflicted."

Today, the psychodynamic theorist attributes psychosomatic illness to some aspect of a disturbed parent/child relationship, the same pattern that underlies other anxiety-based disorders; and psychodynamic therapies, although taking into account the physical aspects of the illness in treatment, approach the individual as they would any other individual with psychological problems.

One group of psychodynamicists, led by Flanders Dunbar and Franz Alexander, evolved a whole series of personality types, different for each of a variety of psychosomatic symptoms. For example, migraine patients were thought to be hard-working, conscientious, or perfectionistic personality types; hypertensive patients were considered to be covertly angry personality types who "defended" themselves against their anger by the symptoms of hypertension.

Research directed by such hypotheses has failed to support them; individuals with those psychosomatic ailments could not be grouped into similar personality types according to the predictions required by the hypotheses. Their personalities were widely heterogeneous. Nevertheless, the relationship between the Type A personality and risk of heart attack, which fits the earlier psychodynamic conceptualization, suggests the possibility that there may yet be discovered a match between personality and certain psychosomatic disorders.

THE BEHAVIORAL PERSPECTIVE

Until recently, the rationale for considering psychosomatic symptoms to be the result of conditioning, either respondent or operant, was difficult to establish. For one thing, autonomic responses were considered to be beyond voluntary control. They therefore would not respond to operant conditioning. Secondly, to hypothesize respondent conditioning as the cause of the illness would require frequent associations between a neutral stimulus to be conditioned and some unconditioned stimulus known to produce the response reflexively. In ordinary living, that eventuality would be a rare occurrence, indeed.

In the 1960s, a principal block to a behavioral interpretation was removed when it was demonstrated that a variety of autonomic responses could be operantly conditioned in a very precise way; at least the theoretical possibility of a causal relationship between operant conditioning and a physical disorder was demonstrated. A powerful result of that research has been the development of a behavioral approach to the treatment of some forms of psychophysiological illness, which is known as biofeedback.

THE COGNITIVE PERSPECTIVE

One major early study (Grace and Graham 1952) relates specific cognitions to specific psychophysiological disorders. For example, before a migraine attack, the individual may be thinking, "I have a million things to do." An asthma patient may be saying to himself or herself, "I don't like what's going to happen. I can't face it." The finding, in a way, harks back to the thinking of Alexander and Dunbar. Until now, it has not been supported by research.

TREATMENT APPROACHES TO PHYSICAL DISEASES AFFECTED BY PSYCHOLOGICAL FACTORS

Psychophysiological illness almost always brings the individual first to a medical doctor; and biological measures, directed mostly to symptom control, are the principal treatments used in such illnesses. In extreme cases—for example, of a heart attack or a bleeding ulcer—hospitalization, either on an emergency basis or for prolonged treatment, may be necessary.

In mild to moderate psychophysiological illness, with no life-threatening features ameliorative medical measures are taken. These include tranquilizers to reduce the exacerbating effect of emotional tensions on the symptoms; antihypertensive medications, usually for a lifetime; or, for ulcer patients, suggested dietary changes.

Of the psychotherapeutic approaches, behavioral and cognitive therapies are more specifically prescribed than are psychodynamically oriented therapies. Three of the most widely used behavior therapies are biofeedback, behavior modification, and relaxation therapy. One approach, Marita therapy, combines a medical and psychological approach.

Biofeedback

One study (Long et al. 1967), describing the use of biofeedback to control heart rate in a group of volunteers, illustrates the main principle involved in that therapy. Subjects watched a visual display of their heart rate and were directed to limit the rate to a prescribed range. As anyone who has taken part in a biofeedback experiment will agree, the subjects could not explain how they did it; but in time, they had learned how to regulate their heart rate.

The technique has been used with limited success in several other psychophysiological disorders. They include hypertension, headaches, and irregular heart beat. Immediately after treatment, patients control or moderate their symptoms. A positive effect is noticeable in mild to moderate illnesses; there are reports, however, that it is not a lasting one.

A variation of biofeedback uses biofeedback—for example, blood pressure as the response to be controlled—and combines it with psychotherapy. Connected into a biofeedback apparatus, the patients discuss, in interview fashion, various aspects of their lives. Whenever the machine beeps, signalling a jump in blood pressure, it also signals an area of life that is causing emotional tension. When followed with further discussion, the individuals can be helped to develop less stressful ways of responding to the troublesome aspects of their life situations.

Behavior Modification

This technique is essentially the application of operant conditioning principles to efforts to reduce or change psychosomatic symptoms. That is, for example, following the symptom either with an aversive stimulus or with the absence of a reward. Such conditioning would, in time, extinguish the undesired symptom. *Time* magazine, in a 1966 issue, reported the control of prolonged and energy-draining sneezing by following each sneeze with a painful, but not dangerous, electrical shock. A sixteen-month follow-up indicated that the sneezing had been controlled (Kusher 1968).

Relaxation Therapy and Systematic Desensitization

Joseph Wolpe, whose therapy approaches have been discussed in chapter 9, has used relaxation therapy, followed by systematic desensitization, as a method of reducing emotional stress associated with headache and ulcer. Once the stress was reduced, the psychosomatic symptoms either disappeared or were reduced substantially.

The therapy is a simple one. Under the guidance of the therapist, the individual has learned to relax. The therapist then encourages the patient to discuss stressful life situations which, it has been learned from a previous history-taking session, tended to trigger the psychosomatic attack. The therapy strategy builds on the incompatibility of tension and relaxation. Talking about situations that ordinarily produce tension while an individual is deeply relaxed seems to disconnect the situation from tension. Wolpe would say that the individual is desensitized to the stressor.

Research establishing the existence of a causal relationship between certain physical diseases and psychological stress clearly suggests that the body and mind work as a unit. The key finding in that research is the demonstration, made possible by modern technical developments, that various unconscious physiological reactions can be brought under voluntary control. With that finding, we may conclude that the body's functioning affects the way we feel and our psychological reactions affect the way in which the body functions.

A prime model for understanding the interaction between physical illness and psychological stress is the diathesis-stress formula, which states that human disorders (physical and mental) result from the presence of a diathesis (a predisposition or vulnerability) which may be genetic, or the result of an early physical illness or injury or disturbed childhood family relationships. The vulnerability in this model is activated by some stressor in the environment; for example, a bereavement or loss of a job.

An external stressor activates the body's alarm reaction which, if maintained over a period of time, impairs the functioning of the body's immune system, comprising the blood, thymus, bone marrow, spleen and lymph glands. With that impairment, there may be a reduction in the number of white blood cells in the bloodstream. These white blood cells function to destroy pathogens (hostile bodily invaders) such as bacteria, viruses, fungi and tumorous growths. As a result of that impairment, the body becomes especially susceptible to a number of physical ailments. Whether an illness will actually develop is influenced by the individual's life-style, "explanatory style" (the way the individual tends to explain what happens to him or her, and various other personality traits.

A hazardous life-style includes bad eating habits, smoking, consuming alcohol, and such personality traits as impatience or a pressing drive to get things done. A pessimistic "explanatory style" is one that attributes bad happenings to fate or "the way things are," explanations that dismiss any possibility of personal control of one's own destiny. The principal personality trait related to the development of psychologically caused physical disease is hopelessness.

The principal physical illnesses affected by those three aspects of the individual's personality are coronary disorder, peptic ulcer, essential hypertension, possibly asthma, anorexia and bulimia, and recurrent headaches, including migraine.

Among the psychological factors effecting coronary disease, the one most widely researched is Type A personality; that is, one that is aggressive, competitive, hostile, pressured, hypersensitive to being successful, and with a strong need to control others. Major large-scale studies have demonstrated a striking relationship between coronary disease and Type A personality. For example, in one study, Type A personalities had twice as many cardiac symptoms as Type B personality (one that is more relaxed and complacent).

In peptic ulcers, although eating heavily acidic foods, alcohol consumption, possibly smoking, and tension-producing occupations all have been implicated in the development of ulcers, prime emphasis has been placed on conflicting dependency needs; that is, conflict between deeply-felt dependency needs and guilt and shame about those needs. The diathesis-stress model seems useful in explaining the development of peptic ulcers.

Essential hypertension is high blood pressure in the absence of an organic reason for it. Two possible psychological causes of it are suppressed rage and an overly inhibited drive for power.

Asthma may be caused by a genetically existing allergy, by an infection, or by such psychological factors (involved in more than one-third of asthmatic individuals) as anxiety, frustration, anger and depression. Psychological factors seem more to act as a trigger for an attack than as the primary cause of asthma.

Emotional distress and tension have at least an anecdotal place in explaining the occurrence of headaches. There is little research to support the anecdotes. Migraine headaches are thought to be based on a genetic vulnerability. Beyond that, research about psychological causation is inconclusive.

Beyond those psychosomatic illnesses, the personality traits of emotional inhibition and hopelessness have, in a small number of research studies, been related to the occurrence of cancer and rate of remission.

Treatment of the mild and moderate psychosomatic illnesses is often ameliorative with the use of the minor tranquilizers (valium or zxanthan). Among the psychotherapeutic treatment techniques are biofeedback behavior modification, use of operant conditioning, relaxation therapy and desensitization (see chapter 7).

Selected Readings

Glass, D. C. 1977. *Behavior Pattern Stress in Coronary Disease*. Hillsdale, N.J.: Erlbaum.

Jeinmolt, J. B., III, and S. E. Locke. 1984. "Psychosocial Factors, Immunologic Medication, and Human Susceptibility to Infectious Disease: How Much Do We Know?" *Psychological Bulletin*, 95: 78-108.

Kessler, R. C. and J. D. McLeon. 1985. "Social Support and Mental Health in Community Samples. " in S. Cohen and S. L. Syme (Eds.). *Social Support and Health*. New York: Academic Press.

Lynch, J. J. 1977. *The Broken Heart: The Medical Consequences of Loneliness*. New York: Basic Books.

Rees, L. 1964. "The Importance of Psychological, Allergic, and Infective Factors in Childhood Asthma." *Journal of Psychosomatic Research*, 7: 253-362.

Rodin, J. 1977. "Research on Eating Behavior and Obesity: Where Does It Fit in Personality and Social Psychology?" *Personality and Social Psychology Bulletin*, 3: 335-355.

Schwartz, G. E. and S. M. Weiss. 1978. "Behavioral Medicine Revisited: An Amended Definition." *Journal of Behavioral Medicine*, 1: 249-252.

Weiner, H. 1977. *Psychobiology and Human Disease*. New York: Elsevier.

11

Personality Disorders

*T*he psychiatric illness personality disorder includes an array of widely
different types of maladaptive behaviors ranging from extreme passivity to
violent antisocial behavior. In between those extremes, an individual with a
personality disorder may characteristically show any one of the following
types of extreme behavior: narcissistic, histrionic, eccentric, hypersensitive,
reclusive, overdependent, or perfectionistic or inflexible behavior.

The common characteristic justifying the diagnosis of personality disorder among those widely differing groups of people is that they have developed,
early in life, sometimes in childhood, personality traits (such as those
described) that are persistent and maladaptive, and that cause either significant impairment in social and/or occupational adjustment or extreme
personal distress. The behavior pattern constituting the disorder can usually
be recognized at adolescence. It persists through adulthood, though sometimes tapering off during the middle years. The behavior of the personality-
disordered individual is not episodic, nor is it notably related to stress. It is
instead a characteristic way of behaving in all or most of the interpersonal
relationships the individual enters.

Personality disorders differ in significant ways from the two other major
categories of psychiatric illness: anxiety related disorders (see chapters 8 and
9) and the psychoses (see chapter 13).

Anxiety related disorders may appear at any time of life; the disorder
manifests itself in specific fears, somatic symptoms, or memory loss. The core
of the disorder is anxiety. Personality disorders are long-established traits of
personality that characterize the individual's behavior from adolescence or
even childhood. The personality disorders involve the whole personality,
permeating all of the individual's thoughts and behavior. Although in certain

types of the personality disorders the individual often appears anxious or fearful, anxiety does not seem to be the central feature of the disorder. In anxiety disorders, the victim acutely feels the pain of his or her disorder; personality disorders usually cause less pain to those with the disorder than to those with whom they are associated, fellow workers, friends and family.

The psychotic individual lives a seriously disordered life, is often disoriented as to time and place, and has seriously loosened contact with reality, which manifests itself in delusions and hallucinations; in contrast, given his or her ways of thinking about human relationships, individuals with a personality disorder lead highly patterned, indeed inflexible, lives; and, although likely to see the world principally through the very narrow perspective of their selfish interests, they usually maintain an adequate contact with reality.

This chapter, following the DSM IIIR, describes the various types of personality disorders, but gives most attention to the one of them about which the most is known, the antisocial personality.

THE TYPES OF PERSONALITY DISORDERS

While the earliest identification of one type of behavior now classified as a personality disorder, the antisocial personality, goes back to the middle of the 19th century, when "depraved," criminal or immoral behavior was labeled "immoral insanity," the first systematic classification of the personality disorders appeared in the American Psychiatric Association *DSM I*, published in 1952. Since its first listing, various refinements have been made in it, and the process of refinement continues. The eleven types of personality disorder are organized into three clusters, labeled here for convenience simply as A, B and C.

Cluster A Personality Disorders

Grouped into one cluster are three personality disorders—paranoid, schizoid and schizotypal—in all of which the characteristic behavior of the individual appears odd or eccentric, although indeed the behavior may take varying forms.

PARANOID PERSONALITY DISORDER

Unreasonable, baseless and persistent suspiciousness is the hallmark of the paranoid personality. The trait shows itself in almost every aspect of the individual's behavior.

Symptomatology. Ordinarily, being suspicious in some life situations can be a prudent response; the normal person gives up his or her suspicions when credible evidence to do so is presented. The paranoid individual ignores such evidence and may develop elaborate reasons to dismiss it or may become suspicious of the person presenting the evidence. The paranoid individual is hypervigilant, always looking for trickery or slipperiness in the behavior of others. Such individuals trust no one's loyalty.

Each new situation they enter must be examined carefully for any possible pitfalls or entrapment. They will seize upon the slightest out-of-the-way occurrence to justify their suspicions. They delight in finding hidden meanings in what someone says or in catching anyone in a misstatement.

Other traits associated with their illness are argumentativeness and litigiousness; absence of sentimental or tender feelings; overseriousness and humorlessness. They are overly concerned with rank and class distinctions, are covertly envious of those in high positions and disdainful of those who seem to be weak or soft people. Although they frequently come close to difficulties with authority figures, an element of their behavior that causes frequent job changes, their very suspiciousness causes them to back away from getting into real trouble. When it threatens, they are capable of covering up their symptoms.

Prevalence. Paranoid individuals rarely trust themselves to the close interpersonal contact of therapy. As a result, little is known about prevalence. The disorder is more frequently seen in males.

SCHIZOID PERSONALITY DISORDER

The outstanding feature of the schizoid personality is an inability to form social relationships, a trait that makes them loners in any society.

Symptomatology. Schizoid persons show a lack of capacity to experience personal warmth or deep feelings; they are, as a result, unable to relate to others. They are insensitive to praise, criticism, or the feelings of others. Self-absorbed, they may appear to others to be absent-minded or off in another world; they are nevertheless free of the eccentricities of behavior, thought or speech characteristic of the schizotypal personality disorder (described next).

Associated with their illness are excessive daydreaming, vagueness about their goals, and indecision and hesitancy about their actions. They are, as one might expect, humorless, dull, cold and uninteresting as human beings. Nevertheless, given a job that allows them to function by themselves, they often make a good occupational adjustment.

Prevalence. Although no reliable statistics exist on the prevalence of schizoid disorder, the *DSM IIIR* ventures to estimate that a notable number of individuals working in jobs that totally and continually isolate them from other people and a good number of people living in skid row communities may have the disorder.

SCHIZOTYPAL PERSONALITY DISORDER

The two separate categories of personality disorder, schizoid personality disorder and schizotypal personality disorder, were developed to distinguish more clearly between two types of schizoid behavior and to separate both of them from schizophrenia. In schizoid personality disorder, the primary symptom is social withdrawal with few if any symptoms of eccentricity. The schizotypal personality disorder is characterized by oddities of perception, speech, thought and behavior which are not extreme enough to meet the diagnostic criteria for schizophrenia. There is evidence of a familial pattern of schizophrenia among the relatives of the schizotypal individual. The schizoid personality is a less disturbed and more adequately functioning individual than the schizotypal personality.

Symptomatology. The oddities observed in the schizotypal person include rambling speech, although not the incoherence of the schizophrenic; borderline illusory experiences, reporting that he or she feels that something illusory was so (the schizophrenic would report it as actually happening); and magical thinking, in which the individual claims to be able to read the thoughts of others or tell the future.

Also present are ideas of reference, in which the individual reports (without foundation) that people are talking about him or her. Other symptoms include extreme superstitiousness, social isolation, suspiciousness bordering on the paranoid, and hypersensitivity to criticism which may be imagined. Under stress, there may be brief episodic psychotic behavior.

Prevalence. The *DSM IIIR* reports no information on prevalence.

Cluster B Personality Disorders

The four disorders gathered here present symptoms that are more dramatic, attention-seeking, impulsive and erratic than are the personality disorders in Cluster A. Three of the four personality disorders of Cluster B will be discussed here, histrionic personality disorder, narcissistic personality disorder, and borderline personality disorder. The antisocial personality disorder will be discussed later in the chapter.

HISTRIONIC PERSONALITY DISORDER

The central concern of the histrionic individual is to be "on stage" at all times.

Symptomatology. Self-dramatization, heightened emotionality, and the need to capture everyone's attention typify their life-style. Their behavior is reactive and intensely expressed in dominating group discussions by dramatic recitals with elaborate exaggerations of events that others might mention in passing. Everything that happens to them is a major event which they seem to assume is of great interest to everyone else. On early acquaintance, they can be extremely charming, but that charm soon grows thin in the face of stormy explosions that often occur and the shallowness of emotion and selfishness of demands which are soon perceived by others.

The histrionic individual often is highly gullible in interpersonal relations, establishing unrealistic dependent relationships and expecting unreasonable favors from others. He or she may be seductive in the attention paid to others, but personal relations are superficial and sexual life is transitory.

Dramatically developed possible catastrophes, including threats of suicide, are manipulatively used by the individual to gain his or her ends. Impaired and stormy relationships follow the individual through life.

Prevalence. The disorder is a common one, more prevalent among women than men.

NARCISSISTIC PERSONALITY DISORDER

The dominating feature of this disorder is an all-consuming self-absorption with grandiose notions of the individual's own unique importance, talent, and right to special consideration.

Symptomatology. There is a total absence of any capacity to empathize with others or to consider their needs. Their self-fascination leads them to make exorbitant demands on others, to be exploitative with no pangs of conscience, and to respond with arrogance, disdain or dismissal when their demands are unfulfilled.

Yet with all of that felt self-importance, there is an underlying lowered sense of self-esteem, which reveals itself in a constant need for reassurance and admiration from others and a quick response of rage or disdain to any proffered criticism. The narcissist may dismiss failure with nonchalance, describing it as an unimportant experience. Some personality theorists consider narcissistic behavior a compensatory and defensive response to deep feelings of inadequacy, perhaps stemming from early childhood experiences of disapproval and rejection. There is also the possibility that parents, through catering to the child and building unrealistic expectations about what he or she should expect from others, creates the narcissistic personality.

Histrionic and narcissistic persons may present themselves to society in highly dramatic ways, but only the histrionic person is aware of or reactive to the other person; narcissistic persons act as if those others did not exist or, at most, were unimportant.

Prevalence. The *DSM IIIR* comments that the disorder seems to be more prevalent in today's society than in the past. It speculates that such increased notice of the disorder may only be due to the greater professional (particularly psychoanalytic) interest in the behavior.

BORDERLINE PERSONALITY DISORDER

The distinguishing characteristic of the disorder is marked instability in interpersonal relations, mood, and even in image of self. Since the borderline personality from time to time shows symptoms of antisocial personality, schizotypal personality, narcissistic or histrionic personality, and occasionally the psychotic symptoms of the mood disorders (see chapter 12), the diagnosis of borderline personality disorder is a challenging problem. Because of the instability of behavior and the wide variations in the way the individual behaves, the diagnosis is in danger of becoming "a kitchen sink" kind of evaluation in which any disorder not readily classified elsewhere is placed.

Symptomatology. To keep the category from becoming such a hodgepodge, the *DSM IIIR* requires that before the diagnosis is made, the individual show at least five of nine types of maladaptive and disordered behavior. The nine behaviors considered diagnostic are impulsive or unpredictable self-damaging emotional behavior, physically self-damaging behavior, instability and inappropriate or maladaptive intensity in interpersonal relationships, spells of intense and uncontrollable anger, self-identity disturbances, emotional instability involving marked and short-term shifts in mood, a high level of irritability or anxiety, intolerance of being alone, and unrelieved feelings of emptiness or boredom.

Prevalence. The Diagnostic Statistical Manual reports the borderline personality disorder is apparently common and appears more frequently in women.

Cluster C Personality Disorders

The third grouping of personality disorders brings together four disorders in which, unlike the other clusters, the individual may experience bouts of anxiety and apprehensiveness. The disorders are avoidant, dependent, obsessive-compulsive, and passive-aggressive personality disorders.

AVOIDANT PERSONALITY DISORDER

Although lonely and desirous of affection and acceptance, the avoidant personality avoids or withdraws from social contacts. Unlike the schizoid personality, who withdraws from social situations because he or she sees no value in them, the avoidant personality prizes social relationships, but self-esteem is so low and sensitivity so high that the person is afraid to reach out and make contact with others.

Symptomatology. The avoidant personality will choose to have lunch in a company cafeteria alone rather than join a table of associates where there is a vacant place. He or she cannot screw up courage to make a phone call, although the person may badly want the phone to ring. They can walk by even a small group of classmates and make no effort to join them. They often interpret even gentle kidding as a dreaded rebuff.

The individual soon finds himself or herself in a vicious cycle, demanding guarantees of acceptance and freedom from even hints of criticism, so that social life soon becomes extremely limited. The failure to make friends lowers self-esteem which, of course, intensifies the anxiety at entering social situations. Left alone, the person worsens the problems by dwelling on shortcomings and magnifying social failings. The avoidant personality's behavior is self-defeating; unwillingness to reach out results in the absence of the very relationships that are desired. As time goes by, any social skills are lost, and the isolation becomes more complete. Career opportunities are limited to those few positions where any social contact is momentary and unimportant.

Prevalence. A common disorder, especially among women.

DEPENDENT PERSONALITY DISORDER

Like the avoidant individual, the dependent personality's illness stems from a seriously low level of self-esteem. In dependency, however, the individual flees into turning over his or her life to other people, meekly carrying out decisions others are pressed to make for him or her.

Symptomatology. Because of a lack of self-confidence, dependent personalities look to other people, such as parents, spouses, neighbors and friends, to make all their decisions: what career to pursue, whom to marry, where to live, how to dress. They tend to think they are too stupid to make their own decisions. Like the avoidant personality, the dependent personality is soon in a vicious cycle. The more passive the person becomes in accepting the decisions (orders) of other people, the more incompetent the individual feels, thus spiraling down into complete passivity, accepting whatever life, in the form of others, brings. Dependent personalities are frequently self-effacing women whose passivity and dependence allows them to tolerate a spouse's drunkenness, infidelities and physical abuse for fear that if she objects, she will be abandoned.

A frequent complication of extreme dependency in an unhappy family situation is reactive depression and loss of interest or pleasure in all usual activities.

Prevalence. Dependent personality is a common disorder, occurring more frequently in women.

OBSESSIVE-COMPULSIVE PERSONALITY DISORDER

Perfectionism, a dominating concern with the rightness of the way things are done, and a crippling preoccupation with detail, much of it trivia, is the all-consuming characteristic of the person handicapped by obsessive-compulsive personality disorder.

The disorder should be distinguished from the obsessive-compulsive neurotic disorder (described in chapter 8). In that disorder, the individual is distressed by the symptoms, sees they are irrational, and would be rid of them if only it were possible. In the obsessive-compulsive personality disorder, the individual takes pride in perfectionism and expects that others will see things as he or she does; the concern of the individual is with getting things right, not the possibility that he or she is sick.

Symptomatology. The obsessive-compulsive personality is so tied to the need to get everything right that he or she has no time to relax and no capacity to find pleasure in life. Life is filled with constant concern for detailed planning of every event, even vacations, to the extent that there is no opportunity to enjoy it by the individual or by others who share the experience. Rigidity, over-conscientiousness, overly controlled behavior, to the exclusion of warmth and spontaneity, characterize the behavior of the individual. Although job success and hard work are of great significance, time-consuming checking of trivia usually makes success difficult or impossible. Although driven to be exacting and demanding of others, the individual is rarely open to the suggestions of others.

Prevalence. The personality disorder is more common, especially in men, than the neurotic illness, which is relatively rare.

PASSIVE-AGGRESSIVE PERSONALITY DISORDER

This diagnosis infers an underlying hostile or aggressive outlook which is expressed covertly by passive behavior which nevertheless effectively blocks compliance with duties or the requisites of others. It is the most controversial diagnosis in the entire category of personality disorders for two possible reasons. It links two seemingly incompatible personality traits, passivity and aggressiveness. Beyond this, research support for this diagnosis as an independent clinical entity is meager.

Symptomatology. The passively resistant behavior can take many forms, including delaying tactics, innocently forgetting to do something, intentional inefficiency, accidental damaging behavior, and stubborn inability to understand what is wanted. Such behavior typically cuts across occupational, family and social situations. The result is evasive and persistent ineffectiveness. The covert resistance persists, even when more directly self-assertive and effective behavior is possible. The *DSM IIIR* provides the following example of passive-aggressive behavior: a person who always comes late to appointments, promises to make arrangements for particular events but never does, and keeps forgetting to bring needed documents to meetings. When such behavior typically occurs in a variety of situations, a passive-aggressive personality disorder is felt to be present.

The diagnosis is inappropriate when such behavior is limited to an assignment the individual considers unfair or unacceptable, but overt resistance is not possible—for example, some assignments in military duty, or the impossible demands of an overbearing and dictatorial parent.

Prevalence. The *DSM IIIR* reports that no information is available on prevalence or sex differences.

OVERVIEW OF PERSONALITY DISORDERS

With the exception of the antisocial personality (to be described later in the chapter), relatively little empirical research has been undertaken on the personality disorders. They are relatively newly-classified clinical disorders which were made a part of the official classification of psychiatric disorders in 1952.

The student of abnormal psychology faces two problems in learning about these disorders. One problem is that not all psychologists agree on their existence as legitimate psychiatric syndromes. The disagreement hinges on the question of whether or not traits as consistent ways of responding across life situations really exist. For example, is an individual an extrovert in all life situations? Behavioral psychologists, on the basis of their research, contend that the existence of cross-situational traits basic to the specific personality disorders is a false premise.

The second problem with the specific personality disorders is the unreliability of diagnosis. In the field trials of the psychiatric manual, the diagnoses of some of the individual personality disorders were considered too unreliable for practical usefulness. One reason for this is the dimensional quality of the characteristics of the disorders, which makes it difficult to decide at what point a disorder really exists. The symptoms of personality disorders range from expressions commonly found in a normal population to severely pathological expressions. Many normal individuals are histrionic to a degree. Dependency of a mild sort is found in the interpersonal relationships of otherwise happily well-adjusted individuals. Further complicating the problem of diagnosis of the personality disorder is the overlapping of their symptoms with other psychiatric illnesses, including other types of personality disorder.

Exemplifying the degree of uncertainty about the personality disorders is the decision of the American Psychiatric Association to postpone entering two other types of personality disorder in their diagnostic manual pending further studies. One delayed category is self-defeating personality disorder, originally labeled masochistic personality disorder. The objection to this disorder was that it could be used to blame the victim—for example, of rape or spousal abuse—for being victimized. The second category only tentatively put forward but not yet entered in the diagnostic manual is sadistic personality disorder, which is, in a sense, a balancing of the first disorder since it is the obverse of it.

ANTISOCIAL PERSONALITY DISORDER

Behavior such as that now described as an antisocial personality was first identified and distinguished from other psychological disorders in 1837 by the British psychologist J. C. Prichard, who considered it to be moral insanity. He described it in old-fashioned language that nevertheless captured the principal symptoms of the disease still recognized today. He wrote that while the intellectual abilities are unimpaired, "the moral and active principles of the mind are strangely perverted and depraved; the power of self-government is lost or greatly impaired; and the individual is found to be incapable, not of talking or reasoning upon any subject proposed to him, for this he will often do with great shrewdness and volubility, but of conducting himself with decency and propriety in the business of life."

History of the Disorder

Clinicians of that day considered it a disorder of the will which made the person incapable of conforming to society's demands. In the late 19th century, the disorder came to be called psychopathic personality, and with the biogenic bias of the day, a hereditary basis for the disorder was assumed. This "bad seed" interpretation held sway until the early part of the twentieth century when social influences were thought to be important causes of the illness and the disorder was named sociopathy. Today the agreed-upon diagnosis is the neutral antisocial personality disorder, although both earlier terms frequently make their appearance. Modern thinking recognizes interpersonal, biogenic and sociocultural factors as possible causative elements in the disorder.

An Example of an Extremely Antisocial Personality

Gary Gilmore, whose criminal behavior and life history are now a matter of public record, is an extreme example of the antisocial personality. His behavior and his reactions to that behavior well illustrate two of the most prominent characteristics of the antisocial personality: purposeless and irrational antisocial behavior with no remorse about the harm done. In his own words, Gilmore describes the murder that led to his death sentence and electrocution: "I pulled up near a gas station. I told the service station guy to give me all his money. I then took him to the bathroom and told him to kneel down and then I shot him in the head twice. The guy didn't give me any trouble, but I just felt like I had to do it." That vicious and purposeless crime was the finale of a long history of assorted antisocial activity beginning during early adolescence.

Symptomatology

Symptoms of the antisocial personality fall into two principal categories, overt antisocial behavior from an early age, and underlying personality traits that provide the basis for that behavior.

OBSERVABLE ANTISOCIAL BEHAVIOR

The diagnostic manual, which rests its diagnosis on observable behavior with no attribution of causality, indicates the following examples as characteristic of the personality disorder: truancy, suspension or expulsion from school; frequent job changes and long periods of unemployment; irresponsible parenting; failure to accept social norms; inability to maintain enduring attachments in heterosexual relationships; irritability and aggressiveness; irresponsibility in meeting financial obligations; impulsiveness and failure to plan ahead; disregard for the truth; reckless behavior such as recurrent speeding or driving while intoxicated.

No one of these tendencies or a single instance of one or two, especially without an early life history of antisocial behavior, justifies a diagnosis of personality disorder. The diagnostic manual specifies that at least four of the patterns be exhibited since the age of eighteen.

PERSONALITY CHARACTERISTICS OF THE ANTISOCIAL PERSONALITY

Psychologists who have studied the antisocial personality go beyond the objective criteria of the diagnostic manual to identify personality characteristics of the disorder that seem to engender the described antisocial behavior. Seven personality traits deeply ingrained in the psychopath's personality have been identified by psychologists.

Emotional Poverty. The antisocial personality seems never to have developed the capacity to feel strong or deep emotional attachments. There is no real capacity for deep love or loyalty to anyone else. The ordinary emotions of anger, grief and despair are absent. Antisocial personalities show no pity or sympathy for the victims of their crimes, not even much sadness about the sorry plight in which they ultimately find themselves as a result of their behavior.

Absence of Conscience. Along with a flat, affective life-style is a nonworking conscience. Although intellectually able to know right from wrong and even ostentatiously mouthing the principles of ethical behavior, they exhibit no remorse about unprincipled behavior, no guilt about irresponsible, sometimes vicious behavior. Nothing seems to affect them about their crimes except perhaps mild unhappiness about having been caught.

Facile Charm, Glibness and Winning Ways. A capacity to be charming and to use winning ways to manipulate or exploit others is characteristic of a person with antisocial behavior disorder. An especially troublesome trait is their glibness and skill in talking others into victimization. Many victims, even after having been exploited, maintain good feelings about the individual who victimized them. The psychopathic personality is frequently able to escape arrest or punishment by their persuasiveness and deliberately projected air of candor and sincerity.

They make friends easily, and just as easily give them up or take advantage of them. They easily persuade others of their good faith, and at times almost delude themselves into believing that what they say is all right.

Inadequately Motivated Behavior. As much as we may deplore criminal behavior, we can still make sense of what the normal criminal has attempted—to make money, to collect on an insurance policy, to make important connections. The antisocial behavior of the disordered individual seems purposeless and spur of the moment: a crime committed, often a heinous one, because the individual felt like doing it. The psychopath is unable to say why he committed the crime. In the place of the usual motives for the crime, there is impulsiveness and the need to seek thrills and excitement.

Inability to Learn or Profit from Experience. Psychopathic individuals go through life without ever seeming to learn from mistakes, to be more calculating in planning their behavior the next time, or to make efforts to avoid detection. The ordinary punishments that most people would fear seem meaningless to them. Their needs are immediate, and memories of past punishments have little if any influence on what they will do today or tomorrow.

Shattered Interpersonal Relations. Initial friendships won by their glibness and exploitative charm are very quickly shattered by the psychopath's soon-to-be-discovered, cynical, ungrateful and unfeeling behavior to the newly acquired friends. Lifetime interpersonal relationships are nothing but a series of short-term contacts, callously looked upon by the antisocial personality as new opportunities for manipulation and exploitation.

Warped Reactions to Punishment. Certain punishments which normal people try diligently to avoid seem meaningless to antisocial personalities. They seem not to be influenced by physical punishment and care not a whit for social disapproval except as it might interfere with an immediate exploitative venture. But at least one experiment demonstrates a concern about loss of money. The proper conclusion to draw here is that punishment is influential with the psychopath only if it specifically interferes with an ongoing goal, and it is therefore especially noxious.

Prevalence

The *DSM IIIR*, supported by other epidemiological studies, indicates the prevalence of antisocial personality to be between 3 and 5 percent of males and less than 1 percent for females. Onset for males is preadolescent; for females, during puberty.

Causative Factors in Antisocial Personality Disorder

Antisocial personality disorder, the first of the personality disorders to be identified, is the most widely researched and the best understood. Although there is some disagreement among psychologists about the other personality disorders, psychologists agree on the principal symptoms of the antisocial personality disorder, and the reliability of the diagnosis is high. There is also substantial agreement that the disorder develops out of some mix of four principal elements: early family relationships and parenting practices; defects in learning; biogenic factors, both genetic and physiological; and sociocultural factors.

EARLY FAMILY RELATIONSHIPS AND PARENTING PRACTICES

Four types of intrafamily experiences seem to be strongly associated with the development of antisocial personality disorder. They are as follows: loss of a parent, inconsistent parental behavior, lack of emotional support from parents, and the modeling of sociopathic parents of the individual.

Loss of a Parent. Greer, in a 1964 study, reported that while 60 percent of a group of psychopathic individuals had lost a parent, in two control groups in the study, the percentage was significantly less—28 percent of a control group of neurotic individuals and an almost equal number (27 percent) of a control group of individuals classified as normal. There can be no doubt that loss of a parent is a catastrophic event in a child's growth, but since so many other children who have lost a parent, or even both parents, grow to maturity with no significant psychiatric illness, such a loss seems to fall short of being an adequate cause of psychopathy in itself. Other research suggests it is the loss of a parent in an already disturbed family situation that is a significant element.

Lack of Emotional Support from Parents. When parents fail to give their children the loving nurturing that healthy growth requires, the child's own emotional growth is stunted, and the emotional poverty of the psychopath may soon result. That emotional deprivation can result from sheer neglect, rejection, or from overintellectualization and coldness on the part of the parent. When the latter is the case, family life, viewed from the outside, can appear to be stable and happy but be unrewarding for the child. Such covert unhappiness at home may account for the occasional psychopathic adolescent who seems to have come from a stable, happy home.

DEFECTIVE EARLY LEARNING EXPERIENCES

Ethical values and principles behavior are normally learned at home. When the models parents offer are inconsistent, children fail to develop any sense of discipline or ethical control.

Inconsistent Discipline. When the reward/punishment practices at home are inconsistent, or when each parent takes a different approach—for example, a stern, disciplinarian father and a mother who compensates (perhaps out of hostility to her husband) by leniency, secretive rewards and giving in to any demands made by the child— the child grows up confused about values, may pick up hostility to all authority as representing a hated father, and learn manipulative and exploitative behavior from the unwitting cooperation of his or her mother.

Inconsistent Values. A 1945 study of Greenacre described a pattern of faulty learning that may account for the development of antisocial personalities from middle-class families. Greenacre describes a family pattern in which the father may be a successful member of the community but distant or fear-inspiring to his children. The mother may be indulgent and often passively contemptuous of her husband's importance. When such families are heavily dependent upon the approval of their communities, it is crucial that they maintain the illusion of a happy family by concealing any evidence of bickering or scandal. The children soon learn that appearances are more important than reality, and they become part of the show window display, in which a premium is put on impressing others rather than on competence and integrity. This need to please and to win social approval for their parents' sakes seems to bring out a precocious but superficial charm in some of these children, together with great skill in handling people for purely selfish purposes.

The son in such a family cannot hope to emulate his successful and awe-inspiring father; but aware of the extension to himself of the high evaluation that is placed on his father, he develops a feeling of importance and of being exempt from the consequences of his actions. Frequently, the prominence of the father does, in fact, protect the child from the ordinary consequences of antisocial behavior. If one additional factor is added—the contradictory influence of a father who tells his son of the necessity for responsibility, honesty and respect for others, but who himself is deceitful and manipulative—we appear to have a family background capable of producing a middle-class psychopathic personality (adapted from Carson *et. al.* 1988, p. 243).

Underarousal and Defective Avoidance Learning. Several early studies of the antisocial personality indicate that they are underaroused by emotional or noxious stimuli which would strongly arouse normal individuals. There is physiological evidence to suggest that their autonomic nervous systems respond at a low level of variability, lowering the level of fear and anxiety they experience. (See discussion under Biogenic Factors.) A series of skillfully constructed and carefully controlled experiments seemed to demonstrate that their low level of arousal not only causes impulsive and stimulant-seeking behavior, but also results in deficient avoidance learning.

To test the hypothesis that the sociopath's low level of arousal impairs ability to learn from negative experiences or punishment (avoidance learning), a group of sociopaths were compared with a group of healthy individuals in learning a mental maze. They were asked to learn which one of four levers turned on a green light. Two of the levers produced the wrong response of red. The fourth lever produced an electric shock. The task was one of considerable complexity. Sociopaths and nonsociopaths, as expected, made the same total number of errors; but while the normal subjects quickly learned to avoid the punishing electric shock, sociopaths took much longer to do so. Their capacity to avoid punishment seemed to be impaired, possibly because the electric shock was not as noxious—that is, punishing—for them as it was for normal subjects.

BIOGENIC FACTORS

Possible biological factors causing antisocial behavior fall into two categories, genetic and physiological, the latter of which may, however, be caused by the genetic anomalies.

Genetic Factors. Much research has been devoted to the question of possible genetic causes of antisocial personality disorder. The safest conclusion to draw from those studies is that sociopathy is the result of a combination of hereditary and environmental influences. A report of two Danish studies will both illustrate the nature of the research conducted and the resultant findings.

Using official Copenhagen registration data and police files, the researcher isolated a group of sociopaths who had been adopted from infancy. He found that the biological relatives of the sociopaths were four to five times more likely than the adoptive relatives to meet the criteria for a diagnosis of antisocial personality. He nevertheless reported that the small differences justified only the conclusion that although there is a genetic factor operating, environmental influences must also be considered as significant. Comparable studies conducted in the United States confirm that conclusion.

In a second Danish study, the criminal records of adoptees were compared with the criminal records of both biological and adoptive parents. The incidence of criminal behavior, as might be expected, was lowest when neither biological nor adoptive fathers had been convicted of a crime. Differing only slightly from that comparison was the rate when the adoptive parent was a criminal but the biological father was not. On the contrary, when the biological father was a criminal, but not the adoptive father, the rate of criminal behavior jumped significantly. However, the highest criminal rate was found among those adoptees both of whose fathers, biological and adoptive, had criminal records. Here is a finding that supports hereditary and environmental influence on criminal behavior.

While this study examined convicted criminals, not necessarily those that had been diagnosed as antisocial personalities, it is likely that a good number of the criminals were sociopaths. In any case, considering only this study, the evidence suggests a genetic factor, but one that interacts with environmental influences. To put it colloquially and loosely, it can be said that although a predisposition to antisocial behavior has a genetic base, the mode of antisocial behavior will be learned from the environment the individual experiences.

Physiological Factors. Given possible genetic causative influence, the question remains, what is it that is inherited to cause the development of antisocial behavior? One strongly supported interpretation suggests that the antisocial personality is born with a physiological deficiency that creates a cortical immaturity. A delayed development of the higher functions of the brain results. Two well-known characteristics of the sociopath give credence to this interpretation. Between 30 and 38 percent of all antisocial personalities show abnormal brain wave patterns (electroencephalographic recordings). The most common feature of the abnormality is a slow brain wave activity characteristic of infants and children, but not of adults. Given time, the immature brain will, later in life, finally mature. With the maturing of the brain, changes in behavior can be expected. Such change does take place in many sociopaths as they grow older, when much of their flagrant antisocial behavior diminishes.

Since much of the abnormal slow brain wave activity comes from the temporal lobes and the limbic system of the brain (the second layer of the brain), areas of the brain that control both memory and emotional behavior, it is thought that genetic influences operate by impairing those parts of the brain. Their impairment would seem to create a physiological basis for the low level of arousal characteristic of the antisocial personalities and their difficulties with avoidance learning.

SOCIOCULTURAL CAUSATIVE FACTORS

The diagnostic manual reports that the antisocial personality disorder is more common in lower socioeconomic groups. In interpreting that statement, care must be taken not to identify poverty with psychiatric illness and not to conclude that poverty by itself is a cause of antisocial behavior. At most, an impoverished home life can be only a contributory cause and only that when other social and biogenic causes are operative.

From an early age, children emulate the behavior of parents. When that behavior is irresponsible and antisocial, it is all too common that they follow the example set for them. The official diagnostic manual relates this causative element to the socioeconomic level of the child in these words: "The disorder is more common in lower-class populations, partly because it is associated with impaired learning capacity, and partly because fathers of those with the disorder frequently have the disorder themselves and consequently their children grow up in impoverished homes." One can add to this statement, with little opportunity to learn different ways of behaving.

Treatment of Antisocial Personalities

There is universal agreement among psychologists that antisocial personalities make poor candidates for treatment, whether the treatment is psychotherapy or medical treatment by electroconvulsive shock or the administration of drugs. Personality characteristics of the antisocial personality, and often their life circumstances, operate against their responding to treatment. Nevertheless, clinicians continue to try new therapeutic approaches. At least one of those, the residential treatment center, seems promising.

NEGATIVE INFLUENCES ON RESPONSE TO THERAPY

Three elements work against successful therapy with the antisocial personality: the ingrained nature of their symptoms, their inability to relate to others, and the involuntary nature of the therapy that society frequently offers them.

Deeply Ingrained Personality Traits. The underlying causes of the antisocial behavior are personality traits that have developed in the individual from early childhood. Lifelong patterns of behavior are resistant to change. Those patterns of the antisocial personality resist even prolonged psychoanalytic psychotherapy.

The Nature of Symptoms. The principal characteristics of the antisocial personality described previously make impossible any interpersonal relationship that is dependent upon mutual trust, and such trust is a requirement of all forms of psychotherapy.

Involuntary Treatment. Antisocial personalities are more likely to wind up in the prison system than in the mental hygiene clinic of the psychiatric hospital. The rehabilitation programs provided are largely involuntary, and they have little impact on the antisocial personality. For them, the penal system seems to be a revolving door; in and out, unchanged.

Promising Treatment Efforts. Despite the discouraging results, psychologists continue to explore other avenues of treatment. A 1978 publication advises therapists attempting to treat antisocial personalities to take three precautions in establishing a therapeutic relationship. They are as follows: be on guard for any attempts at manipulation and exploitation in the therapy relationship; assume that much information provided by the patient will be distorted or even fabricated; and be patient—a therapeutic relationship with a psychopath will take a long time to develop. Aside from that advice for anyone who would attempt one-on-one therapy, programs based entirely on learning principles are being attempted. These programs would first withdraw any reinforcement of antisocial behavior, including the use of attention-providing punishment; secondly, they would use change agents—that is, admired others, including the therapist, upon whom to model the desired behavior, which can then be rewarded when the psychopath responds; thirdly, material rewards are gradually eliminated as the individual finds self-established symbolic rewards effective in motivating behavior.

It is clear that only in a residential treatment center in which the antisocial personality can be supervised continuously could such a program be implemented successfully. In one program with adolescent psychopaths, based on reinforcement learning theory, program leaders report a change in behavior while the individual continues to reside at the center; but, sad to say, the change does not endure after the individual has been released.

The common characteristics of all personality disorders is the development early in life of personality traits that are persistent, maladaptive, and that cause either significant impairment in social or occupational adjustment or extreme personal distress.

The DSM IIIR organizes the eleven types of personality disorder into three clusters. These are Cluster A, which includes the paranoid, schizoid and schizotypal disorders. In all of these, the characteristic symptom is odd or eccentric (but not bizarre) behavior.

Cluster B includes the histrionic personality disorder, narcissistic personality disorder, antisocial personality disorder, and borderline personality disorder. Except for the last, in which wide-ranging instability of behavior is characteristic, they are expressed in self-centered and inordinately selfish behavior.

Cluster C includes avoidant, dependent, obsessive-compulsive and passive-aggressive personality disorders. These have in common the high degree of personal distress experienced by the victims of the disorder.

Of the personality disorders, more is known about antisocial personality disorder than any of the other personality disorders. With respect to the others, there is disagreement among clinicians as to whether or not they truly exist as separate clinical entities. The disagreement rests on controversy about the psychological existence of traits (persistent ways of reacting to the external world) in the expression of personality. Since each personality disorder, except antisocial personality, rests on the presence of an extreme personality trait, if traits as consistent ways of behaving do not exist, neither do the personality disorders that rest on their existence.

The antisocial personality is characterized by emotional poverty, absence of conscience, often facile charm, inexplicable motivation, frequent bouts of violent or criminal behavior, inability to profit from experience, shattered interpersonal relationships, and warped or indifferent reaction to punishment. Both organic and psychological factors are thought to operate in causing the disorder. Treatment is rarely undertaken voluntarily and is rarely successful.

Selected Readings

Kohut, H., and E. S. Wolf. 1978. "The Disorders of the Self and Their Treatment: An Outline." *International Journal of Psychoanalysis*, 59: 413-425.

McGlashen, T. H. 1986. "Schizotypal Personality Disorder. Chestnut Lodge Follow-up Study: VI Long-Term Follow-up Perspectives." *Archives of General Psychiatry*, 44: 143-148.

McGlashen, T. H. 1987. "Testing DSM IIIR Symptom Criteria for Schizotypal and Borderline Personality Disorders." *Archives of General Psychiatry*, 44: 143-148.

Mellsop, G., F. Varghese, S. Joshua and A. Hicks. 1982. "The Reliability of Axis II of DSM III." *American Journal of Psychiatry*, 139 (10): 1360-1361.

Millon, T. 1981. *Disorders of Personality: DSM III, Axis III*. New York: Wiley.

Reich, J. 1987. "Sex Distribution of DSM III Personality Disorders in Psychiatric Outpatients." *American Journal of Psychiatry*, 144: 485-488.

Siguardsson, S., C. R. Clonenger, M. Cohman, A. L. von Knorring. 1982. "Predisposition to Petty Criminality in Swedish Adoptees. III Sex Differences and Validation of the Male Typology." *Archives of General Psychiatry*, 39: 1248-1253.

12

The Mood Disorders

$R$are, indeed, if any, are those individuals who are never "in a mood"—downcast, discouraged, even depressed,; or, on the other hand, elated, optimistic and energetic beyond one's usual feelings. It is normal, occasionally, to be "down in the dumps," a mood that may be triggered by a disappointment, a promotion not granted, a romantic affair broken off, a disturbing family spat. It is just as normal to go through a period of feeling that "everything is rosy," when problems melt away, energy and optimism are high, and much activity, sometimes bordering on the frenetic, goes on.

In the depressed mood, energy drains away, interest in old pleasures wanes, and little is accomplished. In a manic spell, much seems to get done, not always precisely as planned; new projects are begun, resolutions are made, old projects are finished, high hopes are preoccupying, only to fade away too soon when reality is confronted once again.

Among the normal population, these moods have their beginning in some real life situation, and they are terminated by a real life event. Depression disappears after a happy family day or upon receipt of an unexpected compliment. Elation disappears as the reality of life's problems captures our attention. They are both of relatively short duration, and they lead to no drastic or damaging actions.

Such moods are to be distinguished from the extreme moods or mood swings described later in this chapter. They are mentioned in order to reiterate a point that has been made before with other psychiatric disorders: abnormal behavior finds its place on a continuum of behavior from the normal and well-adjusted to the extreme and severely maladaptive.

One other point needs mention here in this introductory statement. The array of diagnoses involving mood disturbances, especially for depression, may seem like hair splitting. But the distinctions made among mood disorders exist because, although on the surface they may seem similar, they represent different disorders that follow their own course, often respond to different therapies and, in extreme cases, lead to markedly different outcomes, including suicide or suicidal attempts.

The chapter first identifies the symptoms of depression and mania as mood disorders, then describes the classification of mood disturbances, and briefly indicates their prevalence. It continues with a discussion of possible causes of mood disorders, and then examines the principal therapies found helpful in their treatment. Finally, it examines the sad phenomenon of suicide, a possible outcome of a severe mood disorder.

DEPRESSION AND MANIA

The two principal affective (emotional) states of the mood disorders are depression and mania. Either can appear alone as the principal symptom of the disorder, or both can appear cyclically. Of the two states, depression is the much more frequent, occurring in 90 percent of the mood disorders. A long-known form of the disorder is one that alternates between depression and mania. It was formerly labeled manic-depressive psychosis.

Sadness, dejection and grieving dominate the life of the disordered individual during the depressed stage. Those feelings may be accompanied by feelings of worthlessness and a sense of the futility of life. There may be profuse weeping or periodic heavy sighing. The loss of a loved one may normally produce many of the same emotional feelings, but the normal individual gradually recovers and returns to normal pursuits. Prolonged grieving of the type described would suggest the presence of a mood disorder.

The individual's posture, stooped over, head down, glum facial expression, flat voice, all signal the depression the individual is experiencing. Spontaneity and expressive movements disappear. Actions are slow and plodding in an overall psychomotor retardation. The person may remain all day in slippers and bathrobe; or, if depressed, clothing will be sloppy and stained, the hair uncombed. Women wear no makeup; men go about disheveled. The behavior of the individual says very clearly, I don't care anymore.

If for no other reasons, the changed lifestyle of the individual will produce physiological changes. There may be loss of appetite and weight; or, on the contrary, the individual will overeat, not a full planned meal, but small servings, all day long. Constipation is a frequent symptom. Sleep patterns are disturbed; there may be difficulty in falling asleep or waking after an hour or two and being unable to sleep. Or, in contrast, there may be excessive sleeping or drowsing in bed all day long. Sexual interest wanes or disappears altogether.

Symptomatology: Mania

As one would expect, in mania the behavior is at the opposite extreme of that of the depressed individual. Characteristically, the manic individual is highly charged, and expends energy uselessly and steadily.

Elation, unrealistic optimism, expansiveness, planning, seemingly backed by endless energy, are the beginning affective symptoms. Blocked or criticized, the manic individual will turn irritable, which mood change can soon becomes belligerency, with abusive and profane language. The individual's strong and unleashed emotions lead to uninhibited behavior, argumentative reactions to others and, occasionally, uninvited and unacceptable sexual advances.

The range of behavior symptoms in the manic have been graded into three categories. Hypomania is the least disturbed. The individual seems supercharged in mood and overreactive in behavior. The push in their affective life leads to bad judgment, but not delusions. They are grandiose and dominating in conversation, and are unprepared to "listen to reason." Although this level of mania is indeed a mood disorder, it is often accepted by those who have grown used to it. They may, for example, simply describe the individual as boorish and unpleasant company, but basically harmless.

At the next level of mania, acute mania, all symptoms are more extreme. Manics become incoherent in speech. They are readily judged to be disordered. Irritability at rebuff, criticism or frustration may be frightening. The acute phase may be an outgrowth of hypomania, but also may spring up quite acutely and with no warning.

In the most extreme form of mania, delirious mania, the individual is completely out of control. The disorder at this stage is the stereotype of the "wild maniac." Hallucinations and delusions are present, and behavior dangerous to the manic individual or to others is possible. Physical restraint or sedation in a hospital setting soon becomes necessary. The principal physiological change is sleeplessness, leading to exhaustion.

CLASSIFICATION OF THE MOOD DISORDERS

In classifying the mood disorders, three major criteria are considered: the cyclical or noncyclical nature of the illness—that is, whether or not there are alternating periods of depression and mania; the degree of the depression or mania—mild, moderate or severe. The difference between the mildest category of the disorder, whether manic or depressive, and the most extreme category, is considerable. The former borders on the normal range of depressive or manic mood, and the latter usually justifies the diagnosis, "with psychotic features," and can require a period of hospitalization. The third criterion, the duration of the illness, categorizes the disorders as acute, chronic or intermittent.

The *DSM IIIR* classification of the mood disorders is presented below.

Bipolar Disorders	Depressive Disorders
Bipolar Disorder	Major Depression
Mixed	Single Episode
Manic	Recurrent
Depressed	Dysthymia
Cyclothymia	

NORMAL DEPRESSION

Although there is no *DSM IIIR* classification for normal depression, the condition is prevalent, and can be alleviated by help from a mental health specialist. Even though normal depression requires no outside help in most cases, when there is any doubt, it is better to err on the conservative side than to take chances.

Grief

Certain events in life bring on the emotion of grief and plunge the individual into the grieving process. The most common cause of grief is, of course, the death of a loved one. There are other grief-causing sorrows in life: the loss of a long-held job (even through promotion or transfer), thereby cutting the individual from a daily network of happy social experiences; the moving away of a lifelong friend; the sale of a home in which one has lived for years. Any of these experiences can bring on grieving. In psychological terms, they are called stressors, that is, any event or situation causing stress.

As long as the grieving process does not go to extreme lengths or last longer than a month or two, it can be a quiet time of recovery from an emotionally affecting loss, and not at all abnormal. It is a frequent and probably useful device to break the grieving period by a treat of some sort; a short trip, a shopping spree, or a small family party.

Life Situations Causing Normal Depression

In some life situations, simple depression can follow very normal life experiences, such as the postpartum depression that sometimes follows the birth of a child. One study reports that almost 50 percent of women after childbirth experience a "down" mood. Students can also experience a kind of postpartum depression. Among doctoral candidates, depression might appear right after their final oral examinations; among undergraduates, a "normal" depression often hits the day after commencement. Throughout the college years, students can be overwhelmed by dependency needs, of feelings of being ineffective or inadequate, with a resulting depressive spell, usually of short duration.

There is no sure antidote for depression caused by those unpleasant but normal and all-too-frequent life experiences. Reaching out to close and supportive friends or relatives, if the individual can mobilize the energy to do so, can be helpful. Also, the knowledge can be reassuring that in most cases (the percentage is difficult to estimate) the stimulation of the normal pleasures and demands of life soon terminate the depression.

MILD TO MODERATE MOOD DISORDERS

There are three mood disorders characterized as mild to moderate: one is cyclical, cyclothymia; the second, dysthymia, is characterized only by depression. A third mood disorder, not included in the mood disorders of *DSM IIIR*, is essentially a depressive response to a recent stressor. In the manual, it is listed as an adjustment disorder.

Cyclothymia

Cyclothymia was at one time considered a personality disorder because it seems to be a lifetime pattern of behavior, in which the individual experiences moods alternating between hypomania (mild to moderate spells of heightened activity) and mild to moderate depressive periods. It is now listed as a mood disorder, not a personality disorder. There is research to suggest that it is a less severe form of bipolar mood disorder (discussed later).

SYMPTOMATOLOGY

The *DSM IIIR* lists as diagnostic criteria for cyclothymic disorder a two-year period of numerous spells of alternating depressive and manic symptoms. The two phases may be separated by months-long periods of normal mood.

Among the prominent symptoms are the following: during the depressed phase, low energy level and chronic fatigue; insomnia or too much sleeping or drowsing; feelings of inadequacy; social isolation; reduced levels of functioning, complicated by concentration, memory, and thinking problems.

During the hypomanic phase, there is a pattern of behavior which is the very opposite of that which exists during the depressed phase, including more energy, less need for sleep; high self-esteem; talkativeness, with much laughter and boisterousness; overoptimism; exaggerated efforts at productivity, including working at unusual hours; heightened social activity, with the possibility of hypersexuality, with little sense of responsibility; foolish activities, such as buying sprees, reckless driving, and baseless boasting.

None of the behavior is extreme enough to justify a diagnosis of a major mood disorder. There are no hallucinations, delusions or loosened associations. Nevertheless, complications of this disorder may lead to major manic or depressive episodes. It is for that reason that cyclothymia is thought to be a mild form of a more serious bipolar disorder.

PREVALENCE

Now judged to be a common disorder, frequently accepted by the individual and family as an extreme way of behaving, without recognition of its disordered nature, cyclothymia begins early in life and has a chronic course. It is more common among women.

Dysthymia

The *DSM IIIR's* diagnostic criterion for the disorder is a two-year period during which the individual suffers much of the time from symptoms of depression.

SYMPTOMATOLOGY

Except for the absence of manic or hypomanic phases, the individual's symptoms are those of the depressed phase of cyclothymia. The depressed moods may be persistent, or interrupted by short periods of normal mood. There is an absence of psychotic features. Dysthymia may be a chronic condition in which a mild depressive mood is a characteristic way of responding to life.

PREVALENCE

A common mood disorder, dysthymia is more frequently found among women. Onset is usually early in life; and for this reason, in the past, this disorder was considered a personality disorder.

Adjustment Disorder with Depressed Mood

Here the depressive symptoms of dysthymia are judged to be a response to a stressor known to have occurred within three months of its onset. The causative stressor can take a variety of forms, such as a single event; for example, a divorce after years of marriage, or a prolonged period of unhappiness caused by marital discord, business difficulties, or unpleasant living circumstances. The stressor may be a catastrophic experience or persecution resulting from racial or religious prejudice. Stressors may simply be times of difficult readjustment: going off to school, having to move away from a longtime neighborhood, marriage under some circumstances, or occupational change.

It is assumed that the disorder will remit by itself when the pressure of the stressor wanes, or when a new level of adjustment is achieved, possibly with the help of short-term psychotherapy.

SYMPTOMATOLOGY

In the adjustment disorder, there is the full range of depressive symptoms previously described for other mild to moderate depressive disorders. Vulnerability to depression, from whatever agents, may cause the disorder, even though the stressor would not normally affect others in the same way. On the other hand, extreme stressors may cause only mild depression or none at all in nonvulnerable individuals.

PREVALENCE

Common. The disorder may occur at any age. No sex differences are reported.

MODERATE TO SEVERE DISORDERS

The two categories of mood disorder discussed here are comparable to cyclothymia and dysthymia, because one, labeled bipolar, is cyclical; and the other, a unipolar disorder, usually labeled major depression, is not, since manic moods do not occur. The major difference between the two groups is that the latter grouping (bipolar and unipolar disorder) present a much more extreme set of symptoms, which may include psychotic features.

Bipolar Disorder

This disorder of alternating patterns of depression and mania was labeled manic depressive psychosis by Kraeplin in 1899. That diagnosis was used for many years, and with it went Kraeplin's belief that there was a generally favorable prognosis. His use of the label "psychosis" suggests the severe nature of the disorder's symptoms in their most extreme form. The *DSM IIIR* now uses the diagnosis "bipolar disorder," and divides it into categories determined principally by the mood dominating the individual's behavior at the time of the diagnosis. The three categories of bipolar disorder are as follows: bipolar, mixed, in which the most recent episode of the disorder exhibits both full depressive and full manic behavior in alternating patterns; bipolar, manic, in which the current or most recent episode is manic, with a past history of depression; and bipolar, depressed, in which the most recent behavior is depressive, but with a history of manic phases.

Unipolar Disorder

In the absence of manic features, a moderate to severe mood disorder is labeled "unipolar disorder." "Major depression" is the more commonly used diagnosis. There are two subcategories of major depression: single episode—that is, without a prior history of depression; and recurrent, in which the individual has had one or more major depressions in the past.

Special Features of Moderate to Severe Mood Disorders

There are two special features of these more serious mood disorders. They are the possible existence of a melancholic aspect to major depression and the presence of psychotic features in the more extreme mood disorders.

MELANCHOLIA

In major depression with melancholic aspects, in addition to the specific symptoms of the typical major depression, the individual shows a loss of pleasure in all activities, even those that were formerly pleasurable. The patient reports not feeling any better, even for the moment, when something good happens.

In addition, for a diagnosis of major depression, melancholic type, the *DSM IIIR* requires that at least three of the following symptoms be present: a depression, regularly worse in the morning; early morning waking; notable psychomotor retardation or agitation; loss of appetite or weight loss; marked feelings of guilt.

The diagnosis, melancholic type, is considered of special significance for two reasons: 1. the psychiatric literature suggests that it is of endogenous causation; that is, it comes from within the individual and seems unrelated to external events; and 2. it seems to respond well to biologically based therapy.

MOOD DISORDERS WITH PSYCHOTIC FEATURES

Extreme types of mood disorders may include such symptoms of psychosis as marked impairment in reality testing, manifested in hallucinations or delusions; or the presence of a depressive stupor, which is signaled when the individual becomes mute or is totally unresponsive.

The delusions or hallucinations may be "mood congruent"— that is, consistent with such depressive themes as personal inadequacy, guilt, deserved punishment, disease, death or nihilism. Or they may be "mood incongruent"—that is, in which the content of the impaired reality testing is unrelated to depressive themes. Included here are persecutory themes and thought insertion or thought broadcasting, [also characteristic of schizophrenia (see chapter 13)].

OVERALL PREVALENCE OF MOOD DISORDERS

In a three-community study, Myers and associates report that for a six-month period, 3 percent of the male population and 7 percent of females had developed a depressive disorder. In a 1987 study, the American Psychiatric Association reports that 26 percent of women and 12 percent of men, at some time in their lives, will show severe depressive symptoms. In extreme forms, mood disorders are one of the most frequently diagnosed psychiatric condition leading to hospitalization. Unipolar mood disorder (depression only) is the most frequently occurring disorder; it has increased in the past fifty years. Bipolar or cyclical mood disorder, with a prevalence of 0.5 to 1 percent, is also reported to have increased. Bipolar disorder is equally common among both sexes. The disorder is principally a disease of the adult years. However, one study reports a 5 percent prevalence among primary school children.

CAUSATIVE FACTORS IN MOOD DISORDERS

Full explanations for the occurrence of mood disorders continue to challenge medical and psychological science. Two broad categories of possible causes have been established: biogenic factors and psychosocial factors. In neither one does there exist an entirely adequate explanation for the etiology of mood disorders.

Biogenic Causative Factors

There are three major factors that medical and psychological research have focused on: genetic, biochemical and neuroendocrine elements. There is research support of varying conclusiveness for the possible causative influence of each. Of the three, the most conclusive evidence is that which relates genetic factors to the development of a vulnerability to mood disorders.

GENETIC PREDISPOSITION

Three strands of evidence tend to establish faulty genes as influential, at least in predisposing the individual to a mood disorder. They are as follows: 1. Blood relatives of those with a mood disorder have a higher incidence of the disorder than is found in the general population; 2. The concordance rate for mood disorders is much higher for identical twins than for fraternal twins (those having different genes).

Neither of those approaches clearly disentangles environmental from hereditary influences. That job has been accomplished by the third type of study: 3. Studies of identical twins who have been reared apart assure that while genetic factors are identical, environmental influences are likely to be varied. High concordance rates for the presence of a mood disorder were found among the identical twins, even though the environments in which they grew up varied. In a variation of this study, a group of individuals with mood disorders was matched with a group of normal individuals. The presence of mood disorders among the blood relatives of the mood-disordered population was eight times higher than among relatives of the normal population.

The most certain conclusion to be drawn about causative factors in the mood disorders is that among a substantial number of those suffering a mood disorder, there exists a predisposing genetic factor that makes them vulnerable to the effect of stressors in their environment.

BIOCHEMICAL FACTORS

Research evidence, accumulating since the sixties, has brought under suspicion biochemical elements as a cause of mood disorders. Those elements seem to affect the neurotransmitters of the brain, which regulate the passage of nerve impulses across the synaptic gap between neurons in the brain.

Attention was drawn to this possibility by the observation that several biological therapies used with mood disorders—for example, electroconvulsive treatment, antidepressant drugs, and lithium—affect the concentration of biochemical substances at the synapses and determine whether particular pathways in the brain facilitate or slow down transmission of brain impulses. Not yet definitely established, the conclusion is still being researched that faulty communication across synapses, as a result of neurotransmitter malfunctioning, is at least a contributing cause of mood disorders. Still uncertain is whether or not that condition is brought about by defective genes.

NEUROENDOCRINAL FACTORS

The body's endocrine glands secrete fluids (hormones), and the effect of those hormonal influences is a focus of much research. One hormonal substance, cortisol, is particularly suspect as having an effect on the development of mood disorders. Hypothyroidism (underactivity of the thyroid gland) seems also to be related to depression.

An important outcome of research in the biological sciences is the suggestion that there is a variety of depressive reactions, traceable to different biological causes and reactive to different forms of biogenic therapy. Such findings tend to increase the role of medicine in the treatment of depression, a development that in no way is antithetical to the positive influences of psychotherapy in the reduction of depression.

Psychosocial Factors

Increasingly, the conclusion is being drawn that when the full etiology of mood disorders is finally understood, the answer will be found in some combination or interaction of biogenic factors (including the predisposing influences of heredity) and psychosocial influences.

The possible effect of a large number of psychosocial factors has been the subject of psychological research, the principal of which are as follows: environmental stress; attitudes held by the individual toward life and the future; learned helplessness; and the defensive value of manic or depressive reactions.

ENVIRONMENTAL STRESSORS

It is well known that environmental stressors produce strong emotional responses that, in turn, affect the body's functioning in a variety of ways. When the stressors are operative over a period of time, or when they are catastrophic, the bodily changes they cause bring about biochemical/hormonal changes, especially in genetically predisposed individuals.

Beck, who has developed his own approach to the treatment of depression, identifies six types of stressors that are especially likely to trigger depression: 1. those that lower the individual's self-esteem— for example, failure in an important endeavor or neglect from loved ones; 2. frustration in achieving major life goals or facing unresolvable conflict; 3. physical disease or illness that brings on thoughts of death; 4. stressors of catastrophic dimension; 5. a series of stressful encounters that suggest a never-ending sequence; and 6. stressors, below the level of consciousness, that nevertheless sap the individual's energies and spirit.

NEGATIVE ATTITUDES

Beck has also reported the prior existence among depressive individuals as a substratum of the individual's personality of a set of negative attitudes: towards the self, the world, and the future. There is the suggestion in the psychological research that such bleak attitudes are frequently found in adults who, as children, have experienced the loss of a cherished parent. Beck's treatment of depressed individuals (described later) is directed at reversing those negative attitudes.

PREEXISTENT PERSONALITY TRAITS

Other research has sought, with mixed results, to identify pre-episodic personality traits among the mood disorders. Where such traits have been identified, as one might expect, the identified personality traits are different for manic-type and depressive-type individuals. The pre-episodic personality characteristics of manic-type individuals tend to be conventional and achievement-oriented. Predepression traits tend toward self-deprecation, with some indications of repressed hostility. Despite the tentative research findings, it is inaccurate to assume that either set of traits predisposes an individual to mood disorders.

LEARNED HELPLESSNESS

A concept that has received much research attention in recent years as a possible cause (some psychologists would say as an effect or, at most, as a concomitant) of depression is learned helplessness. The concept, much favored by those of behavioral/cognitive persuasion, assumes that helplessness is learned in early life experiences in which the child comes to feel that nothing he or she does counts in making life more pleasant or less unpleasant. Given that attitude of hopelessness, the individual subsides into depressive inactivity. Seligman, who has proposed the concept, finds parallels between helplessness and depression. He has also proposed that treatment of depression should provide learning experiences that undo the sense of hopelessness about the effect of what one does.

Although helplessness is certainly congruent with depression, there are two counterpoints to Seligman's concept. 1. Learned helplessness (or hopelessness) may be an effect rather than a cause of depression. In a depressed state, inactive and discouraged, the individual will indeed feel helpless and therefore hopeless. 2. Depressed individuals may not be continuously depressed. The question, then, is what has become of their learned helplessness which, during that period, no longer produces depression?

The least that can be said about learned helplessness is that a life that has taught an individual that he or she is powerless to change things is a depressing thought, but not necessarily one that leads to a state of depression. The alternative might be to learn how to empower oneself (as difficult as that may be). The difference between the two responses may lie in the individual's predisposing vulnerability to depression.

MOOD DISORDERS AS DEFENSE

As maladaptive as it may seem to those not prone to mood disorders, hypomanic or depressive behavior may be viewed as the individual's way of responding defensively to environmental stressors or to negative preoccupations about life and the future. Either the quiet of surrender or the excitement of hypomania may be experienced as a relief to the mood-disordered individual. The common response of reacting to disappointment by intense application to work, or throwing oneself into vigorous physical activity, may be an example among normal people of what the mood-disordered individual is attempting. Some "quiet time in the country" as an escape from life's problems, not an abnormal type of behavior, may be what the depressed individual is attempting in the depressive phase of the disorder.

SELF-DIRECTED AGGRESSION

One psychosocial interpretation of depression, anger turned inward, derived from the early psychoanalytical thinking of Sigmund Freud and Carl Abraham. Freud, in his classic paper, *Mourning and Melancholia,* traces the anger back to an early childhood rejection by a deeply loved person, ordinarily the mother or father. Unable to express the anger because of guilt, the rejected individual identifies with or "incorporates" the rejecting person into his or her own being and then directs the anger against himself or herself. It is, according to psychoanalytic theory, the self-anger that causes the lowered self-esteem. Open self-accusations and expressed need for punishment are characteristic of melancholic depression. In later life, any loss or rejection reactivates the anger (still self-directed) and engenders a depressive reaction.

Although this interpretation is supported by reported experiences of psychoanalysts in their treatment of depressives, the hard scientific evidence to support Freud's hypothesis has not materialized.

TREATMENT OF MOOD DISORDERS

Mood disorders respond to two major forms of treatment, biogenic and psychotherapeutic. There is abundant evidence to indicate that the best approach to the mood disorders is a well-planned combination of the two. For the severe disorders, in which there is likely to be some biological involvement, biogenic treatment, to begin with, is probably necessary. Psychotherapy should accompany it as soon as the patient seems open to it.

Medication, such as that found necessary for the severe mood disorders, has been found to be of limited help with the mild to moderate mood disorders. Emphasis on psychotherapeutic approaches is considered appropriate, with only limited use of the antidepressant drugs.

Biogenic Treatment

Two major types of drugs, the tricyclics and MAO inhibitors, are used in treatment of the moderate to severe mood disorders. In extremely severe cases in which those drugs have not been helpful, electroconvulsive therapy may be tried. Lithium carbonate is the treatment of choice in the bipolar mood disorders.

TRICYCLIC ANTIDEPRESSANTS

One well-supported belief is that unavailability of norepinephrine, a neurotransmitter substance, is a causative factor in depression. Support for the hypothesis is provided by the successful use of the tricyclics in the treatment of depression, especially the endogenous or biologically based depression. The reasoning behind that statement is that an important effect of the tricyclics is an increase in the availability of norepinephrine at the synapses (the gap between one neuron and another) which seems to reduce the depressive reaction.

MONOAMINE OXIDASE (MAO) INHIBITORS

MAO inhibitors are prescribed only for patients who have not responded to tricyclics. It is a secondary treatment because of possible serious side effects. It, too, increases the availability of norepinephrine between neurons.

There is a difference between the ways in which the tricyclics and the MAO inhibitors increase the availability of norepinephrine. The tricyclics block a process in which the sending neuron reabsorbs the norepinephrine present at the synapse (the process is called re-uptake). The MAO inhibitors prevent the MAO enzyme from breaking down the norepinephrine at the synapse, which is that enzyme's work. Although the processes are different, the end result is the same: more norepinephrine is made available to reduce depression.

SIDE EFFECTS OF ANTIDEPRESSANT DRUGS

The two drugs are different in one other important way. Although the tricyclics have side effects, none of them are life-threatening. They are drowsiness, insomnia, agitation, tremors and blurred vision. Possible side effects of MAO inhibitors are quite serious and can be life-threatening.

The MAO inhibitors prevent the MAO enzyme (monoamine oxidase) from carrying out their normal function, which is to break down tyramine, a substance found in cheese, beer, wine and chocolate. Failure to do so triggers what is known as the tyramine-cheese reaction, which causes increased blood pressure, vomiting, muscle twitching and can, if untreated, cause intracranial pressure and death. Patients on MAO inhibitors therefore must scrupulously restrict their intake of the dangerous substances. Sometimes with seriously disturbed individuals, voluntary restriction of diet is a high risk to take. The drug is used only with patients who have not responded to the tricyclics. It is prescribed only with strong precautions about proper diet.

DELAYED EFFECT OF THE ANTIDEPRESSANT DRUGS

Aside from the unpleasant and possibly dangerous side effects of the antidepressant drugs, another potentially serious limitation is their delayed reaction on the depression. At least two weeks must go by before the patient will notice any relief from depression. That delay can be critical with suicidal patients or with restless and impatient individuals whose disappointment in the effect of the drug can cause them to fail to take the medication or to withdraw from treatment.

ELECTROCONVULSIVE THERAPY (ECT)

To some extent, because of the frightening nature of the treatment, but principally because of its disturbing aftereffects and its grossly assaultive nature, electroconvulsive treatment is used to treat unipolar mood disorder only when the depression is extreme and only after antidepressant drugs have been used to no avail. The disturbing aftereffects include short-term memory loss and motivational changes.

LITHIUM TREATMENT OF BIPOLAR MOOD DISORDERS

In an Australian research study in 1949, lithium was discovered to create lethargy in guinea pigs. With that finding, it was then tried on humans to reduce mania. For more than forty years now, lithium carbonate has been used in this country and around the world in treating both manic and depressive symptoms in bipolar disorder. Full or partial reduction of symptoms is reported for more than 70 percent of manic depressives taking the medication. The chemical or physiological reasons for lithium's beneficial effect are unknown. Lithium is considered a lifetime maintenance medication for bipolar mood disorder.

There is one serious problem with its use. For many patients needing the medication, the effective dosage is close to a toxic dose. If too much lithium is taken, the toxicity that results can cause convulsions and delirium. Fortunately, the onset of toxicity is accompanied by the unpleasant symptoms of nausea and vomiting, which warn the patient to discontinue the medication for a time. As a precaution against such toxic attacks, patients on maintenance dosages of lithium are usually advised to monitor the level of lithium in their system by having their blood tested regularly.

Psycho-therapeutic Approaches

Although not the only psychotherapeutic approach used in treating depression, a technique developed by Aaron T. Beck, a cognitive psychologist, has proven successful in treating depression, particularly depressions in the mild to moderate range. It is a good example of a psychotherapeutic approach to depression. Beck uses the technique of rational emotive therapy (see chapter 7).

Beck's therapy is based on his belief that a depressing triad of negative thoughts about the self, life experiences and prospects for the future dominate the patient's thinking. Added to this, Beck states, are five systematic logical errors that further cloud thinking and cause depression.

SYSTEMATIC LOGICAL ERRORS CAUSING DEPRESSION

1. Arbitrary inference: drawing a conclusion without supporting evidence. For example, the patient, without being able to point to any evidence, will nevertheless insist that his wife doesn't respect him.

2. Selective abstraction: The individual accents one relatively unimportant detail while ignoring significant aspects of a situation. For example, although a wife may be full of praise for her husband's talent and hard work, the client may brood over her comment that she doesn't like the ties he picks out for himself.

3. Overgeneralization: Here the patient draws broad conclusions, principally about self-worth, on the basis of a single, sometimes insignificant, failure; for example, brooding over failure to fix a leaky faucet. The average person would settle for calling a plumber and let it go at that.

4. Magnification and minimization: Here, small failures are magnified, and significant achievements are minimized. An example might be castigating oneself for the messiness of a computer room and ignoring the achievement of having created a new computer program.

5. Personalization: incorrectly assuming personal responsibility for bad events that happen around an individual; for example, assuming responsibility for a neighbor's accident because the client never got around to suggesting that the neighbor have the automobile tires checked.

Beck believes that because the individual's cognitive life is dominated by the triad of negative thought and the systematic logical errors, he or she will express negative thoughts to themselves over and over again, even though fleetingly. It is those thoughts, Beck maintains, that support the depression.

BECK'S PROCEDURES IN THERAPY

Beck's therapy begins by his leading the patient to identify negative thoughts and faulty reasoning. His approach in doing so is soft, supportive and encouraging, yet persistent. Once the individual has verbalized a number of those negative thoughts and illogical cognitions, the therapist, in Socratic fashion, questions the individual to draw out the illogicality of the cognitions. When the client has recognized the faultiness of the cognitions, he or she is encouraged to reevaluate real life experiences from a more logical and less depressing perspective. As the therapy progresses and the therapist has been able to build in the patient a more optimistic way of thinking, he or she directs the client's attention to problem-solving thoughts about difficult life circumstances.

AN EXPERIMENTAL TEST OF BIOGENIC AND COGNITIVE THERAPIES

In a study reported in 1989, an interesting comparison was made of the differing effect on depression of tricyclic therapy, cognitive therapy, and both together. Sixty-four individuals with major depression were assigned randomly to one of the three treatment approaches.

The dependent variables (those contingent upon the treatment used) were relief from depression, a change in explanatory style—that is, to what does an individual attribute failure or trouble— and relapse rate after a two-year period.

THE FINDINGS AND THEIR SIGNIFICANCE

On variable 2, explanatory style, there was no relationship between treatment by tricyclics and an improved explanatory style. In the group receiving both treatments, improvement in style was strong. In the group receiving only cognitive therapy, improvement in explanatory style was very strong.

On variable 3, relapse after two years, the most significant variable, evidence indicates that those who did not change their explanatory style showed a higher relapse rate than those who did change.

The findings suggest that drug therapy may only activate patients, but cognitive therapy changes the way in which they look at causes. One can thus speculate that it is that change which produces the lasting effect. Clinicians feel it is desirable to use both antidepressant drugs and cognitive therapy. The results reported suggest clearly, however, that if drug therapy alone is to be used, the only reasons for doing so is resistance on the part of the patient to psychotherapy or other reasons that make it impossible.

SUICIDE

A consideration in all depression is the possibility of a suicidal attempt; and nonoffensive, common sense protective measures should be taken to prevent it. All threats of suicide should be taken seriously; and suicidal talk should be considered as a warning. Yet it must be observed that a person determined to commit suicide is difficult, perhaps impossible, to stop.

The saddest fact about suicide is that, inexplicably to others, it often occurs during the recovery phase, at a point at which the patient seems to be coming out of the deepest gloom of the depression. One possible explanation is that it is only when enough energy has been recovered through an alleviation of the depression that the individual can plan and execute the suicide.

The danger of suicide is at a prevalence level of one percent during the year of depression; it increases to 15 percent during the lifetime of individuals with recurring depression.

The Scope of the Problem

Suicide and suicidal attempts are a significant problem which, in this country, has been increasing steadily in recent years. The increase among women and the young is disproportionate to their numbers in the population. The greatest increase, a tripling since the mid-fifties, has occurred in the age group of 15 to 24 years of age. The increase is considerably beyond their increase in the population. Suicide is the third most common cause of death (after accidents and homicide) in that age group. There is evidence that the increase is drug related.

The most disturbing statistic of all is that two hundred and fifty thousand children, aged five to fourteen, attempt suicide each year, and that number is increasing. The rate of failed attempts in that age group is high.

Studies of the Suicide

Because of its significant consequences to the individual and those left behind, the problem has received a great deal of study. Yet neither the social sciences nor the medical sciences has provided us with any certain answer to the question, why do some people commit or attempt to commit suicide?

Various methods have been tried to find an understanding of the causes of suicide. Among them are examination of notes left behind, psychological autopsies, and biochemical analysis of the functioning of those considered to be at high risk of suicide.

SUICIDE NOTES

Although a number of investigators have studied notes left behind by suicides, other than identifying vital statistic type of information about those who leave such notes (age, sex, marital status), little of significance for understanding motives for the suicide has been revealed. The major conclusion drawn from the study of notes is that the notewriter seems more interested in communicating positive affect to surviving friends and relatives than to leaving behind fully explanatory statements of the reasons for his or her suicide.

THE PSYCHOLOGICAL AUTOPSY

Patterned after a medical autopsy, the psychological autopsy is a post-suicidal study of the individual's life history, drawn from interviews with coworkers, relatives and friends, information gained from presuicide crisis intervention phone calls made by the individual, and public records. Although such studies can help in preventing suicides by others by identifying significant events and personal characteristics of the suicide—information that might serve as warnings of a potential suicide—they have revealed little about the urgent circumstances that lead to the desperation that provokes most suicides.

*Possible
Etiological
Factors in
Suicide*

Factors that are considered to be at least contributory to a suicidal attempt include biochemical factors, social relationships, and adverse life circumstances. Among the complex psychosocial characteristics examined are internalized anger, depression and hopelessness. This section considers each briefly.

BIOCHEMICAL FACTORS

With the strong evidence that links biochemical elements to depression, it is no surprise that biochemical elements have been found in the brains of patients considered more likely than others to commit suicide. It is reported that patients in whom suspected biochemical elements have been found are more likely to choose violent methods of killing themselves and often have a history of impulsiveness, aggressiveness and violence. The finding has raised the possibility of a connection between suicide and aggression.

As with depression, the biochemical fault is attributed to abnormal enzyme activity in neurotransmitters. The chemical abnormality identified as a possible contributory cause of suicide is a low level of five hydrooxyindaleacelic acid (5HIAA), an element produced when serotonin, a neurotransmitter that affects mood and emotions, is broken down. The finding is a tentative one and, in any case, it is unlikely that that biochemical factor is anything more than a contributor to a vulnerability to psychological states that lead to suicide.

SOCIAL RELATIONSHIPS

Emile Durkheim, a French sociologist, in one of the earliest systematic studies of suicide, blames absence of cohesive relationships with others as a primary cause of suicide. In emphasizing the importance of social forces in suicidal attempts, he identified and named three types of suicide resulting from different but troubled social relationships. They are egoistic suicide which results when an individual has too few relationships with others; altruistic suicide, in which the stimulus for suicide is the self-sacrificing wish to dramatize and thereby further an idealistically conceived cause. In this type of suicide, one can suspect that the individual, through his or her suicide, hopes to gain a respected place in society that was not attainable in life. Finally, Durkheim recognized anomic suicide, which he felt resulted from unbalanced or damaged relationships in society, for example, being accused of a crime. Durkheim concluded from his studies that the most powerful deterrent to suicide is a sense of involvement and identification with other people.

ADVERSE LIFE CIRCUMSTANCES

In the Great Depression of the thirties, the suicide rate increased from 10 to 17 per 100,000 people; in the recession of the early seventies, suicides increased to more than 12 per 100,000 people. The suicide rate among black youth in the United States is notably higher than among white young people of the same age. The suicide rate among the divorced, among those threatened with downward mobility, and those living in rapidly changing urban areas, are all higher than in the general population.

There is no question that adverse living circumstances, caused by financial problems, interpersonal unhappiness or severe health problems, increase the likelihood of suicide; but by themselves, those adverse life circumstances do not provide an adequate explanation of suicide. Too many others face equal adversity without resorting to suicide as an escape; most of them, probably, without even considering it.

INTRAPSYCHIC EXPLANATIONS

Early psychoanalytical explanations attributed suicide to rage against a rejecting but introjected love object (a loved but rejecting person with whom the individual identified). The anger has really been caused by the rejecting but loved person; but since this person has been incorporated into the self, the anger becomes a self-destructive force, and suicide may be the result.

Modern studies provide little support for that Freudian hypothesis. Anger and revenge may be among the emotions felt prior to suicide; but shame, guilt, desperation, hopelessness and pain probably occur more frequently.

DEPRESSION AND HOPELESSNESS

The one condition most frequently found prior to suicide attempts is depression. Correlational studies conducted by various investigators among different populations uniformly report high correlation between preexisting depression and suicidal attempts. A sample of the findings: The suicide rate among a depressed population admitted to a psychiatric hospital was 36 times higher than for the general population; 80 percent of another hospitalized population admitted for suicidal attempts were found, upon admission, to be depressed; even among children, depression is a frequent precursor to a suicide attempt.

Among a depressed population, hopelessness about the future (even beyond depression itself) seems to be the more determinative cause of a suicide attempt. A study by Beck provides persuasive evidence for that conclusion. His population was 207 hospitalized psychiatric patients who had expressed suicidal thoughts but who had no history of suicidal attempts. Within seventy-two hours of being admitted to the hospital, each of the patients was assessed on three psychological characteristics: degree of hopelessness, degree of depression, and extent of suicidal thinking. In a ten-year follow-up period, fourteen of the patients had committed suicide.

What differentiated that group of fourteen from the other patients in the study was their high scores on hopelessness. Scores on level of depression and extent of suicidal thinking did not significantly vary between the suicidal group and the larger nonsuicidal group. One study can never be definitive; but Beck's work, consistent with the thinking of other researchers in the field of depression, offers impressive evidence of the critical importance of feelings of hopelessness as a crucial factor causing suicidal attempts. Efforts to prevent suicide surely must take account of that precursor to a suicidal attempt.

Overview of Causal Factors in a Suicide

Suicide attempts have multiples causes. There is, first of all, the possibility of a vulnerability caused by biochemical factors which may be genetically produced. A great variety of life circumstances causes unhappiness which, when prolonged, will lead to depression. Depression itself is a multifaceted psychological disorder, with an unpredictable course, including the possibility of suicide. There are the influences of alcohol and drugs which, in lowering inhibitory controls, may push the individual to the actual suicide attempts. Of lesser importance, but not to be neglected, are the immediate circumstances surrounding the individual during a depressed period; for example, a loaded gun in the house, or being alone in the house after watching a depressing television presentation. The one element that stands out as a crucial impelling force is a feeling of hopelessness in the individual's consciousness, even if circumstances do not justify such feelings.

Efforts at Prevention

The success of any prevention program depends upon our knowledge of early signs of a suicidal effort and the speed with which that information can be communicated to a trained professional who will assume some level of responsibility for intervention. There are known danger signals: a state of extreme depression, mild depression with expressions of suicidal intent, bouts of depression with alcohol or drug abuse, suicide in the family of a depressed individual. Any one of those conditions should trigger a strong effort to get professional help.

CRISIS INTERVENTION

It is believed that most persons who attempt suicide do not really want to die. That belief seems substantiated by the fact that most suicides provide an early warning of their intentions, seemingly a plea for help. Responding to that plea as quickly as possible is the surest way to prevent suicide. Attempts to do that are called crisis intervention. The program seeks to provide immediate, intensive, short-term treatment aimed at resolving the provoking crisis.

Crisis intervention usually involves a short period of hospitalization, where medical treatment and counselling can immediately be offered. Psychotherapy is intensive, sometimes for several hours each day, until the crisis seems resolved, and the patient's panic has been reduced. More traditional psychotherapy, spaced over a period of time, should follow the patient's release from the hospital.

CRISIS PREVENTION CENTERS

In an intensified effort to prevent suicides, hundreds of suicide prevention centers have been established. Making it as easy as possible for potential suicides to reach out for help. Suicide hotlines are made available twenty-four hours a day. At the receiving end of the call, the suicidal person will find a trained individual who is prepared to help. Such individuals are trained to work toward, first of all, maintaining contact and creating a relationship; as that develops, they seek to obtain identifying information—name, phone number, and the name and phone number of a relative or friend. Once those minimal goals have been accomplished, more substantive information about the suicidal risk is sought: an evaluation of the likelihood of an immediate suicide attempt; identifying the principal stressors producing the crisis; searching out possible strengths of the individual and social supports among friends or relatives. A final step is to initiate an action plan, which should describe an immediate action for the individual to take (which might be coming to the crisis center) and a follow-up program; for example, a referral to a social agency the next day for further discussion.

Statistics on the effectiveness of suicide prevention centers are difficult to interpret. For example, how does one interpret the fact that 95 percent of callers never call again? Do they no longer need help? Did they not find it helpful? Or perhaps the effort at prevention failed. Using what researchers might call face validity, we have to believe that such centers serve a good purpose and indeed do prevent some number, not yet counted, of suicides.

Mood disorders are a significant psychiatric problem, affecting millions of people, and causing the hospitalization of the largest number of psychiatric patients. The most common form of mood disorder is depression; in much smaller numbers, the disorder causes alternating spells of depression and mania.

In the more serious depressions, endogenous and biological in etiology, antidepressant drugs and, in extreme cases, electroconvulsive therapy, have proven successful in reducing depression. Psychotherapy is a necessary follow-up. In milder cases, psychotherapy alone may be all that is necessary.

Mounting evidence strongly indicates that a genetic factor causes vulnerability to depression. Biochemical elements, perhaps the result of faulty genes, also seem to be operative. Among the possible psychosocial causes of depression are overwhelming stressors in the environment; negative attitudes toward the self and the future, frequently based on illogical reasoning; preexisting personality traits in the depressed individual—for example, a tendency to deprecate the self; unfortunate early learning patterns of helplessness which leave the individual with little hope of doing anything to reduce the adverse circumstances of his or her life.

Suicide is a major and growing problem in American society, especially among its youth. It is often associated, in that group, with alcohol or drugs. Depression, with a deep-seated feeling of helplessness, seems the most common presuicidal state.

Efforts at prevention include increased efforts to identify the early signs of suicidal risk and the establishment of crisis intervention centers that can work expeditiously with the client to prevent his or her suicide.

Selected Readings

Blatt, S. J., J. P. D'Afflitti and D. M. Quinla. 1976. "Experiences of Depression in Normal Young Adults." *Journal of Abnormal Psychology*, 85: 383-389.

Caryell, W. and G. Winokur. 1982. "Course and Outcome." in E. S. Paykel (Ed.). *Handbook of Affective Disorders*. New York: Guilford Press.

Lewinsohn, P. M. 1974. "Clinical and Theoretical Aspects of Depression." in K. S. Calhoun, H. E. Adams and K. M. Mitchell (Eds.). *Innovative Treatment Methods of Psychopathology*. New York: Wiley.

Stengel, E. 1964. *Suicide and Attempted Suicide*. Baltimore, MD: Penguin.

Steward, J. W., P. J. McGrath, M. R. Liebowitz, W. Harrison and F. Quitkin. 1985. "Treatment Outcome Validation of DSM III Depressive Subtypes: Clinical Usefulness in Outpatients with Mild to Moderate Depression." *Archives of General Psychiatry*, 42: 1148-1153.

Strack, S. and J. C. Coyne. 1983. "Social Confirmation of Dysphoria: Shared and Private Reactions to Depression." *Journal of Personality and Social Psychology*, 44: 798-806.

Stroebe, M. S. and W. Stroebe. 1983. "Who Suffers More? Sex Differences in Health Risks of the Widowed." *Psychological Bulletin*, 93(2): 279-301.

13

The Schizophrenias and Delusional (Paranoid) Disorders

The most disabling of the psychological disorders are the psychoses; they bring with them disorientation, hallucinations, delusions, and social disorganization. Among the most debilitating and complex of the psychoses are the schizophrenias. That disorder is a complex illness, the nature of which is not yet fully understood; and the outcomes of its treatment are not as favorable as clinicians would like them to be. In addition to a detailed examination of the schizophrenias, the chapter describes briefly a psychosis separately classified by DSM IIIR and labeled delusional (paranoid) disorder.

Although, as we shall see later, symptoms vary somewhat from culture to culture, the schizophrenias exist worldwide. One percent of the world's population is afflicted with the illness. There are, in the United States, two million persons diagnosed as schizophrenics, almost all of whom spend part of their lives (for many, most of their adult lives) in psychiatric hospitals. One hundred thousand Americans are stricken with the disease each year.

Emil Kraeplin first identified the illness in 1896 when he distinguished it from the mood disorders. Kraeplin believed that all psychiatric disorders were caused by organic factors, and his experience suggested to him that the onset of the disease occurred early in the life of the individual. Hence, he called it dementia praecox, which means a premature deterioration of the brain.

In 1911, Eugene Bleuler, an eminent Swiss psychiatrist, disagreed with Kraeplin on both points. He had found that onset of the disease could occur in the later years, and he also reported that it was not characterized by a progressive deterioration over the life of the individual, which he felt was suggested by the term "dementia." After an original severe deterioration, many schizophrenics stabilized and remained at the same point in their illness for years.

To avoid any misunderstanding of the nature of the illness that might be caused by what he considered a misnomer, and to give emphasis to its true nature, Bleuler invented the word "schizophrenia," putting together two Greek words meaning "split" and "mind." In that way, he emphasized the most basic feature of the schizophrenias: a splitting of the mental functions; in particular, a splitting apart of the individual's affective and cognitive functioning.

THE SCHIZOPHRENIAS

Students will readily appreciate the complexity of the schizophrenias when they consider the number of perspectives used to describe and classify the disorder. Psychologists first distinguish it from the anxiety-based disorders and the personality disorders. The lost contact with reality and the extreme deterioration make that distinction a relatively easy one. But they must also distinguish it from the mood disorders and the organic psychoses, a diagnostic process which is somewhat more difficult.

Because the disorder is now known to take several different forms, each of which may vary in onset, symptomatology, etiology and responsiveness to treatment, clinicians must then describe the disorder and classify it from several other points of view. They are as follows: the dimensions of the illness, its symptomatology, its course, and the subtypes of the illness. Each is of importance in helping the clinician understand possible causation and the likely future of the illness.

Dimensions of the Schizophrenias

There are three overall characteristics of the schizophrenias that differentiate each form of the illness from the others. These are called the dimensions of the illness. They can be presented as either/or propositions. 1. Is the disease the result of a long-term development: If so, it is called process schizophrenia; Or is it a relatively sudden reaction, apparently to some life crisis? Then it is called reactive or acute schizophrenia. 2. Is the illness manifest by the absence of normal human responses? For example, does the individual show flatness or blunting of affect? If so, the term used is negative symptomatology. Or are there such overt symptoms of disease as hallucinations or delusions? These are referred to as positive symptoms. 3. Is the illness characterized by paranoid symptomatology, or are paranoid symptoms absent or of minor importance?

Before going on to describe each of the dimensions more fully, it needs to be stated that the either/or descriptions of the dimensions describe extreme positions on a continuum. Many schizophrenics fall midpoint between the extremes. Nevertheless, clinicians study their patients carefully to determine, if they can, on which side of the continuum the patient falls, because position on these three dimensions predicts much of the later course of the illness.

THE PROCESS-REACTIVE DIMENSION

Here we first consider process, or Type II schizophrenia, then reactive schizophrenia, sometimes called acute, or Type I schizophrenia.

Process Schizophrenia. Process schizophrenia, also referred to as poor premorbid schizophrenia, may take years in its development, with gradual insidious deterioration and only negative symptoms (absence of normal human response) and few, if any, florid symptoms until later on. Process schizophrenia does not seem to be related to any crisis or major life change.

The process schizophrenic's early history usually reveals a "loner," rejected by family and peers. There is a lifetime pattern of shyness and social withdrawal. Kantor, Wallner and Winder (1953) report that victims of process schizophrenia typically did not belong to a group of friends in school, did not date regularly during the teen years, did not go beyond high school, never held a job for longer than two years, and never married. Their life, in other words, was an extremely maladjusted one which, in time, led to the development of the psychotic symptoms of the active schizophrenic. By the time that period of slow deterioration has led to the development of delusions, a sure sign of psychosis, other easily recognized symptoms of schizophrenia will also be present.

Reactive (Acute) Schizophrenia. Reactive schizophrenia is also occasionally labeled Type I schizophrenia. Its onset is usually sudden and seems to be a reaction to some life crisis. Although florid symptoms of a psychosis are a principal early feature of the illness, they are reversible. In general, because the premorbid history is good, when the schizophrenia does manifest itself, it is still in an early phase of the illness. Whether for that reason, or because of a different etiological background, reactive schizophrenia is a more treatable form of schizophrenia than process or chronic schizophrenia.

DSM IIIR reports an especially poor prognosis when the illness has developed in an insidious and downhill fashion over several years. The reason is stated to be that by the time the individual is brought for treatment, the disease, so to speak, has "settled in."

POSITIVE VERSUS NEGATIVE SYMPTOMS

By the positive dimension is meant the overt manifestation of psychotic symptoms such as bizarre behavior, hallucinations and delusions. Negative symptoms refer to the absence of any adjustive behavior in the important areas of life, a chronic maladaptiveness, flatness of affect, and absence of developed interpersonal relations. There are nevertheless few, if any, of the florid symptoms usually associated with psychosis, which come only in later stages. Reactive schizophrenia is characterized by the early presence of positive symptoms; that is, hallucinations and delusions. In contrast, in process schizophrenia, the individual manifests principally negative symptoms; that is, a generalized lack of adjustment and a flatness of emotional expression.

PARANOID VERSUS NONPARANOID SYMPTOMS

Schizophrenics can also be categorized on the basis of the presence or absence of paranoid symptomatology. There would seem to be a relationship between schizophrenia with paranoid thinking and reactive schizophrenia. Buss (1966) reports that overtly paranoid and reactive schizophrenics "are more intact intellectually, perform better on a variety of tasks, and have a higher level of maturity." Research also indicates that patients suffering from a reactive schizophrenia with paranoid symptoms are hospitalized later than other schizophrenics, stay hospitalized for a shorter time, and have to be rehospitalized less often. The presence of paranoid symptoms early in the disease seems to suggest a good prognosis. Attention to this dimension of the disease is therefore an important aspect of diagnosis. To add to the complexity of distinguishing among the schizophrenias, clinicians report that Type I and Type II schizophrenia may exist as independent processes in the individual at the same time.

Symptomatology   The specific symptom patterns defining schizophrenia have been debated since Kraeplin's early identification of the illness. The most recent authoritative statement was made in 1987 in *DSM IIIR.* With respect to timing of onset, duration and impact on functioning for a diagnosis of schizophrenia, the manual requires that: 1. onset must occur before the age of 45; 2. symptoms must last for a minimum period of six months; 3. there must be an observable deterioration from the individual's previous level of functioning.

Beyond those three criteria, there are two more that have to do with specific symptomatology. There must be a major impairment in the individual's contact with reality. Such impairment would mark the illness as a psychosis. Also, the disturbance must negatively affect several psychological processes from among those listed below.

Major Categories of Impaired Functioning in Schizophrenics

The areas identified by *DSM IIIR* in which maladaptive changes occur in the schizophrenic individual are content of thought, form of thought, perception, affect, sense of self, volition, relationship to the outside world, and psychomotor behavior.

CONTENT OF THOUGHT

Multiple delusions (bizarre and obviously false beliefs) are the principal disturbance in the content of the schizophrenic's thought processes. There are two categories into which the delusions usually fall: persecutory delusions, in which the schizophrenic believes that others are spying on, spreading false rumors about, or planning harm to the individual; and delusions of reference, in which the schizophrenic gives personal significance to totally unrelated events, objects or people. Those thoughts are usually self-deprecatory; for example, a newspaper or magazine may be accused of writing critical articles about the schizophrenic when there is no basis for the accusation.

Common delusions are thought broadcasting, in which schizophrenics believe that their thoughts are being broadcast to the outside world; thought insertion, in which they may think that thoughts not their own are being inserted into their mind; and control by external forces. *DSM IIIR* also notes that less often, other delusions (grandiose, religious or nihilistic) may appear.

FORM OF THOUGHT

To be distinguished from the content of thought is the way in which schizophrenics express their thoughts, a symptom that is labeled "formal thought disorder." Here, associations are loose, ideas shift from one subject to a completely unrelated one, statements meant to be connected are completely unrelated—the individual may shift frames of reference in conversation.

Sometimes there is "poverty of content," meaning that the communication is so vague, overly abstract or concrete, repetitive or stereotyped as to be meaningless to the listener. Neologisms (the creation of new words), clanging (illogically stringing together words that rhyme or sound alike) and perseverative speech may appear in writing or speech.

PERCEPTION

Perceptions of the schizophrenic's world are distorted by hallucinations (a perception in the absence of any appropriate external stimulus). Hallucinations may occur in any sense mode, but they most frequently are auditory. The voices "talking" to the patient may be of several people, of people familiar to the patient, or total strangers. Messages may take the form of commands from, for example, God or the president, and they may be obeyed at high risk to others or to the patient.

Hallucinations may be tactile, as in the form of electric shock, tingling or burning sensations. Somatic hallucinations take the form of living things, such as snakes, crawling around inside the patient's body. Hallucinations in other sense modalities are rare.

AFFECT

The principal and quite pronounced affective symptom is a blunting or flattening or inappropriateness in the individual's emotional responses. The symptoms display themselves in a monotonic voice and immobile facies. An oddity is the extreme lack of concordance between what the individual is saying and the emotion displayed. *DSM IIIR* gives this example: talking of being tortured by electrical shock and smiling or laughing.

VOLITION

Significant ambivalence may paralyze the individual's will to take any action. The schizophrenic has difficulty in pursuing any interest or carrying out a planned course of action.

SENSE OF SELF

Normal people are aware of their own individuality and wholeness. The schizophrenic lacks this sense of self-identity. Victims feel no ego boundaries, have no awareness of the meaning of existence, and experience only perplexity about who they are.

RELATIONSHIP TO THE EXTERNAL WORLD

Victims of schizophrenia are so preoccupied with their own bizarre thoughts that they are "unavailable" to others, a condition that is labeled autism. They literally live in a world of their own fantasies, egocentrisms and illogicalities. They take no notice of events around them or of major world events.

The Course of Schizophrenia

Although not all descriptions of schizophrenia mention it, *DSM IIIR* and others identify three phases of the illness: the prodromal phase, the active phase and the residual phase.

PRODROMAL PHASE

The active or, as one might say, the florid phase, of the illness is usually preceded by a prodromal phase in which there is a notable but not yet acutely psychotic deterioration from the individual's prior level of adjustment, a change that is often commented upon by relatives and friends.

In a 1973 article describing early experiences in schizophrenic breakdown, Freedman and Chapman capture prodromal expressions and feelings of the schizophrenic. Patients are quoted as saying the following:

"I try to think and all of a sudden I can't say anything because it's like I turn off in my mind...."

"Maybe I'm not very sensitive...I keep thinking maybe I'm tired... the other night, in front of the television, I felt a sort of blurring like that."

"My eyes seem to disappear when I look in the mirror."

"Things sound more intense...sound louder. Interesting things sound louder than uninteresting things."

"Say you're talking to another person, I don't understand a word they're saying...if there's more than one person talking, I don't follow them because it goes too quickly."

The length of the prodromal phase varies from a relatively short time (reactive schizophrenia, Type I) to several years of slow deterioration (process schizophrenia, Type II). In the short-term prodromal phase, the onset of illness is preceded by a heightened awareness, foreboding and urgency. Usually that reaction seems to be triggered by some relatively "normal" crisis, such as an ordinary change in life circumstances. The patient may respond to this change with such comments as, "I had nowhere to turn," or, "There was no way out."

As the individual comes closer to active schizophrenia, ideas of reference or of specialness begin to appear as the individual occasionally finds hidden meanings in ordinary events. Other, milder forms of later psychotic symptoms appear. Some of the more frequent are social withdrawal, impairment in role functioning, peculiar behavior, carelessness in personal hygiene, vagueness or circumstantial communication, and occasional bizarre thoughts.

THE ACTIVE PHASE

Here the patient manifests the full array of symptoms associated with schizophrenia which distinguish it from other disorders. Those symptoms were described in the symptomatology section. In the active phase, the individual is frequently described as "floridly psychotic."

THE RESIDUAL PHASE

When the individual passes through the prodromal and active phases of the illness, a residual phase of the illness usually remains. Symptoms here revert to symptoms of the prodromal stage.

The three stages of schizophrenia are not always separated clearly one from another. The patient sometimes seems to fade in and out of different phases of the disorder.

Specific Types of Schizophrenia

In diagnosing the schizophrenias, it is usual practice to diagnose the special type of the illness. *DSM IIIR* recognizes five specific types of full-fledged schizophrenic disorders. They are catatonic, disorganized, paranoid, residual, and undifferentiated (reserved for those cases in which the individual cannot be classified as one of the other types).

CATATONIC TYPE

Two overlapping patterns of behavior appear: excitement and withdrawal.

The excited pattern. In this form of the catatonic reaction, the disordered individual blusters about, talking and shouting, constantly on the move, pacing about or running back and forth until exhaustion takes over. Even in exhaustion, catatonic individuals sleep only for short periods of time. During their agitation, they can become violent, attacking others by throwing things or crashing a chair over their head.

Withdrawn catatonics. Catatonics are often mute, and may adopt strange positions and hold them for long periods of time. At other times, they show a waxy flexibility, holding any position into which an outsider may "arrange" them. Catatonics are, despite their withdrawal, highly suggestible. They will, for example, mimic sounds made by others (echolalia) or the actions of others (echopraxia). Despite exhibiting all the features of an individual totally withdrawn from the world, catatonics nevertheless show, in a variety of ways, that they are aware of what is going on around them.

Catatonics, especially in the withdrawal phase, will not eat or control their bowel or bladder functions.

Some catatonic patients alternate between periods of extreme stupor and extreme excitement. In one study, Morrison (1973) reported that in a study of 250 catatonic patients, almost 50 percent were withdrawn, about 21 percent were predominantly excited, and about 30 percent were mixed.

Because of their uncontrolled excretory functions, their "wildness," and their occasional assaultive behavior, catatonic patients are exceedingly difficult to manage. They are almost always hospitalized; and even in the hospital, they must be closely supervised and controlled.

DSM IIIR states that although catatonic schizophrenia was common three or four decades ago, the disorder is now rarely seen.

DISORGANIZED SCHIZOPHRENIA

Formerly called hebephrenic schizophrenia, and now one of the less common schizophrenias, this type of schizophrenia is the individual at his or her most immature and regressed. Much of the individual's behavior is literally infantile. Cognitive processes are severely disorganized; speech is incoherent; there is much silly behavior and giggling. While systematized delusions (or, for that matter, any systematized cognitions) are absent, bizarre behavior, such as eating feces or finger painting with it, may be expected. The disorganized schizophrenic may masturbate in public or fantasize publicly in weird fashion. There is much grimacing, jumbling words together (word salad), and disconnected associations.

Onset is earlier than in other types of schizophrenia. Ordinarily, the more florid manifestations of the disorder are preceded by a history of oddness, scrupulosity about trivial misdeeds, and preoccupation with religious and philosophical themes distorted from their usual context.

PARANOID SCHIZOPHRENIA

The two most significant psychotic symptoms in the paranoid patient are as follows: 1. Persecutory delusions, in which patients weave bizarre plots about the hostile intentions and acts of relatives, friends or even people who pass them on the street. Being poisoned, watched, followed or influenced by outside forces are prominent in their delusions. 2. In addition, there frequently are delusions of grandiosity, in which the paranoid individual "is," for example, a famed scholar, a millionaire, Christ or Napoleon.

Delusions may be accompanied by hallucinations which fit their persecutory delusions. For instance, God speaks to them, their enemies threaten them, or they hear confirmatory conversations.

The paranoid's delusions of persecution and grandiosity are sometimes interpreted as mechanisms through which the individual provides a sense of identity and importance that reality does not match. Paranoid schizophrenics are notably different from other schizophrenics in that their coping mechanisms and cognitive skills are at a higher level.

Onset of paranoid schizophrenia, although it may be gradual and follow a long history of strained interpersonal relations, rarely goes through a process (Type II) type of development. And occasionally, accomplished people, suddenly in the course of successful careers, break out in the classic paranoid fashion.

UNDIFFERENTIATED SCHIZOPHRENIA

Clinicians use this diagnosis when the patient's symptoms clearly indicate schizophrenia but are so mixed or undifferentiated as to make classification into one of the other types of schizophrenia impossible. Sometimes such an undifferentiated set of symptoms is the prelude to a more fully developed schizophrenia, conforming to one of the specific types of schizophrenia.

RESIDUAL SCHIZOPHRENIA

DSM IIIR advises that this diagnosis be used when individuals have been through at least one episode of schizophrenia (a six-month period of schizophrenic behavior) but now present no extreme symptoms of the disorder. Minor delusions or hallucinations may be present, but they do not dominate the patient's behavior. There may be emotional blunting, withdrawal, eccentric (but not bizarre) behavior, illogical thinking, and loosely connected associations.

SCHIZOPHRENIFORM DISORDER

According to *DSM IIIR*, this disorder is best understood as a schizophrenic disorder that has lasted for more than two weeks but less than six months. It is a less serious diagnosis because it suggests a greater likelihood of recovery to previous levels of functioning. It may be distinguished from other forms of schizophrenia by its sudden onset, a sense of active turmoil and confusion, and the absence of schizophrenia among relatives.

Overall View of the Schizophrenias

It will be reassuring to the student of abnormal psychology to know that the nature of schizophrenia sometimes seems to clinicians and research psychologists to be as complex as it must seem to one approaching the study of psychological disorders for the first time. In summarizing that complexity, we can nevertheless present six statements about schizophrenia with which psychologists generally agree:

1. There is no one symptom or type of behavior that unequivocally points to the existence of a schizophrenic disorder.

2. The symptoms of one schizophrenic patient may be different from those of another.

3. Symptoms may change notably from one stage of the illness to another.

4. Schizophrenics slip in and out of periods of lucidity and contact with reality.

5. Schizophrenics vary in their treatability; but except for the schizophreniform type of schizophrenia, a complete recovery to earlier levels of functioning is rare. Most schizophrenics are left with a relatively stable residual form of the illness.

In giving emphasis to the complexity of the illness whose symptomatology we have just described, it is appropriate to recall Bleuler's very early way of writing about the illness. He described it as "the group of schizophrenias." Today, clinicians generally agree that what they are confronted with is a group of psychiatric patients who share a common diagnosis but who differ widely in the pattern of their symptoms, the etiological factors involved, and even in their treatability.

As attempts are being made to pinpoint the diagnostic signs of the illness (such as the changes in diagnostic criteria for schizophrenia as delineated in early editions of *DSM* and those provided more recently in *DSM IIIR*,), psychologists are expressing concern about the comparability of research using the earlier criteria and more recent research using the revised criteria. Making that point dramatically is a research of Winters and colleagues, who found that of sixty-eight schizophrenics diagnosed according to *DSM* criteria, only thirty-five were diagnosed as schizophrenic when rediagnosed according to the *DSM IIIR* criteria. It may take another decade of rigorous research before we can distinguish clearly the various illnesses now diagnosed as schizophrenia.

Causative Factors in the Schizophrenias

Allowing for the disturbing diagnostic problems mentioned previously, we can still make certain statements about possible causality of the several diseases now called "the schizophrenias." There is general agreement that those illnesses are the result of some interactive combination of biological and psychological factors. The weight given to one or another set of factors varies with the type of schizophrenia being considered.

BIOGENIC FACTORS

Three biogenic factors have been identified as causative in the development of schizophrenia. They are genetic deficiencies, biochemical factors, and neuroanatomical anomalies.

Genetic Deficiencies. This section summarizes the research on the relationship between the schizophrenias and genetic elements. It considers the variety of research designs used to test the hypothesis that genetics plays a part in the development of schizophrenia and reports the findings of each type of research. There are three principal research designs: family studies, twin studies and adoptee studies.

Family Studies. In a summary of published research on schizophrenia and genetics, Gottesman (1978) reports on the prevalence of schizophrenics among relatives of diagnosed schizophrenics. His analysis suggests that the closer the family relationship (and, therefore, the more genes in common), the higher the percentage of schizophrenic individuals. Typical of his results are that 12 to 13 percent of the children of schizophrenics are also schizophrenic; in those cases in which both the schizophrenic and spouse were schizophrenic, the percentage of schizophrenic children jumped to 36 to 37 percent. By comparison, schizophrenia appeared among nephews and cousins at the level of 2 to 3 percent. Prevalence in the general population is 1 percent.

The weakness in drawing a conclusion from this type of study is that it takes no account of the unfavorable environmental influences a child would experience living with one or both parents who are schizophrenic.

Comparison of Monozygotic and Dizygotic Twins. Keep in mind that monozygotic twins have identical sets of genes; dizygotic twins are genetically no more alike than ordinary siblings. An argument in favor of a genetic influence in schizophrenia would be a high concordance rate (both twins having schizophrenia) in monozygotic twins and a significantly lower concordance rate among dizygotic twins. Cohen and colleagues (1972) report concordance among identical twins at the 23 percent level and a concordance rate of 5.3 among fraternal twins. That is a statistically significant difference. Both figures, however, are much lower than other reports, no doubt because the sample was a highly selective group who had been screened for military service.

Gottesman and Shields (1972), with a more representative sample, report results more typical of those found in other studies. Their concordance rates for identical twins was 42 percent, and for fraternal twins, 9 percent. Since the concordance rate between one schizophrenic twin and a co-twin is not 100 percent, there is the suggestion that influences other than genetic operate in the etiology of schizophrenia. Perhaps they are environmental, although it is hard to imagine extreme differences in the life experiences of identical twins who grow up in the same family. In fact, it is just because life experiences for identical twins may be assumed to be very much alike that the twin studies we have cited are criticized. They do not exclude common life experiences (even more so than for dizygotic twins) as a reason for the high concordance levels in identical twins.

Nevertheless, there is, in the studies cited, the very strong suggestion that genetics plays a part in the development of schizophrenia. Even though the genetic factors do not directly transmit the illness, they may create a vulnerability which, when activated by other factors, results in the illness.

Adoption Studies. In Leonard Heston's study (1966) of children raised by foster parents or in adoptive homes, there is more certain evidence of the strong influence of genetic factors in creating a predisposition or vulnerability to schizophrenia. Heston controlled both genetic and environmental influences. Comparing 47 children of schizophrenic mothers who had been placed in foster or adoptive homes prior to one month of age with 50 children in a control group who had been reared in the same homes as the children of the schizophrenic mothers, he found that 16.7 of the 47 children of schizophrenic mothers had received a diagnosis of schizophrenia, but none of the 50 individuals in the control group had done so. In addition, suggesting that the apparent genetic deficiency influenced behavior and pathology in other ways, the study found that 37 of the 47 children of schizophrenic mothers (a substantially larger number than in the control group) had received such other diagnoses as mental retardation, neurosis and psychopathic personality. They also were involved more frequently in criminal activities and spent more time in prison that members of the control group.

In a differently designed study, Katy (1975) added more support for a genetic hypothesis in the etiology of schizophrenia. In his study of schizophrenics and normal adoptees, the critical finding was that there were almost twice as many schizophrenic or schizoidlike relatives in the families of the schizophrenic adoptees than in the families of normal adoptees. The significant point to be made is that though the schizophrenic adoptees had been reared apart from their families, the weakness they carried in their genes resulted in schizophrenia.

Overall View of Genetic Factors in Schizophrenia. Psychologists generally consider that such studies as we have cited, especially the adoptee studies, have provided conclusive proof of a genetic influence in the development of schizophrenia. Since in no study was the supporting evidence at the level of 100 percent, psychologists look to additional factors interacting with genetic elements for the actual development of schizophrenia. Theoretically, these might be other organic mediating influences or, as is more likely, drastically damaging psychosocial factors. That reasoning suggests a diathesis-stress model for the development of schizophrenia.

Biochemical Factors. Among those researchers with strong convictions about the influence of biogenic elements in the development of schizophrenia, interest has focused recently on the dopamine hypothesis. That interest has replaced earlier interest in more simple hypotheses concerning biochemical influences on schizophrenia.

The possibility that there might be biochemical factors involved in the development of schizophrenia has long been the subject of research. Early efforts concentrated on analysis of chemicals in the blood and urine of schizophrenics for comparison with their content in nonschizophrenic individuals. The concept proved simplistic. What differences were found could more accurately be considered the result of dietary differences; for example, between hospitalized and nonhospitalized individuals, or influences other than essential differences directly related to the presence of schizophrenia.

The advent of what has come to be called the antipsychotic medications—also called neuroleptics, or tranquilizing agents, the most frequently prescribed of which are the phenothiazines—has revolutionized the treatment of schizophrenia. In addition, it has led scientists to a new way of considering possible biochemical influences in the etiology of schizophrenia. Phenomena associated with phenothiazine (one of the neuroleptics) treatment of schizophrenics turned attention to the possibility of abnormalities in neurophysiological functioning in that disorder, particularly in the effect of neurotransmitters. That possibility has been expressed in the dopamine hypothesis.

The Dopamine Hypothesis. In treating schizophrenics with phenothiazines, it was soon observed that a course of treatment not only reduced schizophrenic symptoms but also caused side effects resembling Parkinson's disease. It is known that parkinsonism results from too-low levels of the neurotransmitter dopamine, caused by a deterioration in a section of the limbic (or lower) area of the brain (specifically, the substantia nigra), which is involved in emotional behavior. Biochemists hypothesized that excessive dopamine might be associated with the development of schizophrenia. Their reasoning, simply expressed, is as follows: phenothiazine reduces certain symptoms of schizophrenia, but it also induces parkinsonian symptoms which, it is known, are the result of low levels of dopamine. The drug must therefore reduce levels of dopamine and, when it does, schizophrenic symptoms are reduced. High levels of dopamine, the hypothesis concludes, contribute to the development of schizophrenia.

That statement is a very simple description of a complex neurophysiological process. For example, to illustrate one aspect of that complexity, the level of dopamine may result from the density of dopamine receptors or from the action of some agent that blocks the functioning of those receptors.

The dopamine hypothesis has stimulated much research. While a good portion of that research supports the dopamine hypothesis, the hypothesis has not yet been given unequivocal support by either biochemists or psychologists.

Evidence in Support of the Dopamine Hypothesis.

1. There is the initial evidence that when dopamine levels are reduced (indicated by the development of Parkinson-type symptoms), schizophrenic symptoms are reduced. The powerful effect of clozaprine (developed in the late eighties) in reducing the symptoms of schizophrenia—because its primary biochemical effect is to reduce levels of dopamine—adds strong support to the dopamine hypothesis.

2. In large doses, the amphetamines are known to create a psychotic reaction indistinguishable from paranoid schizophrenia. That effect is known to be associated with the increased availability of dopamine caused by the amphetamines. Amphetamine psychosis is treated successfully with the same drug used to treat schizophrenics, the phenothiazines. But as has been stated, that drug blocks the receptors for the neurotransmitter, dopamine, making less of it available. It is thus argued that schizophrenia must result, in some unknown way, from excessive dopamine.

3. Two lines of evidence made possible by PET (positron emission tomography) scans give direct support to the dopamine hypothesis.

In PET scans of the brain of a normal individual and that of a schizophrenic individual of the same age, the latter's brain was shown to have a greater density of dopamine receptors, thus making excess dopamine available.

In 1986, Wong and colleagues compared PET brain scans of three groups of individuals: normal individuals, drug-treated individuals, and totally unrelated schizophrenics. Confirming the dopamine hypothesis, he found that the density of dopamine receptors was significantly greater in the untreated schizophrenics than in either of the other two groups. The research also demonstrated that the effect of phenothiazine treatment was to reduce the density of dopamine receptors and thus to reduce the symptoms of schizophrenia.

More recently, postmortem analysis of the brains of schizophrenics confirm the findings of the PET scans. The postmortem analysis indicated clearly that the brains of schizophrenics have a larger number of dopamine receptors than the brains of nonschizophrenics.

Reasons for Questioning the Dopamine Hypothesis. Those who are still uncertain about the dopamine hypothesis point to two facts which, they believe, do not agree with present statements of the dopamine hypothesis.

1. Dopamine-blocking drugs, which are used so successfully with schizophrenics, are also effective in treating other psychiatric disorders, particularly, for example, some types of organic psychoses. The question asked is, how can excess dopamine be thought to cause schizophrenia when lowering levels of dopamine also has a positive effect on other psychiatric disorders unrelated to schizophrenia?

2. The effect of phenothiazine in reducing dopamine levels takes places quickly (in hours), but any change in the behavior of the schizophrenic takes place gradually, over two or three weeks. If one causes the other, it might be assumed that the effect should be instantaneous.

Overview of the Dopamine Hypothesis. It is important to point out that the dopamine hypothesis applies only in Type I schizophrenia. Type II schizophrenia is unaffected by the phenothiazines, the drug that reduces excessive dopamine.

If dopamine is indeed an etiological factor in Type I schizophrenia, it is hypothesized by some authorities that the excessive dopamine is caused by the genetic abnormality which is strongly indicated to exist.

Psychologists generally take a wary view of the dopamine hypothesis. One of them, Goldstein (1986), points out that the evidence is mostly circumstantial and that the "smoking gun," that is, the evidence which would explain how the dopamine influenced the development of schizophrenia, has not yet been found. The general belief is that if excessive dopamine is involved in the development of certain schizophrenias, more complex biochemical models of the way in which it causes its effect will have to be found.

Neuroanatomical Factors. A third connection between biological factors and the development of schizophrenia grows out of the discovery of structural anomalies in the brains of Type II schizophrenics. So far, three types of structural differences between the brains of nonschizophrenic individuals and Type II schizophrenics have been identified.

1. The ventricles of the schizophrenic brain have been observed to be larger and asymmetrical when compared with normal human brains. Ventricles are tissue-free, cavitylike chambers in the brain which are filled with fluid. Their anomalous enlargement is suggestive of deterioration or atrophy in the brain. The correlation of enlarged ventricles and schizophrenia is suggestive of, but not definitive proof of, a causal relationship between the two. It has also been noted that left-hemisphere ventricles of schizophrenic brains are much larger than those of the right hemisphere. What the effect of that is, or what its cause might be, has yet to be identified, but the temptation is to relate the difference to schizophrenia.

2. Cranium size, cerebrum size, and perhaps most significantly, frontal lobe size, are all smaller in schizophrenics; but again, only in the slow-developing Type II schizophrenia.

3. The highest level of brain function takes place in the cortex. Two 1986 studies report anomalies at that level in schizophrenic brains: neuronal deterioration and reduced blood flow.

With those neuroanatomical anomalies, observed only in the brains of Type II schizophrenics, and with the dopamine hypothesis seemingly relevant only in Type I schizophrenia, it now seems possible to recognize at least two quite different types of schizophrenia, different not only in symptomatology, but also different in etiology. These are Type I schizophrenia, in which biochemical malfunctioning in neurotransmitter activity seems to create at least a vulnerability to schizophrenia, and Type II schizophrenia, in which structural anomalies in the brain have been related to development of the disorder. Differential reactions to treatment adds strength to Bleuler's early belief that there were two clearly distinguishable schizophrenic diseases. We can add here that, happily for them, Type I schizophrenics respond to the antipsychotic medications, the neuroleptics; and, unhappily for the Type II schizophrenics, no effective treatment has yet been discovered for this seemingly structurally based disorder.

PSYCHOLOGICAL FACTORS IN THE DEVELOPMENT OF SCHIZOPHRENIA

The biogenic factors associated with the development of schizophrenia, as we have just described, provide a reasonably solid basis for believing that there is a biologically caused diathesis or vulnerability in the schizophrenic individual such that he or she can be thought of as schizophrenic-prone. That vulnerability does not always cause a schizophrenic breakdown. To understand why it does in some individuals and not in others, we need to know what psychologically stressful circumstances which, when imposed on a vulnerability to schizophrenia, actually push the individual into a schizophrenic breakdown.

An obvious candidate for consideration is a life crisis immediately preceding the schizophrenic breakdown. But Bowers (1974), in a careful study of developing schizophrenic breakdowns, reports that the so-called life crises preceding the schizophrenic breakdown seem to be no worse than life crises faced by most young adults in our society; and, according to Bowers, such crises have not occurred immediately before the breakdown.

To psychologists considering the collapse of the individual in the face of only normal life stresses, it seemed that the answer must lie in earlier life experiences that were so psychologically crippling and disabling to the schizophrenic-prone individuals as to make it impossible for them to cope with any, even normal, later life crises. And it is a fact that most, if not all schizophrenics grow up in disturbed and seriously crippling family settings.

The search for early life experiences so psychologically damaging as to cause a schizophrenically vulnerable individual to break down and move into a full schizophrenic psychosis has centered on four aspects of the schizophrenic's life experiences: parent-child relationships; the authenticity of interpersonal life in the family; communication patterns in family relations; and the way in which emotion is expressed in the family, labeled in the research as "expressed emotion."

Parent-Child Relations. An early attempt to understand more fully the psychological causes of schizophrenia built upon a concept developed in 1948 by Frieda Fromm Reichmann, a psychoanalytically oriented clinician who specialized in the treatment of schizophrenia. She coined the term *schizophrenogenic* mother and applied it to those mothers whose pathological relationship, particularly with their sons, was likely to induce a schizophrenic breakdown. To this term was later added that of *schizophrenogenic father*, and the family as a totality was named a *schizophrenogenic family*.

Schizophrenogenic Mother-Son Relationships in Schizophrenogenic Families. The mother in such families, Fromm Reichmann said, was unfeeling, rejecting and cold, yet overprotecting and overcontrolling. Indifferent or hostile to her husband, she binds her son to her and seeks emotional satisfactions from him rather than from her husband. The son is thus bound into a conflicting relationship with his mother; rejected, yet overprotected and made dependent upon her.

Although initially received enthusiastically, doubt has been expressed about this interpretation of the psychological etiology of schizophrenia. A principal reason is that such mothers are often found in the families of individuals who develop a variety of other psychological disorders unrelated to schizophrenia; nor does the interpretation relate at all to the particular symptomatology of schizophrenia, particularly the disturbed cognitive functioning and split-away, affective life. Finally, the concept of the schizophrenogenic mother-son relationship does not tell us much about the cause of schizophrenia in daughters.

Father-Son Relationships. Exacerbating the influence of the so-called schizophrenogenic mother, it was stated, was a father who is a weakling and passive in family relationships or who, indifferent to his spouse and son, relates to his daughter in a seductive way. But here, too, it is a fact that such fathers can be found in the families of individuals with a variety of disorders other than schizophrenia.

Lack of Authenticity in Family Relationships. Wynne and colleagues (1958) have created the term *pseudomutuality* to describe a different pattern of family life experienced by some schizophrenics. Here, an outer semblance of mutual understanding and acceptance conceals a tangle of feelings that are at sharp contrast to the public face such families present.

Such a nonauthentic, indeed, fraudulent set of emotional relationships experienced in the intimacies of family life on a daily basis will surely be confusing to a young child and be likely to undermine his or her understanding of what is real and what is not.

To add further confusion to the interactions of family members, families characterized by pseudomutuality assign to their children caricatured, even allegorical, roles to which they are held inflexibly. Such roles simplify family relationships into the "good" and the "bad" and keep them in their artificial place without genuine feeling or authenticity. The role assignments fill out the pseudomutuality that is part of all the family's interpersonal relationships. Living in such a contrived world, some members of such a family will fail to achieve a self-identity in which they can believe, and will slip into a schizophrenic breakdown.

Communication Deviance. Given the known centrality in schizophrenic symptomatology of cognitive confusion, attentional difficulties, and weakness in distinguishing between the real and the unreal, more recent psychological research on the development of schizophrenia has focused on the total system of family relationships and the characteristics of those relationships that cause distortions in reality interpretation.

Relationships among family members are developed through the communications that they exchange. Singer and Wynne (1965), in an early study of the types of thinking and communicating existing in the families of schizophrenics, state that when communication between parent and child is ambiguous or confusing, it causes the intellectual confusion that is a weakness of the schizophrenic individual.

The researchers provide this example of deviance in communication between a schizophrenic patient and her parents.

Patient: "Nobody will listen to me. Everybody is trying to still me."

Mother: "Nobody wants to kill you."

Father: "If you're going to associate with intellectual people, you're going to have to remember that "still" is a adjective and not a verb."

That type of what psychologists call communication deviance, Singer and Wynne report, is not an occasional thing, but a characteristic of the parents' distorted way of thinking, which regularly expresses itself in family communications. Years of being misunderstood in that fashion and of having meanings mixed up in that way, the researchers stress, will lead the schizophrenic-prone individual to the cognitive distortions of schizophrenia.

Wynne and colleagues, in a later report, identify three ways in which parents engage in communication deviance: they inject meanings, conceal or cloud meanings, and simply deny truth.

Injecting a Different Meaning. Here a parent rejects, overtly, subtly, and possibly as an expression of his or her own distorted thinking processes, a clear meaning of a child's message, and substitutes (injects) a different meaning. The verbal exchange cited previously between a daughter and her parents is a bizarre example. Less bizarre but nevertheless damaging is the following example. A child asks to stay over at a friend's house, and Mother says, "You are always wanting to do things that upset me." If Mother persists, and amplifies that injected meaning, the effect on the child is confusion and self-doubt about his or her own motives.

Concealing or Clouding a Clear Meaning. Parents may hide information and leave children confused about what they thought they knew; or parents may answer in such a way that they put their child off in a way that causes blurring or vagueness about what the child thought was a known fact. Parents may deliberately keep silent on the request of a child for information and thus give the impression that there is no basis to the request.

Denying the Truth. Parents may also be more deliberate about their deceptiveness—for example, by consciously lying about negative aspects of family life. Rosenhan and Seligman (1984) give an example of denial that resulted from a thought distortion of the parents themselves. They report that a young patient complained that his parents were "somehow talking" about him, which both parents denied doing. Yet the therapist, in an interview with the parents and son observed both parents, in an "on stage" fashion, winking and nodding to each other as if they could not be seen by the child. They effectively denied a reality that the child was experiencing. One has the feeling from this case report that the son's way of describing his parents' behavior ("somehow talking" about him) suggests that he was already within the schizophrenic range of behavior.

In concluding their discussion of communication deviance, Rosenhan and Seligman stress the special significance of distorting communication for the development of schizophrenic illness. The meaning-distortions described prevent the achievement of a consensually validated reality. Without that, a child's belief in his or her own capacity to accurately perceive reality is weakened, and the foundation if laid for schizophrenic cognitive disarray.

Care must be taken to distinguish between the pathological communication deviance just described, which is characteristic of family disturbances and which is likely to induce schizophrenia in vulnerable individuals, and the quite different and only occasional deceptions of normal parents who are behaving in ways that they believe are protective of their children's welfare.

Research Support for the Communication Deviance Hypothesis. Research support for the hypothesis that communication deviance is likely to be an inducing cause in the development of schizophrenia comes from one of the relatively few long-term longitudinal studies of schizophrenia.

In the mid-sixties, M. J. Goldstein and colleagues studied sixty-four intact families that had applied to a psychological clinic for help with a behaviorally or emotionally disturbed teenaged child. They describe the teenaged children for whom help was sought as mild to moderately disturbed but not close to schizophrenia at the time of the initial evaluation. The teenagers and their sibling were periodically contacted for the following fifteen years.

At the time of the initial evaluation, parents of the teenagers completed the Thematic Apperception Test, a projective test in which the individual is asked to tell a story in response to a relatively ambiguous exposed picture. All parental stories were scored for communication deviance; that is, for the degree to which the stories were fragmented, with unconnected associations and discontinuities in the flow of the story. Each family was given a communication deviance score and was classified as high deviance, intermediate deviance or low deviance.

In the fifteen-year follow-up, fifty of the sixty-four families were located and available for assessment. In fifteen of the fifty families, at least one child had developed schizophrenia or a disorder in the schizophrenic disorder spectrum (with schizoid symptomatology). Those diagnoses were made by clinicians unaware of the family's communication deviance scores as initially determined.

The authors report that in families with high communication deviance, there were fourteen schizophrenic disordered offspring, but only five in the intermediate families, and one in those families with low deviance scores. They concluded that their results indicate that a high communication deviance between parents and young children can be said to be predictive of probable schizophrenic spectrum disorder later in the life of the child.

Double-Bind Communication. Gregory Bateson, one of the first researchers to identify the confusing communication patterns to be found in schizophrenic families, in a series of theoretically oriented papers (1956, 1959, 1960), described one pattern that he considered of special significance and which he called double-bind communication.

Double-bind communication takes place: 1. when an individual has so intense a relationship with one or the other parent that he or she feels it is urgent to understand communications from that parent so that he or she can respond properly; 2. when that parent expresses two messages, one incompatible with the other; 3. and finally, when the individual does not feel secure enough to press for clarification, yet cannot withdraw from the situation or ignore the message.

It is easy to feel compassion for the individual in such a dilemma and to understand the confusion and conflict that results. When double-bind communication is a regular pattern in family life, it induces, Bateson felt, role ambiguity and confusion about self-identity, problems that, over time, could induce a schizophrenic reaction in a schizophrenia-prone individual. An example frequently used to illustrate double-bind confusion is a mother who seems to want loving expressions from a child but then rejects them.

Equally powerful in causing confusion would be a father who presses a son to be independent but then criticizes him for making decisions on his own.

Although Bateson provided illustrative case reports from his own work with schizophrenic patients, subsequent research has not supported a conclusion that double-bind communication is any more common in schizophrenic families than in other families, one or more of whose members have a nonschizophrenic psychological disorder. But, it should be pointed out, those families may have no genetically caused vulnerability to schizophrenia.

Expressed Emotion. One other family communication pattern has been related to the development of schizophrenia.

The way in which family members communicate their emotions, negative and positive, has been related to the development of schizophrenia. In a pattern called *expressed emotions,* in schizophrenic families, research suggests, family members express their feelings openly and intensely in ways that negatively affect schizophrenia-prone individuals. Two elements of those emotional expressions are particularly crucial in causing a pathogenic effect: emotional overinvolvement and excessive criticalness or hostility.

The effect of expressed emotion on the schizophrenic was first reported in a series of studies by Vaughn and associates that attempted to predict the course of a schizophrenic psychosis prior to release from a period of hospitalization. As possible predictors, they considered such factors as nature of onset (gradual or sudden), the prior social adjustment of the patient, symptomatology during the active phase of the illness, and quality of the emotional life and its communication in the patient's family.

Nine months after the studied patients had been discharged, the researchers followed them to identify those who had relapsed. Of all the factors studied, the quality of emotional life in the family to which they returned was the best predictor of relapse rate. Patients who returned to families in which there was a high degree of expressed emotion—that is, a high degree of criticalness or overemotional involvement with the patient or overprotectiveness—were three or four times more likely to have been rehospitalized than those patients who lived in low expressed emotion homes.

Those early studies were not directed toward identifying the original cause of the schizophrenic breakdown. Yet was it not possible that if a highly charged emotional climate at home was related to later relapse rates after discharge from a hospital treatment program, it might also be related to the original schizophrenic breakdown? In a later study of the precursors of a schizophrenic breakdown (Rodnick and colleagues 1984), just such a relationship was established. They found that when the key elements of expressed emotion were a feature of family communication—that is, over-criticalness of or emotional involvement with one of the children in a family—that child was more likely to develop symptoms within what they called the spectrum of schizophrenia.

The coincidental finding of their research, which is that communication deviance and high expressed emotion are correlated, suggests that it is the combined presence of the two that is the critical factor in inducing a schizophrenic breakdown.

Overview of Psychological Causes of Schizophrenia. As an earlier section has reported, research has identified three biological factors in the etiology of schizophrenia: a genetic factor, a biochemical factor, and neuroanatomical anomalies. Those biological elements are considered to produce a vulnerability to one or another of the schizophrenias.

In addition, during the last twenty years, research efforts of psychologists have caused them to suggest a variety of psychological disturbances in the backgrounds of schizophrenics as possible causes of the disease. (The foremost of those disturbances have been described in the preceding section.) Despite such a considerable body of research, it is not yet possible to describe one specific set of psychological dynamics that psychologists generally will agree precedes and is causative in the development of schizophrenia. One significant reason for that is the fact that (as we have pointed out earlier) the illness is not one illness, but several different illnesses with different vulnerabilities and probably different psychological causes.

What is widely accepted among clinicians and other authorities in the field is the view that with our present knowledge of the illness, a diathesis-stress model is the most useful way of thinking about the disorder.

For that purpose, Goldstein (1984) has suggested replacing the original diathesis-stress model, which he considers too simple and static, with a more complex and dynamic version. He suggests that what fits the accumulated evidence better is a cyclical model of the way in which schizophrenia develops. In that model, diathesis and stress are constantly interacting across the early years of the individual's life. A heightened vulnerability and the periodic intervention of one or another stressor ultimately induces schizophrenia.

Goldstein suggests that due to a genetic predisposition and long-term exposure to a pathogenic family environment, the individual fails to develop adequate coping mechanisms. Without adequate mechanisms for adjusting to normal life problems, he points out, as the demands of life increase, the individual falls further and further behind in adjusting to them. Finally, he suggests, with pressures for autonomy from the family, for self-assertion, and heterosexual relations that develop in early adulthood, the vulnerable individual is incapable of dealing with them, and succumbs in the shelter of a schizophrenic breakdown.

SOCIOECONOMIC AND CULTURAL FACTORS IN THE DEVELOPMENT OF SCHIZOPHRENIA

One might assume that the influence of socioeconomic class member-ship and cultural environment would have a more remote and weaker impact on the development of schizophrenia than would the influence of more intimate relationships within the family; yet there are statistical findings that relate the prevalence and type of schizophrenia to just such sociocultural factors.

Schizophrenia and Socioeconomic Level. At least a half-dozen solid studies (Murphy 1968) show a relationship between schizophrenia and social class level; the lower the socioeconomic class or occupation, the more prevalent is schizophrenia. These studies suggest that the prevalence of schizophrenia is eight times higher in lower socioeconomic individuals than in middle or upper socioeconomic classes.

Unresolved is the question of what is cause and what is effect. Do the hardships and struggle of poverty add such burdens to an individual already burdened with a genetic predisposition and a troubled family that it makes escape from schizophrenia impossible? Or does the presence of schizophrenia or tendency to schizophrenia lead to a downward social class drift? We don't know yet. We know the prevalency facts, but not the relationship between those facts and the development of the disorder.

Cultural Factors and Schizophrenia. Cultural factors seem to be related to the prevalence of schizophrenia and to the form that it takes.

Prevalence. There are many cultures around the world in which the reported prevalence rate is significantly different from the worldwide mean of 1 percent, some significantly higher, others significantly lower. That fact has caused one authority (Carson et al.) to speculate that just as there are schizophrenogenic families, there may be schizophrenogenic cultures and others that are, to coin a word, nonschizophrenogenic. Considering the known cultural impact on aggressiveness, ambition, family and sexual life, religion and fantasy life, the thought is worth further consideration. Doing so will have to take account of a simpler interpretation: cultures may differ in the inclusiveness of their diagnoses of schizophrenia. *DSM IIIR* suggests, for example, that studies in Europe and Asia use a relatively narrow concept of schizophrenia, while in this country, clinicians use broader criteria.

Cultural Influences and Types of Schizophrenia. The evidence from a variety of studies (for example, Carothers 1953, 1959; Torrey et al. 1984) suggests that cultural differences do influence symptom formation and the type of schizophrenia that develops. For example, Japanese schizophrenics are often described as rigid, withdrawn and passive, which symptoms seem, in exaggerated ways, to reflect the values that Japanese place on conformity. Among Chinese schizophrenics, in recent years, delusions relate to the social problems following the Cultural Revolution in the sixties. Among

African tribal groups, the disorganized type of schizophrenia is the most common form of the disease.

Treatment of Schizophrenia

Reflecting the dual nature of causative factors in schizophrenia, clinicians take two interacting and complementary approaches to the treatment of schizophrenia: biological, largely pharmaceutical, and psychological.

Primarily as a result of the development of tranquilizing drugs in the 1950s, which reduced the florid symptoms of schizophrenic patients and made them much more available for psychological types of therapy, today's schizophrenics and their families can enjoy a more hopeful prognosis.

In this section, after a brief description of pre-1950 treatment efforts for schizophrenic patients, we first examine biological treatment of schizophrenia and then modern approaches to psychological help for the disorder.

PRE-1950 TREATMENT OF SCHIZOPHRENIA

Prior to the revolutionary changes in treatment of schizophrenics made possible by drug therapy, the future of the individual after a schizophrenic breakdown usually was quite bleak. Hospitalization, which was usually required, brought the patient into a huge, highly institutionalized setting, in which care was largely custodial, leaving the patient bored and hopeless. Low staff-to-patient ratios, very low mental health-care budgets, and a limited knowledge of effective treatment resulted in long periods of hospitalization and brief visits home, followed by seemingly inevitable relapses and return to the hospital. The result was a slow but steady decline into extreme deterioration.

That period of hopelessness was occasionally interrupted by the efforts of clinicians to attempt more active treatment. During the three decades prior to the development of antipsychotic medication, two radical organic treatment techniques were widely used: prefrontal lobotomy and insulin shock treatment. Although initial success was reported for both, they were soon stopped, and for good reason. Although a prefrontal lobotomy reduced the extreme agitation of the schizophrenic patient, it was soon discovered that it left him or her in a tragically passive and only vegetative state. Insulin shock, a high-risk therapy, was discovered to be more appropriate as treatment for depression than for schizophrenia. Electroshock convulsive therapy has since been substituted as a treatment of last resort for extremely depressed patients; it is not used in the treatment of schizophrenics. In 1923, Harry Stack Sullivan initiated the use of intensive psychoanalytically oriented treatment for schizophrenics. Following him, Frieda Fromm Reichmann and John Rosen used modified psychoanalytic psychotherapy. Here, again, although initial success was reported, it was soon discovered that insight therapy of the type being used was not helpful in the treatment of the schizophrenic. With the arrival on the scene of drug therapy, more supportive psychotherapeutic approaches were being used successfully in the aftercare programs for schizophrenic patients.

MODERN TREATMENT FOR SCHIZOPHRENICS

The modern treatment of the schizophrenic patient takes a two-stage approach. In stage one, the goal is the reduction of the positive symptoms (hallucinations, delusions and agitation) of the patient, the initial stages of which take place immediately after hospitalization. Successful control of those symptoms usually requires that the patient continue the antipsychotic medication for long periods after discharge from the hospital. In stage two, the goal is to help the patient develop the ability to function socially. Pursuit of that goal begins before the patient's discharge and is continued out of hospital in carefully nurtured aftercare programs. It should be pointed out that in stage one, the treatment is almost entirely biological; in stage two, it is psychological with continued maintenance of drug therapy.

Symptom Reduction and the Antipsychotic Medications. In using the newly synthesized antihistamines for the relief of asthma and other allergies, clinicians soon took note of their strong tranquilizing effect on patients. Experimentally, at first, psychiatrists began to use the drug with disturbed psychiatric patients. It was soon discovered that the drug they were using, chlorpromazine, had a dramatic tranquilizing effect on schizophrenic patients. And so a revolution in the treatment of that disorder was begun.

Effect of Drug Therapy. The pharmaceuticals (chlorpromazine, phenothiazines and butyphenones), also called neuroleptics, antipsychotic medications, or tranquilizing agents, were standard treatment until the late seventies in the initial phase of caring for schizophrenics. In the late eighties, the new drug clozapine was experimentally tested and found to be highly effective in the treatment of schizophrenia. At the introduction of the drug for the regular treatment of schizophrenics, a number of psychiatrists reported that "it worked wonders" in making it possible for schizophrenics to return to their families, even to find employment. Although without the usual negative side effects, the drug causes a fatal blood disorder in a small number of patients, requiring that they be followed up with an expensive monitoring program. The biochemical effect of the antipsychotic drugs is to lower levels of dopamine in the brain. Clinically, that change reduces fear, agitation, thought disorders, delusions and hallucinations, which are the most acutely disruptive of the patient's symptoms. Once those symptoms are alleviated, the patient is readied for the second phase of treatment and discharge from the hospital, usually in a period of two to three weeks.

Hospital statistics reveal the dramatic effect of drug therapy. In 1955, prior to widespread use of drug therapy, there were, in round numbers, 560,000 patients in psychiatric hospitals. By 1982 (Witkin 1981), a report for the Department of Health and Human Services stated that that number had decreased to 160,000. The effective use of drug therapy was what made that reduction possible. But there are costs involved.

Negative Consequences of Drug Therapy. Negative factors associated with drug therapy are of two types: negative physical side effects and unhappy social consequences.

Negative Side Effects. One set of troublesome side effects is the development of Parkinson-type symptoms: muscle rigidity, immobile facial expression, and tremors. These symptoms are unquestionably the result of lowered dopamine levels produced by the medication. In some patients, there may also develop itching in the muscles, which leads to a constant need to move around. To relieve that discomfort, patients resort to pacing about restlessly.

In time, use of the drugs leads to an exceedingly unpleasant disorder (tardive dyskinesia) in which patients continuously smack their lips and move their tongues in what have been described as flycatching movements. One quarter of those patients who have been on the drug for seven years or more, especially those with Type II symptoms, develop the reaction. The symptoms, which are, as can be imagined, extremely discomforting to the patient, grow worse as the patient ages. The new drug, clozapine, has done much to reduce the negative side effects.

Unhappy Social Consequences. In past years, schizophrenics remained in the hospital for long periods, sometimes until their death. With the use of the antipsychotic medications, most patients can be discharged well before a year passes. But, as a consequence, readmission rates have soared, leading to a phenomenon nicknamed "the revolving door effect." In 1986, Hogarty and associates reported that the readmission rate within a two-year period was 79 percent. One explanation for that increased readmission rate is that in past years, many patients now discharged would never have been out of the hospital. Whether or not that high relapse rate will continue with the new drug has not yet been determined.

Trying to look on the bright side of things, we can say that at least 21 percent of hospitalized schizophrenics now are able to stay out of the hospital for at least two years. For those who remain on medication and live in benign facilities at home or elsewhere, that two-year period might be even longer. For others, perhaps most of the discharged patients, the period out of hospital may not have been a pleasant one. Unknown numbers of discharged patients become part of the urban homeless population; others, while not homeless, may spend their time out of the hospital with the same disruptive and fractious family that provided the setting for the initial schizophrenic episode. A high rate of relapse among such released patients is predictable.

Post-Hospital Care and Relapse Rate. Studies of discharged schizophrenics have identified four conditions that influence the length of time before a relapse and return to the hospital occurs: 1. whether or not the patient continued to take the antipsychotic medication; 2. the quality of family relations in the home to which the patient returns; 3. the availability of out-of-home activities for the patient; 4. the extent to which the patient has developed useful social skills and the availability of nonfamily interpersonal relations.

Maintenance Drug Therapy. Substantial research (Hogarty and Goldberg 1973, for example) has related length of time before relapse and whether or not the patient has continued medication after hospital discharge. In their study, in a two-year period, 30 percent of discharged patients who continued medication were back in the hospital, whereas 68 percent of those who were given a placebo had relapsed. That study also tells us that, as important as continued medication is, it is not enough to lengthen the period before relapse for some patients. Other factors, principally psychological factors, play a part.

Many patients, either to avoid negative side effect of the drugs or because of negligence, stop taking the drug. When they do, a shorter interval before relapse is the almost certain result.

Family Therapy. A number of studies (for example, Goldstein and colleagues 1978; Faloon et al. 1981; and Leff et al. 1982) indicate that a combination of continued medication and family therapy can be a powerful influence in lowering the relapse rate. In the Leff study, for example, in the nine months following discharge, the rate of relapse for discharged patients who were drug-maintained and who were given family therapy was 8 percent; for a comparable group receiving only drug therapy, it was 50 percent.

All three studies cited above further indicated that when the family therapy (reinforced by continued medication) focused on the problems associated with the patient's return and current real life problems, more favorable results were obtained than when the therapy attempted more drastic approaches; for example, unraveling problems of the distant past or attempting to restructure long-established family relationships. Those findings were consistent with other reports (Gunderson 1984) which indicate that reality-focused, supportive therapy is more beneficial than exploratory, insight-oriented therapy in a psychoanalytic mode.

Successful family therapy stresses family relationships; how emotions are expressed, patterns of communication between the patient and other family members, and role relationships within the family. The therapist, working with the family as a unit, helps members recognize the damaging effect on the patient of intensely expressed emotion, whether the emotion surrounds the patient with emotional overprotection or emotionally offers criticism to "help" him or her. The therapist works toward improving intrafamily communication to avoid communication deviance and gently identifies maladaptive role relationships between the patient and parents or siblings.

Importance of Time Away from the Family. For some schizophrenics who are returning to difficult home situations, the opportunity to get away from the family, at least for some hours during the day, can reduce the likelihood of an early relapse. Arrangements for the patient to spend some time in a halfway house, or, when the patient is capable of it, in part-time employment, can be a helpful alternative to unalleviated time in a disruptive home setting.

Social Skills Training. Ordinary social skills used in relating appropriately to others or in seeking their help—asking directions, for example—which are skills that most people use routinely with little difficulty, often have been completely lost during the schizophrenic illness; yet any successful attempt to resume a somewhat normal interpersonal life is dependent upon those skills. Once the individual's most disturbing symptoms have subsided, training can begin while the patient is still in the hospital and continue after discharge at an aftercare clinic.

One well-conceived and carefully implemented program, described by Wallace and colleagues (1982), eased the patient's reentry into normal out-of-hospital social settings and enabled the patient to more comfortably meet life's ordinary social demands. The program divided social skills into three phases: 1. accurate perception of the social situation; 2. planning choice of response options; and 3. implementing the chosen response. Through therapy, the patient was trained in each separate step, and then the patient integrated and practiced the steps in role-playing situations—in the beginning, with the therapist, and later in group situations, with other patients.

For more lasting effect, the patient should have an opportunity to "test" the new social skills in real life interpersonal situations, followed by a discussion with the therapist about any problems that may have developed.

Milieu and Therapeutic Communities. In the sixties and seventies, two full-time residential communities, providing a post-hospital experience that created a totally therapeutic environment for the patient, served as examples of what can be accomplished in such a setting with skilled and dedicated staff. Both programs used only psychosocial therapy without antipsychotic drugs.

The Lodge. In 1969, George Fairweather and a group of associates, dissatisfied with the high relapse rate of recently discharged schizophrenics, created The Lodge, a short-term (six months) residential community for recently discharged schizophrenics to test the hypothesis that what schizophrenics needed was the opportunity to develop a sense of self-responsibility. In The Lodge, former patients were assigned major responsibilities in managing the household affairs of the community. As their capabilities increased, they were given additional responsibilities, until the entire community was patient-managed.

After six months, a group of the seventy-five patients who volunteered to live at The Lodge was compared with a matching, nonvolunteer group who had received an in-hospital treatment program that included psychotherapy as well as drug maintenance and help in community adjustment and foster home placement. After six months, 65 percent of Lodge patients, but only 27 percent of the control group, remained free of a relapse requiring hospitalization.

Even more impressive are the figures on full-time employment. Fifty percent of Lodge patients held full-time jobs during this six-month period, compared with only 3 percent of the control group. Fairweather and his group reported that those favorable results held up even after three-and-a-half years.

Soteria House. In the 1970s, four dedicated nonprofessionals set up a family living experience for six individuals who had been diagnosed as schizophrenics but who were not hospitalized. They named their house Soteria, meaning "deliverance." The four staff members all had previous experience with schizophrenics and had learned to view a schizophrenic episode as a valid reaction to intolerable life circumstances; terrifying as the episode was, it nevertheless contained a strong potential for leading the individual back to normal adjustment.

Staff and recovering patients served as caretakers and parental surrogates for the most disturbed patients. Through interacting with these caretakers, the disturbed individuals worked through emotional and communication difficulties that they faced in their own family lives. The emphasis in the treatment was to use the symptoms of schizophrenic breakdown constructively to create a new sense of reintegration and growth.

In 1975, Mosher and associates evaluated the results of a six-month stay at Soteria. They report that the six patients showed equal symptom reduction when compared with a regularly hospitalized group and, in addition, made superior adjustments in living away from home. There are two other considerations to bear in mind when evaluating the program. All patients were kept off their medications during the six months; apparently, a totally supportive environment without drugs can serve as well as a hospital environment with drug support. Although no actual cost figures are available, one can speculate that Soteria House's cost per patient was far lower than for those patients in the hospital.

A disappointing follow-up of the Soteria House experiment was the inability of several subsequent attempts with different staff to replicate the experience. Those efforts revealed that routine treatment in a local community health center provided more positive results than did the various Soteria House programs. As an explanation of that finding, Goldstein et al. (1984) point out that often the beneficial effects of alternative treatment programs disappear when the charismatic leadership of earlier programs is no longer present. Charisma is something that we have not yet learned to teach.

OVERVIEW OF OUTCOMES IN THE SCHIZOPHRENIAS

There are various ways of describing outcomes following an initial schizophrenic episode, some of them pessimistic, others more optimistic.

On the optimistic side, we can say that since the introduction of drug therapy, almost 90 percent of those individual suffering a schizophrenic episode and entering a psychiatric hospital for the first time will improve and be discharged in a short time—for some, in a few weeks, and for others, in months—but for practically all of that 90-percent group, in less than a year. To balance that optimism, it is necessary to report that many will have to be rehospitalized within the subsequent two years.

DSM IIIR provides what seems to be the most pessimistic report, stating that a complete recovery to preschizophrenic functioning is unlikely. Such a recovery is so rare, *DSM IIIR* states, that some clinicians would be uncertain of the diagnosis if such a recovery did take place. It concludes on a slightly more optimistic note and concedes the possibility of full recovery, but also points out that the frequency of such recoveries is unknown.

Carson et al., in their 1988 publication, without citing specific research, offer a less bleak picture, which, while not contradictory of the *DSM IIIR* statement, describes outcomes for schizophrenic patients in a different way. They report that one-third of hospitalized schizophrenics "recover," which they define as being symptom-free for five years. This is not quite the same as saying that they return to premorbid levels of functioning. At the sad end of the scale are the 10 percent of the schizophrenic population who go into a steady decline toward deterioration and lifetime disability. The remaining 60 percent of the schizophrenic population go through life in and out of hospitals after occasional reoccurrence of schizophrenic episodes and weakening of their personality.

DELUSIONAL (PARANOID) DISORDER

In addition to the schizophrenias and mood disorders, there is a third type of functional (nonorganic) psychosis, labeled in *DSM IIIR* as Delusional (Paranoid) Disorder. It is occasionally referred to as paranoia. Although often featured in motion pictures and occasionally headlined in newspaper accounts of unusual crimes, it is a rare psychiatric disorder. Scant published research about the illness is available, and we describe it here only briefly.

Types of Delusions

The central (and, for the most part, only) symptom is a well-established and often ably defended delusion. *DSM IIIR* lists five specific types of delusion characteristic of the disease.

1. Persecutory type, in which the individual believes he or she is being threatened or mistreated by others.

2. Grandiose type, in which victims of the disorder believe that they are extraordinarily important people or are possessed of extraordinary power, knowledge or ability.

3. Jealous type, in which the delusion centers on the suspected unfaithfulness of a spouse or sexual partner. This delusion is more common than the others.

4. Eroticmanic type, in which individuals convince themselves that some person of eminence, often a movie star or well-known political figure (often one they have never met but to whom they have written frequently) is in love with them.

5. Somatic type, in which the false belief focuses on a delusional physical abnormality or disorder.

An odd and extremely rare form of the disorder has been called *folie à deux*. The disorder is occasionally used as a central feature of a novel or motion picture. The distinguishing feature of this form of delusional disorder is that it results from a close relationship with someone else who already has a delusional disorder. The most common pairing for the disorder is two sisters, one of whom initially develops a delusion. Living closely together, often in isolation from other social contacts, the sisters develop common ways of thinking, including the central delusion. *Folie à deux* may also develop from one spouse to the other, between brothers, or between parent and child (Gralnick 1942).

Diagnostic Criteria

For a diagnosis of the disorder, *DSM IIIR* requires that, at least for the duration of one week, the individual display one of the disorders named, behave and respond emotionally in a fashion consistent with the delusional belief, and be free of hallucination, incoherence or loosened associations.

The disorder is distinguished from paranoid schizophrenia, in which there would ordinarily be an array of other symptoms not found in delusional disorder, such as hallucinations, agitation, or social disorganization. It is also distinguished from paranoid personality disorder, in which paranoid thinking takes the form of suspicion of the motives of others but in which there is an absence of the elaborately developed and patently false delusions of the delusional disorder.

Associated Symptoms

Generally, all other symptoms are associated directly or indirectly with the central delusional belief. There may be resentments and anger, which occasionally cause violence. Especially in the persecutory type, there is likely to be social isolation, seclusiveness and behavioral eccentricities. In defense of the delusions or consistent with them, the individual may initiate court actions, write long and involved letters to people he or she does not know, or become involved in long and complex conversations, even with strangers.

These patients rarely seek treatment; and when they are forced to do so by relatives or social or legal organizations, they do not participate effectively in the treatment effort. The disorder is one of middle or later adult life. It is a chronic illness, free both of further deterioration or remission.

Causative Factors

Although little systematic research has been done on the delusional disorder, clinicians generally believe that it has no genetic or other physical basis, but grows out of pathological early life experiences. Supporting that belief is a study of Kendler and Davis (1981) which reports that relatives of these patients are no more likely to develop schizophrenoform symptoms than are individuals in the general population. The few researchers reporting on etiological factors in delusional disorder suggest a childhood characterized by aloofness, secretiveness, and resentment of criticism or punishment. Family experiences are reported to be authoritarian, domineering and critical.

The schizophrenias, a group of psychoses that distort the thought processes and cause anomalies (distortions) in the behavior and affective life of the individual, make up some of the most debilitating of psychiatric disorders. They affect 1 percent of the world's population. In the United States, two million people suffer from one or another form of schizophrenia.

The various schizophrenias are distinguished by a set of three dimensions: 1. the nature of the onset; 2. the presence of positive symptoms—for example, delusions or hallucinations,— or negative symptoms, an absence of florid symptoms but serious deficiencies in normal functioning—for example, flatness of affective reactions; 3. the presence or absence of paranoid elements in the symptomatology.

The schizophrenias are also divided into two broad categories. There is Type I schizophrenia, which is characterized by a short or sudden onset and the presence of delusions and hallucinations. Type II schizophrenia, also known as process schizophrenia, has a long and insidious onset, ultimately causing withdrawal, blunted affective response, and a dwindling of any motivational energy.

Maladaptive changes in the schizophrenic individual include bizarre thought content, anomalies in the form of the individual's thought processes, warped perceptions of the world, flattening or inappropriateness in emotional expression, paralysis of will, a loss of any sense of self-identity, and withdrawal from the outside world. There is no one symptom or type of behavior that unequivocally identifies the schizophrenic.

In the development of schizophrenia, clinicians recognize three phases: the prodromal or early stage; the active stage, which brings on florid symptomatology; and the residual stage, which is what the schizophrenic is left with after a schizophrenic episode.

DSM IIIR classifies five specific types of schizophrenia: catatonic, disorganized (formerly called hebephrenia), paranoid, residual and undifferentiated.

In considering the causes of schizophrenia, psychologists agree that the disorder results from some interactive combination of biological (including genetic) and psychological factors. There would seem to be a genetically caused predisposition to schizophrenia.

Most schizophrenics are hospitalized for treatment. Initially, antipsychotic drugs are administered, followed by some form of supportive therapy. The rate of relapse and rehospitalization is exceptionally high. DSM IIIR concludes that recovery to the preschizophrenic level of functioning is unlikely; but, many clinicians would add, not impossible.

Selected Readings

Bellak, L. 1979. "Introduction: An Idiosyncratic Overview." in L. Bellak (Ed.). *Disorders of the Schizophrenic Syndrome.* New York: Basic Books.

Bowers, M. B., Jr. 1977. "Clinical Components of Psychotic Disorders: Their Relationship to Treatment." *Schizophrenia Bulletin*, 3: 600-607.

Goldstein, M. J. (Ed.). 1982. *Preventive Intervention in Schizophrenia: Are We Ready?* Washington, D.C.: U.S. Government Printing Office.

Harrow, M., B.J. Carrone, and J. F. Westermeyer. 1985. "The Course of Psychosis in Early Phases of Schizophrenia." *American Journal of Psychiatry*, 142: 702-707.

Levine, I. S. 1984. "Service Programs for the Homeless Mentally Ill." in H. R. Lamb (Ed.). *The Homeless Mentally Ill: A Task Force Report of the American Psychiatric Association*, (pp. 173-200), Washington, D.C.: American Psychiatric Association.

Meehl, P. E. 1962. "Schizotaxia, Schizotypy, Schizophrenia." *American Psychologist*, 17: 827-838.

Spitzer, A. L., A. E. Skodal, M. Gibbon, and J. B. W. Williams. 1983. *Psychopathology: A Case Book.* New York: McGraw-Hill.

14

Substance-use Disorders

The problem of drug abuse is a central concern at all levels of American society. Along with poverty and racism, drug abuse has been targeted by national mental health authorities as one of the principal causes of mental health problems. Two of the three major institutes of the United States Public Health Service concern themselves exclusively with alcoholism and drug abuse.

Neighborhoods in major urban centers are beset by the thousands of drug peddlers on street corners; and even in so-called good neighborhoods, certain houses are known as "drug drops," visited regularly by street peddlers. At the family level, there are few households that are not familiar with the problem, either because of its presence in their own home or in the families of relatives or neighbors.

The effects of substance abuse are devastating for the individual, his or her family, and society. We cite only a few examples of those effects here, leaving more details of their effects to later discussions of each of the addictive substances. Half of all suicides, more than half of all fatal automobile accidents, and almost half of all murders are alcohol-related. Almost all street crimes involve drug users. The dreaded AIDS question has now become a problem for women and children, as well as men, chiefly because of contaminated needles used in intravenous administration of drugs.

Despite the negative effects of excessive use of alcohol and other psychoactive substances, they are, as the Diagnostic and Statistical Manual of Mental Disorders points out, frequently used to modify mood or behavior, in a recreational way, under circumstances that are considered normal and appropriate. There exist subcultural groups who, in opposition to those practices, forbid, or at least strongly discourage, any use of alcohol, and by strong implication, all other psychoactive drugs.

Ill effects and all, the practice of using various substances to reduce pain and emotional tension, or to induce euphoria, is, as far as we can tell, an ancient practice. The virtues (if that is the right word) of wine were sung in the poetry of the Greeks and the Romans; the royalty of Persia and Egypt were subject to its influences. Persian history gives Cambysis, a sixth-century B.C. member of the royal family, the dubious distinction of being the first alcoholic in recorded history.

This chapter, although giving principal emphasis to alcohol, a substance negatively affecting many more individuals than all other drugs combined, will describe the principal addictive substances, their effects, possible causes, and treatment programs.

THE DSM IIIR *AND SUBSTANCE ABUSE*

Psychological disorders that are the result of substance use are divided into two types by the *Diagnostic and Statistical Manual:* substance dependence and substance abuse. As with other psychological disorders in the manual, the categories relate to behavior caused by the substance use and not to any etiological factors.

Substance Dependence

According to *DSM IIIR,* an individual is diagnosed as substance dependent when any three of the following nine types of symptoms or behavior patterns are characteristic of his or her behavior.

1. When the substance is taken in larger quantities or over a longer period of time than the individual planned.

2. When despite a strong desire to reduce or control substance use, the individual fails to do so in several attempts.

3. When the individual spends inordinate time in trying to obtain the substance.

4. When obligations are not met, or when the individual fails to appear at school or for work because of intoxication or withdrawal symptoms.

5. When important social, occupational or recreational interests are given up or neglected.

6. When substance use is continued despite the knowledge of having a persistent social, psychological or physical problem that is caused or exacerbated by the use of the substance. Examples are as follows: exacerbation of an ulcer by continuing to drink alcohol; provoking a major family dispute because of drug abuse; or continuing use, even though it is followed by a severe depression.

7. When a marked tolerance of the substance causes the individual to increase use of the substance.

8. When there are significant withdrawal symptoms.

9. When the substance is taken to relieve or avoid withdrawal symptoms. (Adapted from *DSM IIIR*.)

Substance Abuse

A less severe reaction than substance dependence, substance abuse is diagnosed by *DSM IIIR* when there is a pattern of pathological use, accompanied by impaired social or occupational functioning, for at least a month's time.

An extension of substance dependence is the diagnosis of organic mental disorder by psychoactive substance use when severe mental symptoms, such as delirium tremens, accompany withdrawal symptoms.

ETIOLOGICAL FACTORS IN SUBSTANCE-USE DISORDERS

More than any other psychological disorder, the development of substance-use disorders seems to be dependent upon of the ready availability of the substance and its use by the individual's peers. Both biological and psychological factors have also been explored as possible causes of substance-abuse disorders. Alcohol use has been studied most extensively.

Essential Conditions for the Development of Substance-use Disorders

Not all individuals who have access to psychoactive substances or whose friends use one or more of them become victims of the substance. To those two conditions, there is usually added either a set of life circumstances that are so unhappy for the individual as to cause him or her to seek escape from them, or life circumstances so boring and unexciting as to provoke the need for artificial stimulation. Once individuals are tempted to try the substance, its immediate psychological effects draw them into regular use of the substance and hence into addiction.

To understand the etiology of substance-use disorders, we begin by describing the way in which most psychoactive substances work.

Characteristics of the Way in Which Psychoactive Substances Work

Richard Solomon (1977) describes three characteristics or phases of substance abuse that create a strong motive to continue using the substance. He has called his analysis the "opponent-process" model of addiction. It is so named because of the opposition between two phases of substance abuse. In all, there are three phases to Solomon's model: affective pleasure, affective tolerance, and affective withdrawal. Initially, the user seeks the pleasure of the substance's first phase. As the substance user moves into the third phase, going without the drug, and experiences withdrawal symptoms, he or she is drawn back into substance use to avoid the unpleasantness of withdrawal. The oppositional nature of the two processes is easy to see. They are, in a sense, opponents of each other.

AFFECTIVE PLEASURE

All psychoactive substances causing addiction, in their initial stages, provide positive emotional experiences. The nature of those experiences vary from one substance to another, but they are all, in one way or another, pleasing to the user. Alcohol releases inhibitions, overcomes shyness, and pushes current problems out of consciousness; heroin gives the user a "rush," bathing the individual in a warm ecstasy; cocaine provides a thirty-minute period of euphoria, well-being and tirelessness. Those pleasant experiences invite the individual to come back again.

AFFECTIVE TOLERANCE

But users soon find that they develop a tolerance for the substance. The initial dosage no longer produces its initial "high." In the beginning, for example, two or three drinks would set the individual "on top of the world." Some time later, that amount no longer provides the desired effect; it then takes five or six to get the same effect. At that point, the individual moves toward addiction.

AFFECTIVE WITHDRAWAL

Individuals, after a period of heavy substance abuse, may develop feelings of guilt about their habit; there may be pressure from a spouse, parents or employers. They may then decide to give up their habit. If, by that time, their body's physiological processes have become dependent upon use of the substance, they will develop withdrawal symptoms. These are feelings of panic or heightened irritability. The reaction is a very unpleasant one, and now drives the individual, not so much to seek pleasure, but to reduce the unpleasantness of the withdrawal symptoms. The more frequently relapses occur, the more drastic are the withdrawal symptoms, causing users to frantically seek "a fix," sometimes at any cost. They have moved from drug abuse to drug dependence, with dire effects upon their lives, including possible criminal acts to obtain money for purchasing the drugs upon which they have now become dependent.

Are there biogenic factors or personality characteristics that make the individual vulnerable to substance abuse? Recent research (1991) suggests that these may be brain irregularities making some people quicker to become addicted than others, and harder to cure.

TYPES OF PSYCHOACTIVE SUBSTANCES

This section describes five categories of psychoactive (that is, affecting cognitions, feelings or behavior) substance: alcohol, narcotics (derived from opium), sedatives (principally the barbiturates), stimulants (principally cocaine and the amphetamines), and the hallucinogens (including marijuana).

Alcohol

Consumption of alcohol is a major characteristic of the contemporary American social scene. We discuss here prevalence, effects, causative factors, and treatment approaches.

PREVALENCE

According to a 1985 survey, 86 percent of the population reported using alcohol in the recent past; 12 percent reported using it at least twenty days each month. Prevalence of alcohol use has risen steadily since the repeal of Prohibition. Twenty years ago, in 1970, prevalence of alcohol use was at the level of 68 percent as compared to a prevalence rate of 86 percent today.

The *DSM IIIR* reports that 20 percent of men are alcoholics at some time during their lives. That figure for women is 5 percent. Overall, the National Council on Drug and Alcohol Abuse reports that there are now nearly eighteen million alcoholics and alcohol abusers in this country.

The social and economic damage caused by drinking alcohol is extreme. The National Council on Alcoholism estimates that in 1983, the overall cost of alcoholism, including work absences and health costs, came to more than 116 billion dollars. It is difficult to quantify the cost of disrupted family life and neglected children and the personal suffering of the alcoholic individual.

THE EFFECTS OF ALCOHOL

There are both physiological and behavioral effects of drinking alcohol.

Physiological Effects. Alcohol acts quickly. In a matter of minutes, alcohol is absorbed into the bloodstream through the walls of the stomach and the small intestine. It then goes to the liver, which has the capacity to metabolize (that is, to convert into energy) one ounce of 100-proof alcohol (percent by volume) in one hour. In theory, if a person drank just one ounce of 100-proof alcohol every hour, there would be no alcohol available to the blood, and hence to the brain, to effect any behavioral changes. What alcohol that is not metabolized remains in the bloodstream and is carried to the brain. Some remnant of alcohol taken into the body remains in the bloodstream for up to twenty-four hours.

Although often considered to be a stimulant, alcohol is a narcotic. Its stimulating effect results from its narcotizing effect on cortical control of emotion and behavior. It turns an overly inhibited individual into a relatively uninhibited one. With continued drinking, initial amiability may be converted into depression or aggression.

Behavioral Effects. Even moderate doses of alcohol impair coordination and slow reaction time. It also interferes with speech, vision, and the higher mental processes, such as judgment and calculation. Alcoholics typically have trouble adding up the bill for the cost of a night's drinking.

Social Effects. Two socially significant effects of alcohol are their impact on aggressive behavior and sexual behavior. The combination can be especially upsetting to those around them. Small doses of alcohol cause aggression to be expressed in assertively arguing contrary political, ethnic or religious views. With increased drinking, the individual may "look for a fight," or, indeed, become assaultive. With respect to alcohol's effect on sexual behavior, psychologists enjoy quoting Shakespeare, from Macbeth: "Lechery, Sir, it provokes and it unprovokes; it provokes the desire, but it takes away the performance."

The Influence of Expectations. There is research support to indicate that much uninhibited behavior, resulting from a drink or two, comes more from what the individual believes will be the effect of alcohol than from the alcohol itself. For example, in two separate studies, groups of males and females were given what they thought were alcoholic drinks. Their behavioral reactions were then observed. With respect to aggressive behavior and to amorous behavior, both males and females behaved in notably uninhibited ways.

The Drinking Cycle's Influence on Effects. There is also research to indicate that the effect of alcohol varies with the timing of the drinking cycle. Using tests of abstract problem-solving and memory, Jones and Parsons (1971) were able to show that with identical levels of alcohol in the blood, those moving toward intoxication were much more intellectually impaired than those on their way to sobriety, that is, on the downward cycle of the drinking episode. In either phase, performance was lower than performance without alcohol.

Long-term Effects. The effects of alcohol discussed so far are those within a single drinking episode. With frequent drinking bouts over a prolonged period of time, there will be more damaging and long-term effects. Chronic alcoholism affects almost every tissue of the body. The most damaging long-term effects of chronic alcoholism are as follows: 1. Malnutrition. The calories of alcohol are empty of nutritive value; because alcohol is substituted for food, the body soon breaks down from the absence of nutrients essential for health, especially the absence of protein. 2. Severe psychiatric disorders develop. Korsakoff's syndrome (see chapter 16) is a direct result of the absence of B-complex vitamins that results from the diet of the chronic alcoholic. 3. Cirrhosis of the liver is a likely possibility. This serious illness, in which fat replaces healthy liver tissue, impairs the liver's functioning and causes inflammation. Cirrhosis of the liver is often fatal, ranking eighth among the principal causes of death.

One sad long-term effect of alcohol affects not only the woman alcoholic but, if she is pregnant, the fetus, as well. A report (1978) by the U.S. Department of Health, education and Welfare states that alcohol consumption by pregnant women is the third leading cause of birth defects.

SPECIAL FACTORS IN THE ETIOLOGY OF ALCOHOLISM

Psychological research has focused on two possible causative factors in alcoholism: genetic and other biogenic causes, and personality characteristics. Certain psychosocial factors, such as ethnicity, occupation and social class, seem to be associated with alcoholism. They are not considered to be primary causes of the alcohol addiction.

Genetic Causes of Alcoholism. Although the genetic mechanism has not yet been described, there is clear evidence, from family and twin studies, that genetic factors play a part in causing alcoholism. Early research has suggested that the culprit gene predisposing an individual to alcohol abuse was a specific dopamine receptor gene. Subsequent research (Gelernter 1991) has provided reason to reject that hypothesis. The individual's heredity causes a vulnerability to alcoholism; the effect is not that of a dominant gene, such as that which determines eye color. Something more, environmental factors working in conjunction with the genetically caused vulnerability, is needed to cause the disorder.

The evidence for the genetic influence may be summarized as follows:

1. From animal laboratories comes evidence that animals can be bred to show a preference for alcohol over other beverages. That is strong evidence of a genetically caused weakness for drinking alcohol.

2. With humans, there is less certainty. The weakest, but nevertheless suggestive, evidence of a genetic factor in alcoholism is the number of studies that report a higher incidence of alcoholics among the relatives and children of alcoholics than would be expected on a chance basis.

Cloninger and associates (1986) report the following figures of the family histories of alcoholics: In a population of males with one alcoholic parent, the rate of alcoholism in family members was 29.5 percent, compared to 11.4 percent in the general population; with two alcoholic parents, that percentage jumps to 41.2 percent. Comparable rates in females were 9.5 to 5.0 percent with one alcoholic parent, and 25 percent with two alcoholic parents. The weakness of this evidence is the fact that common heredity is not the only variable operating. Relatives, including children of alcoholics, may have been surrounded by an alcohol-drinking environment.

3. Stronger evidence is provided in a study by Godwin and others (1973). That study reported that when children of alcoholic parents were raised apart from their parents by adoptive parents, the rate of alcoholism at the age of

twenty among the adopted children was almost twice as high as among a matched control group. Comparing children of alcoholic parents raised by their own parents with those raised by adoptive parents, Godwin's group, in a second study, found statistically insignificant differences between the two groups; that is, 25 percent and 17 percent. Those figures suggest some small influence from the home environment. But what is most significant in causing alcoholism is the parents to whom you were born, and not the parents who raised you.

On the other hand, there is one study that reports no significant differences between children of alcoholics and a matched control group (Schulsinger et al. 1986).

Etiological Factors, Genetics, and Type of Alcoholism. The reactions of psychologists to those mixed studies are to suggest that there may be two types of alcoholism:

1. Milieu-limited alcoholism, affecting both males and females, in which some alcohol dependence by parents, combined with an impoverished home environment, may result in a high incidence of children with alcohol dependency; and

2. Male-limited alcoholism, in which environmental factors seem to play no part. It is that type of alcoholism, it is suggested, that Godwin studied. Differing environmental influences would have little impact on the development of this type of alcoholism.

Physiological Factors in Alcoholism. Volpicelli (1987) has suggested that alcohol dependence may result from the same physiological relationships that cause other narcotic addiction. Psychoactive drugs, he states, "mimic" the way in which the brain's naturally producing compounds prevent the feeling of pain. That experience results naturally from the release of endomorphins in the brain. When certain types of psychoactive drugs are used, they cause the same physiological changes in the brain as do the presence of endorphins, that is, a sense of pleasure. It is that pleasure, now artificially produced by the psychoactive substance taken into the body, that is sought by the individual. One suggested cause of alcohol consumption is the need to compensate for reduced endorphin activity. Such lessened activity would result when life is an unhappy experience for the individual; endorphin production is low and there are few, if any times, when the individual feels pleasure. Alcohol produces that missing pleasure.

Personality Characteristics in the Etiology of Alcohol Use. Two markedly different approaches have been taken to seeking an understanding of the alcohol-prone personality. One is the psychoanalytic approach. It offers a number of hypothecations based largely on the descriptions of alcohol-dependent patients seen by the analyst. The second is a set of longitudinal studies that followed into adulthood a group of children whose behavior patterns had been observed. Two predictive characteristics stand out: hyperactivity in childhood is an important predictor of later alcoholism; even stronger in its predictive accuracy is early antisocial behavior. When early antisocial behavior is linked to similar behavior on the part of natural parents, predictive accuracy, not only for alcoholism, but for drug abuse generally, is high.

The consensus of psychological opinion is that no one alcohol-prone personality has been identified. That finding, as later discussion will reveal, is generally true for other substance abusers as well. The one common background factor found in the case histories of alcohol abusers is a pattern of maladjustment, principally in interpersonal relationships, but also including career and financial areas. That, of course, is not a personality trait, but a state of unpleasantness that the alcohol abuser is attempting to escape.

Although a prealcoholic personality has not been identified, common personality traits have been identified in those who are already alcoholics. These are negative self-image, feelings of inadequacy, low tolerance for stress, isolation, and depression. As the problem worsens, the alcoholic shows low impulse control, a lack of responsibility, and extreme foolishness. There are no reported studies that report those traits as being present prior to alcohol abuse.

Psychosocial Factors. There are ethnic, occupational and socioeconomic correlates of alcoholism. Such factors cannot be causative in any real sense; they are likely to be environmental conditions that make it easy to drink alcohol, and social conditions in which peers drink alcohol.

In France, the national consumption of alcohol for each person aged fifteen or older is the highest in the world. The French also apparently have the highest rate of alcohol abuse in the world. About 15 percent of the French population have alcohol problems. As a major wine-producing country, France's high rate of alcoholism is perhaps understandable.

From an occupational perspective, prevalence of alcohol abuse is highest in such occupations as railroad workers, sailors, bartenders, waiters, and liquor salesmen. Here, too, availability and peer group practices provide the environmental impetus for drinking.

Not so easily explained is the high prevalence of alcoholism in the middle socioeconomic class when compared with the lower class. Perhaps it is too simplistic to say that lower socioeconomic classes do not have the money necessary to pay for alcohol. In the worst cases of alcoholism, a drop from middle-class to lower-class family income can be the result.

TREATMENT FOR ALCOHOL ABUSE AND ALCOHOL DEPENDENCE

The principal hurdle for all treatment programs is the prevention of a relapse. Professional treatment for alcoholism usually takes place in three stages. An important adjunct to professional treatment is the help of such groups as Alcoholics Anonymous.

Stage One of Treatment. Hospitalization for a minimum of a month begins the process. That period is sometimes called a drying-out time. In any case, the time in the hospital should be long enough to give the individual a significant period of time without using alcohol. The discovery that he or she has done without alcohol, even though in a protected environment, can give the individual a sense of accomplishment.

Stage Two of Treatment. At the end of that initial period, the individual must be confronted with his or her alcohol problem, which may, up to this point, have been denied. The alcoholics are led to admit that they have been alcoholics and that they may have a vulnerability to the problem. That possible vulnerability requires an "on guard" defensive stance for the rest of their lives.

Stage Three of Treatment. At this point, a period of psychotherapy is initiated, often in a group setting. A principal emphasis here is identification of the types of situation that usually lead to heavy drinking. In therapy, many approaches focus on the development of cognitive strategies to handle situations that put the alcoholic at risk. These strategies may range from how to graciously refuse an offered drink (that is, if the goal is abstinence, which it may not be) to dealing with tension-provoking situations at home or on the job.

Cognitive-Oriented Therapy. In one widely-used cognitive therapeutic approach, the individual is first weaned away from any tendency to believe that his or her alcoholism results from a craving for alcohol which the individual may blame on some poorly understood physiological condition. Instead, individuals are encouraged to believe that their weakness is a matter of self-indulgence and that the goal must be to strive for control of that self-indulgence. The longer individuals are able to maintain that control, the greater the sense of self-mastery and confidence. With those feelings strong, the more likely it is that they will triumph over their excessive drinking.

Unanticipated Consequences After Therapy. Once a short-term program is concluded, two possible developments may take place that tend to destabilize the individual.

1. Therapists report that the danger is not that there will be a sudden major alcoholic episode, but that through a series of seemingly harmless "minor" decisions, alcoholics will gradually head toward a relapse. Sometimes a spouse will unwittingly elicit such a decision. For example, the simple statement, "Helen and Joe are coming over for dinner tonight"; in the interest of being a hospitable host, such a comment may lead the husband to bring home a bottle of Scotch, saying to himself, "I know Joe likes Scotch." With that act, temptation is brought home. Warning about such mini-decisions can help alcoholics see their danger and avoid making such decisions.

2. A second problem occurs if, in therapy, the goal of absolute abstinence has been set. Alcoholics may accidentally, in the course of a social evening, or by deliberate choice, take a single drink. Stopping after a single drink is a victory; but if the goal was abstinence, alcoholics may not perceive their accomplishment, but assign such significance to that one violation that their confidence is destroyed and they lose their past determination to avoid heavy drinking. This is another important area in which advance warning about such possibilities can be helpful.

Aversive Substances in Treatment. In the course of the treatment program, the therapist may use the help of an aversive deterrent to drinking, antabuse. This is a chemical that disrupts the metabolic processing of alcohol for two days after it is taken. If the individual is in a total abstinence program, and he or she drinks alcohol during the two-day period, the consequences are very unpleasant: flushing, increased heartbeat, and severe nausea, an event likely to deter the desire to take another drink during the two crucial days following a dose of antabuse. The rationale behind the use of antabuse is that is stops impulsive, unplanned drinking. If the alcoholic decides to resume drinking, he or she has to plan two days ahead to do so. In that time, therapists believe, there is a good chance that the determination not to drink will have become reestablished. The problem with such aversive therapy is that unless underlying problems motivating the drinking are solved, the alcoholic will simply decide to give up antabuse once out of the hospital.

Programs comparable to the three-stage program described are now offered in Veterans Administration hospitals and in more than four hundred residential centers throughout the country.

Self-Help Groups. The most widely known, and for some 20 percent of those who seek its help, the most effective self-help program, is Alcoholics Anonymous. With no professional staff, AA offers alcoholics the opportunity to meet in groups with other problem drinkers and also with those who have completely and securely reformed. In the course of the meetings, those who have reformed (often well-known personalities) describe the indignities and unwholesomeness of their lives while drinking as an example to avoid and as an example of the possibility of overcoming a drinking problem.

Alcoholics Anonymous uses the "buddy" system, which enables an alcoholic who feels the urge to drink to call his or her "sponsor" for help. Ordinarily, in quick order, a healthy member will arrive and stay with the individual until his or her desire to drink disappears. It is a part of the AA philosophy that in this practice, both individuals are helped; the buddy is reinforced in maintaining an alcohol-free life, and the newcomer survives a crisis.

Established in 1935 by two former alcoholics, the program has developed its own philosophy of treatment based on three propositions: 1. Once an alcoholic, always an alcoholic. The weakness is always there. 2. No one can stop drinking without help. 3. A spiritual but nonsectarian approach to life is helpful to everyone, and is especially needed by alcoholics.

When the program works, cured individuals are generous in their praise of it. Unfortunately, a dropout rate of 80 percent limits its usefulness to the 20 percent who persist.

Overall View of Alcohol Treatment Programs. Treatment programs for those who use excessive amounts of alcohol get mixed reviews, and how one interprets the research findings depend upon one's expectations of what should happen.

The most extensive research on the effects of treatment is that reported by Polich and colleagues in a 1981 report. They reported the negative side of the pictures as follows: only 7 percent of a group of 922 males studied had not used alcohol in the four years following treatment; 54 percent of the group continued to have alcohol-related problems during that time.

When the statistics (drawn accurately from the study) are presented differently, one can feel more encouraged about the possibility of treating alcoholics. Of the 922 men in the study, more than 90 percent had serious drinking problems to start with; only 54 percent continued to have problems with alcohol. That is a substantial reduction.

Conditions for Effective Treatment. Carson et al. (1988), describe conditions that improve the likelihood of favorable treatment outcomes. They are early recognition of the problem, acceptance by the individual that he or she has a problem and needs help, the availability of adequate treatment facilities, and the use of a criterion of reduced alcohol consumption, not abstinence.

Other Types of Psychoactive Addictive Substances

Here we consider three major types of psychoactive drugs: the depressants, the stimulants, and the hallucinogens. Various of these drugs may be taken orally, by sniffing, smoking or "snorting," or intravenously. We examine the nature of the various substances, their effects, etiological factors, and possible therapies.

THE DEPRESSANTS

In addition to alcohol, the depressants are categorized as narcotics, sedatives, and tranquilizers. All have similar characteristics: the user grows tolerant of them and requires increased dosages to produce the desired relaxing effects; withdrawal symptoms develop when the substance is unavailable; and overdoses of the substances depress the functioning of various bodily systems; for example, blood pressure and rate of respiration.

Extreme overdoses of any of the depressants can cause death by reducing vital activities to the point where they can no longer support life.

OPIUM

A principal source of substance abuse, it has been around at least since the Sumerian civilization in 7,000 B.C. Opium is derived from the seed of the poppy plant. The principal forms of its modern use are morphine and heroin.

Morphine. Morphine is a powerful sedative and pain reliever. Prior to knowledge of it addictive powers, it was used widely in patent medicines and as a means of reducing pain. It is still used occasionally, under strict medical supervision, when intractable and unbearable pain is present.

Heroin. This opium derivative was developed as a means of controlling the use of morphine, but was soon discovered to have stronger addictive power than morphine, and other negative physiological and behavioral effects, as well. Opposition to its use was led by Theodore Roosevelt; and with his help, in 1914, the Harrison Narcotics Act made illegal the unauthorized use of morphine or heroin.

Widespread use of heroin by young people as a kind of daring recreational and escapist activity developed in the 1960s, despite its illegality. Its use has decreased in the seventies and eighties. By 1983, 58 percent of those requiring emergency treatment for the drug were over thirty years of age, a statistic that suggests a large proportion of those who use heroin today are leftover members of the sixties' generation.

Effects of Morphine and Heroin. Both drugs produce euphoria, reverie and drowsiness. In addition, heroin causes a "rush" effect from intravenous injections, in which the individual is suffused with feelings of warmth and ecstasy. For four to six hours, the individual is in a stupor and seems "out of things."

Heroin's appeal is explained well by Solomon's opponent-process model. In that model (as earlier discussion reported), the first appeal is pleasure; when later withdrawal symptoms develop, heroin is then sought to escape the extreme discomfort of withdrawal. Withdrawal symptoms result when neither the drug nor the body's natural processes are at work to produce a sense of well-being.

Prevalence. A report from the National Institute on Drug Abuse reports that heroin use, as indicated by emergency hospital admissions, has dropped from a high of 47 percent to its present level of 37 percent. In estimates of public bodies and scientific researchers, the number of heroin users ranges from 350,000 to 450,000. Many more young people, survey reports reveal, have experimented at least once with the substance.

SEDATIVES

The principal sedatives are the barbiturates (phenobarbital, secobarbital and amobarbital). There are two types of barbiturates, a long-acting type for prolonged periods of sedation, and the short-acting type, which has an immediate effect, causing short-term sedation or sleep.

Prescriptive Use of Sedatives. As prescribed medically, barbiturates relax muscles and provide a sense of well-being. When used excessively, they cause loss of motor coordination, slurring of speech, and concentration and cognitive difficulties. As the effect of the drug continues, there is a loss of emotional control and periods of verbal hostility and aggressive behavior.

Types of Users. The problem of excessive use of barbiturates affects two quite different populations: 1. Young antisocial poly-drug users. 2. So-called respectable middle-aged and middle-class men and women, who originally take the drug on a doctor's prescription. Their gradually developed tolerance for small doses causes them to increase dosages to an addictive level, with the possibility of withdrawal effects. At that point, they have become addicted to the substance. 3. Doctors and medical workers who begin by taking advantage of the ready availability of the drug, only to soon find that they cannot do without it.

STIMULANTS

There are two principal stimulants: amphetamines and cocaine. They are notably different in the types of users they attract. The amphetamines were available initially as a nonprescription inhalant for clogged nasal passages. Their use as artificial stimulants was soon discovered by a mixed population looking for "kicks." Since 1970, the substance has been made a highly restricted prescription medication; yet since it is widely available illegally, it has become a much-used drug.

Amphetamine Users. Because of its stimulating effect—a user seems, at least for a brief time, to be more alert, have more energy, and feel stronger—its use by soldiers in World War II was encouraged by both Germans and Americans. For the same reasons, it now appeals to long-distance truck drivers and night-shift workers. Among the eighteen-to-twenty-five age group, it is frequently taken as "a shot in the arm" by college students cramming for exams and by athletes, including Olympic stars and professionals. Most recently, since one of its effects is to depress the appetite, it has become a means of controlling weight, principally by women. Using it for that purpose, without medical supervision, is a dangerous practice. Excessive use of amphetamines will have serious deleterious effects on one's health, including the possibility of death.

Amphetamines can now be obtained in three different prescription formulations: Benzedrine, Dexedrine, and the more potent and therefore more dangerous Methedrine. They all cause both physical and psychological changes.

Effects of Amphetamines. The drug is addictive whether taken orally or intravenously. Exceeding the small dosages usually prescribed medically causes increased heart rate, a jump in blood pressure (sometimes to levels high enough to cause death), impaired intestinal functioning, and constriction of the blood vessels on the surface of the body and in bodily membranes. Heavy doses cause such psychological states as nervousness, agitation, heart palpitations, dizziness and sleeplessness. Beyond those changes, the individual under the influence of the substance may become suicidal or hostile and dangerously assaultive.

Cocaine. Like opium and marijuana (to be described later), cocaine is a plant product; it is extracted from the leaves of the cocoa plant, which is grown extensively in some South American countries.

Prevalence. Its use in the United States is described in surveys as being of epidemic proportions, especially among middle- and upper-income groups. Problems created by its use are increasing rapidly. In reports of the National Institute of Drug Abuse (confirmed by independent researchers Kozeland and Adams 1980), active users of cocaine currently number 5.8 million, a jump of 260 percent over the figure of 1.6 million for 1974. In the general population, some 21 million Americans admit to having used cocaine at least once.

Effects of Cocaine. The drug acts rapidly on the cortex of the brain, sharpening sensory awareness and suffusing the individual in a haze of euphoria. It accentuates sexual desire, feelings of well-being, and tirelessness. Taking an overdose results in psychoticlike hallucinations and paranoid thinking and other such physical changes as nausea, chills, and sleeplessness. Inveterate cocaine users soon isolate themselves from former friends by their irritability and paranoid thinking. Heavy users frequently find themselves in a hospital emergency room with a heart attack resulting from a myocardial infarct (see chapter 16).

Varieties of Cocaine Use. Because of the tolerance effect following regular use, cocaine addicts seek to intensify its effect. One way of doing so is to heat the cocaine with the highly inflammatory ether (a highly dangerous practice), which purifies the cocaine as it produces what is known as a "free base," sometimes labeled "white tornado" or "snow." The practice is a frequent one among long-time users of the drug.

A recent and rapidly growing addition to the various ways of using cocaine, introduced initially on the streets of New York City around 1985, is crack. Crack is a free-base form of cocaine, readily available in small doses at relatively low cost. That diabolically clever marketing scheme has made it an increasingly used form of drug addiction. Professional groups concerned with drug abuse consider crack to be the most dangerous and addictive drug now in use.

HALLUCINOGENS

Here we will discuss the two most widely used hallucinogens: LSD (lysergic acid diethylamide) and marijuana. There are others: mescaline, psilocybin, and PCP, or angel dust. Since their effects are generally within the range of those produced by the principally used hallucinogens, we discuss here only those two.

Psychedelic Drugs. LSD and related drugs are frequently labeled "psychedelic" drugs. They were first studied during the 1950s because they were believed to produce psychotic reactions, and it was thought that their study might shed light on certain psychotic disorders. The importance of LSD and its attractiveness to a small, highly specialized fraction of the drug-using population grew out of a research decision made by Timothy Leary and Richard Alpert at Harvard (1957). They became interested in the possibility that one of the hallucinogens might have a positive effect on antisocial behavior. Their early, very tentative studies on a population of prisoners suggested that an experience with psilocybin reduced the number of postprison arrests in the same sample population.

Seemingly attracted by what they thought were the mind-expanding effects of the drug, Leary and Alpert began to use it themselves and encouraged a small group of others to do so. The activity soon attracted the interest of law enforcement authorities. The two left Harvard and set up their own organization to study the so-called mind-expanding properties of LSD and its associated hallucinogens. Following the publicity given to Leary and the promise of mind expansion, a number of well-known artists, writers and composers took to using the hallucinogenic substances, and an LSD movement developed.

It soon became apparent to the group that the psychedelic drugs had no power to increase anyone's creativity. Today the use of psychedelic drugs is a relatively minor problem in the field of drug abuse. About 1 or 2 percent of the population use the drugs, and their use of them is limited.

Effects of the Psychedelic Drugs. The effects of LSD can be produced by minute dosages; larger dosages are required for mescaline and psilocybin. The drugs are taken in liquid form or absorbed into sugar cubes, which are then ingested by the user. Effects last from six to twelve hours.

As with alcohol, the psychological effects that follow use of the psychedelic drugs depend to a considerable extent upon what the user expects to happen. Expect a "trip," get a "trip." There is a very real danger of a "bad trip" which occasionally results. Panic and profuse anxiety occur; for a small group of users, the result can be a psychotic episode.

A typical trip, about eight hours long, brings on kaleidoscopic sensory experiences, shifting emotional experiences, and feelings of detachment and depersonalization. There is little or none of the euphoria of other drugs. Without the expectation and readiness for a mind-expanding experience (which research has demonstrated does not occur), to a non-user, there would seem to be little reason to use psychedelic drugs, with the possible exception of the appeal of belonging to a cult whose practices include the use of such substances.

Flashbacks. One unusual and unpleasant effect of the psychedelic drugs is the occasional occurrence of "flashbacks." Soon after a trip, without further use of the substance, there is a short-term but dramatic reoccurrence of the original psychedelic experience. Flashbacks may occur repeatedly for one or two months after use of the substance. Fifteen to 30 percent of psychedelic users have flashback experiences. They are not accompanied by physiological changes that might explain their occurrence. For most individuals who experience them, they are an upsetting, perhaps even frightening, event.

The expectation factor as an influence on what will actually happen would suggest that the psychedelic user is extremely suggestible. If so, and if flashbacks are expected, they may simply be triggered by ordinary changes in consciousness such as we all experience; but psychedelic users give them a more dramatic interpretation.

Marijuana. This hallucinogen is smoked as a cigarette, usually referred to as a "joint." As with other hallucinogens, its effect is influenced by what individuals expect. For most users, it produces a "high" different from the use of alcohol. The user is euphoric and experiences a pleasant sense of being relaxed and drifting or floating. Marijuana stands apart from the other substances discussed here in that there has been a strong movement to legalize its use.

Arguments in Favor of Legalizing Marijuana. The argument for legalizing it is that marijuana is a source of pleasure and relaxation which is no more damaging than alcohol. As with alcohol, it is psychologically but not physiologically addictive and has no extreme withdrawal effects. Advocates of legalization would say that its worst negative effect is that it causes only the same obnoxious, noisy, overly talkative, argumentative behavior as the alcoholically intoxicated person; and, as they point out, drinking alcohol is legal.

Arguments Against Legalizing Marijuana. The argument against legalization is, to some degree, reminiscent of the arguments for the prohibition of alcohol prior to passage of the Volstead Act, which made alcohol consumption illegal in 1919. Opponents of the legalization of marijuana point to the following possible negative side effects of smoking marijuana.

Marijuana does not always provide a pleasant experience. Smoking a "joint" while in a downcast mood will frequently exacerbate that mood, causing depression and intense anxiety. It may also cause psychotic-like behavior. Marijuana, it is argued, impairs safe driving. There is much evidence to indicate that long-term marijuana users develop problems in marriage and on the job. Other psychological problems may be part of the postmarijuana life of marijuana users, and they may drift into using other drugs.

Physical Effects. Regular use of marijuana negatively affects the reproductive processes. In males, it reduces the sperm count; in females, it shortens the fertility period and interferes with ovulation. It raises blood pressure slightly and will create damage to the lungs, since marijuana brings into the lungs many of the same carcinogens as cigarettes; and because it can raise the heart rate dramatically, it will impact on those with potential heart trouble.

Treatment for Drug Abuse and Dependence

There are two principal therapies for drug addiction. One is substitution therapy, in which the addict is given a harmless drug capable of relieving withdrawal symptoms. The second mode of treatment is the residential treatment center.

SUBSTITUTION THERAPY

An essential first step in treating addicts is detoxification; that is, completely withdrawing the addict from drug use. The major challenge here is limiting the pain of withdrawal symptoms. The most successful substitution program is the use of methadone for heroin addiction.

Methadone Treatment. Methadone is a synthetic narcotic developed by Dole and Nyswander in 1966 at Rockefeller University. It is related to heroin and is addictive, but does not have heroin's negative psychological effects.

Advantages of Using Methadone. Most heroin users who stay in the methadone program find that while taking methadone, they can do without heroin and yet not experience the withdrawal effects of giving it up. Since reducing the withdrawal effects is the strong second-stage reason for taking a drug, that effect of methadone has significant value.

There are secondary advantages to the methadone program. Its pharmacological effect, that is, its helpful effect in preventing withdrawal symptoms, lasts for more than twenty-four hours, in contrast to a four-hour effect produced by heroin. The advantage of that is to give the former heroin user a longer period of time when he or she has no reason to visit old haunts in pursuit of heroin. During that twenty-four-hour period during which, in the past, the individual sought contacts from whom to obtain heroin, the repeated pairings of environmental cues, followed by the reinforcement of taking heroin, are eliminated. Thus, in conditioning terms, their motivational value for triggering a heroin trip should be extinguished, or at least reduced significantly.

Another advantage of methadone is that with high doses of methadone, over a period of time, intravenous heroin no longer produces the sought-after high. Thus, should the individual have a relapse, the heroin would not provide a satisfactory experience.

Disadvantages of Methadone. Methadone substitution does have some serious limitations. For one thing, it keeps the individual drug dependent and requires that he or she visit a hospital or clinic daily to be given the methadone, which is usually taken orally and always supervised by a staff member. And it does have some negative physical effects, such as insomnia, constipation, and diminished sexual performance.

The negative physical effects and probably the absence of a high following methadone causes a high drop-out rate in most methadone programs.

Many methadone programs are accompanied by psychotherapy. Contrary to what one might expect, methadone users not in psychotherapy seem to do as well, socially and psychologically, as do those users who received psychotherapy (Rounsaville 1986).

There are no substitution programs for drugs other than heroin.

RESIDENTIAL TREATMENT CENTERS: THERAPEUTIC COMMUNITIES

Drug abusers are sometimes treated individually on a private basis by psychiatrists, psychologists and social workers. Treatment offered is similar to what would be offered to individuals with any other psychiatric disorder. Little is known about how extensive or effective such treatment is.

The best-known approach to drug use treatment that attempts to restructure the individual's personality is the residential therapeutic community fashioned in the model of the original Synanon program, which has since, for irrelevant reasons, been effectively discontinued. The original program was established by Charles Dederich in Santa Monica, California, in 1958. Other well-known therapeutic communities are Daytop Village, Phoenix House and Odyssey House. Such programs have as their goal the restructuring of the individual's life perspective so that drugs of any sort no longer have a place in his or her life. The use of methadone is usually discouraged.

CHARACTERISTICS OF SUCCESSFUL RESIDENTIAL TREATMENT

Davison and Neale (1990) describe five features of such therapeutic communities that seem to promote success. Therapeutic programs are successful when:

1. They surround individuals with a drug-free environment in which former drug addicts are supported psychologically as they seek to establish a drug-free existence.

2. Former addicts who are successfully living free of drugs serve as models and describe their past problems and how they solved them. This is one of the successful techniques also used by Alcoholics Anonymous.

3. Confrontational encounters occur in which former drug users are challenged to accept responsibility for their problems and are pressed to take charge of their lives.

4. Each resident is respected as a fully independent and worthwhile human being and is not stigmatized or criticized for past failures.

5. The residential nature of the treatment center separates the individual from former friends and old haunts and, in that way, breaks up the person's old drug-dominated social network.

EFFECTIVENESS OF THERAPEUTIC CENTERS

Residential therapeutic centers pride themselves on the success of their alumni. Nevertheless, it must be recognized that they are relating to a very select segment of the drug-user population. All participants volunteer to join the community, which means that they come in with high motivation. Even so, the drop-out rate is exceptionally high, an occurrence which leaves an even more select group who eventually go on to become alumni. One of the few research reports (Jaffe 1985) on therapeutic communities concludes that for those who spend a year or more in the center, the experiences helps "a large number" of them.

*D*rug abuse is a central concern at all levels of American society. The DSM IIIR distinguishes between 1. substance dependence, which is diagnosed when the individual manifests three of nine symptoms, all of which clearly indicate that the individual's loss of control of substance use has seriously disrupted life; and 2. substance abuse, a less severe pattern than dependence, which interferes with social or occupational functioning for at least a month.

Four causative elements operate in the development of substance use disorder. They are ready availability of the substance and use of the substance by peers. When to these two conditions are added unhappy life circumstances or a life that is unexciting or boring, a substance disorder frequently develops.

The "opponent-process" model describes the motivations for the development of a substance disorder. At first the relaxing or euphoric effect (in either case, a pleasant one) of the drug attracts the individual and continues to motivate substance use. In time, growing tolerance of the substance causes the individual to take larger doses. Guilt feelings or external pressures from family or friends cause the individual to withdrawn from substance use. Withdrawal symptoms cause the individual to return in desperation to drug use. Initially, the individual seeks pleasure; later on, he or she seeks to avoid pain. These are antagonistic or opponent processes.

There are five generic types of psychoactive substances. They are alcohol, narcotics (derived from opium), sedatives (principally barbiturates), stimulants (principally cocaine and the amphetamines) and the hallucinogens, which include marijuana.

Alcohol. Twenty percent of men and 5 percent of women are alcoholics. The use of alcohol has increased from 68 percent of the population in 1970 to 86 percent today. Alcohol produces both physiological effects, principally affecting the liver and the brain, and psychological effects, mainly a dampening effect on the individual's inhibitions. Long-term use of alcohol causes malnutrition and severe psychiatric disorders, including Korsakoff's syndrome. Alcohol use by pregnant women is a principal cause of birth defects.

Alcoholism may be caused by genetic factors and personality traits such as low self-esteem, and seems to be related to such psychosocial factors as ethnicity, occupation, and social class level. Middle-income groups seem to be especially vulnerable.

Treatment is best undertaken in a residential center. There are three stages of such treatment. They are a drying-out period, a confrontational period, during which the individual is helped to recognize the problem, and a prolonged period of psychotherapy, in which the goal is to restructure the individual's personality. Self-help groups, such as Alcoholics Anonymous, play a prominent and helpful part in treating alcoholism.

The principal depressants are opium, morphine and heroin. Use of the depressants has decreased in recent years. Particularly affected by the sedatives are members of the middle socioeconomic class, for whom a barbiturate is initially prescribed, and doctors and medical workers, to whom the drug is readily available.

Stimulants. The principal stimulants are amphetamines and cocaine. Users are principally those who, for whatever reason, seek to find new sources of energy. Heavy doses cause major and dangerous physiological changes and psychological tension. Overdoses can cause suicide or assaultive behavior. Estimates indicate there are about six million cocaine users in this country, an increase of 260 percent since 1974.

The hallucinogens. Two well-known hallucinogens are lysergic acid and marijuana. The psychedelic drugs, principally mescaline, psilocybin (PCP) or angel dust are used by a relatively small portion of the drug-using population. These drugs cause varied and unusual sensory experiences and feelings of detachment and depersonalization.

Marijuana should be considered separately from the other hallucinogens. Its effects, although clearly harmful, are less extreme than other drug substances. Arguments pro and con for legalization of marijuana have been advanced for several years without resulting in legalization of its use.

There are two principal therapies for drug use. They are substitution therapy, principally the use of methadone for heroin use, and residential treatment centers. The first of these centers was Synanon House, since allowed to close down. Other widely known centers are Daytop Village, Phoenix House and Odyssey House.

Selected Readings

Critchlow, B. 1986. "The Powers of John Barleycorn: Beliefs About the Effects of Alcohol on Social Behavior." *American Psychologist*, 41: 746-751.

DeLeon, G. and S. Schwartz. 1984. "Therapeutic Communities: What are the Retention Rates?" *American Journal of Drug Abuse*, 10: 267-284.

Nowlan, R. and S. Cohen. 1977. "Tolerance to Marijuana: Heart Rate and Subjective 'High.'" *Clinical Pharmacology and Therapeutics*, 22: 123-132.

Peele, S. 1984. "The Cultural Context of Psychological Approaches to Alcohol. Can We Control the Effects of Alcohol?" *American Psychologist*, 39: 1337-1351.

Shener, M. A., Km. M. Kumor, E. J. Cone and S. Jaffe. 1988. "Suspiciousness Induced by Four-Hour Intravenous Infusions of Cocaine: Preliminary Findings." *Archives of General Psychiatry*, 45: 673-677.

Solomon, R. L. 1977. "An Opponent-Process Theory of Acquired Motivation: The Affective Dynamics of Addiction." in J. Maser and M. Seligman (Eds.). *Psychopathology: Experimental Models*. San Francisco, CA: Freeman.

Steel, C. M., L. Southwick and R. Pagano. 1986. "Drinking Your Troubles Away: The Role of Activity in Mediating Reduction of Psychological Stress." *Journal of Abnormal Psychology*, 95: 173-180.

15

Sexual Disorders

*P*sychosexual disorders react on the individual sufferer in one way that distinguishes them from most other psychological disorders. A common response of the individual, male or female, with a sexual disorder, are feelings of shame and guilt. While victims of most other disorders feel that they are sick, troubled or even abnormal in their behavior, they are not especially motivated to keep it secret, nor do they feel guilty, shamed or disgraced by it. Because the sexually disordered individual feels shamed by what should properly be recognized as an illness, to be treated as are other psychological disorders, he or she frequently keeps the ailment hidden. It is probable that until recent years, those feelings kept the individual from seeking treatment either because of shame and embarrassment or because the sufferer did not think it was something that was treatable.

Society's understanding of normal sexual behavior and deviations from it have been changing gradually, partially in response to two pioneering and courageous studies: one, the "Kinsey Report" on frequency of various forms of sexual behavior; the other, the Masters and Johnson studies of sexual disorders. Attitudes towards normal sexual behavior have broadened, and different ways of expressing sexual needs are given more understanding. Today, individuals troubled by sexual problems are increasingly seeking treatment for those problems.

The DSM IIIR categorizes sexual disorders into three groupings: psychosexual dysfunctions, in which inhibitions prevent or reduce the individual's enjoyment of normal sex and prevent or reduce the usual physiological changes brought on normally by sexual arousal; the paraphilias, in which the individual associates sexual release with objects or situations not part of normal sexual arousal behavior; and ego-dystonic *homosexuality, in which there is an absence of or significant weakness in heterosexual arousal and a long-term pattern of homosexual arousal, which is strongly stated as undesired by the individual and a source of psychic distress.*

After a brief description of normal sexual activity, the chapter describes the symptomatology of each subtype of the sexual disorders. Possible causes and therapies are described separately for each disorder. The chapter adds rape and incest to the disorders listed in the DSM IIIR. *The chapter also includes an examination of current perspectives on homosexuality.*

ASPECTS OF NORMAL SEXUAL ACTIVITY

In its most rudimentary aspects, sexual activity can satisfy two important and related (but not congruent) human needs: the procreation of children and the experiencing of a unique, sensory, physical, and emotional pleasure. As practiced by almost all human beings, the primary motivation for sexual activity is the pleasure it provides; only occasionally in the sexual lifetime of the individual is procreation the primary purpose of sexual activity. Both functions are important, one because of the unique pleasure one receives and is able to give a partner; the other because it fulfills a much-desired goal of family life and, in a less personal but more instinctive sense, because it continues the life of the species and maintains membership in particular social groups, principally those of religions and nations.

In that part of the world which is influenced by the Judeo-Christian traditions, normal sex, as prescribed in their religious writings and moral codes, is sex in which the goal is penile/vaginal intercourse (coitus). The partner, of course, is expected to be a member of the opposite sex. That standard for normal sex was also presented in the scholarly works of scientists in the field, principally Kraft-Ebbing and Havelock Ellis, but also emphasized by Freud. And although there are endless variations in the ways in which coitus is approached, that form of sexual activity prevails in societies that wish to survive.

We know from the Kinsey Report of 1948 that substantial fractions of a normal population occasionally engage in sexual activities other than penile/vaginal intercourse, some of which lead to orgasm. In its most recent version, the American Psychiatric Association's *Diagnostic and Statistical Manual* (1987) stopped listing homosexual (same-sex sexual activity) as a sexual disorder. A safe conclusion to reach is that normal individuals find sexual pleasure in a great variety of ways not conforming to the limited definition prescribed in traditional religious writings and not conforming to the Freudian dictum or the writings of earlier scholars.

CLASSIFICATION OF SEXUAL DISORDERS

The *DSM IIIR* lists two principal categories of sexual disorder: sexual dysfunction, inability to participate fully and enjoyably in coitus; and the paraphilias, in which sexual arousal is stimulated by unusual objects, situations or behavior. Most textbooks in the field add to those two, gender identity disorders and such extreme sexual behavior as rape or incest. The *DSM IIIR* lists four sexual dysfunctions and eight paraphilias. These are discussed separately in the chapter.

SEXUAL DYSFUNCTIONS

The sexual dysfunctions are grouped into three broad categories according to the phase of the sexual cycle in which they occur. They are disorders of the desire phase, of the arousal phase, and of the orgasm phase. Sexual pain disorders of male and female are grouped separately.

Disorders of the Desire Phase

There are two levels of this disorder: hypoactive desire and aversion to sex.

HYPOACTIVE DESIRE

Here, the dysfunction is a disinterest in sex. In its milder form, the diagnostic term "hypoactive desire" is used and means simply lack of interest in sex. Since desire for sexual intercourse is so variable a characteristic, problems sometimes develop between spouses who differ in their desire for sex. It would not be accurate to dismiss a mate as having a sexual disorder simply because he or she desired sex three times a week and not seven.

The sexual disorder hypoactive desire refers to a complete or almost complete lack of interest in sex, resulting; for example, in routine or uninvolved participation in sexual intercourse simply because it is a marital duty. Here, too, a too-quick diagnosis may be out of order, since the fault might lie in the technique of the individual's sexual partner.

AVERSION TO SEX

Hypoactive sex desire must be differentiated from aversion to sex, in which sexual approaches or imposed sexual activity causes repulsion and apprehension. Aversion to sex most frequently is the result of earlier traumatic sexual experiences, such as childhood molestation, incest or rape.

Disorders of the Arousal Phase

Sexual desire normally leads to specific physiological changes preparing the individual for sexual intercourse. In the male, the penis fills with blood and becomes enlarged and erectile. In the female, an increased flow of blood causes the woman's genitals to swell; in addition, the walls of the vagina secrete a lubricating fluid. When those changes do not occur or occur weakly, the disorder, in males, is erectile disorder; and in females, female sexual arousal disorder.

Disorders of the Orgasm Phase

The peak of sexual activity toward which normal sexual behavior leads is orgasm. At this point, rhythmic contractions of the muscles in the genital region occur, accompanied by heightened sexual excitement. The male orgasm disorder is premature ejaculation, too early for his partner to have achieved her orgasm. A delay or absence of orgasm in women is diagnosed as inhibited female orgasm.

Sexual Pain Disorders

There are two sexual pain disorders. One is dyspareunia, in which pain occurs during intercourse. It is predominantly a female complaint, although it occasionally occurs in men. The second, vaginismus, is exclusively a female disorder. The symptoms are involuntary spasmodic muscle contractions at the entrance to the vagina when an attempt is made to insert the penis into it. Ordinarily, the result is an inability to proceed with intercourse. If the attempt is made to persist with intercourse, a painful sexual experience results.

Special Factors in Understanding Sexual Dysfunction

The diagnosis of sexual dysfunction is made only when the disability persists. Such dysfunctions can occur occasionally in all sexual relationships. Fatigue, worry, sickness or alcohol or drugs may interfere in any phase of the sexual relationship. Inexperience in sexual relations may cause anxieties and concern about performing well, with a resulting failure in performance or desire. An embarrassing failure in sex may cause a lingering effect on subsequent sexual attempts.

In diagnosing sexual dysfunction, the *DSM IIIR* distinguishes between lifelong dysfunction and acquired dysfunction; different etiological factors produce the two types of dysfunction. It also distinguishes between dysfunction in all sexual situations and situational dysfunction. Examples of the latter are these: a man may successfully masturbate to ejaculation but not be able to ejaculate in sexual intercourse; or one partner in a marriage may experience orgasm only in an extramarital affair.

Sexual dysfunction is often diagnosed in both members of a marriage; particularly frequent in marriages are premature ejaculation by the husband and orgastic dysfunction in the wife. The cause-and-effect relationship in that relationship is easy to understand.

Causative Factors in Sexual Dysfunction

Sexual desire and sexual functioning may be influenced by both psychosocial and physical factors.

PSYCHOSOCIAL INFLUENCES ON SEXUAL DYSFUNCTION

A variety of psychosocial influences can cause sexual dysfunction: faulty learning, negative emotional feelings related to sex, faulty interpersonal relationships between partners, early-life sexually traumatic experiences, egotistically oriented attitudes toward sexual relations by one of the partners, and, finally, such a "remote cause" as failure to resolve the Oedipal or Electra complex.

Faulty Learning. Behavioral theorists, in particular (but most other clinicians join them), focus on the importance of early respondent conditioning, in which sexual events are associated with negative emotional experiences of shame, fearfulness, feelings of inadequacy or expectations of failure. Those feelings cause the individual to approach sex tentatively, uncertain about performance. Masters and Johnson state that these feelings cause the individual to adopt a "spectator role" in sexual relations. The individual, on guard, instead of relaxing and enjoying the sexual experience, is more concerned about whether or not performance is adequate. That very concern interferes with the adequacy and enjoyment of the performance.

Negative emotions producing that effect may have been picked up from parents, from other misguided elders, or from punishments administered following early childhood sexual play. Concern about sexual performance may also result from lack of knowledge or experience. Here, especially, the individual is likely to assume the spectator role. An early failure because of that behavior may increase the concern and make it impossible later to enjoy sex fully.

Relationship Problems. Absence of love, closeness, respect, of feelings of admiration for the physical being of the other person in a marital or other relationship, can cause any one of the sexual dysfunctions, at least in that relationship. Dysfunction can develop in a relationship that has previously been satisfying when strong disagreement about other issues becomes heated. Couples may fight over financial matters, ways of raising children, jealousy or the existence of an extramarital affair on the part of one of the couple. The result can be a sexual dysfunction in one or both partners.

The negative feelings toward the other person in other areas of life soon overshadows the desirability of sex and impairs sexual performance. Once such failures occur, their very existence threatens future sexual relationships, and the dysfunctional behavior sets in and becomes a longtime pattern.

Early Parent/Child Relations. Helen Kaplan, in her 1974 publication, *The New Sex Therapy,* has set out a widely accepted view of the causes of sexual dysfunction. She regards sexual dysfunction as the result of immediate causes and remote causes. She identifies the immediate causes as performance anxiety, overconcern about pleasing one's partner, poor technique on the part of either person, lack of communication between partners about what is pleasing in sex, and marital conflict. The remote causes she names are infantile needs, deeply rooted guilt, and, especially, fixations in childhood psychosexual development. Those intrapsychic conflicts stem mainly from unsatisfactory early childhood relationships and are similar to patterns which those of the psychodynamic perspective consider as causes of other psychological disorders. They may be said to create a vulnerability to sexual dysfunction which is then triggered by one of the immediate causes.

PHYSICAL CAUSES OF SEXUAL DYSFUNCTION

Nonpsychic causes of sexual dysfunction fall into two categories: external substance absorbed into the body's chemistry and hormonal imbalances. The former, for the most part, cause only transitory dysfunction; the latter, most probably, are predisposing in their effect but not, in themselves, causative.

External Substances. Heavy drinking before sexual activity impairs sexual performance. Certain hypertensive medications sometimes limit sexual desire and performance. And drugs that suppress levels of testosterone, such as barbiturates and narcotics, decrease sexual desire in males. In addition to such external elements, certain medical conditions (for example, a heart condition) will reduce sexual drive because of the debility they cause.

Hormonal Influences. Abnormal distribution of male and female hormones may cause a vulnerability to sexual dysfunction in affected individuals. There is no strong evidence that this condition alone produces the dysfunctions.

Treatment of Sexual Dysfunctions

Masters and Johnson and, some time later, Helen Kaplan, have been leaders in developing treatment techniques reported to show a high degree of success, at the 80 to 90 percent level in some reports. Also significant about sex therapy is the fact that so many more of those who suffer from the disorder are now seeking treatment. And beyond that, other scientists in the field continue to develop new approaches to therapy.

THE MASTERS AND JOHNSON PROGRAM

Following a comprehensive study of sexual dysfunctions, Masters and Johnson developed their program of direct sex therapy. It differs in three principal ways from earlier efforts at treating the problem. First, it avoided the approach taken principally by psychoanalysts and other clinicians with a psychodynamic perspective who would consider first deeper problems ordinarily associated with other psychological disorders. The sexual dysfunction was considered a symptom of the diagnosed disorder and was treated as such by probing into background factors.

Masters and Johnson offered a simpler explanation: The individual has, for example, inhibitions of sexual arousal, which should be treated by eliminating the reasons for the inhibitions.

Second, Masters and Johnson treated couples, not individuals, on the premise that sex is a cooperative and interactive process. They felt there existed the possibility that either individual could enable sexual fulfillment or block it.

Third, they believe that couples should be encouraged to practice sex in ways that remove anxiety and apprehension. Graded exercises were recommended to lead the couple from simple touching and caressing, with no expectation of intercourse or orgasm, eventually to the culmination of a mutually satisfying sexual experience. The pace of advancement in the exercises is set by the couple's progress in finding enjoyment in what they are doing. Enjoyment at an early level of sexual enjoyment leads to taking each next step. In treating premature ejaculation, for example, the woman is encouraged to stimulate the penis but to stop just before the moment of ejaculation. In this way, through desensitization to sexual stimulation, the male will learn to delay ejaculation to accommodate the pace of his partner.

A major postulate of the Masters and Johnson therapeutic approach is that anxiety blocks sexual excitement and performance by interfering with the preliminary physiological changes that normally precede sexual enjoyment. These are, in the female, vaginal enlargement and lubrication and, in the male, erection. Without those changes, coitus is neither possible nor enjoyable. Clients are encouraged to avoid being spectators of their own sexual activity and to focus on the sensual pleasures of the graded sexual exercises in which they are engaged.

SENSATE FOCUS IN TREATMENT

Clients are taught that there are three stages in what therapists call "sensate focus": giving pleasure, achieved principally through stroking and caressing the body; tender, genital stimulation; and finally, nondemanding intercourse; that is, intercourse that is enjoyed with no other demands from one's partner.

Taking each treatment exercise one step at a time desensitizes the individual and gradually lifts the oppressive anxiety, making pleasure in coitus possible.

Masters and Johnson originally reported very high rates of success. In recent years, these reports have been challenged; nevertheless, their theories and therapeutic practices have led the way to sensible attitudes toward sexual dysfunction and ready access to treatment for the disorder.

THE PARAPHILIAS

In earlier editions of the *DSM IIIR,* the label "sexual deviations" was used to describe what are now called the paraphilias. The authors of the manual now prefer to use the Greek roots, *para,* meaning beyond or to the side of, and *philia,* meaning preferred, as more descriptive of the disorder and less pejorative. The *DSM IIIR* describes the paraphilias as sexual disorders in which unusual or bizarre objects or acts are required for sexual excitement. It sorts the paraphilias into three types of behavior: 1. those in which there exists a preference for nonhuman objects for sexual arousal; for example, shoes; 2. repetitive sexual activity with human beings involving real or simulated suffering and humiliation; and 3. repetitive sexual activity with nonconsenting partners. (See chapter 21 for a listing.) This section describes symptomatology, cause and treatment of all the paraphilias except frotteurism (seeking sexual pleasure by rubbing against someone else's body; what might be called, "the subway syndrome"), about which too little is known.

Types of Paraphilias

The paraphilias include a group of psychological disorders that range widely in their impact on other people. The spectrum extends from those that affect only the suffering individual, or that individual and his or her partner, to those that threaten the well-being of other unrelated individuals. In all, the *DSM IIIR* recognizes eight paraphilias, which are grouped into three broad categories, as described below.

SEXUAL AROUSAL AND PREFERENCES FOR NONHUMAN OBJECTS

There are two: fetishism and transvestism.

Fetishism. A fetish exists when a person is aroused by a nonliving object. Fetishes may be manifest in one of two ways, one more seriously disordered than the other. One form of fetish is associating coitus with some object, most frequently women's panties or other undergarments. Here the individual, usually a male, seeks to intensify sexual urges by preceding coitus by talking about or holding and fondling the object; for example, a pair of silk panties. It is relatively harmless if the action is taken playfully and is acceptable to his partner. If, on the other hand, the man persists even when the sexual partner objects to or resents the use of the object as a substitute for herself, the fetish must be considered a disorder and harmful, at least in its effect on the individual's partner.

Focusing on the parts of the female body (hair, toes or ears, for example), except as part of the pleasurable foreplay, can become fetishistic in its hold on the individual.

...ore ...eme form of fetishism is one in which an inanimate object completely substitutes for a human partner. The most common articles used in such fetishes are female underwear, boots and shoes, and such textured objects as rubber, silk or velvet. Here, ejaculation is achieved when the individual is alone, fondling the cherished article. Fetishism can cause trouble with the law when it leads to shoplifting special articles, which it occasionally does. Such activity—that is, the shoplifting—seems to cause sexual excitement in the individual.

Transvestism. This paraphilia exists when sexual excitement is achieved by cross-dressing; for example, a male dressing as a female. Two quite different purposes seem to be served in different individuals by transvestism. In one, the individual seeks to intensify sexual excitement in coitus with a partner by partially dressing as a woman. In the other form of transvestism, in which the male, for example, moves about in the full regalia of a woman, the disorder suggests some type of gender identity problem but not necessarily homosexuality. Transvestites usually report less frequent homosexual urges than do average American males.

The transvestite describes his problem as one in which he is both a "he" person and a "she" person, with the she person gaining expression only through cross-dressing. Transvestism is ordinarily kept secret from others, so there is little known about its prevalence. Estimates suggest that it occurs in 1 percent of the male population. It is extremely rare among females.

Causal Factors in Fetishes. Much has yet to be learned about the causes of fetishism and transvestism. Etiological factors in fetishism probably operate at two levels. Primarily existing is a set of early life experiences leading to maladjustment, lowered self-esteem and feelings of inadequacy, especially in sexual roles. A fetishistic direction is usually given to expressions of that psychic disturbance by some triggering experience. That is often a conditioning event in which orgasm has been stimulated, sometimes accidentally, by strong emotional reactions to some inanimate object. More often, the fetish is traceable to the use of some object, such as female underwear, to increase sexual intensity in early masturbatory activities. Since much masturbation is performed with some stimulating object— a sex picture, a garment, perhaps a perfume bottle—and relatively few males seem to develop a fetish from that activity, the suggestion is present that some underlying psychopathology might exist in the background of individuals who develop such fetishes.

Causal Factors in Transvestism. Causative factors in transvestism are quite different from those described above for fetishes. Extensive studies indicate that transvestites are frequently married men who have children. Psychological testing of transvestites indicates that they show no more evidence of psychiatric disorder than would be found in the general population. Their problem is more likely to be marital conflict and divorce because of a spouse's objection to marriage to someone who dresses up like a woman.

Transvestites do frequently have an early history of being dressed up like a girl in early boyhood by unwise mothers, and perhaps by emotionally overinvolved female relatives. Such happenings suggest either the absence of a father with whom the boy can identify or, if a father is present, that he must be either very weak or not very interested in his son's upbringing. Childhood cross-dressing that meets the approval of a mother or other well-regarded relative brings operant conditioning into the picture, that is, rewarding and thereby reinforcing the wearing of female dress. Given certain patterns of reinforcement, such behavior would be difficult to overcome.

SEXUAL AROUSAL AND PREFERENCES FOR SITUATIONS CAUSING SUFFERING

There are two such disorders: sadism and masochism. They are complimentary in nature: what the sadist needs to inflict, the masochist needs to receive. They are best discussed together.

Sadism and Masochism: Symptomatology. Although sexual activity fundamentally is, or should be, a loving and tender activity, there appears to be an element of aggressiveness in much sexual activity among normal individuals. Some who are neither sadist nor masochist have sexual fantasies about suffering or humiliation in sex. Kinsey found that about 20 percent of his male sample and 12 percent of his female sample reported sexual arousal on hearing stories about rape, bondage, chains, whips and imposed hardships.

Two points need to be raised here: 1. Kinsey's sample was a group of individuals who volunteered to be interviewed about their sex lives. It may be assumed that their attitude toward sex would be freer than those individuals who would not volunteer; and 2. Of more significance is the apparent absence of any need, prior to sexual arousal, for such fantasies. The sadist or masochist finds essential to his or her sexual arousal either inflicting suffering or receiving pain or humiliation.

The terms *sadist* and *masochist* apply correctly only to suffering associated with sexual arousal. The terms are often used much more loosely to describe socially punitive individuals or long-suffering martyrs. The behavior of neither type of individual comes at all close to that of the disorders. The terms, as psychological disorders, refer to the repeated and intentional infliction on another person of suffering (sometimes a nonconsenting person) in association with sexual arousal; or, for masochism, it requires that an individual ask for the infliction of pain or humiliation in order to be aroused sexually.

The terms are derived from the reported sexual ex[...] de Sade (1740–1814) and the writing of Leopold [...] (c.1831), whose male characters sought out women wh[...]

Sadists may seek relationships promiscuously wit[...] who have masochistic needs; masochists often relate to pr[...]utes who encourage or accept a masochistic clientele. But stable coupling of sadists and masochists also takes place in heterosexual and homosexual life. In certain areas of this country, where such demand exists, shops provide suitable equipment, and there are publications that run classified ads that openly suggest invitations for sadomasochistic activities.

Among sadists, there exists the possibility that, over time, the individual will need to inflict increasingly more pain and suffering, occasionally the final result of which is torture, rape and murder. Masochists may also need to increase their suffering, with the possibility that their relationship will lead to their own injury or murder. The course of the disorder is chronic and may continue to exist throughout the sexual lifetime of the individual, either promiscuously or in a stable relationship. The *DSM IIIR* provides no prevalency statistics for either disorder.

Causative Factors in Sadomasochism. Sadism and masochism will be considered separately here.

Sadism. The causes of sadism are similar in pattern to the causes of fetishes. Strong emotions of any sort can trigger involuntary feelings of sexual arousal. When there is early association of such emotional feelings in response to someone inflicting pain or even torturing an animal, and when the experience is a vivid, even a haunting one, the result may be a relatively stable linking of inflicting pain with sexual arousal. It would nevertheless seem unlikely that one such experience would have so drastic and lasting an effect without more basic psychopathology being present.

Sadism may also be caused in a prudish, narrowly restricted personality with negative attitudes toward sex, perhaps developed on a religious basis. Here the sadism may be seen as a warped, perhaps even bizarre, attempt to punish the woman who is permitting or even enjoying sex. One can speculate that the occasional individual who makes the headlines for murdering a number of prostitutes is manifesting that kind of motivation.

Masochism. Masochism would seem to be triggered by an early life experience of extreme pain (with strong emotion) which, in some, perhaps accidental way, is associated with a satisfying sexual event. The literature, for example, reports in the history of a masochistic individual this experience: A boy having a bone painfully set without an anesthetic becomes aware of a nurse in attendance caressing him and holding him close to her breast in a consoling way. For the boy, the experience produced a sexual reaction immediately following severe pain. The case report suggests that the experience also later provoked a sadistic response. Again, one feels compelled to believe that there must have been some predisposing personality traits to cause even so powerful an experience to have so lasting an effect.

SEXUAL AROUSAL AND PREFERENCE FOR NONCONSENTING PARTNERS

This category of paraphilia includes exhibitionism, voyeurism and pedophilia (child molesting). All three are considered crimes in this country, and all three are almost exclusively male crimes, although occasionally a female is arrested for voyeurism.

Exhibitionism. Indecent exposure is the most common sexual offense leading to arrest. It accounts for one-third of all sexual crimes. Oddly and inexplicably, it appears only in Western society and is totally absent in such countries as Japan, Burma and India. Another anomalous feature of exhibitionism is that, in American society, it can be a crime only when committed by a male. When women exhibit themselves, excluding total nudity, they are seen as victims of male voyeurs.

As a crime, exhibitionism is exposure of one's genital organs in a public place. From a psychological point of view, it should be noted that there is a pattern, almost standardized way, in which males exhibit themselves. There are three characteristic features of the exhibition: 1. it is always performed for unknown women; 2. it always takes place where sexual intercourse is impossible; for example, in a crowded shopping center; and 3. it seems designed to surprise and shock the woman. There are reports that when a woman shows no reaction, the act lacks the power to produce sexual arousal in the individual.

Favored settings for exhibitionistic activities are outside of churches and schools, in shopping centers, in the dark of a movie theatre, in the middle of the relative seclusion of a park, or any place where the individual can find victims likely to be shocked and where there are no supervising police officers. The exhibitionist usually exhibits an erectile penis, but that does not seem to be an essential for the activity. Ejaculation may occur at the moment of exposure or develop later with masturbatory stimulation.

Exhibitionists are not assaultive and are considered to be more of a nuisance than a danger.

Voyeurism. A relatively common, apparently normal activity, is that of looking at sexually arousing pictures or situations. Today's off-mainstream marketplace is full of opportunities to do so. One television channel features erotic films, and "adult" videotapes are readily available. Bars with "erotic" dancing are not far from many neighborhoods, and there are magazines featuring naked and erotically posed women and men.

The difference between those activities and voyeurism lies in the function served by the viewing. In normal watching, the viewing is ordinarily a prelude to more usual sexual activities. Some married couples view erotic films both to learn and to increase the intensity of their sexual activities. For the voyeur, the "Peeping Tom" experience replaces normal sexual activity. Nevertheless, voyeurism may exist in a person who also engages in normal heterosexual activity. One report states that 30 to 50 percent of voyeurs are married, with no more marital conflict or more frequent divorces than exist in the general population.

For whatever reason, voyeurs are more likely to have a juvenile history of minor offenses. "Peeping Tom" behavior requires somewhat the same kind of covert climbing as does burglary; and although it may be stretching a point, looking through a window into an apartment is a kind of vicarious "breaking and entering" for sexual robbery.

Pedophilia. This paraphilia, because of its damaging impact on the nonconsenting partner, a child, is radically different from exhibitionism and voyeurism, and the strongly condemnatory attitude of the public reflects their concern about the hurtful effects on the child.

Pedophilia is the act of fondling a child sexually or attempting intercourse with one. Contrary to a common view, pedophilics do not skulk about waiting to pounce on an unaccompanied and helpless child, nor is assaultive behavior an important part of the problem. Violence occurs in no more than 3 percent of pedophilic activities; some coercion or force is nevertheless used in more than 15 percent of the cases.

Ordinarily, the pedophilic, usually in his thirties, is someone who has ready access to the child; he may be a close male relative, a teacher, a recreational leader, occasionally a clergyman. The child or parent would have no reason to suspect the possibility of a pedophilic orientation.

The pedophilic activity itself may begin with the individual exposing himself to the child or alternately taking the child on his lap. Occasionally it involves picture-taking of naked or posing children. Several children at a time may be involved. Some plausible explanation may be given to the child, who may be unsuspecting or very frightened. Sexual aspects include fondling the child's private parts or having the child fondle the man's penis. Coercive aspects come into play when they are used to pledge the child or children to secrecy.

Causative Aspects of Paraphilia with Nonconsenting Partners. A common psychological characteristic shared by personalities who become exhibitionists, voyeurs or pedophilics is social isolation, low self-esteem and, particularly, feelings of sexual inadequacy. Not psychologically at ease in usual heterosexual relationships, or not willing to risk the rejection of their attempts to create more mature relationships, paraphiliacs resort to abnormal sexual activity. There is emotional immaturity, and one can also suspect the remote causes specified by Kaplan; that is, more deep-seated personality conflicts and frustrations from which relief is sought.

Theoretical Perspectives on the Paraphilias

Two conflicting perspectives on the paraphilias, both of importance in abnormal psychology, offer interpretations of the paraphilias: one drawn from the psychodynamic perspective, the other from behavioral theory.

THE PSYCHODYNAMIC INTERPRETATION

In Freudian theory, during the phases of psychosexual development, fixations rooted at one level of sexual adjustment prevent normal progress to the next stage of development. In the process of fixation, object-cathexes (attachments) are formed in which strong, positive or negative feelings are attached to objects that are otherwise neutral. The selected object is charged with psychic energy. In the case of a positive cathexis, sexual feelings become attached to the object. Fetishes can result from such early positive attachments. When the cathexis is negative, fears develop, as in phobias. The explanation can less elegantly be used to understand the other paraphilias. A problem with the explanation is that one has to go back into the psychodynamic forces leading to fixations and cathexes and then ask, even given these maladaptive developments, why are particular objects or activities selected to be connected with sexual activity? Any attempt to answer that question comes close to the behavioral explanations.

BEHAVIORAL INTERPRETATIONS

The basic behavioral interpretation is that sexual arousal has been linked with some unusual object or some activity such as watching (for voyeurs) or exposure in exhibitionism through either a Pavlovian-type conditioning process or operant conditioning. Pavlovian conditioning seems to fit the fetishist better. A stimulus (for example, a shoe) is associated with the strongly emotional response of sexual arousal.

But for paraphilias that cause the individual to carry out some extreme action to arouse sexual feelings (exhibitionism, for example), the formula may be that of operant conditioning; a response—for example, exhibiting oneself—is reinforced by the pleasure of the resultant sexual activity. When those conditioning events occur in the early life of an individual who, for other reasons, is dominated by feelings of inadequacy and low self-esteem, which limit social life and tend to isolate the individual, a paraphilia readily develops.

Completely convincing psychological evidence has not yet developed to support fully the hypothesis of either psychodynamic or behavioral interpretations. Perhaps the answer will come as we discover which treatment is more successful.

Treatment of the Paraphilias

Some successful treatment results are reported for behavioral therapeutic approaches, but also many failures. The paraphilias do not respond readily to treatment. When it has been successful, treatment has most often involved some form of aversion therapy; that is, pairing the paraphilic object or activity with either an actual aversive consequence, such as electric shock or a nausea-producing agent; or, in covert sensitization, pairing the object with vividly imagined aversive consequences.

Case reports of successful psychodynamic treatment of paraphilias occasionally appear in psychoanalytic journals, but they are infrequent and are more anecdotal than research-oriented.

SEXUAL IDENTITY DISORDER

A sexual identity disorder exists when individuals, male or female, experience confusion, vagueness or conflict in their feelings about their own sexual identity. There is a sharp struggle between the individual's anatomical sex gender and subjective feelings about choosing a masculine or feminine style of living.

Elements in Sexual Identity

In understanding this disorder, it is helpful to distinguish among the terms *gender identity*, *gender role*, and *sexual partner choice*.

GENDER IDENTITY

Awareness of being male or female, of knowing "I am a girl (or woman, or boy, or man)," is called gender identity by psychologists. Children can distinguish maleness and femaleness by the age of two. Between their second and third birthdays, they will, when asked, readily identify themselves as girl or boy.

SEXUAL ROLE

Reminiscent of Shakespeare's, "All the world's a stage..." role is the public living of a part. Between their third and fourth birthdays, children can identify a variety of gender differences and have learned that boys and girls behave in somewhat different ways. They begin to assume a male or female sexual role.

SEXUAL OBJECT CHOICE

This aspect of gender relates to what will arouse sexual feeling in the individual: the types of people, the part of the body, and the specific situations to which the individual will respond sexually. It is not until a child completes the pubescent process at age fifteen or so that sexual-object choice becomes definite.

Influences Affecting Gender Identity

Both psychosocial and biological factors affect gender identity.

PSYCHOSOCIAL INFLUENCES

Etiological answers are by no means certain; some psychologists call them speculative. Nevertheless, psychologists tend to believe that for most individuals with gender identity problems, two elements of growing up are influential in shaping gender identity, sexual role, and sexual-object choice: 1. how parents relate to the child; that is, do they treat the child as a girl or as a boy? and, 2. the emotional relationship between the child and the same-sex parent.

Parental Behavior. With a young boy, for example, if parents allow his hair to remain long with a feminine coiffure, frequently dress him in girl's clothing, or allow him to wear such clothing long after infancy, that behavior will cause confusion in the child's feelings about his proper sexual role. Often collateral members of the family take a leading role in inducing such reactions. A favored aunt, often unmarried, may spend special time with the little boy, applying cosmetics and dressing him up in mother's dresses and high-heeled shoes. The problem here is not necessarily that the boy will become homosexual, but that he will develop effeminate mannerisms in assuming his sexual role and become uncertain as to whether he is really, at heart, a girl. With girls, fathers can encourage tomboy behavior and skill in principally male activities, leaving the girl with mixed feelings about sexual identity and masculine ways of behaving.

Same-Sex Relationships. The boy's relationship with his father (or the girl's relationship with her mother) holds even greater significance in the formation of sexual identity. If the father is domineering or hostile to the boy, or remote and indifferent, the boy moves away from male identification. In the process, he moves closer to his mother and often takes on her feminine mannerisms. In the average, normal family, a more usual and natural process of bonding between father and son takes place, in which the son, often unconsciously, identifies with the father and internalizes (takes into his personality as his own) paternal values and ways of behaving. He becomes a man and knows with certainty that he is a man. The same process will usually take place between daughter and mother, with comparable results.

BIOLOGICAL INFLUENCES ON GENDER DISORDER

Biological factors operating during the fetal stage can cause the malformation of genital organs so that, in appearance and function, they are neither fully male nor fully female. The result is an individual who has been scientifically labeled as a pseudohermaphrodite. The condition principally affects females.

During the fetal stages, the mother's body surrounds the embryo with a fluid of mixed hormones. Those hormones promote development and differentiation of parts of the embryo's body. When the fluid is overly rich in androgens, the male hormone, it makes an hermaphroditic child of a female embryo. In the most thorough study of embryos born after such an embryonic occurrence, the researchers report that when compared with matching normals, the hermaphrodites expressed more dissatisfaction with the female role and behaved in ways more typically masculine than feminine.

VARIATIONS IN GENDER DISORDERS

Before focusing on the more extreme forms of gender identity disorder, transsexualism, two milder manifestations of the disorder need be mentioned.

Transitory Cross-Sex Behavior in Young Children. There are children who, before the age of four, will show cross-sexual behavior; for example, boys who exhibit softness in emotion, gentleness in play, enjoyment of dolls as toys. Most often, with no other efforts at change, psychosocial pressures, especially those with playmates outside the home, will cause that type of behavior to taper off, with no carryover into later life.

Problems of Gender Identification in Adults. Research suggests a correlation between strong gender identification in men and women with effective functioning leading to success. Successful men are likely to be fully identified with maleness; successful woman are fully identified with femaleness.

On the other hand, many individuals with weak gender identification and the resultant confusion and vagueness about sexual-role behavior find successful functioning in a career difficult. Their psychic energies seem to be invested elsewhere.

TRANSSEXUALISM

In this most extreme form of gender identity disorder, the individual, if a male, feels he is a woman trapped in a male body and wishes to change his genitals, become a woman, and behave like a woman. If the individual is a woman, she likewise feels trapped and unreal as a woman and would like to develop a penis and become a man. Their anatomical gender at birth has fit them with a set of genitals that disgusts them. Those feelings are accompanied by depression and suicidal thoughts. Transsexualism is a totally disheartening illness, bringing the individual close to desperation.

Nevertheless, many such troubled people settle for deceptively living life as a member of the opposite sex. Until the 1950s, for the most part, they had little other choice.

In 1953, the sex-change operation of Christine Jorgensen was publicized extensively. Since then, by 1977, some 2,500 individuals with transsexual problems have undergone similar sex-change procedures. In the male operation, hormonal injections stimulate breast development and inhibit beard growth. Surgery removes the penis and testicles and constructs a partial vagina.

In the female, hormones affect vocal changes and stimulate beard growth. A nonfunctioning penis is constructed from other parts of the body. Despite some research reports of satisfaction among those undergoing the change, the Johns Hopkins University Gender Identity clinic, which performed some of the earlier sex-change operations, ended its operations with the statement that, "Sex reassignment confers no advantage in terms of social rehabilitation." A number of research reports suggest that most sex-changed transsexuals live unfulfilled social and sexual lives, most often separated from their families and having poor relationships with others.

HOMOSEXUALITY

Here we consider first social attitudes and public policy, then the current status of homosexuality in the *DSM IIIR*, characteristics of homosexual and lesbian behavior, and, finally, explanations for homosexual behavior and problems of treatment.

Social Attitudes and Public Policy

Social attitudes toward homosexuality vary widely across time and place or culture. Homosexuality has been practiced throughout time immemorial. The Old Testament suggests its early existence by condemning it in Sodom and Gomorrah. On the other hand, Greek, Roman, Moslem and Persian civilizations all condoned it if practiced in discreet fashion; that is, not between two members of the upper classes. A number of eminent historical figures have been homosexual or lesbian, including Alexander the Great, Sappho, Michaelangelo, Oscar Wilde (who was imprisoned for it), Gertrude Stein and Virginia Wolfe.

Attitudes in Western societies vary from country to country. The British in modern times seem more tolerant. Scandinavian countries disapprove strongly. In America, a large majority of the population condemns it strongly. A 1974 survey reports that 70 percent of Americans believed that homosexuals are "sexually abnormal." In that survey, 50 percent said they believed homosexuals are perverts, and 40 percent said that they are mentally ill. Nevertheless, following the civil rights revolution of the mid-twentieth century, homosexuals in an increasing number of jurisdictions, along with other minority groups, are finding their civil rights, particularly in employment, protected by law. The military services, however, do not accept known homosexuals.

The DSM IIIR *and Homosexuality*

Two forms of homosexuality may be distinguished. One, labeled ego-syntonic homosexuality, is a sexual adjustment in which individuals, men or women, are content with their sexual orientation and have no desire to change it. Abnormal Psychology textbooks in the past have listed that form of homosexual as a paraphilia. The American Psychiatric Association, in preparing its most recent classification, removed it from its listing of disorders in the *DSM IIIR*. That manual continues to list the second form of homosexuality, ego-dystonic homosexuality, in which the individual is distressed about having a homosexual orientation and would like to change it. It now lists ego-dystonic homosexuality as Psychosexual Disorder Not Otherwise Specified.

The APA's reasons for delisting ego-syntonic homosexuality are the absence of personal discomfort about homosexual behavior, the absence of other psychopathology, and the apparently good level of personal adjustment of most ego-syntonic homosexuals.

One opinion among some psychiatrists is that treatment should not be offered to ego-dystonic homosexuals because now, under the revised classification system, they suffer no psychiatrically recognized disorder. Most psychologists, however, consider the personal discomfort of such individuals as sufficient basis for compassionately and ethically offering those individuals treatment when they request it.

Types of Homosexuality

Homosexuality may be divided into two broad categories: male homosexuality and lesbianism. It is inaccurate to consider the two alike in either the form of the relationship or in the needs which the behavior fulfills. Lesbians place much more emphasis on emotional support and similarity of values. The consequence is that they put less emphasis on overt sexual activities than do male homosexuals.

Prevalence

Prevalency estimates suggest that male homosexuality is much more common than lesbianism. In terms of known lesbian relationships, larger numbers are now being reported than previously. This may simply be an effect of a change in social attitudes toward self-sex orientation, with more lesbians admitting to that sexual orientation.

Those males who engage in homosexual activities cannot all be grouped together. They vary widely in the nature of their sexual activities. Kinsey's 1948 study was the first extensive report on the range of homosexual activities. The figures are for males. His study indicates that only 4 percent of his male population were exclusively homosexual as adults; eighteen percent were bisexual; and 37 percent had at least one homosexual experience as adults. What is important about these figures is not the percentages, but the range of the differences among those who engage in any form of homosexuality. No comparable figures are available for women.

One extrapolation from Kinsey's figures suggests that, if accurate and representative, there would be 2.6 million men and 1.4 million women who are exclusively (or principally) homosexual. A figure for the combined male and female population who have a long, but not exclusively self-sex, history of homosexual activities is estimated to be 25 million, a sizeable fraction of the nation's adult population.

Homosexual Life-Style

There are two facets of life-style that are of psychological interest: relationships with sexual mates and form of sexual activity.

RELATIONSHIPS WITH SEXUAL MATES

In a 1978 study, Bell and Weinberg identified five styles of homosexual living among both homosexuals and lesbians. An attitude that seems to lie at the basis of their classification system is that the closer the individual comes to a stable, two-person relationship, the closer to normality is the relationship. The distribution of the five life-styles is as follows: Twenty-eight percent of lesbians and 10 percent of male homosexuals lived in closed-couple relationships and were content with that homosexual adjustment; 18 percent of males and 17 percent of females were open couples and lived with a primary mate but participated in outside sexual relationships.

So-called functionals remained single with no commitment. Their attachment seemed to be to the gay world and the cause of homosexuality. The sexual breakdown for this group was 15 percent for men and 10 percent for women. The possibility of contracting AIDS has significantly complicated sex life and choice for that group.

The researchers reported that 12 percent of males and 5 percent of females reported a dystonic aspect to their homosexuality. They had no settled relationships, regretted their homosexuality, and described other adjustment problems. However, an oddity of the study was that it could not categorize 29 percent of the research population.

Homosexuals and lesbians cannot be known by their physical appearance. They look like other men and women; some are strong and muscular, and others are not; lesbians do not characteristically look masculine. Among both males and females, some are striking in appearance and others very average.

The change in attitudes and public policy now make it easier for homosexuals, to use a colloquialism, "to come out of the closet." But the decision to reveal their sexual preference is fraught with problems. There are parents to tell, not all of whom are understanding; lifelong friends who "never knew"; employers who may change their attitudes and hesitate about promotions. There is even the possibility of loss of employment opportunities, despite laws that seek to prevent discrimination.

FORMS OF HOMOSEXUAL SEXUAL ACTIVITIES

There is no mystery about how homosexuals relate sexually to each other. In many ways, with one or two exceptions, their practices are similar to a large fraction of the nonhomosexual population.

For those with stable relationships, there is love, commitment and tenderness. For males, orgasm results frequently from fellatio (oral sex). Manual stimulation of the penis is an alternative. Anal intercourse is a third possibility. The fear of AIDS has introduced the use of condoms in homosexual intercourse. For lesbians, there are also deep feelings of love and tenderness and commitment in stable relationships. Sexual activity to orgasm involves oral-genital sex, manual stimulation, and possibly, in imitation of heterosexual intercourse, there is the rubbing of genitals of each partner against the other to arouse clitoral orgasm. There is no research on the subject, but homosexuals probably experience the same levels of sexual dysfunction as do heterosexuals. Yet, the fact that they are more familiar with what is sexually arousing in their mates may make homosexuals and lesbians more successful sexually than are average heterosexuals.

The Causes of Homosexual Orientation

There is no explanation of homosexual behavior that is universally accepted by psychologists. "Speculative" best categorizes the status of etiological factors in homosexuality. Explanations, as with many other personality characteristics, fall into two categories: psychosocial and biogenic. The latter are generally given less weight than the former. A 1991 study (described later) may significantly change that judgment.

PSYCHOSOCIAL FACTORS

There are two principal psychosocial explanations of homosexuality. One is a warped relationship with the boy's mother which rebounds and disturbs his relationship with his father. The sequence may be reversed, beginning with a bad relationship with the father which pushes the child into a more intimate relationship with his mother. For lesbians, less study has been devoted to etiological factors, but the likelihood is that a converse set of relationships with her father can lead to female homosexuality.

The second major interpretation of homosexual orientation is faulty early learning in which there is an early pattern of conditioning that brings together sexual arousal and a person of the same sex. Aversive conditioning resulting from failed heterosexual experiences can also influence both males and females toward homosexuality.

Mother/Son Relationships. There are two principal mother/son relationships that many psychologists believe create conditions favorable for later homosexuality. One, the psychodynamic explanation, has been called "smother love"; the other is almost the opposite—a cold, rejecting, punitive and controlling mother. There is research to support both interpretations.

Smother Love. Here is a classical version of Freudian theory. The son fails to resolve the Oedipal complex, and that failure blocks the son from identification with his father. This interpretation blames faulty psychosexual development for the son's failure to achieve genital maturity and normal heterosexual interest.

The history of such a development, described in a widely influential 1962 study by Bieber, unfolds as follows: A disturbed relationship between parents (perhaps infidelity by the father) causes the mother to turn her affection toward her son, in an oversolicitous and seductive fashion, offering much physical coddling, hugging and kissing. The mother's behavior pushes her husband further away and also sours his relationship with his son. That reaction prevents a male identification for the son. As part of her special relationship with her son, the mother tends to deprecate the male role as exemplified by her husband.

An early history of such smothering expressions by his mother damages the son's ability to become a man. Instead, in rejection of his father, he turns away from the male role, feeling more comfortable as a homosexual. In that role, he can safely continue to repress earlier erotic feelings aroused by his mother's behavior. Heterosexual intercourse would tend to rearouse them and produce feelings of guilt.

A Hostile Mother. Here the mother's behavior is not seductive, but rather controlling. Again, there is a disturbed marriage that causes deep resentment in the mother, who disrupts the son's relationship with his father and leads him into activities that are more feminine than masculine. She may keep him in girl's clothing far beyond infancy, encourage feminine play and female friendships, and object to "rough" masculine activities.

The result, according to one 1969 research study, is a child who grows up frail, clumsy and "wimpish," with few or no masculine skills. Although given a behavioral slant, the hostile-mother theory overlaps considerably with the Freudian and psychodynamic perspectives.

LEARNING SAME-SEX PATTERNS IN SEXUAL ACTIVITIES

From a behavioral perspective, homosexuality may be learned either from reinforced early same-sex sexual activities or from negative or aversive conditioning associated with heterosexual activity.

Positive Reinforcement. Several studies of both homosexual males and females report early satisfying same-sex sexual activities that are then frequently reinforced. Those studies report such findings as these: Two-thirds of a group of lesbians had willingly experienced a satisfying homosexual relationship before the age of twenty; 4 percent of the group had proceeded to orgasm. In a San Francisco study of male and female homosexuals, more than 50 percent had experienced a homosexual relationship before the age of nineteen; two-thirds of them reported enjoying the experience. In another study of 79 male homosexuals, the single common background event was an adolescent homosexual experience that was enjoyed.

Those studies, in reporting a cause of homosexuality through early conditioning, may, in fact, be reporting an effect of predisposing homosexual tendencies. There is here a "chicken-or-an-egg" dilemma: Did the early homosexual experience cause the later fixed homosexual orientation, or did it occur because of rudimentary homosexual leanings that led the individual to the early homosexual relationship?

Negative Conditioning. When early heterosexual experiences are found unsatisfying because of failure, or because they were ridiculed, rebuffed or even punished, the individual may turn to homosexual behavior to avoid the aversive outcomes of heterosexual behavior. Examples of such aversive experiences are parental punishment when a little boy is found playing at sex with a little girl, or a heterosexual venture in which the partner rejects an amateurish first-time sexual effort. Among lesbians, paternal rape may turn the individual to homosexuality, or disenchantment with a faithless lover may cause the woman to seek more loyalty in a lesbian relationship.

BIOGENIC CAUSATIVE FACTORS

The principal biogenic variable considered as a possible biogenic cause or contributory agent in homosexuality is some combination of genetic, hormonal and neurological elements that interferes with the full masculinization of the male fetus. The most widely accepted explanation of that effect is a 1989 study of Ellis and Ames. Their findings apply only to male homosexuals and therefore hardly seem an adequate explanation for all homosexual behavior.

Ellis and Ames report the possibility that some time between the second and fourth months of pregnancy, a disruption in neurochemical elements in the mother produces a weakness in development of fully masculine characteristics. When later in the life of the individual pubertal changes effect other hormonal activities, the inadequate masculine elements express themselves in homosexual behavior.

Causes listed as initiating the process are as follows: 1. a genetic hormonal defect in which receptors for androgen, the male sex hormone, are inadequate; 2. an oversupply of progesterone drugs (those that increase femininity) taken by the mother during pregnancy; and 3. maternal stress, such as bereavement or divorce, at an early stage of the pregnancy.

The Ellis and Ames hypothesis has been partially supported by other research but needs fuller substantiation. In any case, it would explain only a fraction of male homosexuality and none of female homosexuality.

In August 1991, Simon Levay, a neurobiologist at the Salk Institute, reported in *Science* a study suggesting that there is a significant structural difference between the brains of homosexual men and heterosexual men. Levay states that in homosexual men, one segment of the hypothalamus, a key neural structure at the base of the brain which affects both emotion and motivation, is only a quarter to a half the size of the same region in heterosexual men. The special significance of this finding in understanding the etiology of homosexuality is that prior research on animals has found that injury to this portion of the brain causes male animals to lose interest in females while continuing to express sexual interest in masturbation. The conclusion Levay suggests is that his finding would mean that there is a possible biological influence—even if only in creating a predisposition—in the development of homosexuality.

The finding elicited lively responses from members of the homosexual community and from the scientific community. The *New York Times*, in reporting scientific comment, offers the following samples:

> "Unprecedented and very provocative, Levay is a world-class neuroanatomist."

> "This [study] just points in a possible direction."

> "Biology is clearly not destiny and this shouldn't be taken to mean that you are automatically homosexual if you have a structure of one size versus a structure of another size."

> "The consensus in the scientific community is that it is likely to be a combination of [inborn and environmental factors] that cause the development of homosexuality."

In any case, it must be pointed out that the Levay sample was a small one, all male, and his finding, as yet, is only a one-time event.

TREATMENT OF HOMOSEXUALITY

Treatment for ego-syntonic homosexuality and ego-dystonic homosexuality must be considered separately. Since the ego-syntonic homosexual does not choose to become heterosexual, he does not seek treatment.

When the desire to change sexual orientation is strong, as in ego-dystonic homosexuality, two small-scale studies report success with aversive conditioning in 60 percent of the cases. In the therapies used, homosexual fantasies are followed by either actual aversive consequences, such as electric shock, or such consequences as can be imagined vividly by the individual. Masters and Johnson report success by using sensate focus exercises with a heterosexual partner. The reaction of some psychologists to that reported success is that the treated individuals were not fully homosexual but actually bisexual.

RAPE AND INCEST

Although both of these forms of sexual activity are ignored in the most recent revision of the official diagnostic manual, most textbook authors consider them in their discussions of sexual disorders.

Sexual activity imposed on an unwilling partner, either by actual force or threat, is labeled rape. From a legal point of view, two types of rape are distinguished: forcible rape, which is defined as an attempt to penetrate an opening of the body by a penis or other object; and statutory rape, which is sexual involvement with a minor, whether or not that minor has participated willingly.

Here we consider the motivations for rape, characteristics of the rapist, legal and social issues, and prevalence.

Motivations, Characteristics, and Issues of Rape

POWER AND ANGER IN RAPE

In 1977, Groth, Burgess, and Holmstrom completed the most systematic study to date of rapists. They divided motivation for rape into four categories: 1. Power assertive rape, in which the attack is motivated by a desire for conquest, which is sought by sexual penetration. Forty-four percent of the rapes studied fell into this category. 2. Power-reassurance rape, in which the conquering of the female is sought to provide reassurance to an individual who has weak feelings of his own masculinity. Twenty-one percent of the group exemplified that motivational basis for rape. 3. Anger-retaliation rape, the most dangerous form of rape, which often results in the murder of the victim when the rape has been completed, grows out of a generalized hatred of women. That hatred of women, the source of which can only be surmised, and not a desire for sexual release, was the motivation of 30 percent of the rapes studied. 4. Anger-excitation rape can be seen as an extreme form of sadistic behavior in which sexual arousal comes from the violence, not the intercourse, which may or may not take place. Five percent of the rapes were of this type.

OTHER TYPES OF CAUSATION IN RAPE

Two other types of rape need to be discussed: gang rape and date rape.

Gang rape. A gang rape widely covered by newspaper accounts was an attack by a gang of ten to twenty young males, some of them still in their teens. The woman was attacked while jogging in New York City's Central Park and was sexually assaulted and beaten viciously. Not all of those present participated in the sexual attack; some mauled her with their hands; others attempted intercourse; still others combined sex with a vicious physical attack. As reported, there also seemed to be racial overtones. Here, the motives that brought the group together must have varied widely, including, perhaps, variations of those motives identified in the Groth study. Peer pressure might also have been present.

Date Rape. Research on date rape describes these rapists, frequently college undergraduates, as "sexually very active, successful and aspiring." In the study, the motivations the date-rapist verbalized were that the rapist was given "the come-on" by a sexual tease or notoriously promiscuous woman, and he was not to be "put on" in that way. Once sexually aroused, he was not to be frustrated. Perhaps previous experience of finding dates who were willing to "have sex" poorly prepared the rapist for refusal.

Such males are astonished and enraged by such a refusal, and they resort to force. Added to this explanation could be the frequent association in the media of sex and violence, a phenomenon that, it would seem, can only weaken any sense of responsibility and control an individual might have been brought up to exercise.

OTHER CHARACTERISTICS OF RAPISTS

Police reports of arrested rapists (by no means all rapists) indicate that they are most often under twenty-five years of age. Thirty percent of arrested rapists were in the age bracket eighteen to twenty-one. In this available (because arrested) sample of rapists, 50 percent were married and living with their spouses. The group studied was predominantly of low intelligence, had low occupational skills, and earned low-level salaries. Those statistics say more in answer to the question, Who gets arrested for rape? than to the question, Who are the rapists?

LEGAL AND SOCIAL ISSUES

Legal issues relate to the incidence of arrest for rape and the weight to be given to the rapist's mental condition in determining punishment. There is a relatively low conviction rate, principally because of the difficulty in identifying the rapist. It is accurate to state that more rapists are free in the community than are behind bars. Yet rapists are ordinarily repeat offenders. Perhaps we should be asking, Is rape today being judged seriously enough?

A principal destructive effect of rape is the serious damage it causes in the victim's later adjustment. A 1983 study reports that raped women are seven times more likely to experience depression than other women. Almost always there is a disruption in their normal sexual life, and they often live unbearably apprehensive lives.

Beyond those disturbing consequences, there is the humiliation the victim may experience at the rapist's trial. It is fair enough that an accused rapist be considered innocent until proven guilty, but some laws and some judicial behavior suggest that the woman herself is on trial. In an effort to prevent a vengeful woman from falsely charging rape, the law has perhaps gone too far in the opposite direction and made it too difficult to prove guilt. The law in New York State formerly required that there be a witness. Occasionally, a judge will prejudicially inquire into the provocativeness of the woman's attire. To avoid such humiliation, many women do not report attempts at rape.

A Michigan law now in effect designates rape as "criminal sexual conduct" and places heavier responsibility on the arrested individual to defend himself. A majority of other states have developed similar laws to reduce the likelihood of victims being humiliated.

PREVALENCE OF RAPES

The FBI reported that there were more than 85,000 rapes reported in 1985, a 53 percent increase in nine years. Still other estimates suggest that there may well be ten times as many. When hospitalization is required, the police will ordinarily demand that the crime be reported, although the woman may still refuse to press any specific charges. The victim's behavior in detailing the circumstances of a widely publicized rape in 1990 and her willingness to answer questions about her own prior sexual behavior suggests that perhaps as a result of the women's rights movement, more women will report and prosecute rapes.

Incest

Legally and narrowly defined, incest is coitus between parent and child or brother and sister. Almost universally across time and cultures, incest has been forbidden. There are sound reasons for this taboo. This section briefly examines three reasons, considers causative factors, and comments on the prevalence of incest.

REASONS FOR THE UNIVERSAL TABOO ON INCEST

There are three negative effects of incestuous sexual relations: biological, familial and psychological.

Biological Reasons. Coitus (leading to pregnancy) between blood relatives increases the likelihood that defective recessive genes will be present in both sexual partners and will be matched. The result of that matching will be the likely appearance of defects in the offspring. Evidence of that fact is reported in a 1967 study of eighteen children of either father/daughter or brother/sister pregnancies matched against a carefully constructed control group.

Among eighteen offspring of an incestuous pregnancy, the following sad outcomes were reported: in six months, five children born of such a pregnancy died; two were severely mentally retarded; three were of borderline intelligence; and one was born with a cleft palate. Seven of the infants were normal, suggesting the absence of defective recessive genes. Among the children of normal pregnancies, two children had defects, one physical, the other intellectual.

Familial Reasons. Incestuous sexual activity, whether between parent and child or between siblings, introduces highly emotional and divisive strains into family life. Wife and husband can hardly be comfortable with each other when father and daughter are sharing sexual relations. Among siblings, tensions and rivalries divide the family. The taboo against incest is necessary to keep families intact and a positive force in the functioning of society.

Psychological. Women who have experienced an incestuous relationship, especially with their fathers, are prone, in later life, to distressing emotional reactions: depression, guilt, anxiety, and lowered self-esteem. Their capacity to develop warm interpersonal relationships is lost or badly damaged, and they often carry with them hostile and vengeful feelings toward the opposite sex. When incestuous relations have been frequent or with several relatives, the individual often drifts into prostitution, a form of sex without feelings.

CAUSATIVE FACTORS IN INCEST

Seductive behavior by a daughter occasionally provokes incest, but only rarely, and, of course, only when, for whatever reasons, the father is receptive to the seduction. Discovering what those reasons might be requires that we examine the characteristics of the paternal participant.

One might jump to the conclusion that such fathers would have to be amoral and indiscriminate in their sexual behavior. What research has been conducted on the problem suggests a contrary conclusion. An early study (1965), for example, indicates that such fathers are frequently moralistic with fundamentalist religious beliefs. There is invariably a troubled marriage that serves as a precipitating cause. A number of clinicians report father/daughter sex growing out of a longtime, loving and tender relationship between father and adult daughter in a situation in which the mother has died or is absent from the home. It is, nevertheless, a reasonable conclusion to draw that some fraction of incestuous activities occur in severely pathological families or are attempted by irresponsible or sexually promiscuous fathers.

PREVALENCE

Estimates of prevalence vary widely in this infrequently researched area of the sexual disorders. Data from the "Kinsey Report," now more than forty years old, indicates a figure of 3 percent. Two other more recent studies suggest much higher levels. The one study in which interviews were conducted in a representative sample of the general population reports a prevalence figure of 16 percent. Other details of that study are that 40 percent of the incidents were carried to abusive lengths; much of it was at the level of child molestation, in which uncles were most frequently involved. Although many of the occurrences were single events, more than half were multiple; and in a small number of cases, several relatives attempted incest.

The DSM IIIR *divides sexual disorders into three major categories: First, is sexual dysfunctions in which inhibitions prevent or reduce the individual's enjoyment of normal sex and/or the physiological changes normally brought on by sexual arousal. The dysfunction may be manifest at any of the three stages of sexual activity: the desire stage, the arousal stage, or the orgasm stage.*

Disorders of the desire stage are hypoactive desire, a disinterest in sex, or the more extreme form of the disorder, aversion to sex. Disorders of the arousal stage manifest themselves in an absence or weakness of the specific physiological changes that prepare the individual for intercourse. In the orgasm stage, the male disorder is premature ejaculation; in the female, it is an inhibited orgasm. There are two sexual pain disorders: they are dyspareunia, which is pain during intercourse, predominantly a female disorder, and vaginismus, exclusively a female disorder, which produces contractions at the entrance to the vagina and prevents penile entry.

There are both psychosocial and physical factors that may cause sexual dysfunction. Among the psychosexual causes are faulty learning, negative attitudes toward sex learned in early traumatic sexual experiences, early disturbances in the individual's psychosexual development, or friction or hostility between the two sexual partners. The physical causes of sexual dysfunction include the effect of ingested external substances such as alcohol or marijuana. The principal internal factor is hormonal imbalance.

Treatment of sexual dysfunctions is much more frequently sought today than in earlier decades. Illustrative of treatment approaches are those suggested by Masters and Johnson, who prescribe graded sexual exercises and encourage partners to focus on the sexual pleasures (sensate focus) rather than on whether or not they are "performing" satisfactorily. High levels of success are reported for such treatment approaches.

The second major category of sexual disorders are the eight paraphilias, which can be grouped into three broad clusters.

Cluster 1 includes fetishes and transvestic disorders, in which there is a sexual preference for nonhuman objects. A fetish is an attachment to such objects as shoes, female clothes or textured material, either as a supplement to coitus or as a substitute for it. Transvestism is finding sexual excitement by cross-sex dressing.

Fetishes occur in those persons with lowered self-esteem and feelings of sexual inadequacy. The fetish is usually triggered by an early conditioning experience in which the fetishistic object stimulated, often accidentally, an orgasm. When followed by planned use of the object, the fetish soon becomes established. Transvestites often have early experiences in which a boy is dressed as a girl or a girl as a boy.

A second grouping of paraphilias is those disorders in which there is a preference either for causing suffering as an aspect of sex (sadism) or desiring to have pain inflicted (masochism). Both are developed out of early life experiences which relate pain (given or received) to an orgasm, very much in the same way that fetishes are developed.

Another major grouping of the paraphilias is that of sexual preference and arousal with nonconsenting partners. These paraphilias may take the form of pedophilia (child molesting) and exhibitionism or voyeurism (secret viewing of sexual scenes). All of them involve the participation of nonconsenting individuals in some aspect of a sexual activity. The basis for these paraphiliac activities is profound feelings of sexual inadequacy and fear of being embarrassed or rebuffed in normal heterosexual activities.

The paraphilias do not respond readily to treatment.

The third major sexual disorder, gender identity disorder, exists when individuals, male or female, express confusion, vagueness or conflict in their feelings about their sexual identity. Those disturbing feelings may relate to gender identity, gender roles, or choice of sexual partner. Here, as with transvestism, early prolonged experiences in being treated as a child of the opposite sex can have drastic later effects on the individual's sense of gender identity. Biological influences on the developing fetus can cause malformation of the sex organs and predispose the individual to an identity problem.

Transsexualism is the most extreme form of gender identity disorder. In that disorder, the individual, either male or female, feels trapped in a body of a non-preferred sex. Since 1953, almost 3,000 persons suffering from transsexualism have sought sex-change operations. Research reports that most sex-changed transsexuals continue to live unfulfilled social and sexual lives.

Historically, social attitudes toward homosexuality have varied widely across time and culture. In its 1987 revision of their classification, the American Psychiatric Association has removed homosexuality from classification as a disorder. It has substituted ego-dystonic homosexuality, which is a sex identity disorder in which the individual is dissatisfied with a homosexual or lesbian disorder and would like to change. Clinicians usually offer therapy only to this group. Ego-syntonic homosexuality is not considered a disorder, and individuals in that category usually do not seek treatment. Extrapolations from Kinsey's study suggest that there may be 2.6 million homosexuals men and 1.4 million lesbian women in the United States.

Individuals with same-sex sexual preferences differ widely in appearances, life-style and reasons for their sexual orientation.

There is no universally accepted explanation for homosexuality. Both psychosocial factors, including parent/child relationships and early conditioning, and biogenic factors, such as genetic, hormonal and neurological factors, are considered as possible causes.

Although rape and incest are not listed as disorders in the DSM IIIR, most textbook authorities consider them in their discussion of the sexual disorders. Strong feelings of need for power and anger against the female are considered primary motivations for rape.

Official reports indicate that in 1985, there were more than 85,000 rapes committed in the United States. The reluctance of many women to report rape attacks suggests that the actual number is much higher.

Incest is coitus between parent and child or brother and sister. Kinsey's figures suggest a prevalency rate of 3 percent; more recent studies cite a higher rate.

There are good reasons for the universal taboo against incest—biological, familial and psychological. Pregnancies resulting from incest, because of the greater likelihood of matching recessive and defective genes, result in a high rate of physical and intellectual defects in the offspring. Incest, especially that between parent and child, profoundly disrupts family harmony. Women who have experienced incestuous sexual relations often, later in life, suffer depression, guilt, anxiety and lowered self-esteem. The result is extreme difficulty in establishing satisfying interpersonal relations. Research indicates that incestuous fathers can be members of a strongly disciplined but unhappy family. Many incestuous situations also develop in pathological families or are attempted by irresponsible or sexually-promiscuous fathers.

**Selected
Readings**

Frank, E., C. Anderson and D. Rubinstein. 1978. "Frequency of Sexual Dysfunction in "Normal" Couples." *New England Journal of Medicine*, 299: 111-115.

Green, R. 1985. *The "Sissy Boy Syndrome" and the Development of Homosexuality*. New Haven, CT: Yale University Press.

Kaplan, H. S. 1974. *The New Sex Therapy: Active Treatment of Sexual Dysfunctions*. New York: Quadrangle Books.

Kaplan, H. S. 1979. *Disorders of Sexual Desire*. New York: Simon & Schuster.

Money, J. 1987. "Sin, Sickness or Status? Homosexual Gender Identity and Psychoneuroendocrinology." *American Psychologist*, 42: 384-399.

Rekers, G. A. 1977. "Assessment and Treatment of Childhood Gender Problems." in B. B. Lahey and A. E. Kazdin (Eds.). *Advances in Clinical Psychology*, vol. 1, 286-306, New York: Plenum.

Wise, T. N. 1985. "Fetishism-Etiology and Treatment: A Review from Multiple Personalities." *Comprehensive Psychiatry*, 26: 249-257.

16

Organic Mental Disorders

*A*ll human behavior, normal and abnormal, has its basis in the activities of the nervous system. The organizing, executive, and most crucial part of the nervous system is the brain. To reflect the two different ways in which the brain effects the development of abnormal behavior, mental disorders are grouped into two broad categories: 1. organic disorders, those mental disorders known to be caused directly and primarily by pathology in the brain itself; and 2. functional disorders, which result from abnormal life experiences imposed on a normal brain. Organic disorders account for 25 percent of all first admissions to mental hospitals.

The other mental disorders described in this book (except for mental retardation) are, for the most part, functional disorders; in this chapter, we discuss the principal organic disorders. As has been indicated in other chapters, functional disorders can result from vulnerabilities that grow out of organic defects. But such defects create only predispositions for particular mental disorders and not the illness itself.

In a demonstration of mind/body interdependence, functional disorders, with no physical basis for causing them, can manifest themselves in physical symptoms; for example, the somatoform disorders; and the behavioral symptoms of organic disorders may be affected by psychosocial aspects of the environment. Two individuals with the same brain pathology may show different symptoms because of their differing life circumstances.

Functional disorders are generally considered the province of psychologists and psychiatrists; neurologists diagnose and treat the organic disorders. Depending upon the needs of the patient, a team of all three may work together to help the individual.

This chapter considers the following: the various parts of the brain and their functions; characteristic symptoms of organic disorders; the problems of distinguishing between organic and functional disorders; causes of organic disorders; the principal organic disorders; and neurological approaches to treatment.

The DSM IIIR *classification of organic disorders is of more value to medical students than to students of abnormal behavior. For that reason, it is not outlined in this presentation.*

THE HUMAN BRAIN

Human superiority to animals rests principally on the superiority of the human brain. The human brain is the best-protected organ in the body. The bony structure of the skull and three enveloping layers of tissue afford protection from many, but not all, of life's accidents or illnesses.

The brain is described by neurologists as the most complex biological structure in existence. They also say we know more about the brain than we know about any other organ of the body, perhaps because there is so much more to know about so complex an organ; but they say further that there is so much more that we don't yet know. For that reason, learning all about how the brain functions is one of the most challenging goals of both medicine and psychology.

Here we consider the following: the neuron, the basic functioning unit of the brain; localization of function; spatial organization of the brain; and the effects of brain damage.

The Neuron

There are said to be billions of these hard-working units of the brain. The neuron consists of 1. a cell body, which provides the life support of the neuron; 2. dendrites, a system of fine branches that receive electrochemical impulses (messages) from other neurons; and 3. terminal endings that transmit messages to other neurons. The gap between one neuron and another is the synapse. Messages are enabled to cross that gap by the neuron's release of neurotransmitter substances into the synapse. The transmitters, as enabling agents, either activate or inhibit the functioning of other neurons.

The importance of the transmitter enzymes is exemplified in Parkinson's disease, a debilitating disease affecting older people. The disease is caused by a degeneration of brain cells (neurons), which degeneration limits the supply of the transmitter agent dopamine. In the absence of dopamine, the message telling certain groups of muscles to flex or to expand is not transmitted across the relevant synapses, and movement is impossible or severely limited. The symptoms of Parkinsonism can be alleviated by the administration of a synthetic form of dopamine.

Localization of Function

Bundles of neurons controlling similar functions are located in the different regions of the brain; thus, there is correlation between behavioral symptoms produced by brain damage and location of the damage.

Collections of neurons serving similar functions are located in one or another of the lobes of the cerebral cortex (the surface layer of the cerebrum, which is the main part of the brain). The four lobes are named frontal, parietal, occipital and temporal. The entire cerebrum is separated into two symmetrical hemispheres.

The cell bodies of neurons of the brain are concentrated in what is called the "gray matter" of the brain. That gray matter makes possible the higher mental functioning of the human being. The axons, wirelike structures called the "white matter" because of their white myelin sheath, are bundled into tracts that connect areas of the gray matter.

A convenient way of thinking about the structure of the brain is to consider the gray matter as a group of modules, each with a specialized job to do. The white matter, or bundles of axons, serves to connect the various modules. Some modules—for example, those in the frontal lobes—control wide-ranging functions, such as processing of information. Others are limited, for example, to receiving sensations from the various sense receptors.

Spatial Organization and Brain Function

There are three axes or ways of thinking spatially about the brain: front/back, left/right, and up/down. Those axes relate to various human functions.

FRONT/BACK ORGANIZATION OF THE BRAIN

Motor functions are generally located in the front of this axis and sensory functions at the back. Various aspects of both activities will also be located on the up/down axis in the front and back of the brain.

Illustrative of this localization of function in the cerebral cortex is a description of two higher functions of the brain provided by the Russian neuropsychologist Alexander Luria. He named one of those functions the information-processing activity, and he located the place where it was controlled in the back portion of the cerebral cortex. Damage to that part of the brain will cause loss of sensation; damage at other levels of the back portion of the brain will cause such symptoms as poor representation of space or even inability to identify common objects. The condition is known as *agnosia*.

Luria named the other function planning-verification, and located that function in the front of the brain. The area controls the actions the individual takes in his environment. One result of damage to this area is perseverative behavior, in which the individual repetitively makes the same response instead of taking the next step in the normal way of responding.

LEFT/RIGHT ORGANIZATION OF THE BRAIN

This axis separates the cerebrum into two symmetrical hemispheres. The left hemisphere receives sensory input from and controls actions of the right side of the body. The right hemisphere serves the left side of the body in a similar way. Damage to either hemisphere will affect the opposite side of the body.

Aside from that basic localization of function, there is a qualitative difference in the way each hemisphere functions. The left hemisphere contributes an analyzing ability and organizes the perceptual world; it sorts things out. The right hemisphere is better at synthesizing; that is, reassembling discrete information into units. Damage to either hemisphere will affect its normal functioning; the particular malfunction will depend upon the up/down location of the damage.

UP/DOWN ORGANIZATION OF THE BRAIN

The vertical organization of the brain affects functioning in a hierarchical way. The upper levels of the brain have to do with cognitive and voluntary behavior. That level builds on and moderates functions of lower levels. There is evidence that in such general disease of the brain as that of the degeneration caused by aging, there is greater vulnerability to dysfunction of the upper levels of the brain. In senility, for example, the first functions to be affected are the higher cognitive functions, such as memory, adjusting to new situations, or keeping things in sequence. Only later are more basic biological functions disrupted. A sad example is the individual in a coma who goes on living vegetatively.

MAJOR SYMPTOMS OF ORGANIC DISORDERS

There are three clusters of symptoms that suggest the presence of organic disease: defects in basic mental activities, impairment in higher intellectual functioning, and certain types of affective disorders.

Defects in Basic Mental Activities

Memory loss is a significant indicator of brain dysfunction, although it may also be a symptom of a functional disorder. It is one of the earliest signs of cerebral deterioration associated with senility. A prime example is the impairment of memory that is a primary symptom of Alzheimer's disease. The memory impairment in functional disorders manifests itself in markedly different ways from that produced by cerebral degeneration (see chapter 9).

An even more severe indication of brain damage, and one on which initial diagnosis can more confidently be based (although psychosis would also have to be considered), is loss of orientation, in which the individual cannot locate himself or herself in space, has no awareness of the date or even the season, and may not be able to report self-identity.

Impairment in Higher Mental Functioning

Persons with brain disorders have trouble in making decisions. They make them only after much hesitation and uncertainty, or make foolish decisions about everyday activities. They also make gross errors in financial matters. There can be slowness and inaccuracy in calculating. Their fund of general information is reduced, and knowledge of common items, such as who is the president, can be lost.

Affective Disorders

There may be lability of affect in which the individual shifts suddenly and inappropriately from one emotion to its opposite; for instance, from unpleasantness to hostility, or from laughing to weeping. Included in this type of symptom is a loss of resilience. When fatigued or emotionally upset or puzzled, the necessity of making a decision, or solving even a simple problem is just too much for the individual.

All of the symptoms described above can be suggestive of possible organic involvement; a number of them also are present in functional disorders. A diagnosis of organic damage can be made only after careful neurological and psychological study.

DIAGNOSING ORGANIC MENTAL DISORDERS

With the possible overlap in symptoms of functional and organic disorders, diagnosis can be a problem. Mistaking one for the other will, of course, block effective treatment. In organic disorders of some types, delayed treatment can result in death.

Correct diagnostic practice requires that even for apparently minor symptoms that cannot be explained, a thorough physical examination be undertaken before a diagnosis is made. A good dictum to follow is to exclude physical causes before exclusively psychological causation is diagnosed.

Sometimes doing that is easy; for example, a long-time specific phobia, with no other symptoms, is not likely to have an organic cause. On the other hand, even a brief loss of consciousness is quite another matter. Such an event could be caused by physical exhaustion, high temperature, or the early sign of a brain tumor.

Fortunately, recent advances in medical technology, especially advances in brain imaging techniques such as computer-assisted tomography, (CAT) scan or the more recently-developed magnetic resonance imaging (MRI) make diagnosing brain damage an easier process than in the past. Accurate diagnosis in pinpointing specific performance defects is now also possible with the help of specially developed psychological tests; for example, the Halsted-Reitan Neuropsychological Battery. The performance profiles of those tests can help locate the region of the brain damage and also the extent of the damage.

ETIOLOGICAL ASPECTS

There are broad categories of agents that cause brain damage. They are, as we will discuss them, a degenerative process in the brain, brain tumors, brain trauma, vascular accidents, nutritional deficiency, and endocrine disorders. A separate category of organic disorders is epilepsy. For each of the disorders, the extent of behavioral disruption, and the specific nature of the symptoms depends upon the amount of brain damage and the location of the damage.

Before discussing the specific causes of organic disorders, we consider broadly the types of effect the causes can produce, factors that affect the vulnerability of certain parts of the brain to damage, and the availability of redundant systems that can take over lost functions.

The Range of Effects of Brain Damage

The agents of brain damage may cause acute symptoms, some lasting only a few months (for example, some strokes), or chronic symptoms, which may handicap and disrupt the individual's functioning for the rest of his or her life, or indeed cause death; for example, neurosyphilis. The symptoms of brain damage may be localized and affect only specific functions, such as speech and/or mobility, as in many strokes; or they may, when extensive areas of the brain are affected, as in the degenerative disorders, cause generalized debility and disorganization of functioning. Symptoms may come on suddenly, as, for example, the early signs of brain tumor or appear gradually with increasing severity, as with senile dementia.

Most damage to the brain causes negative effects; that is, there is an impairment in the functioning of the affected area. In particular instances, the damage may also increase the activity of the adjoining area. For example, the increased irritation caused by the damage may have the "positive" effect of exciting and activating the nearby area. The effect may nevertheless be disruptive. The convulsive seizures of epilepsy (periods of heightened activity) are explained in this way.

Vulnerable Parts of the Brain

Since an adequate supply of blood is essential to the proper functioning of a neuron, positioning of a neuron cluster that limits access to a supply of blood or that makes it exceptionally susceptible to stroke increases the likelihood of brain damage in the area. The area controlling speech is one such area, and speech impairment is a frequent symptom of brain damage.

Even the axial length of the neuron may make it more vulnerable than a neuron of shorter length, since the greater length requires more than average nourishment for its full functioning. A vitamin deficiency, for example, would have stronger impact on the functioning of a long neuron than it would have on a shorter neuron. Parts of the brain involved in memory are particularly vulnerable for such reasons. As a result, memory is frequently affected by concussion of the brain.

Redundancy

Redundancy in the brain is the presence of multiple cerebral pathways performing the same function. Redundancy is common in the human body. The two kidneys are an example; one is all that is needed. Cellular redundancy makes it possible for a partial liver to function adequately.

Three possible redundancies in the human brain make it possible for damaged functions to be maintained or shifted elsewhere. They are as follows: 1. A surplus of neurons for a particular function. If only some are damaged, the remaining undamaged neurons can maintain the function. 2. Alternative pathways are available for some functions. For example, left-hemisphere damage can be mitigated by a neural passage going between hemispheres. Some functions (for example, basic biological activities) can be carried on from either hemisphere. 3. Finally, the individual can design behavioral strategies to compensate for disabilities caused by brain damage. Such adjustment would be comparable to the blind person learning to depend more heavily on hearing in order to avoid obstacles.

CAUSATIVE AGENTS IN BRAIN DAMAGE

Here we identify seven principal agents of brain damage and illustrate the types of symptoms that result from each.

Brain Degeneration

The wear and tear of living is hard on the organs of the body. Biologists report that the wearing out of the body begins virtually at birth. When one is young, the worn-out cells of the body are replaced regularly by new growth. As the individual grows older, in a process commonly called aging, the replacement process slows down, and a generalized degeneration of the body's tissues gradually takes place. The brain is as affected as are other parts of the body. The rate of biological aging varies among individuals and seems to be related to the individual's genetic heritage. Science has not yet learned to understand the full nature of aging.

When this degeneration process produces changes in the brain, certain alterations in intellectual functioning gradually appear. For most people, these changes initially affect daily life only in minor ways; for example, occasional memory lapses, the inability to recall a name, or failing to remember what the individual set out to do just a moment ago. As the individual grows older, in a normal and to-be-expected way, the disabilities increase. Examples are a slower way of walking, lessened capacity to handle complex information, and decreased efficiency of memory and in the learning of new tasks.

Aside from this normal aging of the mental and motor processes, in 4 percent of the population over age sixty-five, a condition called dementia develops, which brings on a progressive loss of a variety of the higher mental processes. The percentage increases with age, so that beyond eighty years of age, 20 percent of the population show varying degrees of senile dementia. There are two types of senile dementia: Alzheimer's disease and multi-infarct disease.

ALZHEIMER'S DISEASE

There are two symptom patterns to expect in Alzheimer's disease. In half of the group, the illness follows the pattern of simple deterioration. In others, a system of paranoid thinking may develop.

Simple Deterioration. Here, various mental capacities begin to fail. Memory loss is usually first. Loss of memory is followed by periods of disorientation, poor judgment, indifference to personal hygiene, and ultimately a complete loss of contact with reality.

The behavioral expressions of the disease may vary. None of them make caring for the individual any easier. Some typical examples of Alzheimer behavior are repetitive asking of the same question, walking out of the house and getting lost, or forgetting to turn off running bath water or appliances around the house.

There may be genial amiability (but also irritability) and a busyness about useless but harmless activities, for instance, saving string or ritualizing household activities to a painful extreme.

Paranoid Reactions in Alzheimer's Disease. Much more difficult to deal with is the Alzheimer patient who develops paranoid thinking. Although this is a less frequent reaction pattern than simple dementia, when it occurs it is the symptom about which most caretakers complain and the one which they find the most difficult to manage. The individual is suspicious and busy concocting plots of the nefarious activities engaged in by the very people who are providing care. Strangely, with this symptom pattern, deficiencies in cognitive functioning seem to be less noticeable. The individual becomes more observant about the behavior of others and uses those observations to justify suspicions. Although rare, paranoid thinking can lead to assaultive behavior. Most often, however, the feebleness of the individual prevents much harm being done.

Causes of Alzheimer's Disease. The cause or causes of the disease are unknown. Two hypotheses have been offered: high concentrations of aluminum in the blood and genetic deficiencies.

Increased Aluminum. A notable number of studies of the disease report high levels of aluminum in the patient's blood, especially in those areas of the brain known to be involved with the disease. Since such heavy metals as aluminum are known to accumulate at sites of neural damage, the question of cause and effect has been raised. Prevailing opinion is that the brain damage causing the disease is the cause rather than the effect of the accumulation of aluminum.

Genetic Factors. Brain damage of some Alzheimer patients is caused by genetic defects. Such a genetic basis for Alzheimer's disease is nevertheless hard to justify since, for the majority of Alzheimer patients, there is no family history of the disease, yet the belief in genetic causation persists. And it is a fact that, from time to time, bits and pieces of evidence surface which support this conclusion. This evidence has not yet been collected and summarized in a way to provide an adequate explanation of how genetic factors work to cause Alzheimer's or even whether or not there is a genetic cause of most cases of the disease.

Nevertheless, there would seem to be agreement among neurologists that some genetic basis, not now entirely understood, is a cause of some forms of the disease. They believe that there is sufficient evidence of familial occurrence of the disease to support that view.

Prevalence. With an increasing aging population, Alzheimer's disease has become a major health problem with troublesome corollary social problems. About 15 percent of the American population over sixty-five have the disease. Since there is no known cure for it and proper management of the illness at later stages is difficult, nursing homes carry much of the burden. Estimates report that 30 to 40 percent of all nursing home residents suffer from the disease.

MULTI-INFARCT DEMENTIA

Symptoms similar to those described for Alzheimer's disease can also result from multi-infarct disease. That disease is not as specifically age-related as is Alzheimer's disease. It is a vascular (blood vessel) disease which may occur earlier in life than is likely with Alzheimer's disease. Brain degeneration in multi-infarct disease results from the cumulative damage of multiple small strokes, which are caused by a blockage in the supply of blood to a specific area of the brain. The cause of the blockage is usually a blood clot. The impacted area is called an infarct, which loses its ability to function and soon begins to degenerate. As those small strokes grow more frequent and the neural damage spreads, dementia ultimately results.

The condition is associated with hardening of the arteries. In that condition, calcified fatty substances accumulate on the interior arterial walls, narrowing them and slowing the flow of blood through them. Eventually, a blood clot forms, and the resulting blockage ruptures the blood vessel, allowing blood to hemorrhage into the brain. A single stroke of that type may result in a variety of psychological and physical symptoms. As they occur more frequently, dementia follows.

A sudden onset of symptoms occurs in 50 percent of the cases, presumably as a result of a major stroke involving extensive areas of the brain.

OTHER DEGENERATIVE DISORDERS

There are two other degenerative disorders, Huntington's chorea and Parkinson's disease. Both involve specific but unrelated areas of the brain at subcortical levels.

Huntington's Chorea. This organic disease is transmitted genetically by a dominant and defective gene of either parent. Its presence can first be observed only when the individual is in his or her thirties. The brain area affected is the basal ganglia, which are bundles of neurons deep within the cerebrum. The characteristic symptom, for which the illness is named, is a spasmodic jerking of the limbs. The disease is a serious one, causing bizarre behavior and loss of bodily functions, resulting in death, usually some fourteen years after the onset of the first symptoms.

Parkinson's Disease. The disorder results from a degeneration of the neurons in the substantia nigra, a part of the basal ganglia. The absence of the neurotransmitter dopamine makes conduction of impulses across the synapses impossible in the affected area. Characteristically developing in later life, in the sixties, it appears occasionally as early as the forties. Symptoms include muscular rigidity, tremors, and a masklike fixedness of facial expression. In severe cases, in the latter phases of the disease, dementia may be present.

Although the disease cannot be cured, symptoms can be greatly moderated by regular doses of a synthesized substitute for the missing dopamine. The problem with that drug is that the body gradually accommodates to it, therefore requiring that the dosage be increased gradually, with the danger that its effect may be lost altogether.

Brain Tumors

A tumor is an abnormal growth of body tissues. Some tumors are benign, affecting the individual only because of the pressure they exert. Upon removal of the tumor, symptoms usually disappear. Others are malignant, and unless removed in time, will cause the individual's death. Tumors may appear in many parts of the body, including the brain.

TYPES OF BRAIN TUMORS

Brain tumors are of two types: primary tumors, which originate in the brain itself and may be malignant; and secondary tumors, usually cancerous, originating in other parts of the body and carried to the brain through the vascular system. As the brain tumors grow in the cerebrum of the brain, they increase intracranial pressure and cause a variety of serious physical and behavioral symptoms; and unless removed or reduced, eventually cause death. The secondary tumors are just as dangerous as primary tumors; they simply arise from a place outside the brain, metastasize (that is, break up), and travel to the brain through the blood vessels.

SYMPTOMATOLOGY

Intracranial tumors show their presence initially in relatively minor symptoms—headache, visual problems, a brief loss of consciousness. As the tumor continues to grow and affects other parts of the brain, symptoms increase and more seriously affect the health and mental functioning of the individual. Higher mental functions deteriorate, abnormal reflexes develop, emotional expression is blunted, memory and concentration are affected, and disorientation as to time and place results. When brain tumors cannot be removed because of their location or size, they eventually cause unbearable pain and extreme personality changes. The patient ultimately becomes floridly psychotic, sinks into a coma, and dies.

Many brain tumors can be removed by surgery or reduced by radiation therapy.

Brain Trauma

There are three types of brain trauma: concussion, contusion and laceration. They most frequently result from falls, automobile or motorcycle accidents, blows to the head, or penetration of the brain by a foreign object such as a bullet. The critical elements in each type of injury are the extent of the injury and its location in the brain. The most frequent victims of brain trauma are young males. With speed and violence on the increase in our society, it is remarkable that brain trauma occurs no more frequently than it does, which is 200 per 100,000 of the population in any one year.

CONCUSSION

In concussion, the brain is momentarily jarred and shifted from its position. The result is usually nothing more than a brief loss of consciousness, lasting only seconds, or perhaps a minute or two. The longer the period of unconsciousness, the more severe and longer-lasting will the symptoms be. When the individual regains consciousness, he or she may not be able to recall events immediately preceding the accident. Post-traumatic symptoms may continue for several weeks. Those symptoms—their nature, length and severity—reflect pretrauma personality characteristics, hypersensitivity to pain, or preoccupation with bodily symptoms. The range of such symptoms includes headache and dizziness (most frequent symptoms), memory and concentration difficulties, irritability and insomnia. Doctors usually recommend a period of quiet for the individual and close observation of behavior. The extent of the brain damage may not be immediately observable.

Damage to the brain from a number of concussions, such as those experienced in prize-fighting, have a cumulative effect, eventually matching the symptoms caused by a more serious brain injury.

CONTUSION

Contusion is a more serious jarring of the brain, forcing it out of position and pressing it against the skull. Brain tissue on the cerebral cortex (exterior surface of the brain) may be damaged. The result will be more serious symptoms than those that occur from concussion.

Contusion will cause a longer period of unconsciousness, sometimes for days. The individual may experience convulsions and speech impairment when coming out of the coma. Confusion and some disorientation may also be present. Repeated concussions or contusions may result in permanent brain damage.

LACERATIONS

When a foreign object passes through the skull and enters the brain itself, the injury is a laceration. It is the most serious of brain traumas. The severity of the injury depends upon its location and the extent of the collateral damage the object causes as it passes through the brain. The effect of laceration varies widely, from death to intellectual, sensory or motor impairment. In rare cases, there will be only minor residual impairment.

Cerebral Vascular Accidents

There are two distinguishable cerebral vascular accidents: cerebral occlusion and cerebral hemorrhage.

CEREBRAL OCCLUSION

A blood vessel of the brain may clog from an embolus, that is, a ball-like clump of clotted blood or fat may move through a blood vessel until the vessel becomes too narrow for its passage. When the blood from that blocked vessel no longer provides adequate support for an area of the brain, the brain cells in that area degenerate and can no longer function. The same result can be caused by a thrombus, which is a buildup of fatty material on the inner surface of the vessel. As the buildup continues, it gradually reduces blood supplied to that area of the brain. When a cerebral vascular accident produces a sudden and dramatic set of symptoms, such as paralysis or inability to talk, an embolus, producing an instant clogging of the vessel, is likely to be the cause. A thrombus grows slowly at the same spot in the vessel, gradually reducing the supply of blood and progressively causing the development of symptoms. Cerebral vascular accidents cause a variety of symptoms, from death to such handicaps as aphasia, agnosia, apraxia (see glossary in Appendix) and a right- or left-sided paralysis.

CEREBRAL HEMORRHAGE

Here, a blood vessel ruptures, and blood pours out onto brain tissue, limiting the capacity of the brain to function. It is that kind of accident about which the individual with high blood pressure should be concerned. The rupture is usually caused by an aneurysm, which is a bulging in the blood vessel. Cerebral hemorrhaging is a serious condition that may cause the death of the victim immediately or in a matter of days. In less extensive hemorrhaging, the symptoms can nevertheless be quite disabling. They may include memory loss, impaired judgment, speech impairment and/or paralysis. As always with brain damage, its expression in symptoms depends upon its location and the extent of the damage.

Nutritional Deficiency

In this type of brain damage, the cause is the lack of certain vitamins necessary for brain function. The principal disorders resulting from vitamin deficiency are Korsakoff's syndrome, pellagra, and beriberi. The latter two are practically nonexistent in Western societies.

KORSAKOFF'S SYNDROME

This disease is a direct result of the inadequate diet that accompanies chronic alcoholism. In particular, a deficiency of vitamin B1 and thiamine causes the disease. It causes foolish thinking and talking and, in time, generalized weakness and gross intellectual impairment. Damage caused by the disease is irreversible.

PELLAGRA

An organic disease that has all but disappeared in this country, pellagra results from a diet deficient in niacin, a B vitamin. In the early part of this century, it was a principal cause of admission to state psychiatric hospitals in the South where, at that time, the principal diet ingredient, corn meal, provided inadequate amounts of vitamins.

Early symptoms are rash and diarrhea. If the diet deficiency is uncorrected, more serious psychological symptoms may develop, ranging from depression and anxiety to psychosis. When detected early enough, massive doses of the needed vitamin can correct the disorder.

BERIBERI

The disorder is most prevalent in Far Eastern countries, where vitamin-deficient polished rice is a major part of the diet. The critical missing ingredient is thiamine. Symptoms are lassitude, irritability, and concentration and sleep disorders.

Endocrine Disorders

The endocrine glands secrete hormones that are critical for such important bodily functions as growth, energy level and sexual activity. Oversecretions or undersecretions of some hormones can produce serious physical and mental disorders. The two glands in which that problem occurs most frequently are the thyroid and adrenal glands.

PROBLEMS OF THE THYROID GLAND

In the thyroid gland, either oversecretion or undersecretion can cause problems. Hyperthyroidism, that is, too much secretion, causes Graves' disease. The increase in thyroxin creates bodily changes that ordinarily accompany anxiety: sweating, apprehensiveness and hyperactivity. In extreme cases, hallucinations may develop.

Hypothyroidism, a deficiency of thyroxin, may cause myxedema, which, as might be expected, causes symptoms the opposite of those produced by hyperthyroidism. Its principal symptoms are sluggishness and depression.

In both disorders, patterning of symptoms will be influenced by the individual's personality before onset of the disorders; for example, a worrying type of person will show more of it with the hyperthyroidism, while a depressed and gloomy person will become more so in hypothyroidism.

Brain Damage from Infection

A number of infectious diseases can produce brain damage. They are encephalitis, meningitis and neurosyphilis.

ENCEPHALITIS

The term is a generic one meaning inflammation of brain tissue. The source of the infection can be any of a number of living and nonliving agents. The principal culprits are mosquitoes and ticks. The disease can also be caused by infections that travel from other organs of the body to the brain, principally from the ears and sinuses.

A particular epidemic of encephalitis, encephalitis lethargica, occurred in this country and in Europe during the period of World War I. The most prominent symptom, that which gave it its name, sleeping sickness, was an extreme lethargy, causing the infected individual to sleep for days, even weeks. The disease is not seen often now.

Encephalitis causes a number of physical symptoms, including vomiting, stiffness of neck and back, fever and tremors. In its acute phase, with high fever, delirium and disorientation will also occur. Most victims recover completely, although some may be left with paralysis of an arm or leg, severe tremors, and sensory and speech disorders. In infants, the disease may cause mental retardation.

MENINGITIS

Bacterial infection may inflame the three layers, or coats, that envelope and protect the brain. Such inflammation of the meninges causes symptoms similar to those of encephalitis. The principal epidemic form of the disease results from a menincoccal infection, which is worldwide in its occurrence, tending to reappear in an eight- or twelve-year cycle.

NEUROSYPHILIS

This disorder, the most devastating of the infectious disorders, results from a long-term and untreated infection caused by the syphilis spirochete. Since the development of the Wassermann test, which makes possible the early and reliable diagnosis of syphilis, neurosyphilis has largely been brought under control.

The syphilis infection is contracted by either coitus or oral-genital sex. It may also be transmitted from mother to fetus. The early symptom is a small sore at the site of the infection, which develops during the first three weeks after the event causing the infection. That early indication is followed by a darkish rash covering much of the body. Accompanying the rash will be fever, headache and fatigue, sore throat, and open sores in the mucous membranes of the mouth and genitals.

The insidious and dangerous aspect of untreated syphilis follows as the disease seems to abate or even disappear. Bitter disappointment is in store for the individual who believes so. The spirochetes are busy invading other organs of the body, including the heart and the cerebral tissues. About 30 percent of those infected in this way develop neurological impairment. In this paretic phase of the illness, the individual becomes paralyzed, inarticulate and convulsive, and gradually declines into a horrible death.

TREATMENT OF ORGANIC DISORDERS

As might be expected, the treatment of organic disorders is notably different from the treatment of functional disorders. It is principally a medically administered problem and makes use of skilled and delicate surgery, pharmaceutical drugs, such as the antibiotics, and medical procedures for maintaining the individual's general health. A course of psychotherapy is frequently recommended, along with neurological treatment, to help the patient with functional symptoms that develop in reaction to the neurological symptoms.

We consider here basic characteristics of neural tissue and neural damage that affect treatment, and then the principal approaches to treatment of the organic disorders.

Characteristics of Neural Tissue and Neural Damage that Affect Treatment

Neurologists attempting treatment of organic disorders take account of three characteristics of the nervous system: 1. the impossibility of creating new neural tissue; 2. the recoverability of damaged neurons; and 3. the existence of redundant areas.

An example of taking account of those characteristics in neurological treatment is consideration of the fact that when neural tissue in an area of the brain has been completely destroyed, only if there are redundant areas matching the function of the destroyed area is there hope of recovering the lost function.

Another example illustrates a different consideration. When arteriosclerosis or pressure on the brain reduces the supply of oxygen or other nutrients, the affected neural tissue is damaged. In such cases, the appropriate intervention, such as surgical removal of the pressure-causing tumor, can resume the supply of nutrients, after which the neurologist's focus will be to strengthen the general health of the individual in the hope that doing so will enable the damaged neural tissue to recover.

Neurological Treatment Approaches

There are three possibilities:

1. The most urgent is to remove or contain the condition causing the damage. Examples are surgical removal of a brain tumor; treatment of an infection with antibiotics; or drainage of fluid that is causing intracranial pressure. The possibility of attempting such procedures depends upon the extent of the neural damage and its accessibility.

2. A second approach is to treat the symptoms so that they interfere less with normal living. The treatment of Parkinson's disease by controlled doses of synthesized dopamine, which ameliorates the symptoms, is an example.

3. A third approach is to modify the patient's mode of carrying out everyday activities. The help of family members here is usually necessary. Strong motivation is a vital ingredient in order for such an approach to succeed.

When considering prognosis, three factors will be uppermost: extent of the damage; its location; and such secondary factors as the general health and age of the individual, energy level, personality and living circumstances.

EPILEPSY

Epilepsy is best considered apart from the other organic mental disorders. In most victims, it manifests itself during childhood, sometimes before the age of four. Occurring in 0.5 percent of the population, no cause for the illness can be identified in more than three-quarters of the affected group.

Epilepsy is known principally by its most prominent symptom, the epileptic seizure, but an assortment of the other organic disorders also cause convulsions or seizures. In most cases, such seizures are distinguishable from the typical epileptic seizure. Seizures from known pathology other than epilepsy are sometimes loosely referred to as acquired epilepsy; they are the result of very different causes, and should more properly be diagnosed for what they are, i.e, brain tumor, encephalitis, etc. Apart from such convulsion-causing organic conditions, there is what might be called a true epilepsy, which is diagnosed as idiopathic epilepsy. The cause of that condition has not yet been identified.

Four types of epileptoid seizure have been identified: grand mal (or major sickness), petit mal (or small sickness), psychomotor epilepsy, and Jacksonian epilepsy.

Grand Mal Epilepsy

The grand mal epileptic attack is preceded by a visual or auditory aura, signaling the impending occurrence of the attack. The aura is generally a distinctive pattern of changing lights or sounds. The patient will then cry out and lose consciousness.

There are four distinguishable phases to the grand mal attack: 1. the aura stage; 2. the tonic phase; the individual becomes rigid, with arms tightly flexed and legs outstretched. Muscular contractions continue for a minute or so, and breathing is interrupted briefly; 3. the clonic phase; jerking motions take the place of the tonic, or rigid, phase. A danger during this phase of the seizure is that the strong jerking movements will cause bodily injury; and 4. soon after, the individual falls into a coma.

Coming out of this coma, the individual is confused and responds weakly. There is no recollection of events preceding the attack.

Petit Mal Epilepsy

In one sense, petit mal has been well-named. Compared to the grand mal attack, it is indeed a small illness. For some seconds, ten to thirty, without warning, the individual is "absent," sitting or falling, staring, unaware of what is going on, and usually immobile. The attack is so fleeting, with so brief a period of unconsciousness and so few external symptoms, that those around the patient may be unaware of the attack. The individual may also give no sign of being aware of it, picking up the uncompleted activity begun before the attack.

The critical element of the small attack, like the proverbial dripping of water, is the wearing effect of repetitive seizures. Some patients may have literally a hundred petit mal "absences" in a day. That frequency of seizure ultimately can have profound consequences.

Psychomotor Epilepsy

This combination of motor and psychic disturbance is the most unusual of epileptic seizures. Following the advance warning of an aura, the attack consists of a loss of consciousness, during which there will be repetitive, seemingly automatic activities. Despite the reduced consciousness, the individual is frequently aware enough to resist attempts to control his or her activities. A grand mal attack may follow a psychomotor seizure.

An unusual feature of the psychomotor attack is the assortment of confused, sometimes psychoticlike, mental content that may accompany the episode. These include perceptual changes, in which ordinary objects take on different shapes and sizes; changes in self-awareness, causing the individual to experience depersonalization; and extreme cognitive and affective reactions. Schizophreniclike experiences, such as hallucinations or delusions and irrational behavior, are occasionally part of a severe psychomotor seizure. Assaultive behavior, although possible, is rare, and most often takes the form of resistance to efforts to control the bizarre behavior of the patient.

Jacksonian Epilepsy

Named for Hughlings Jackson, who first reported it, this type of epilepsy is more limited in behavioral and mental change than either grand mal or psychomotor epilepsy. Its symptoms principally are tingling and twitching of hands or feet, which may then spread to other parts of the body. Its cause has been localized in a small area of the brain, which may be excised to control the disorder.

*M*ental disorders may be grouped into two major categories. There are organic disorders, which are known to be caused directly and primarily by specific pathology in the brain, and functional disorders, which result from abnormal life experiences imposed on a normal brain. Organic disorders account for 25 percent of all first admissions to mental hospitals.

The functioning unit of the brain is the neuron. It consists of: 1. a cell body, providing the neuron's life support; 2. the dendrites, a system of fine branches that receives impulses from other neurons; and 3. terminal endings that transmit messages to other neurons. The gap between one neuron and another is the synapse. Impulses are transmitted across synapses by neurotransmitters.

Localization of function. Various human activities are controlled by highly specific areas of the brain. In localizing function, we may consider its three axes. They are front/back, left/right, and up/down.

In the front part of the brain is located the planning-verification functions; the information-processing unit is located in the back part of the brain. The left side of the brain (the left hemisphere) receives sensory input from the right side of the body and controls motor behavior of the right side of the body, and vice-versa. The left hemisphere sorts things out; the right hemisphere synthesizes. The higher levels of the brain have to do with cognitive and voluntary behavior.

There are three major symptom clusters in organic disorders. They are defects in basic mental activities, such as memory; impairment in higher mental functioning; and affective disorders.

The principal causes of organic disorders are brain degeneration—that is, deadening of brain cells (neurons)—brain tumors, vascular accidents, nutritional deficiency, endocrine disorders, and infection.

The effects of brain damage range from short-term memory loss to death. Vulnerability of the brain to behavioral impairment depends upon the presence of multiple cerebral pathways (redundancy).

Four organic mental disorders result from brain deterioration. They are: 1. Alzheimer's disease, initially manifesting itself in severe memory loss; 2. multi-infarct disease, resulting from blockage in the blood vessels of the brain, the primary result of which is a stroke, producing partial to extensive paralysis, with later signs of dementia; 3. Huntington's Chorea, which is transmitted by a dominant defective gene. Its symptoms are spasmodic jerking of arms and legs, bizarre behavior and loss of bodily function. It is a terminal illness; and 4. Parkinson's disease, which causes limited mobility, rigidity of facial and body muscles and, in later stages, dementia.

Brain tumors, which may develop within the brain or move from other parts of the body, may be benign or cancerous. A full array of psychiatric symptoms and death results if the tumor cannot be excised.

Brain trauma includes: a concussion, or slight jarring of the brain; contusion, or jarring which produces a displacement of the brain; and laceration, or penetration of the brain. Impairment depends upon location and extent of the damage.

Clogging of a cerebral blood vessel, either from clotted blood or fat moving into a narrow blood vessel or accumulation of fatty material on the interior of the blood vessel, is called cerebral occlusion and causes the paralysis and associated symptoms of a stroke. A ruptured cerebral blood vessel causes the same symptoms. Either can be fatal.

The principal organic mental disorders resulting from nutritional deficiency are: 1. Korsakoff's syndrome, which is caused by a deficiency of vitamin B1 and thiamine, brought about by bad dietary habits of alcoholics; and 2. pellagra, which results from diets deficient in niacin, a B vitamin.

Overactivity of the thyroid gland can cause such psychological symptoms as anxiety, sweating and hyperactivity. The condition is known as Graves' disease. Undersecretion of the thyroid gland causes lassitude and depression.

The principal infectious diseases resulting in organically-caused psychological disorders are encephalitis, meningitis and neurosyphilis.

Treatment of organic mental disorders is principally a medical problem, which may be accompanied by a course of psychotherapy to help the individual and his or her family to adjust to new limitations on behavior and personality changes that occur.

Epilepsy is known principally by the epileptic seizure. There are four types of epileptic seizure. They are grand mal (or major sickness); petit mal (or small sickness); psychomotor epilepsy, causing automatic repetitive motor activities; and Jacksonian epilepsy, the symptoms of which are severe tingling and twitching of hands and feet. The causes of idiopathic (or true) epilepsy are unknown.

Selected Readings

Casson, I. R., O. Seigel, R. Sham, E. A. Campbell, M. Tarlou and A. DiDomenico. 1984. "Brain Damage in Modern Boxers." *Journal of the American Medical Association,* 251: 2663-2667.

Cummings, J. L. 1985. *Clinical Neuropsychiatry.* Orlando, FL: Grune & Stratton.

Ewen, D. 1956. *Journey to Greatness: The Life and Music of George Gershwin.* New York: Holt, Rinehart and Winston. p. 298.

Hecan, H. and M. C. Albert. 1978. *Human Neuropsychology.* New York: Wiley.

Slater, E. and P. W. Beard. 1971. "The Schizophrenia-like Psychoses of Epilepsy." in J. Shields and I. J. Gottesman (Eds.). *Man, Mind and Heredity: Selected Papers of Eliot Slater on Psychiatry and Genetics.* Baltimore, MD: Johns Hopkins Press.

Volpe, A. and R. Kastenbaum. 1967. "TLC." *American Journal of Nursing,* 67: 100-103.

17

Mental Retardation

*K*nown in earlier years as feeblemindedness and mental deficiency, mental retardation is said to exist when an individual fails to develop the various skills requisite for independently and adequately solving the problems of ordinary living. If such impairment develops after the age of eighteen, it is an altogether different disorder, which is categorized as dementia.

The American Association on Mental Deficiency, a national association that provides information on mental retardation and promotes research in the field, education, and proper care for the mentally retarded, defines mental retardation as, "significantly subaverage general intellectual functioning existing concurrently with deficits in adaptive behavior and manifested during the developmental period." There is general agreement among educators and psychologists that of the two aspects of development included in the definition, adaptive behavior is a much more significant criterion than the formal measurement of intelligence. Approximately 1 percent of the population can be classified as mentally retarded.

TYPES OF MENTAL RETARDATION

There are two distinguishable types of mental retardation: 1. cultural/familial retardation, which is caused by some combination or interaction between normal genetic variation and an impoverished and unstimulating environment; and 2. organic retardation, the result of some physical condition that limits the development of the brain.

Cultural/ Familial Retardation

The condition usually results in a mild retardation (in the upper range of those classed as mentally retarded). Cultural/familial retardation accounts for the majority of those with a mild degree of retardation. Individuals with this type of retardation have good, normal physical growth, are normal in appearance, and fall within the normal range in physical abilities. Most of them learn to function in a marginally independent fashion if they are provided with suitable living accommodations. This type of mental retardation appears more prevalently in families at the lower end of the socioeconomic scale.

Organic Retardation

This form of mental retardation affects about 25 percent of the mentally retarded population. It results from a physiological or anatomical anomaly affecting brain development. Individuals with this form of mental retardation typically are different in appearance and behavior from others, characteristics that result from the underlying organic malfunction. They are often more seriously retarded, but this evaluation may be the result of the physical and behavioral anomalies that may mask intellectual functioning.

MISCONCEPTIONS ABOUT MENTAL RETARDATION

Despite the general awareness most adults have of the existence of mental retardation, they often include in that awareness misconceptions about the characteristics of the mentally retarded. In a compassionate article in the professional journal *Social Work,* I. R. Dudley identifies five common misconceptions which, in large measure, underestimate the capacity of the mentally retarded individual to understand his or her problem, and attribute to them undesirable characteristics that do not commonly exist. Common misconceptions are:

1. *The mentally retarded have little or no understanding of their limitations.* Except for the extremely retarded, most retarded individuals have a common sense awareness of their limited capacities and readily admit that they cannot do many things as well or as fast as others. They frequently describe themselves as "slow" at catching on.

2. *The mentally retarded are all alike.* That belief should be given the same status as the distasteful and obviously inaccurate statement, "All Chinese look alike." The mentally retarded vary in their physical appearance and in their personality characteristics as widely as do normal individuals. Some are cheerful and active; others are glum and lazy; some are handsome or beautiful, and others are not.

3. *They have little or no feeling about what people call them.* In fact, their preferred term for themselves is "slow."

4. *They have little understanding of how their limitations affect them in everyday life.* Quite the contrary! Most of the mild to moderately retarded ask advice and assistance; they slowly and prudently approach new situations or new problems.

5. *They are dangerous.* The mentally retarded are not assaultive. They occasionally have temper tantrums, as do other children of their mental age. Faulty judgment may cause them to appropriate property of others, but that is easily rectified; they train easily in property rights. If their behavior is at all criminal, it is a direct result of what they see in the behavior of others around them.

LEVELS OF RETARDATION

The *DSM IIIR* recognizes four levels of mental retardation. For want of a more adequate measure, the manual distinguishes levels on the basis of IQs. At the margins between different levels, there may be disagreement on classification, depending upon the nature of the observations available to the diagnostician. The four levels are:

Types of Mental Retardation	IQ Level	Population Estimates
Mild	50 to 70	5 million
Moderate	35 to 49	600,000
Severe	20 to 34	200,000
Profound	Below 20	90,000

(Estimates are based on the *DSM IIIR* percentage reports.)

Mild Mental Retardation

This level of retardation may not be diagnosed certainly until the child is three or four years old. In many cases, it is first officially diagnosed soon after the child begins school. For purposes of educational planning, this group is diagnosed as "educable," which means that they can benefit from academic schooling. Even before the time of school attendance, with a caring home environment (which, unfortunately, is often lacking for these children), the mildly retarded can develop simple social and communication skills. Their vocabulary will be notably limited and their enunciation poor. There is no notable impairment in sensorimotor areas, although learning to walk and talk will be delayed. They make progress very slowly, and in their late teens they can learn academic skills up to the sixth-grade level. As adults, given the motivation, they will usually develop sufficient social and occupational skills to provide some portion of their own support. They will continue, however, to require guidance and social support throughout their lifetime.

The mildly mentally retarded comprise 80 to 85 percent of the total mentally retarded population.

Moderate Mental Retardation

From the point of view of expected achievement level, this group is distinguished from the mildly mentally retarded as "trainable" (rather than educable). The term means that with care at home, they can be trained in simple communication skills but will respond poorly to schooling in academic subjects and are usually unable to progress beyond the second grade level. The schooling experience, under the best circumstances, can provide occupational and social skills that enable them, as adults, to work under supervision in sheltered workshops. Here they work at unskilled or semiskilled jobs and are able to earn some money for their own maintenance. Placement in the sheltered workshop not only provides some income, but provides, as well, supervision during the daytime hours. Twelve percent of the mentally retarded population fall into the category of moderate mental retardation.

Severe Mental Retardation

In every criterion of performance, this group falls behind the less severely retarded. Their retardation is manifest at an earlier age,; there is poor motor coordination and meaningless speech. Later in childhood, they acquire simple speech skills, sometimes only monosyllables, and can be taught rudimentary habits of hygiene. Never developing vocational skills, they can find employment, if at all, only in highly protective environments, where they may be taught simple, useful tasks; for example, putting items into containers.

Profound Mental Retardation

During the preschool years, these children develop little sensorimotor capacity; for example, coordinating what they see with hand movements. As time goes on, they will show further motor development and rudimentary self-care behavior. As adults, they continue to require constant aid and supervision, ultimately learning some useful self-care habits. This 1 percent of the mentally retarded population will continue, throughout their lifetimes, to be almost totally dependent upon hour-to-hour aid and constant supervision. Whether that care can ever be provided at home is questionable; but only the parents of a sadly handicapped child can make that decision, and they usually need professional support and guidance to do so.

SPECIAL SYMPTOMATOLOGY (OTHER THAN INTELLECTUAL DEFICIT) OF THE MENTALLY RETARDED

Such symptoms vary with the severity of the disorder.

Mild to Moderate Retardation

Here the symptoms are likely to be such personality traits as dependency, passivity, low tolerance for frustration, depression, and self-injurious behavior.

Severe or Profound Retardation

Here the special symptoms may be speech disorders, vision and hearing problems, cerebral palsy or other neurological disorders.

COURSE OF MENTAL RETARDATION

In planning for the mentally retarded, not only should the level of the retardation be considered, but also the long-term course of the disorder. The course followed by mental retardation varies with the two types of the disorder: cultural/familial retardation and organic retardation.

Course of Cultural/ Familial Retardation

Given a stimulating environment along the way, mentally retarded individuals, especially those with the two lesser degrees of impairment, will justify their own preferred name for themselves; i.e., "I am slow at learning things." By adulthood, they may show a notable improvement in adaptive behavior. Their problem is that it takes them longer to reach that point and requires a more caring environment. Sometimes that spurt in adaptive behavior appears when they are freed from the more restrictive demands of school attendance. That possibility should not cause parents to remove a child hastily from a good (tolerant) school setting. There will be enough time for that.

Course of Organic Retardation

When the cause of the retardation is a specific biological abnormality, the expected course is bleaker. In these types of retardation, the disorder is likely to be chronic and without remission and with little hope from treatment. Symptoms may become more severe.

MENTAL DISORDERS ASSOCIATED WITH MENTAL DEFICIENCY

The mental retardation of the individual may be made even more complex when it is accompanied by other mental disorders. The *DSM IIIR* lists three such mental disorders that appear three or four times more frequently in the mentally retarded group than in the general population. They are stereotyped movement disorder, infantile autism, and attention deficit with hyperactivity. They are described briefly here and more fully in chapter 18.

Stereotyped Movement Disorder	This developmental disorder is characterized by abnormal gross motor activity, tics (which are involuntary twitches) and repetitive movements or vocalizations.
Infantile Autism	This developmental disorder manifests itself during the first year-and-a-half of life, in which there is a lack of responsiveness to others, extremely limited communication skills, and bizarre behavior.
Attention Deficit Disorder	The principal feature of this developmental disorder is inappropriate attention deficits accompanied by hyperactivity.

CAUSATIVE FACTORS IN MENTAL RETARDATION

The pattern of etiological factors and the effects of those causal factors are notably different for the two major types of mental retardation, cultural/familial and organic.

Cultural/ Familial Retardation	Both severe environmental impoverishment and possible hereditary influences must be considered here.

IMPOVERISHED ENVIRONMENT

A 1962 report of the President's Panel on Mental Retardation assigns causation of this type of mental retardation in the following way: The majority of the mentally retarded are the children of the more disadvantaged classes of our society. This extraordinarily heavy prevalence in certain deprived populations suggests a major causative role, in some way not fully understood, for adverse social, economic, and cultural factors.

More recent studies of this usually mildly retarded group only confirms the belief that a multiply impoverished home is a principal causative factor in cultural/familial retardation; recent studies are beginning to suggest ways in which impoverishment impairs intellectual development. There are four especially significant adverse conditions that block intellectual developments in impoverished homes. They are as follows: 1. Inadequate diet that leads to malnutrition can produce low levels of energy and weak motivation. There is, in addition, an absence of medical care which, for example, by leaving sensory deficits in vision and hearing unattended, can seriously handicap an individual's development. 2. Parents who are so beset and distracted by the struggle to make ends meet may have little time available for their children. The resulting emotional impoverishment and the absence of a rich communication and social exchange among family members provide no stimulus for intellectual growth. Verbal ability, so much a part of intellectual functioning, is stunted. 3. Impoverished parents have low expectations for their children and offer them little stimulation for problem-solving activities, curiosity, reading or even social conversation, which are all significant aspects of middle-class family life. 4. Children growing up in impoverished homes soon develop the lowered self-esteem of their parents, which discourages them from making any effort to advance.

Entering school with those handicaps and performing poorly, they soon fall further and further behind, causing their teachers to develop low expectations of any progress from them. There is little in society or the classroom that interrupts that slide down to a lifetime diagnosis of mental retardation.

POSSIBLE HEREDITARY INFLUENCE

The mental retardation we are discussing here is not randomly distributed among families living in poverty; it seems to be concentrated in certain families. One study reports that 80 percent of the children with IQs below 80 had mothers with IQs below 80. The report further indicates that the lower the mother's IQ, the greater the probability that her children will have low IQs.

It should be noted that such a correlational finding does not necessarily indicate causation. It does not, by itself, establish a hereditary factor. The mother's low intelligence may only worsen the conditions which impoverishment imposes. And it is certainly true that a parent of low intelligence can offer less stimulus for intellectual development than a parent with normal intelligence, regardless of the level of impoverishment in the home.

Organically Caused Mental Retardation

The 25 percent of the mentally retarded whose retardation is organically caused have more severe levels of retardation than those who fall into the category of cultural/familial, and they also show more associated physical anomalies. Their retardation may be caused by genetic abnormalities, metabolic abnormalities or by such environmental factors as brain trauma, severe malnutrition, infection or premature birth.

GENETIC FACTORS

There are two types of genetic influence on the development of mental retardation: chromosomal anomalies and defective recessive genes which, when matched from both parents, produce the disorder. In 1991, two studies, one conducted in England and the other in this country, identified gene mutations on chromosomes 19 and 21 as contributory to the development of mental retardation.

Chromosomal Anomalies. In humans, there are twenty-one pairs of differentiating chromosomes (called autosomal chromosomes), and one pair of sex chromosomes. Mental retardation may result from abberations in either type.

Autosomal Aberrations. Here the normal splitting and matching of each parent's chromosomes (meiosis), the mother's in the egg and the father's in the sperm, does not occur normally; for example, the failure of one parent's number one chromosome to split. When fertilization takes place, there are then three number 21 chromosomes, giving the fetus one more chromosome than the normal forty-six. The aberrant process is known as trisomy-21. The result is a type of mental retardation known as Down's syndrome. The chances of a mother conceiving a child with Down's syndrome is age-related. One study reports that the chance of a woman under the age of twenty-nine conceiving a Down's syndrome child is one in every fifteen hundred births; by the age of forty-five, those chances become one in thirty. Down's syndrome results from a spontaneous defect in the mother's egg, not passed on in the standard hereditary pattern.

A medical procedure called amniocentesis can now identify the presence of this anomaly in the growing fetus. That medical possibility confronts the mother with the choice of preventing the birth of a Down's syndrome child with an abortion.

The Down's child is born with three types of handicap: 1. Shortened life expectancy. Because of vulnerability to cardiac and respiratory illness, these children are at high risk during the first six months of life. Advances in medicine have increased the survival rate during those months, and many Down's children now live to adulthood. At age one, having survived the early risks, their life expectancy is twenty-two years. 2. Physical appearance. There are well-known physical characteristics that mark the child as a Down's child. They include unusual almond-shaped eyes (which in past years led to these children being called "Mongoloid"), a flattened nose and broadened face, enlarged tongue with deep grooves, and stubby fingers. Cosmetic surgery reduces the abnormalities, particularly that of the tongue. Such an operation considerably improves eating habits and speech and makes interaction with other children more normal. Growth remains stunted.

Most, but not all, Down's children have IQs below 50 and are therefore moderately mentally retarded. About 10 percent of the moderately to severely retarded suffer this syndrome.

Sex Chromosome Anomalies. There are three types of sex chromosome anomalies: one occurring only in females, another occurring only in males, and a third affecting both sexes. The twenty-third chromosome, which is responsible for the determination of the embryo's sex, normally has two X chromosomes in the female, and an XY pair in the male. Aberrations in this pattern can occur in both sexes. In the female, a condition known as Turner's syndrome results when there is only one X chromosome. Such physical characteristics as retarded growth and absence of secondary sexual characteristics result. Only 20 percent of this population are mentally retarded; others may show a variety of perceptual deficiencies.

In the male, a comparable anomaly results when there are more than two X chromosomes. Known as Klinefelter's syndrome, the disorder causes mental retardation in 25 percent of the children affected.

The third sex chromosome anomaly results from what is known as the fragile X syndrome. Here a genetically induced malformation of the X chromosome produces the disorder, which is estimated to cause 10 percent of all mental retardation. There are anomalous physical characteristics such as elongated face and prominent jaw and forehead. Of more significance is its seeming relationship to childhood autism. Ten to 15 percent of autistic children also have fragile X chromosome. Because females have two X chromosomes (XX), the stronger one seems to compensate for the fragile X chromosome, and, as a result, females are less frequently mentally retarded.

Recessive and Defective Genes. A recessive gene is one whose effect on the physical being of the child can only appear when it is matched with another identical recessive gene from the other parent. This is more likely to occur in the children of married relatives. Defective recessive genes have been identified as responsible for three types of mental retardation: phenylketonuria (PKU), Tay-Sachs disease, and cretinism. In all of these conditions, the recessive genes produce a malfunction in the metabolic processes.

Phenylketonuria (PKU). In this genetic disorder, the matched recessive genes leave the child with an excess of phenylalanine. The end result is serious damage to the developing central nervous system, in turn causing mental retardation, seizures, hyperactivity and erratic behavior.

Early diagnosis, which is now possible and likely because tests for the condition are routinely performed soon after birth, will initiate a regimen of feeding begun during the first months of life and continued until the child is six years old. The diet keeps from the child all foods high in phenylalanine. Because of the possibility of eliminating necessary nutrients in the diet of the child, such a diet must be supervised by a competent physician.

When PKU goes untreated, the condition produces severe to profound mental retardation, with the IQ typically below 40, and such other problems as to require institutionalization. On the other hand, when the condition has been treated successfully and an appropriate diet maintained, if a treated woman should become pregnant, there is a high likelihood that her children would be born healthy and with normal intelligence. In any case, where the possibility of PKU exists, genetic counseling should be sought prior to pregnancy.

Tay-Sachs Disease. Another genetic disorder transmitted by matched recessive genes and impacting on the body's metabolic processes is Tay-Sachs disease. The disorder damages metabolism as a result of the absence of the enzyme hexosaminidase A in the cerebral tissues. Although not manifest at birth, it is usually detected between the eighth and twenty-fourth month, when the infant shows progressive muscle weakness, expressed in inability to roll over, to raise the head or torso, or to initiate movement. There is a lack of appetite and loss of sight and hearing. Death usually occurs between the second and fourth years.

The disease is confined to those of Eastern Europe and Jewish ancestry.

Cretinism. This type of mental retardation results from a deficient secretion of the thyroid gland. The principal cause of it is a lack of iodine in the blood. Other causes may be operative: birth injury which produces bleeding into the thyroid gland; infectious diseases such as diphtheria, measles and whooping cough; or occasionally a genetic defect causing the thyroid to be underactive.

Public health measures taken both in this country and in most other countries affecting the distribution and use of iodized salt have largely eliminated absence of iodine in the body as a cause of cretinism.

ENVIRONMENTAL CAUSES

Environmental causes of mental retardation fall into three categories: those that operate in the prenatal environment, those resulting from injuries at birth, and postnatal causes.

Prenatal Causes. There are two principal prenatal causes of mental retardation: 1. Viral or bacterial infections of the mother during pregnancy which are transmitted to the fetus through the placenta (protective membrane lining the uterus). Such infections create inflammation of the brain and degeneration of brain tissue. Rubella, or German measles, when contracted by pregnant women, although only a mild illness in the mother, with low temperature and a rash, can cause mental retardation when transmitted to the child. The danger to the fetus is greatest during the first three months of pregnancy. During that period, 50 percent of infected mothers transmit the disease to the fetus. The result, depending upon the severity and location of the resulting brain damage, can be mental retardation, sensory defects and congenital heart disease. 2. Fetal alcoholic syndrome (FAS). This pathetic preventable condition results from heavy use of alcohol during pregnancy. (Any consumption of alcohol during pregnancy is unwise.) Alcohol present in the mother's body acts directly on the child, causing brain damage and the possibility of various physical and mental defects. One of the effects can be microcephaly (development of a small brain). Microcephaly causes mental retardation, mild to moderate. Apart from mental retardation, which is not always present in FAS, other symptoms are likely, including attention and academic problems, hyperactivity and behavioral problems.

Incidence estimates of FAS in children of alcoholic mothers range from 26 to 76 percent, depending on the strictness of the diagnosis. It is now estimated that one case of FAS occurs in every 750 live births. That statistic indicates use of alcohol by pregnant women as one of the most common causes of organically caused mental retardation.

Birth Injuries. A variety of conditions existing during the birth of a child can damage the brain and cause mental retardation. They include prolonged birth, which can deny the fetal brain necessary oxygen and inflict pressure on the head, and physical trauma. Birth injuries account for a relatively small fraction of organically caused mental retardation. Among premature infants, approximately 20 percent show some signs of neurological problems. They range from later difficulty in learning to mental retardation. Markedly low birth weight shows a correlation with lower-than-average intelligence.

A nasty cause of brain damage after birth, seemingly on the increase, is child abuse. Statistics are lacking, but one authority suggests that child abuse should be considered a major cause of organic brain damage in children, which condition becomes mental retardation in many cases, especially among infants.

CARING FOR THE MENTALLY RETARDED

Since almost 90 percent of the mentally retarded fall only marginally below the IQ requirement for classification within the normal range of intelligence (an IQ of 68 or above), and since an even larger percentage of them, despite below-normal IQs, are able to adapt and to manage in simple environments, the goal of caring for the mentally retarded should be to bring them as close to normal living as their capacity (latent as well as manifest) makes possible.

Considerations for doing that can be examined under three principal headings: the role of parents; society and the mentally retarded; prevention and treatment.

The Role of Parents

Issues here are initial response of parents to the birth of a retarded child; problems of rearing; and dealing with emotional problems.

INITIAL RESPONSE

Disappointment and hurt in the hearts and minds of parents are the frequent, perhaps universal, greeting that meets children born mentally retarded. For the organically and severely retarded, with notable physical signs, that disappointment, undoubtedly accompanied by anguish for the child's illness, may appear early in the life of the child. For the mildly mentally retarded with no physical stigmata, the disappointment may come gradually as the child fails to meet benchmarks of normal development. The disappointment may be expressed in the way in which parents hold the child or talk to him or her.

Those initial responses are a natural, human response. What matters for the future of the child is what feelings follow that initial disappointment. Later responses are dependent upon characteristics of the parents themselves—their own feelings of self-esteem and adequacy, the state of their marriage, their socioeconomic status, the place of intellectual development in their value system, and, indeed, their own intellectual level.

Studies of parental reactions report certain responses to be common. 1. Parents may persistently deny that their child could be mentally retarded. That denial can cause individuals to go from one doctor or psychologist to another, seeking a different opinion. Rose Kennedy, mother of President John F. Kennedy, despite the competent medical and psychological opinions available to her, continued to believe that her daughter would grow out of her retardation, until the emotional changes of adolescence caused such problems that the girl was institutionalized. 2. Parents may covertly feel guilt and, or, anger. All sorts of past actions will be dredged up; in some cases, used to feed guilt; or in others, to fuel anger at a spouse. 3. Parents may feel that the retardation of their child is punishment for past misdeeds or sins.

The best resource parents can have is the comfort they can give each other; that, with the help of a professional counselor, clergyperson or physician, can draw the parents back to their child and the love and care the child will need.

CARING FOR THE CHILD

Professionals familiar with the needs of the retarded and their special problems will point out to parents that the needs of their child are the same as the needs of the normal child: physical care and proper nutrition, love, and a relationship that builds the child's self-esteem and provides opportunity for social life as they grow. A need that may be more pressing for the retarded is the satisfaction of discovering what they can do for themselves. Achievements, although they may be at a lower level than those of siblings or normal children, are nevertheless rewarding to the retarded; and a significant part of that reward is the pleasure parents find in their child and the special ways that are created to give recognition to such children for their special accomplishments.

Parents face a problem in the achievement area; the achievements of retarded children should be measured by a standard that is all their own. Achievement is an advance over previous behavior; simple things such as feeding themselves, learning to walk independently, and first efforts at communication. For the mildly retarded, as they approach school age, there will be learning to recognize the meaning in a picture, the interpretation of symbols, and then simple words. A big accomplishment will be in writing their own name.

The care parents must take is to encourage their child to stretch toward his or her potential, always on guard not to show disappointment at slowness and faltering steps the retarded child will take toward more advanced behavior. There should not be pressure, but "soft" challenge, admiration and pleasure, even when the child takes only half a step in the right direction.

When siblings are present, they, too, must be taught the proper standards for judging performance of a handicapped brother or sister. Yet the siblings' own efforts at growth and accomplishment must also be recognized. It is indeed a happy family when the retarded child and his or her normal brothers and sisters take pleasure in each other's different accomplishments.

Choosing a school and knowing what to expect is an anguishing problem. Parents need preparation for this decision, as does the child. Schools in different communities and in different parts of the country vary widely in accommodating the retarded. Parents will profit not only from talking to experts in the field, but also from speaking with other parents of retarded children, especially if their children are similar in adaptability and if parents have the reputation of doing a good job.

EDUCATION

As early as the 1920s, schools in some parts of the country set up special classes for the mentally retarded. In New York City, for example, they were called Classes for Those of Retarded Mental Development (CRMD). A twofold problem existed: such classes did not exist countrywide, and there was no legal requirement that such children attend classes. In 1975, Congress passed Public Law 94-142, which mandated for every citizen under the age of twenty-one free public education matching his abilities or handicap.

For handicapped children, including the mentally retarded, teams of educators, including administrators, psychologists and teachers, now develop for each child an individualized educational program (IEP). Once the group has approved the program, it is committed to writing. The school system is then required to provide the necessary resources. Progress reports are submitted periodically to the original committee for whatever additional recommendations they consider necessary.

Unfortunately, as educational resources are strained, the standards of what must be provided are often lowered. The Supreme Court, in the case of a deaf child seeking a sign-language interpreter (the Rowley decision), has supported the school district's right to determine "a basic floor of opportunity" in its educational programs. Going beyond that to achieve higher levels of academic performance is a matter for the school system (and ultimately the community) to decide.

EMOTIONAL PROBLEMS

The life of a retarded child, even in a home with caring parents, is a more emotionally trying life than that which most children normally experience. It is no surprise, then, that the mentally retarded suffer emotional disorders, from anxiety-based disorders to schizophrenia, more frequently than do normal children. Parents of mentally retarded children can expect "down" periods that can approach depression, feelings of inadequacy, and apprehension about venturing into new environments. More serious disorders—schizophrenia, alcoholism or severe behavior disorders—occur in the retarded at a level of 15 percent.

Parents who have come to accept the retardation of their child may find the additional burden of emotional problems that develop as the child grows older a heavy burden, indeed. There is help to be found. Increasingly, professionals who specialize in the field of mental retardation are coming to recognize that it is in the mental health area particularly where they can be especially helpful to parents. As a result, mental health centers, especially for the retarded, are now available in most metropolitan areas across the country.

As the mentally retarded individual approaches adolescence, emotional problems become more acute, for the child and for the parents. Now the need for increased independence and peer contact, male and female, becomes more important; physical changes bring on sexual urges. It will be easier for the parent to deal with such problems if he or she has learned how to deal with the intellectual problems. The same common sense, prudence, and supervision that parents of normal children must use are also useful in responding to the retarded adolescent. With such children, it all requires a lot more time and greater attention.

SOCIAL ATTITUDES AND PUBLIC POLICY

For much of the first half of the twentieth century, neglect and denial dominated society's attitudes toward the mentally retarded, and there were few laws protecting their rights. Improvement in those attitudes and passage of federal and state laws came as an extension of the civil rights movement of mid-century. As black members of American society began to use civil disobedience and protest to attract national attention to their problems, and as those actions effected changes, principally through federal court decisions, other neglected or suppressed groups adopted the same techniques for their own ends, particularly women and the physically handicapped, soon joined by the parents of the mentally retarded. The latter group organized themselves into the National Association for Retarded Citizens (NARC). A major advance for the mentally retarded was the Alabama federal court decision (*Wyat v. Stickney*) mandating an individualized treatment program for each hospitalized retarded person, skilled staff to administer such treatment, and a humane psychological and physical environment. Although governing only hospitals in Alabama, the decision provided a precedent for other hospitals, and they have moved ahead to try to implement the decision.

The result of those efforts has been the establishment of a policy platform of human rights for the mentally retarded that has molded programs of care and reshaped social attitudes. This platform asserts that, as human beings, the mentally retarded have the right to be protected from abuse of any sort, to receive an education individually customized, and to live in the least restricted environment appropriate to their adaptive capacities. If institutionalization is required, the institution is mandated to provide continuing treatment. Beyond those basic principles, social policy now vigorously encourages independent living, service programs that are individualized, a system of reports to indicate progress, and mainstreaming the retarded individual in school, employment, and social life as fully as is possible.

The Special Problems of Mentally Retarded Adults

As a result of the changes in social policy and the changes in social attitudes affected by that policy, it is now easier for the adult retarded individual, especially those with only mild or moderate levels of retardation, to solve problems of adult adjustment, the principal ones of which are independent living, employment, and the possibility of marriage.

INDEPENDENT LIVING

Beginning in the sixties, the establishment of small residential centers for groups of mentally retarded adults now provides one of the most helpful resources for the parents of the mentally retarded. Here, in locations close to the homes of the residents, it is possible to offer them a family atmosphere and some sense of independence with whatever level of supervision is necessary. The centers, at their best, offer four levels of care: supported living arrangements, in which residents work during the day in sheltered workshops and return to the center in the evening; centers that provide community living facilities and 24-hour supervision; and for the severely retarded; small-scale nursing home type care. Yet, a large number of the most severely retarded must still be provided mainly custodial care in large hospitals.

EMPLOYMENT

Perhaps the greatest progress in helping adult retardants to live an independent existence is in the area of employment. Their right to employment is now protected by both federal and state laws. Many of the least retarded work in industrial settings at regular wages; others find employment in sheltered workshops, where speed and complexity of job is set to match their capabilities.

MARRIAGE

In the past, stable relationships between male and female retarded adults were discouraged, marriage was forbidden, and involuntary sterilization was practiced in many states. A more tolerant attitude now exists, with recognition given to the rights of retarded individuals to set up appropriate heterosexual relationships consistent with their ability and sense of responsibility.

*M*ental retardation affects one of every one hundred live births. Some live only a few years after birth, and others die early in adulthood. The DSM IIIR recognized four levels of retardation: mild, with IQs ranging from 50 to 70; moderate, with IQs of 35 to 49; severe, with IQs of 20 to 34; and profound, with IQs below 20.

There are two major types of mental retardation, separated on the basis of etiological factors. They are as follows: 1. cultural/familial retardation, in which causation is judged to be a result of cultural deprivation during early upbringing, and the possibility of hereditary influences; and 2. organically related mental retardation. The cultural/familial type of retardation accounts for the majority of those with mild retardation. Organic factors are operative in 25 percent of the mentally retarded population.

Organically caused mental retardation may result from genetic abnormalities, metabolic abnormalities, or environmental influences, such as birth injuries or brain injuries. The principal types of organic retardation are Down's syndrome, Klinefelter's syndrome, Turner's syndrome, Phenylketonuria (PKU), Tay-Sachs disease, and cretinism. Fetal alcohol syndrome, related to alcohol consumption during pregnancy, causes the development of a small brain (microcephaly). Children of such pregnancies are usually at least mildly retarded.

In recent years, as a result of both federal and state court decisions, attitudes toward the mentally retarded have changed; and with that change have come major improvements in the type of care mandated for the mentally retarded. An important outcome is the establishment of a policy platform of the human rights of the mentally retarded. That platform now shapes policies in schools, hospitals, employment, and social life.

Selected Readings

Carter, C. H. 1970. *Handbook of Mental Retardation Syndromes.* Springfield, IL: Charles C. Thomas.

Cegelka, P. T. and H. J. Prekin. 1982. *Mental Retardation: From Categories to People.* Columbus, OH: C. E. Merrile.

Cheseldine, S. and R. McConkey. 1979. "Parental Speech To Young Down's Syndrome Children: An Intervention Study." *American Journal of Mental Deficiency,* 83: 612-620.

Gold, M. 1976. "Task Analysis of a Complex Assembly Task by the Retarded Blind." *Exceptional Children,* 43: 78-84.

Kiely, J. L., N. Paneth and M. Susser. 1981. "Low Birth Weight, Neonatal Care and Cerebral Palsy." In J. Mittler and J. M. deJong (Eds.). *Frontiers in Mental Retardation: II Biomedical Aspects.* Baltimore, MD: University Park Press.

Nihira, K., F. Foster, M. Sheehaas and H. Leland. 1974. *AAMD Adaptive Behavior Scale: Manual* (rev. ed.). Washington, D.C.: American Association on Mental Deficiency.

Richardson, S. A. 1978. "Careers of Mentally Retarded Young Persons: Services, Jobs and Interpersonal Relations." *American Journal of Mental Deficiency,* 82: 349-359.

18

Abnormal Behavior of Children and Adolescents

Sensitivity to the differences between childhood psychological disorders and adult psychological disorders is a fairly recent development. Early theories tended to view children as small adults and did not recognize the cognitive and emotional differences between the two age groups. The developmental processes of childhood and adolescence had not been studied closely; and it was therefore difficult to achieve an accurate understanding of what constituted normal and abnormal behavior for children.

More recently, theorists have acknowledged those processes, and substantial progress has been made in the study of childhood disorders. This increased understanding has led to improved treatment facilities for children and to a more meaningful classification system for maladaptive behaviors. This is reflected in the difference between the DSM I, published in 1952, and the DSM IIIR, published in 1987, which is much more comprehensive. The need for this increased attention to abnormal childhood disorders is indicated by their prevalence, which most experts place at 13 percent of all children in the United States.

SPECIFIC DIFFICULTIES IN STUDYING CHILDHOOD DISORDERS

Three possible difficulties are considered here: the influence of adults, developmental considerations; and defining "abnormal."

The Influence of Adults

It is impossible to understand a child's behavior without understanding the role of the important adult figures in the child's life. Children rarely seek help for their psychological problems on their own, so it is up to adults to act on behalf of the child. Parents, other relatives and school personnel are the obvious key people. Parents can be reluctant to seek help for their child because they may feel that any problems reflect upon their ability as parents. They often view the difficulty as a "phase" though which the child is going, with the expectation that the child will soon "outgrow" this stage. This is particularly true of the less impairing disorders such as fears, simple phobias, and social anxiety.

Sometimes, however, too much parental intervention can be a problem. By focusing undue or excessive attention on a difficulty, parents can exacerbate a problem that might be only transitory.

The start of school is frequently the time when a child's psychological problems are first recognized. One reason for this may be that behavior that is acceptable at home cannot be tolerated in a school setting. An attention-deficit hyperactivity disorder (to be discussed later) is an example of this type of problem.

Furthermore, teachers and other educational personnel are exposed to a broad range of children and can use this exposure, in addition to their training and experience, to assess abnormal behavior.

Developmental Considerations

The behavior of children must be evaluated within the developmental context in which the behavior occurs. Normal development involves the interaction of three areas of individual functioning: the cognitive-intellectual; interpersonal and emotional; and physical-motor areas. Development proceeds in stages in these areas, with one stage building upon an earlier stage. Difficulties or disruptions at one stage can lead to more serious problems at a later time. It is therefore important to recognize and treat any developmental abnormalities as early as possible.

A complicating factor in this process is that children often develop at varying rates, and it is often difficult to differentiate between what is just slow development and what is disruptive or abnormal behavior.

What is "Abnormal"?

In most cases, the differences between normal and abnormal behavior are not as clearly defined in children as they are in adults. All children, at times, display maladaptive behavior, such as bedwetting or temper tantrums. Such behavior may be a result of specific stress and be a normal response to that stress for a child at a certain developmental stage. Most theorists in this area state that any behavior should be viewed as a problem if it occurs repeatedly and interferes seriously with the child's, or another person's, functioning.

Classifying Children's Disorders

Until very recently, diagnosis and classification of the psychological disorders of children have been a woefully neglected and confused area of abnormal psychology. For example, the first *Diagnostic and Statistical Manual,* issued in 1952, listed only two categories of children's disorders: childhood schizophrenia (which is now considered an inappropriate diagnosis) and a catch-all type of category which was labeled "adjustment reaction of childhood."

Eighteen years later, with the publication of the *DSM III,* most clinicians still found the proposed system unreliable and inappropriate. Not until the 1987 revision, *DSM IIIR,* was a generally accepted classification system provided for children's disorders.

Although the *DSM IIIR* now lists nine categories of children's disorders, they can, for our purpose, be most conveniently discussed under five headings: disruptive behavior disorders, affective (emotional) disorders, special symptom disorders, developmental disorders, and gender identity disorders, which we have discussed in chapter 15 and therefore do not include in this chapter. For each of the other four principal groupings and their subtypes, we describe symptomatology, possible causes, and treatment.

DISRUPTIVE BEHAVIOR DISORDERS

Under this heading, the *DSM IIIR* lists three subtypes of disruptive behavior: attention-deficit hyperactivity disorder (usually abbreviated as ADHD), conduct disorders, and oppositional-defiant disorder. All have in common the child's frequent disregard of the rights of others.

Attention-Deficit Hyperactivity Disorder (ADHD)

Behavior of the ADHD child is troublesome to parents and teachers; because of its disruptive effect in the classroom, it is a frequently used diagnosis.

SYMPTOMATOLOGY

The behavior of children diagnosed as having attention-deficit hyperactivity disorder is characterized by impulsiveness, inattention, and physical hyperactivity that is inappropriate for the child's age. These highly distractible children have difficulty remaining still and will race from one activity to another. Nothing seems to hold their attention for very long. They frequently act with little thought of the consequences of their actions and are disruptive when engaged in social activities. In the classroom, they do not attend to directions, are frequently out of their seats, and will call out at inappropriate times. While these children often have average or above-average intelligence, they are underachievers in school and often exhibit specific learning disabilities. Because of their poor scholastic achievement and social difficulties, ADHD children often display low self-esteem. In addition, their relationship with their parents is frequently strained by their inability to follow rules and their high level of motor activity.

ADHD is the childhood problem that is most often referred to mental health workers. One study (Anderson et al. 1987) reports the prevalence of this disorder at about 7 percent of all preadolescents. As with most childhood disorders, the number of boys diagnosed as ADHD greatly exceeds the number of girls receiving this diagnosis.

PROGNOSIS

An important issue in studying this disorder is whether or not it persists into adolescence and adulthood. The answer is far from conclusive. In one study (Hechtman and Weiss 1983), adolescent boys with ADHD and adolescent boys without ADHD were compared. The results suggested that the ADHD boys had a substantially higher rate of delinquent behavior. The study also revealed, however, that most of the ADHD adolescents did not become habitual offenders as adults. Milder symptoms, such as impoverished interpersonal relationships and poor self-concept, did persist into adulthood.

Many researchers believe that when evaluating long-term prognosis, it is important to differentiate between subjects who exhibit pure ADHD symptoms and those who also display aggressive symptoms. A study by Satterfield (1982) initially demonstrated that hyperactive boys were twenty times more likely to be in trouble with the law than was a sample of "normal" boys. He then divided the hyperactive group into two subgroups, one with aggressive symptoms and one without, and determined that the nonaggressive group had no more legal problems than did the normal population.

It can be generalized from these and other studies that while many ADHD children exhibit improvement in their behavior as they enter late adolescence, the subgroup with aggressive behavior in addition to ADHD symptoms will continue to have significant problems as teenagers and adults.

CAUSES OF ATTENTION-DEFICIT HYPERACTIVITY DISORDER

No one definitive cause of ADHD has been discovered. A recent study (Greenhill 1990), however, has provided evidence for a biological basis for ADHD. The study determined that ADHD subjects utilized 12 percent less glucose, a source of fuel for the brain, than did normal subjects. The brain area most deprived of glucose was an area associated with attention and motor control, which are the central problems of ADHD children. The study does not clarify whether ADHD is caused by the glucose imbalance or whether other brain chemicals are also involved.

Other researchers have focused on the central nervous system as a factor in the development of this disorder. Zentall and Zentall (1983) have posited that ADHD children are underaroused, and without adequate motivation, they find it hard to focus attention. Coleman and Lewis (1988) have hypothesized that a genetic predisposition, along with environmental stress, may lead to ADHD.

Feingold (1977) ties attention-deficit hyperactivity disorder to the child's diet. He focuses particularly on food additives such as food coloring. Sugar has also been cited as a contributing factor; but there currently is little evidence to suggest that food plays a significant role in the development of ADHD.

Another possible factor is a genetic, or hereditary, basis. A study by Rie and Rie (1980) reported that the relatives of ADHD children have a higher rate of personality disorders than does the normal population. On this basis, they hypothesized a possible genetic basis for the disorder.

Other theories suggest that difficulties during pregnancy and delivery of these children may contribute to the development of ADHD.

TREATMENT

There are three main treatment approaches for ADHD. These are pharmacological, cognitive-behavioral, and dietary.

The Use of Medication. The use of drugs to treat the symptoms of ADHD is probably the most common form of treatment. The drugs most frequently used are central nervous stimulants such as Ritalin and Dexedrine. These stimulants have the paradoxical effect of reducing motor activity and thereby improving a child's ability to focus and maintain attention. Studies (Ottenbacher and Cooper 1983) indicate that these drugs achieve their results without impairing the child's cognitive abilities. School performance is often improved. Not all ADHD children respond to medication; about 35 percent of this population receive no benefits. Some researchers believe that those ADHD children who also exhibit symptoms of conduct disorder are also those who are least likely to benefit from medication.

There are many critics of the use of drug therapy. Gadow (1986) questions the long-term benefits of medication, especially when the underlying causes of the disorder are neglected. In most instances, when the medication is discontinued, the symptoms reappear. A troublesome result of medication is the physical side effects they produce, such as insomnia, slowed growth and impaired appetite, which are particularly attributed to the use of Ritalin and other stimulants. Furthermore, the long-range physical effects upon children of these medications have not been studied fully.

Cognitive-Behavioral Therapies. The use of behavior modification techniques has proven effective in the treatment of ADHD. These include token economy systems, which involve providing a clear explanation of expected behavior to the child and then a tangible reward system for satisfactory performance. Behavior modification systems have achieved positive results (Kazdin 1977) in the classroom, such as increasing concentration and decreasing disruptive behavior. A problem with token economies, however, is that they do not adapt easily to other situations. Another criticism of this technique is that it can have a negative impact on the child's belief that he or she can control his or her own behavior (Horn 1983).

Cognitive-behavioral approaches also attempt to teach ADHD children the use of verbal self-instructions to increase attention span and decrease impulsive actions. The children are taught to stop before acting impulsively and to utilize learned self-instruction to monitor and modify their behavior (Meichenbaum 1977); for example, saying to themselves before taking action, "Hold up, now; let me think about this for a minute."

Many researchers report that the use of drug therapy, in conjunction with cognitive-behavioral techniques, is most effective in treating ADHD (Gittelman-Klein et al. 1980).

Dietary Modifications. This type of treatment focuses on removing food additives and sugar from the child's diet. While anecdotal findings suggest some positive benefits from this type of diet, research studies have provided little support for a dietary method of treating ADHD (Milich 1986).

Conduct Disorder

This diagnosis may be considered a more extreme type of disruptive disorder than ADHD and includes antisocial and occasionally delinquent behavior. It must, however, be considered a separate disorder with its own etiology.

SYMPTOMATOLOGY

The *DSM IIIR* defines conduct disorder as "a persistent pattern of conduct in which basic rights of others are violated or major societal norms are violated." The characteristics include problems at home and in school, poor frustration tolerance, and the destruction or theft of the property of others. These children are often involved in physical fights and are at increased risk for developing early substance abuse and precocious sexual activity. It is not unusual for a conduct-disordered child to suffer from emotional problems, particularly depression.

It is estimated that about 3.5 percent of children can be diagnosed as conduct disorders. This figure rises to about 9 percent for adolescents (Gittelman et al. 1985). Again, males are much more likely to be diagnosed as conduct disorders. The *DSM IIIR* reports that boys are four-and-a-half times more likely to suffer from this disorder than are girls.

PROGNOSIS

Unfortunately, conduct disorders often persist into late adolescence and adulthood. One study (Kazdin 1987) reports that children with conduct disorders, later on as adults, in many cases continue the pattern in criminal activities. As adults they have difficulty maintaining employment and frequently experience marital problems.

Another study reports that a child diagnosed as conduct-disordered is significantly more likely to become an alcoholic or to become an antisocial personality as he or she grows older than are children with other emotional problems (Rutter and Garmezz 1983).

Many theorists believe that the diagnosis of conduct disorder more accurately predicts impaired adult functioning than does any other factor or diagnosis, except for childhood psychosis.

CAUSES OF CONDUCT DISORDERS

The family environment is viewed as an important factor in the development of conduct disorders. These families are often disrupted by marital problems, emotional instability, and inconsistent displays of affection and support. Discipline is often inappropriate and is characterized by particularly harsh or extremely lenient methods. Patterson (1986) addressed the matter of disciplining techniques in a study with conduct-disordered children. His results indicated that the parents of these children are inconsistent in punishing misbehavior and fail to teach skills necessary for social and academic success.

There is some support for the role of genetic factors in the development of conduct disorders. Mednick (1986), in a comprehensive study of more than fourteen thousand adopted children, concluded that adopted children are more likely to have engaged in criminal behavior if their biological parents were criminals, even if they had never lived with their biological parents.

TREATMENT

Since family influences are important in the development of this disorder, many treatment methods focus on treating the family unit. These include teaching effective parenting techniques and family therapy to reduce discord in the home. Given the problems and stresses in many of these families, this approach has had limited success.

Educating the conduct-disordered child in the use of cognitive-behavioral skills is another treatment approach. These skills include the identification of problems, the use of self-statements to modify behavior, and the development of more appropriate behavior. The method appears to be most effective with preadolescent children.

It often becomes necessary to remove the conduct-disordered child from the home and place him or her in a residential treatment setting. This is most common with adolescents. Many of these settings utilize behavior management techniques and control the child's complete environment. The child must comply with rules and demonstrate appropriate behavior in order to achieve specific privileges and rewards. It is also important, through the use of various methods such as role playing, to teach new ways of behaving and important social and academic skills.

Oppositional-Defiant Disorder

This diagnosis is used for children who show negative, argumentative or hostile behavior. Such children lose their tempers frequently, object to doing chores, and ignore rules. The behavior is most frequently expressed in family settings, but may also be carried over to school or other settings involving authority figures. Occasionally, the child will be relatively subdued at home and act out his or her disruptive behavior only elsewhere, usually in the classroom. One can surmise that such behavior is a displacement of anger felt about a home problem that cannot be expressed there.

The diagnosis is a relatively new entry into the classification system for children's disorders and has met with some resistance from some clinicians who feel that giving a child a psychiatric diagnosis for such behavior is an example of overkill that may handicap a child in later years.

Many parents of teenagers or preteens will recognize the behavior described as a phase their children have "gone through." How long such a phase lasts depends principally upon how parents handle it and how rich a social and recreational life is available to the child. In the average stable family, it usually does not involve the more serious antisocial behavior of the conduct-disordered child. Many clinicians consider it an unattractive and upsetting phase that is experienced by many children on their way to a normal maturity.

EMOTIONAL DISORDERS

Emotional difficulties exhibited by children differ in several ways from disruptive disorders. The incidence of emotional disorders is about equal for boys and girls and becomes more common in girls during adolescence. Emotionally disordered children do not manifest the academic and legal difficulties that occur in children with disruptive disorders. Treatment prognosis is generally more optimistic for emotional disorders; and frequently, problems receiving no treatment do not persist into adulthood.

Children are subject to a variety of disturbing emotional disorders, some of them similar to adult psychiatric illnesses; for example, childhood depression, anxiety-based obsessive and compulsive disorders, other anxiety states, and even preoccupation with bodily symptoms, as in hypochondriasis (see related chapters). Here we consider five lesser emotional disorders to which children may be subject: separation anxiety, fears and phobias, school phobias, avoidant disorder, and overanxious disorder.

Separation Anxiety Disorder

Some degree of emotional pain at being separated from parents is shown by many children, especially in close-knit families in which the child has developed an emotionally dependent relationship with his or her parents (particularly the mother). However, when excessive anxiety, to the point of panic, is shown by the child, he or she is said to be suffering from a separation anxiety disorder. Extreme manifestations of the illness are shadowing the parent around the house, refusing to stay alone in a room at home, extreme difficulty in falling asleep without a parent being in the same room, and the appearance of physical symptoms when threat of separation from parents exists. Physical symptoms may range from stomach disorders to heart palpitations and dizziness. The *DSM IIIR* comments that the disorder is "apparently not uncommon." Anderson and colleagues (1987) provide a more specific prevalency estimate of 3.5 percent among preadolescent children. They also report it as much more common in girls than in boys.

Although the symptoms of separation anxiety can be controlled by drugs, they should rarely be used because of harmful side effects. Such behavioral therapies as modeling and systematic desensitization are considered helpful psychotherapeutic approaches (see chapter 7).

Fears and Phobias

Fearfulness about many things is a common problem in childhood. There are three age periods during which specific kinds of fear are most characteristic: 1. Preschool children often develop fears of insects and animals; for example, spiders and dogs. 2. During preadolescence, their fears shift from the concrete and visible to the hidden and imaginative; for example, the dark, frightening shadows may be imagined as ghosts or hidden, perhaps murderous villains. During this period, there will also be fears of possible disasters in elevators or airplanes, even in approaching a department store escalator. 3. Soon after puberty, when social life becomes important, their fears come closer to resembling those of insecure adults; they worry about not being accepted by "the group" and fear new social situations. They may also suffer lowered self-esteem and develop concern about their self-identity.

Unless those emotional reactions seriously disrupt a child's functioning, they can be dealt with by parental understanding and sympathy. Rational explanations and protected direct experiences with the encouragement of parents and the support of childhood friends can reduce the intensity of the child's fears.

When the fears are disabling or take on the irrationality of a phobia, professional help may be needed. Anderson and colleagues (1987), in a comprehensive discussion of children's disorders, report that 2 to 3 percent of children develop real phobias. The most effective therapy is modeling in imitation of other children of the same age, who may or may not be friends. In extreme cases, the therapist may attempt systematic desensitization (see chapter 7).

School Phobia

Although not separately classified as a childhood psychological disorder by the *DSM IIIR,* school phobias are a frequent symptom, early or late in the school years. Such phobic children refuse to go to school, develop illness to avoid going, hide out instead of going to school, and even, at older ages, play truant and walk the streets until the hour arrives for going home.

School phobias may develop in children at three points in their development: 1. for the first one or two years after starting school, when the phobic reaction is likely to be an expression of separation anxiety; 2. later on in school, in the fifth or sixth grade, when school achievement is increasingly emphasized. The phobia paradoxically occurs more frequently among children earning good grades, whose concern about maintaining those grades makes school an unpleasant place. But children who are earning failing grades may also become school phobic to avoid being in school situations where the embarrassment of failing or "not knowing the answer" to teachers' questions may be overwhelming for the child; and 3. soon after transfer to an upper school, when children are thirteen or fourteen, are emotionally insecure, uncertain about fitting into new social groups or made fearful by the sterner demands of upper school teachers, a child may also become school phobic. In the last case, the truancy must be distinguished and treated differently from the truancy of antisocial children.

The maxim suggesting that a thrown rider get right back on the horse is the best one to follow with school phobias. It is important to get school-phobic children back in regular attendance at almost any cost. It is frequently necessary for a parent, ignoring all complaints of physical ailments, to walk or drive the child to school and see him or her through the classroom door. A word or two, after hours, to a sympathetic teacher, can sometimes do wonders. Along the way, a parent can find a means of explaining to the child why going back to school is the "only way."

Avoidant Disorder

These children exhibit extreme shyness around strangers and are withdrawn in social situations; for example, in school. They attempt to limit their social involvement to people they know very well and go to great lengths to avoid strangers. This disorder might be labeled a social phobia in adults. Avoidant-disordered children do not usually manifest difficulties at home and do not suffer many of the symptoms of separation anxiety. As a result of their social inhibitions, they have limited social contacts and therefore do not develop the age-appropriate skills normally learned in ordinary social situations.

Overanxious Disorder

The anxiety experienced by these children is less specific than the fears experienced in other emotional disorders. They can be described as generally anxious, spending an excessive amount of time worrying about future events. They are concerned about past performance and expect most situations to work out badly. They worry about being accepted by their peers and anticipate social rejection. They are extremely self-conscious and require constant reassurance about their abilities. Physical complaints are common, as are sleeping problems, particularly delayed sleep onset. The *DSM IIIR* requires that these symptoms be present for at least six months to establish the diagnosis.

Causes of Anxiety-Based Emotional Disorders

Many theorists focus on maladaptive learning patterns to explain the development of anxiety disorders. A number of studies (Gittelman and Klein 1984; Last et al. 1987) suggest that parents of anxiety-disordered children frequently, themselves, suffer from anxiety disorders. Parents are obviously important role models for their children, and an anxious parent will model anxious behavior. A genetic basis for anxiety disorder is not ruled out by the studies conducted thus far.

Some parents may communicate to their children a belief that above-average achievement is necessary in order to be loved and accepted by them. Such children may react by being intensely self-critical and excessively anxious about their performance.

Another theory, based on Bowlby's (1980) work, suggests that anxiety disorders are a result of difficulties in establishing a secure attachment during the first two years of life.

There is also some support for the theory that a child is born with characteristics that predispose him or her to develop certain behavior. Such a predisposition interacts with familial and environmental factors to create specific disorders such as anxiety disorders (the diathesis-stress model).

Overview of Childhood Emotional Disorders

The general prognosis for children's emotional disorders is good. Many difficulties improve with time, while others require treatment. Drug therapy, using antidepressant medication, can alleviate many of the symptoms of anxiety. These drugs, however, often have unacceptable side effects, and their use is therefore limited.

The major treatment modality for these disorders is behavioral. Techniques include relaxation training, systematic desensitization, modeling, and assertiveness training (see chapter 7). Training in social skills is also utilized as an ancillary treatment for avoidant disorder.

SPECIFIC SYMPTOM DISORDERS

Here are grouped a number of behavior disorders that have in common three characteristics: 1. the disorder is expressed in a single symptom and does not usually involve a pervasive maladaptive pattern of behavior; 2. that symptom is a troublesome physical expression in the eliminatory function, in speech, motor behavior, or eating; and 3. most often, the symptom is troublesome to the individual because it tends to embarrass him or her and bring on social tensions that interfere with the young person's normal social development.

Here we discuss briefly the eliminatory problems of enuresis and encopresis, the speech disorder of stuttering, motor tics, and the eating disorder resulting in obesity.

Eliminatory Problems

There are two: enuresis, which is involuntary urinating, and encopresis, which is bowel movements in culturally inappropriate ways.

ENURESIS

Involuntary voiding of urine may occur in the daytime or at night. Occasional involuntary daytime voiding, often referred to in the family as "an accident," is common soon after the child has been toilet trained, most often when the child is absorbed in a pleasant activity which the child chooses not to leave or during a time of emotional or otherwise exciting play.

Ordinarily, the term *enuresis* refers to nighttime bedwetting. It is formalized as a behavioral disorder, according to the *DSM IIIR*, when a child of five or six wets the bed at least twice a month; for older children, the criterion is once a month.

Enuresis is more prevalent among boys (7 percent), double that of girls at early ages (five or six years of age). It remains higher, at a diminishing rate, through young adulthood.

Causes of Enuresis. A variety of psychological factors have been associated with enuresis. None is given special prominence. Among possible causes of enuresis are 1. regression on the birth of another child; 2. emotional immaturity that causes a child to retain babyish habits; 3. frequent emotional upheavals in the child's home life; and, according to psychodynamic theory, 4. feelings of hostility toward the child's parents. Enuresis does introduce a bothersome laundering problem, an effect that can be seen as an expression of hostility.

Treatment Approaches to Enuresis. Two notably successful treatment programs are available to the parents of the enuretic child.

The first and simpler method, developed by Mowrer in 1938, requires a special bed pad which, when moistened by the child's urine, sets off a loud signal, waking the child and sending him or her off to the toilet.

The second method uses a form of aversive therapy and requires only a very short training period, usually less than a week. Azrin and colleagues (1974), who developed the program, prefer an outside trainer rather than the parents to accomplish the program. Before any training, the "dry bed" program is explained to the child and parents. In phase one, the child drinks a preferred beverage and lies down in his or her bed, and counts to fifty; then, in an unhurried fashion, walks to the toilet and tries to urinate. After several such trials, in phase two, the child is given more to drink and told that he or she will be awakened hourly to urinate. Accidents result in the child being required to change the sheets and to begin training all over again. In the Azrin report on outcome, the group reports that all trained children were continent for at least six months after four nights of training.

In both behaviorally oriented therapies, a success rate of 90 percent has been regularly reported.

ENCOPRESIS

A habit disorder that is much less common than enuresis, encopresis is said to exist if a child older than four years passes feces in inappropriate places, including his or her clothing, at least once a month. The problem occurs in 1 percent of five-year-olds, more frequently in boys than in girls.

When involuntary rather than deliberate (a determination not always easy to make), the cause may be constipation or a tendency to retain fecal matter. When it is deliberate, there is the possibility of oppositional or antisocial tendencies or even more severe pathology. Whether involuntary or deliberate, a physical examination is in order to identify any organic problem that may be present.

Inconsistent or overly rigid toilet training may contribute to development of this problem. Although there is a paucity of research on encopresis, Levine and Bakow (1975) do report a better than 50 percent success rate when they combined medical and behavioral therapy. The *DSM IIIR* reports laconically that the disorder "rarely becomes chronic."

Speech Disorders

As a child grows beyond infancy, speech becomes a principal tool in the child's developing social life. When speech is seriously impaired, there will be upsetting limitations in the child's social life; and when that impairment persists to school age, it can impair classroom performance. There are two principal speech disorders: stuttering and immature speech.

STUTTERING

Also occasionally referred to as stammering, stuttering is the most disturbing psychologically caused speech disorder. It is a marked disturbance in speech rhythm, resulting in frequent repetitions, prolongations or hesitations in producing sounds, syllables or words that may have special emotional connotations for the child. It may be less the word than the tension of the situation for the child.

Symptomatology. A characteristic blockage in stuttering is repetition of an initial consonant, which the child repeats perhaps five to ten times before being able to complete the word. Explosive sounds cause particular difficulty.

Many children three or four years of age experience transitory periods of stammering. In 4 or 5 percent of children, the problem may persist for as long as six months. Usually, if parents and others scrupulously avoid calling the problem to the child's attention in any way, the speech dysrhythmia simply disappears as the child moves along in his or her development. About 1 percent of all children continue to stutter into adolescence. The problem occurs four times more frequently in boys than in girls and seems to run in families.

Social and Educational Consequences of Stuttering. When marked stuttering persists to school age, it can have substantial impact on the child's interactions with peers and interfere seriously with classroom performance. Other children respond quickly to another child's stuttering, often making fun of the child or mimicking the stutterer in ridicule, or sometimes simply avoiding the child because of his or her problem. Teachers sometimes respond to stutterers protectively by not calling on them in class. Either type of response, in play or in the classroom, intensifies the child's anxiety about speaking. Stuttering tends to feed upon the response it creates in others.

Causation in Stuttering. There was a time when much was made of changing a child's handedness as a cause of stuttering and more sophisticated theorizing about mixed cerebral dominance, and there are still some who espouse organic explanations for stuttering. But most psychologists today believe stuttering has its roots in anxieties the child is somehow made to feel in association with his or her speech. Parents sometimes unwittingly show their alarm about transitory hesitations in the child's speaking and transmit their anxiety to the child. The child may sometimes be made anxious by demands for better enunciation or in other ways be made to feel insecure about speaking. Precise psychological causes of stuttering have not been identified, but most psychologists agree that anxiety that has been focused by the child on speaking is a major component of the etiology of stuttering. Once the problem begins, there are environmental stimuli to increase the child's awareness of a speech problem. It is that awareness of a speech problem that maintains and aggravates stuttering.

IMMATURE SPEECH

Many times more prevalent than persistent stuttering, immature speech occurs when a child, by the age of three or four, regularly fails to correctly mouth the sounds for certain consonants. The three that seem most troublesome are K, L and R, but other consonants may also be affected. When the child has trouble with S, he or she is said to lisp.

Immature speech usually results from relatively minor faulty relationships between child and parent, such as parents who learn too well a child's mispronunciations and respond quickly to them, baby talk on the part of parents, or parental responses that encourage immaturity.

The problem is troublesome when the child begins to spend more time with other children, who will have difficulty understanding the child's speech (which difficulty may force the child to work harder at enunciation and thus cure the problem). However, such a reaction from other children may also have the effect of embarrassing the child and lead to shyness or retreat from normal play activities.

Parents can help by gently insisting on more clearly articulated speech; but the help of an outside speech therapist is usually a better way of dealing with the problem.

DEVELOPMENTAL DISORDERS

Developmental disorders are the most serious of psychiatric disorders affecting children. They have a pervasive effect on every aspect of the child's behavior, and often are best cared for in a hospital-like treatment center.

The two principal developmental disorders are mental retardation and infantile autism. We have discussed mental retardation in chapter 17. Here we present a full discussion of infantile autism.

INFANTILE AUTISM

Among the saddest and most devastating of the childhood disorders is autism; fortunately, it is a relatively rare disorder. Two to four children in ten thousand develop the disorder. Onset is very early in the life of the child and is indicated by a marked delay in motor development and a failure to show responsiveness to parental love. In view of its early onset, the illness is officially labeled infantile autism.

Because of its extreme impact on a child's behavior and the disheartening plight of the parents of an autistic child, researchers in the field of childhood behavior have devoted considerable research effort to understanding its etiology. Despite that effort, there is much yet to be learned about causative factors. Treatment is most uncertain, although certain therapies, largely behavioral, have been found somewhat effective in reducing the more extreme symptoms of autism. The *DSM IIIR* reports that one child in six of those affected will make an adequate social adjustment and will be able to do some kind of regular work by adulthood; another one in six makes only a fair adjustment; but two-thirds remain severely handicapped and are unable to lead independent lives.

Leo Kanner (1971), who specialized in the treatment of autism, offers this plaintive portrait of an autistic child as he appeared in the doctor's office: ". . . he wandered aimlessly about for a few moments, then sat down, uttering unintelligible sounds, and abruptly lay down, smiling. Questions and requests, if reacted to at all, were repeated in echolalic fashion. Objects absorbed him, and he showed good attention in handling them. He seemed to regard people as unwelcome intruders. When a hand was held out before him so that he could not possibly ignore it, he played with it as if it were a detached object. He promptly noticed the wooden form boards and worked at them spontaneously, interestedly and skillfully."

This section considers the symptomatology of autism, the present status of our understanding of its etiology, and therapies used with the autistic child.

Symptomatology   Among autistic children, 70 percent are mentally retarded, 40 percent severely so, with IQs below 50. The *DSM IIIR* lists six diagnostic criteria, the first of which is onset before thirty months. A description of the other criteria follows:

1. Disturbance in relating to others. Autistic children avoid interaction with other children and adults. This is not simple shyness, but an attempt at total exclusion of people from the child's world. The preference of autistic children is for inanimate things, which seem to preoccupy them. One father

describes his child's behavior in this sentence: "When Robert turned to you, he looked through you as if you were transparent." (Kaufman 1976, p. 11)

A particularly disconcerting aspect of their behavior is their unwillingness (perhaps inability) to maintain eye contact. Clinical speculation (Hutt and Ounstead 1966) suggests that since eye contact is the essence of interaction with others, that is the one response that the autistic child must avoid at all costs.

The *DSM IIIR* reports that some of the least handicapped children later on develop a sham and deceptive sociability; for example, they may run along with a group of other children, but they nevertheless remain aloof from them.

2. Delayed language development. About 50 percent of autistic children remain mute or use only three or four necessary phrases, which may later disappear. The remaining 50 percent of the autistic group are limited to echolalic expression, repeating words someone has said to them in parrot-like fashion.

3. The use of speech oddities. Autistic children confuse pronouns; for example, using "you" for "I," which is rarely used. Parents must learn that repeating the parental question, "Do you want your dinner?" means "Yes, I do." Autistics will use parts of an object or event for the whole, referring to dinner, for example, as milk. When they do use words or react to them, they will be very literal in their usage; for example, correcting the expression, "Please put your coat on the chair," to "Lay your coat on the chair." Their language may be metaphorical, such as the use of a prohibiting command learned from parents; for example, "Don't crayon the walls," as a universal expression for "No" or "Don't do that." Speech is high-pitched and monotonous, with inappropriately emphasized words.

4. Idiosyncratic or odd responses to the environment. Autistic children develop peculiar attachments to inanimate objects; for example, carrying around a toy mechanized truck as a normal child might carry around a cuddly teddy bear, or exhaustively fingering a light switch.

5. Absence of delusions, hallucinations or loosened associations. Autism is distinguished from childhood schizophrenia, which it resembles in some of its symptoms, by the absence of such schizophrenic symptoms as delusions, hallucinations or incoherent associations.

Additional Symptomatology in Infantile Autism

There are two other notable characteristics of the autistic child, which are reported by clinicians but not given particular emphasis in the *DSM IIIR*.

Concern About Sameness. The first characteristic is the child's concern about sameness. With surprising perceptual acuity and spatial memory, autistic children will order and reorder their world to maintain things as they were, frequently going into temper tantrums when changes caused by others are first noticed. The need for sameness may carry over to the food they choose to eat, the toys with which they play, and the arrangement of their room or bed.

Strange Movements and Play Activity. The second peculiarity, also absent from the *DSM IIIR*, are the bizarre and stereotyped movements of autistic children. Included are tiptoeing around the room, sudden starts and stops, flapping of their arms, body rocking or whirling, head rolling, and playing with their fingers pulled up close to their eyes. Objects may be endlessly twirled or fingered in detail. Autistic children may play with pieces of a game but actually play no game.

Causative Factors in Autism

Much less is known about the etiology of autism than is known, and what is known makes it difficult to choose between biological and psychological causative factors.

PSYCHOLOGICAL INTERPRETATIONS OF AUTISM

Bruno Bettelheim has been the strongest advocate of a psychogenic interpretation of autism. In his 1967 book, *The Empty Fortress,* in itself a forbidding title for the parents of autistic children to hear, Bettelheim writes that parents of an autistic child "wish that the child did not exist" and reject the child, refusing to respond to its signals at critical points of the child's development during the first year. Kanner, before Bettelheim, had coined the expression "emotional refrigeration" to describe the child's early experiences as he thought them to be. Behavioral theorists (Ferster 1961) regard parental failure to reinforce prosocial behavior as a significant causal factor in autism.

But extensive research tends to reject those conclusions. For example, Wolff and Morris (1971) and others did not find the parents of autistic children to be "emotional refrigerators." McAdoo and DeMyer (1978) make two important points in rejecting both Bettelheim's and Kanner's interpretations: they report that they did not find parents of autistic children significantly different from the parents of children with other types of disturbances; and secondly, they report that mothers of autistic children had significantly fewer psychological problems than mothers who were patients in a mental health clinic.

Nevertheless, those findings do leave open the possibility that, given a biological predisposition toward autism, even the relatively minor personality flaws they report as present in the parents of autistic children might tip the child's balance and cause the development of an autistic disorder. We now examine the question of possible biological causes.

BIOLOGICAL FACTORS RELATED TO AUTISM

There is evidence that the autistic child is a different biological organism from the normal child in pathological biological characteristics and, apparently, genetically.

Biological Differences. Rosenhan and Seligman (1989) state that 30 percent of autistic children late in life develop epileptic seizures. Such seizures are known to be biologically caused. Autistic children show a higher rate of abnormal brain waves than do normal children; but not all autistic children do so. Campbell and colleagues (1975) indicate that almost one-third of autistics have abnormal serotonin levels. Serotonin is a neurotransmitter related to perception and memory. Both of those functions may be affected in autism.

Genetic Factors. Folstein and Rutter (1978) provide strong evidence for the existence of a genetic factor in autism. In a study of twenty-one pairs of twins, among whom at least one of the twins was autistic, eleven of the twin pairs were identical (with identical genes). Of those eleven, four co-twins were also autistic; in addition, five co-twins showed abnormalities in speech and language usage (a problem in the autistic child). Among the nonidentical twin pairs, none of the co-twins were autistic. The researchers report that autistic twins also experienced much more difficult births than the nonautistic twins. Folstein and Rutter concluded that in the development of autism, biological (possibly genetic) factors play an influential part.

SUMMARY STATEMENT ON CAUSATION OF AUTISM

Although much good research has been directed at understanding autism, much about the disease is not yet known. In a general way, what we do know about it can be summarized in the two statements that we quote here. One set of authorities in the field (Goldstein and colleagues 1986) puts it this way: "The autistic child quite likely enters the world biologically different in some ways [from other children], but the biological consequences probably vary with the way the child's environment, especially his mother, responds to that difference." It is a statement with which most clinicians are likely to agree. DeMyer, Hingtgen and Jackson (1981), in concluding their studies, express the thought less definitely and with a somewhat different emphasis: Autistic children are "beings with an inborn defect or defects in brain functioning, regardless of what other causal factors may subsequently become involved."

Treatment of Infantile Autism

Beginning with the work of Bruno Bettelheim at the Orthogenic School at the University of Chicago, clinicians working with autistic children have developed a variety of treatment approaches, a number of which report at least partially successful results. Despite their efforts, the prognosis for the autistic child is still considered bleak. Typical of that opinion is the estimate of Cardon et al. (1988) that less than one-fourth of the autistic children who receive treatment attain even marginal adjustment later in life. Rosenhan and Seligman (1989), while agreeing that treatment for autistic children is slowly improving, nevertheless predict that most autistic young adolescents and young adults will still need access to residential facilities.

Response to treatment is correlated directly with the autistic child's measured IQ and with the presence of intelligible language before the age of five. Both those factors are, of course, related, and both indicate a less severe form of autism. What the relationship between those two factors and response to therapy means is that children with mild to moderate autism may respond to treatment. But even for those treatable autistic children, the course of treatment is prolonged (two to three years) and intense (in some programs, as many as forty hours a week). The cost of such programs is out of the reach of many, perhaps most, families with autistic children.

Rutter, in an early review (1968) of treatment approaches to autism, reports that insight therapy of a psychodynamic nature has not proven effective with autistics. On the other hand, there are many reports of success with a variety of behaviorally oriented treatment efforts that focus intensively on the correction of specific deficits in the child's behavior. Examples of such approaches are teaching specific sounds and identifying them with specific objects; helping a child to give up objects to which he or she has become pathologically attached, so attached that the attachment interferes with developmental progress; and helping two autistic children to make even rudimentary physical contact with each other. That type of training makes extensive use of behavioral principles; for example, reinforcing desired responses, even though they move only generally or slightly in the right direction (see "Shaping" in chapter 7).

Some therapists use graded educational approaches adapted to the specific needs of the child in an attempt to remove specific perceptual, cognitive or motor deficits.

Almost all of the successful programs make use of one-on-one, long-term treatment approaches that build warm, loving and accepting interaction between therapist and patient.

Despite the occasional reports of successful treatment, experts on autism advise caution in adopting too optimistic an outlook on outcome of treatment.

*R*ecognition of the presence of mental disorders among children and adolescents and research on those disorders has lagged behind the efforts at understanding adult mental disorders. Not until the revision of the third edition of the DSM was a completely adequate listing presented of development disorders of children and adolescents.

Three special difficulties exist in trying to understand the mental disorders of the young: 1. attitudes of adults in the home who so significantly shape their children's personalities and often deny the existence of problems; 2. developmental considerations, which would cause behavior considered normal at one age but which would be considered abnormal at a later age; and 3. the great difficulty in delineating between the normal and the abnormal in children.

The DSM IIIR now lists nine categories of children's disorders; for convenience and clarity, the chapter has discussed them under four principal headings.

Disruptive Behavior Disorders. There are three such disruptive mental disorders. They are attention-deficit personality disorder (ADHD), which is characterized by impulsiveness, inattention and hyperactivity inappropriate for the age of the child; conduct disorders, which are a more extreme form of ADHD and include antisocial and delinquent behavior; and oppositional-defiant disorder, which is manifest in negative, argumentative or hostile behavior.

Emotional Disorders. There are five types of emotional disorders. They are separation anxiety disorder, in which the child shows emotional pain, sometimes extreme, when separated from home and family; fears and phobias, which in the disorder are more overwhelming to the child than normal, e.g., inappropriate apprehensiveness; school phobia, which is such a fear of school as to cause the child to seek out various ways of not going to school; avoidant disorder, in which a child avoids or finds extremely painful all social contacts with persons other than close family; and over-anxious disorder, in which a child shows generalized anxiety and foreboding about upcoming events.

Specific Symptom Disorders. This disorder is usually limited to a specific troublesome symptom which embarrasses and handicaps the child in social and educational life. The principal symptom disorders are the eliminatory disorders of enuresis and encopresis (bowel movement problems); and speech disorders, the principal of which are stuttering and immature speech. The disorder also includes specific academic problems.

Developmental Problems. There are two. They are mental retardation (discussed in chapter 17) and infantile autism, which is a relatively rare but most serious childhood mental disorder in which the child shows a marked delay in motor development and a failure to respond to parental love or any interpersonal contact.

Etiological factors cut across a wide range of psychosocial factors, principally involving parent/child relationships, particularly for ADHD and autism. There are also strong indications of the causal influences of genetic factors.

**Selected
Readings**

Achenbach, T. M. and C. G. Edelbrock. 1978. "The Classification of Child Psychopathology. A Review and Analysis of Empirical Effects." *Psychological Bulletin*, 85: 1275-1301.

Cantwell, D. P. 1982. "Childhood Depression: A Review of Current Research." in B. B. Lahey and A. E. Kazdin (Eds.). *Advances in Clinical Child Psychology*. New York: Plenum Press.

Douglas, V. I. and K. G. Peters. 1979. "Toward a Clearer Definition of the Attentional Deficits of Hyperactive Children." in G. A. Hale and M. Lewis (Eds.). *Attention and Cognitive Development*. New York: Plenum Press.

Ross, D. M. and S. A. Ross. 1976. *Hyperactivity: Research, Theory and Action*. New York: Wiley-Interscience.

Rutter, M. and E. Schopler (Eds.). 1978. *Autism: A Reappraisal of Concepts and Treatment*. New York: Plenum Press.

Sperling, M. 1963. "Dynamic Considerations and Treatment of Enuresis." *Journal of the American Academy of Child Psychiatry*, 4: 19-31.

Werry, J. S. and H. C. Quay. 1971. "The Prevalence of Behavior Symptoms in Younger Elementary School Children." *American Journal of Orthopsychiatry*, 41: 136-143.

19

Legal Issues and Social Policy

Throughout this book, our focus has been the individual: the nature of his or her illness, possible causes of the illness, and treatment approaches. Other people, when they were considered at all, were those who were directly affected by the abnormal behavior, particularly spouses and children. Here we shift our focus and consider larger societal issues: legal issues posed by abnormal behavior and social policy questions related to it, what might be considered the conscience issues that the problems of mental illness create for all of us.

Those issues fall into three categories: 1. Legal issues—those concerning the questions, broadly put, what are the rights of patients, and how can they be protected, and, at the same time, how can we protect the entitlement of the general public to a safe and secure society in which to live? 2. The issue of prevention; what is society doing now to prevent mental illness, and what more must it do? and 3. What organized efforts on behalf of the mentally ill exist now, and how can more Americans be drawn into those efforts?

LEGAL ISSUES

Abnormal behavior, as we have seen, occasionally causes an individual to violate society's norms, sometimes in ways that are criminal. When a mentally ill person commits a crime, especially a serious one, several questions have to be answered: Is the mental condition a defense against being punished? Is the individual competent to stand trial? When the threat of criminal or dangerous behavior is present, how can an involuntary commitment be achieved in ways that are fair to all? How can treatment be provided to an unwilling mentally ill person?

Some of those questions have confronted the U.S. Supreme Court and, along the way, various lower courts, federal and state. The decisions handed down have not always pointed the way to practical and universally accepted answers to the questions raised. Psychologists and psychiatrists are often drawn into attempts to find answers to these questions; their testimony in court is often required.

The Insanity Plea

Placing an individual on trial for criminal behavior is based on the belief that he or she chose to commit a crime knowingly and was therefore responsible for it and should be punished. Punishment for criminal behavior has as its rationale the effect of deterring others who might be contemplating a crime; the hoped-for deterrence on the individual's future behavior; and, when punishment involves incarceration, the guarantee that at least for the term of imprisonment, the individual will not commit a similar crime. But the rationale rests also on an ancient Judeo-Christian ethic that mandates equitable punishment after bad behavior. To the average person, punishment after criminal behavior seems appropriate and, indeed, necessary.

But what happens to that reasoning if the individual was not responsible for the crime in the way in which a normal person is responsible for his or her behavior? What does society do if it can be demonstrated that the individual was "insane" at the time of the crime? What a plethora of problems a plea of insanity makes for a society with a conscience!

Two of the most significant problems are these: How does one support a diagnosis of such mental disorder as to persuasively exonerate the individual from responsibility for the crime? and, What follows the decision that the individual cannot be held responsible because of insanity at the time of the crime? The first question has a long legal history, the second question addresses the issue of involuntary commitment to a psychiatric facility for an unspecified period of time.

ESTABLISHING A DIAGNOSIS OF "INSANITY"

An early court decision (1834) in this country ruled that individuals should not be held responsible for their crimes if it could be established that, as a result of mental illness, they were unable to resist the impulse to commit the crime. An example might be obeying "a command from God," which an insane person might hear and feel compelled to obey. In this ruling, the issue must be resolved by a jury of the individual's peers, presumably with the assistance of the testimony of experts.

The motivation for this court decision is easy to understand: "If the individual had to commit the crime as a result of irresistible psychic forces, how could he or she be held culpable?" The problem, of course, lies in determining when is an impulse irresistible, and when is it not. Since the 1834 decision, three other criteria have been offered for the determination of responsibility: The McNaghten rule; the Durham test; and the *United States* v. *Brawner* decision, which adopted criteria established by the American Law Institute.

The McNaghten Rule. Although handed down in an English court, this decision has also set the standard for American court decisions. In the McNaghten trial, defense counsel admitted that McNaghten had murdered Drummond, whom he had mistakenly identified as the British prime minister, who was the intended victim. The defense contended that McNaghten believed that the voice of God had directed him to kill the prime minister, and that McNaghten suffered delusions of persecution under which he felt bound to obey the command.

The trial set a precedent for many criminal trials that followed because, for the first time, the testimony of experts had been officially received into the proceedings of the trial.

McNaghten was acquitted. In defense of their decision, the judges laid down the "McNaghten rule," which has been labeled in legal circles as, "the right-wrong test." The essential reasoning of this ruling is expressed as follows: It must be proved clearly that at the time of the commission of the criminal act, the defendant was laboring under such a defect of reason, caused by disease of the mind, that he did not know the nature and quality of the act he was committing; or, if he did know, did not know he was doing wrong.

The ruling became known as the right-wrong test because of that language. It was considered a rather narrow basis for the determination of responsibility for criminal behavior.

The Durham Test. In a federal district court in 1954, the McNaghten rule was broadened significantly and given a totally different perspective. In the words of the judge who enunciated the criteria, "An accused is not criminally responsible if his unlawful act was the product of mental disease or mental defect." The legal basis for successful use of the insanity plea was widened in two regards by this decision. It introduced the concept of mental disease, a condition that could be certified only by a trained specialist, and also explicitly included mental defect, which could also be certified only by an expert.

The attempt to use the criterion, "product of mental disease or mental defect" lasted from 1954, the time of its enunciation, until 1972, when it was withdrawn as an experiment that had failed. Two reasons are thought to have been operative in causing the demise of the Durham test: 1. It gave almost exclusive weight to the testimony of professional experts, psychiatrists and psychologists, in determining responsibility, thereby effectively removing that determination from judge and jury; and 2. With the likelihood of disagreement among those experts, determination of the question of responsibility became a matter of choosing sides; that is, which side, defense or prosecution, most persuasively presents what are essentially, or should be, objective determinations. The professionals themselves are often uncertain of achieving agreement on the diagnosis of "mental disease," especially if such a diagnosis implies an absence of responsibility for one's behavior.

The *United States* v. *Brawner*. Modifications of the American Law Institute Formulation. The rule that now guides judges in federal courts and in a majority of the state courts when instructing a jury on the matter of a criminal's responsibility for criminal behavior sets two criteria for making that judgment: When the individual, by virtue of either mental disease or mental defect, lacks substantial capacity either, 1. to appreciate the criminality (or wrongfulness) of his or her conduct, or 2. to control that conduct, the person may then be deemed not responsible for the criminal act. Careful reading of that language leads one to the conclusion that the presence of mental disease or mental defect in and of itself, without a demonstration of the conditions specified in the ruling, would not lead to an acquittal.

Perhaps to placate that public opinion that considers the law "soft" on crime, the rule, as it is used in the courts, does not include, in its understanding of a mental disease, an abnormality that is manifest only by frequency of criminal or other antisocial behavior. In other words, a lifetime of crime cannot be used as a demonstration of "insanity."

Guilty but Mentally Ill. With the newly created verdict of "guilty but mentally ill," some states have found still another way of dealing with the so-called insanity defense. This legal definition seems to have developed in reaction to the national outrage that followed the acquittal of John W. Hinckley, Jr., who, after an attempt to assassinate the president of the United States, was granted a verdict of "not guilty by reason of insanity." The assassination attempt was concocted by Hinckley for bizarre reasons, in order to cause a young actress, whom he had never met but with whom he had become infatuated, to "love and respect" him.

The verdict surprised the judge and Hinckley. The jurors explained that the prosecution had not proved beyond a reasonable doubt that Hinckley had the mental capacity to be responsible for his crime. There was no question about his making the assassination attempt; many thought the burden of establishing his mental illness should have been borne by the defense.

In any case, the fallout from public reaction was the passage of legislation in several states creating the new verdict, "guilty but mentally ill." The virtue of that verdict, in the opinion of many who were concerned about the legitimacy of the Hinckley verdict, is that while an individual, having committed a crime, might escape a prison sentence, he or she would nevertheless be incarcerated in a secure hospital setting.

Once incarcerated, what criteria should be used for granting freedom to the individual? The Supreme Court, in 1983, ruled the permissibility of keeping an insanity-acquitted individual hospitalized indefinitely.

One other result of the Hinckley proceedings was a change in the federal courts that shifted the burden of proof with reference to mental illness from the prosecution to the defense. In those courts, the defense must now prove insanity, rather than the prosecution being required to prove sanity.

Diminished Capacity. In addition to all of those considerations, the New York State Department of Mental Hygiene in 1978 proposed an entirely different way of considering the issue of criminal responsibility. One can paraphrase the department's argument as follows: The presence of a mental illness, while it may not entirely remove the individual's awareness of right from wrong, does reduce the capacity of the individual to appreciate the full nature of the crime committed. If that is so, the best approach, the department argued, would be to admit evidence of any abnormal mental condition that would affect the degree of culpability for which an individual is being tried. For example, those crimes requiring intent or full knowledge of the criminal nature of the act, that is, its "wrongness," could be reduced to such lesser offenses as reckless or criminal neglect in the case of a mentally ill person.

There is no evidence that this concept has received formal judicial acceptance. Nevertheless, one can speculate that in some of the many cases of plea bargaining about which one now reads, the basis for a reduced charge is the mental condition of the individual at the time of the crime.

PREVALENCE OF THE INSANITY DEFENSE

No doubt, when in the trial of an individual charged with a particularly heinous crime, the defense lawyer is reported in the newspapers to be planning an insanity defense, many newspaper readers jump to the conclusion that the case is one of many in which proper punishment will be escaped or, at least, reduced appreciably by such a defense. But a 1980 study reports that the insanity defense has been attempted in less than 2 percent of criminal cases, a percentage that is probably far lower than the number of mentally disturbed individuals in the criminal court system. Other studies indicate that it is used successfully in less than 1 percent of felony cases.

There are two other reports that might give those who are critical of the criminal justice system support for their criticism. One report indicates that those acquitted of a criminal charge on the basis of an insanity plea spend less time in psychiatric hospitals than criminals convicted of a similar crime spend in prison. The second report reveals that in the past quarter of a century, the frequency of use of the insanity defense has increased. One can only speculate about the reasons for that increase.

Competency to Stand Trial

The competency of the individual to stand trial, that is, whether or not he understands the nature of the charges and can participate rationally in his or her own defense, is also a matter of concern to the judiciary. It is a more narrow issue than the question of an individual's criminal responsibility for the crime. Competency has nothing to do with uncontrollable impulses or right and wrong; a compassionate judiciary system requires only that the individual have a basic understanding of the charges and be reasonably able to cooperate with counsel. Even though psychotic at the time of the crime, an individual may be judged competent to stand trial.

The issue of responsibility is related to the individual's mental condition at the time of the criminal offense; the competency issue is relevant only at the time of the trial, when mental condition can be examined adequately. The judgment about mental condition at the time of the crime can be only retrospective. Individuals may be judged to have been insane when committing the crime, but psychiatrically competent later, when the trial is to take place; or they may have been judged to have been sane when the crime was committed, but not sane at the time of the trial. Trials are often held long after a crime has been committed, sometimes years later. It occasionally happens that the defendant's mental state has changed radically, for better or for worse.

MISUSE OF THE COMPETENCY ISSUE

While competency is a relatively easy condition to determine, it is often used in a loose way by both prosecution and defense. When pleading incompetence, the defense attorney usually is interested only in delay, hoping that time will give his client a better chance of acquittal. In a weak case, the prosecution may have something at stake in pressing for or allowing a ruling of incompetence.

Once judged incompetent, individuals may nevertheless remain incarcerated for a long time, even though they have not been judged guilty and may, indeed, be innocent. The injustice of that situation finally received the attention of the U.S. Supreme Court, and in 1972, it ruled that a person judged to be incompetent at the time of trial could be held in custody on the grounds of incompetency only as long as it would reasonably take to determine whether or not the individual would become competent in the foreseeable future. In the case of a psychotic flare-up, that period might be a short one. For a person judged to be mentally retarded and therefore incompetent, competence would never be achieved.

When the probability of the individual ever achieving competence is, in professional opinion, slight, the court ruled that the individual must be committed to a mental institution under legal commitment procedures or released.

COMPETENCY AND ANTIPSYCHOTIC MEDICATION

Since the development of antipsychotic medication, a difficult problem presents itself to the judge and attorneys. If the individual is allowed to continue on the medication, the medication will reduce or eliminate symptoms and, in that way, might cause the jury to reject an insanity defence. If the individual is denied medication, incompetency, with all of its hazards, may be ruled. Most often, competency gained through medication is considered acceptable, no matter what effect the individual's apparent normality during the trial might have on the jury.

The Problem of Civil Commitment

More than half of the commitments to state mental institutions are involuntary. While a hospital is not a prison, involuntary hospitalization does deny individuals their freedom against their will. Once committed, hospitals or prisons do not provide much of a difference in how individuals will spend their time and live out their lives for years, or even until their deaths.

Such considerations have caused some mental health professionals to demand, for psychiatric patients facing involuntary commitment, the same legal protections granted to an individual on trial for criminal behavior. Those rights are as follows: 1. decision only after a hearing by jury; 2. the assistance of counsel; 3. freedom from self-incrimination; and 4. proof beyond a reasonable doubt of the necessity of commitment.

Because commitment to a hospital, even though protested by the individual, is considered (although not always accurately) a compassionate act and not a condemnation, and because goals other than punishment motivate the decision, adequate protection of those rights has not yet been legally established.

PROVIDING A JURY TRIAL

A jury trial is not now provided to a psychiatric patient facing involuntary commitment, and, in the opinion of those in the field, it is not likely to be introduced in the near future. One reason is that peer review of the issues involved in such a commitment is not given much weight by the professionals who might have to live with any decision made. There are practical problems as well: trials are expensive and time consuming, and juries are difficult to select. One answer to the problem, widely practiced in many hospitals, is to provide the individual with at least the benefit of judgment made by a panel of experts, and not one made by an individual, no matter what the individual's apparent qualifications.

PROTECTING THE INDIVIDUAL AGAINST SELF-INCRIMINATION

It might seem inappropriate for mental health advocates to appear to be equating psychiatric illness with criminal behavior. Nevertheless, one can see the point of their talking about self-incrimination. An illustration makes the point: Should a patient be counseled to be passive, indifferent, and silent during the commitment process? Such behavior might indeed be considered pathological in an individual confronting so crucial a judgment. If, on the other hand, he or she does not do so, it is all too likely that the tension of the situation might exacerbate symptoms that, in usual surroundings, would not justify hospitalization.

THE ASSISTANCE OF COUNSEL

The right to counsel is respected almost universally in commitment procedures in this country. The problem lies in how counselors see their role. The two extremes of such a role might be described as follows: 1. The lawyer's usual legal responsibility of acting in order to require the authorities to make out a *prima facie* case for enforced hospitalization, or 2. the lawyer proceeding in such a way as to "force" the authorities to agree to return the individual (one might say, at all costs) to the community.

Most lawyers who agree to take on the responsibility will, to the best of their abilities, try to determine what is best for the client. But here, of course, they are trained in law, not in psychiatry or psychology. Some of those in the field of mental health would choose to define the patient's best interests as what he or she would choose to do if there were complete freedom to do so. More wisdom even than Solomon's seems to be required to know what to do. What is right varies with every patient: the need for hospital-administered treatment, its availability and, as well, the quality of the resources available to the patient outside the hospital.

REQUIREMENTS FOR COMMITMENT

Society is not irrational or punitive in requiring involuntary commitments, although some individuals involved in making commitment decisions may operate in a hurried or callous way. Involuntary commitment, at least insofar as policy is described, requires that one or more of four conditions be met.

Presence of Mental Disease. The individual must be suffering from a mental disease. Usually, no clear definition is provided of which mental diseases qualify. For example, would a severe phobic reaction qualify, or a somatoform disorder? Even an elementary knowledge of those diseases would cause most individuals to think not. But that does not guarantee that circumstances would never arise to cause just such disorders to be used as grounds for involuntary commitment; for example, extreme pressure from families, perhaps exhausted, by efforts to take care of the individual.

There is, however, a safeguard available to the patient. All states require that in addition to the presence of a mental disorder, at least one of a set of described characteristics also be present. They are impaired judgment, need for treatment, danger to self or to others, and grave disability.

Impaired Judgment. What is principally meant here is that the individual's judgment is so impaired by the mental illness that he or she is unable to recognize the need for treatment. It is argued that in such a case, compassion and a sense of social responsibility require that someone else make that decision for the patient.

Need for Treatment. In 1975, A. A. Stone proposed a way of thinking about the need for treatment as grounds for involuntary commitment that has won some support from the mental health community. The proposal has earned for itself the label of "the thank you" proposition. Stone argues that if a person is suffering a mental disease, and if a recognized treatment is available, and if, for whatever irrational reason, the patient refuses to undergo treatment—for example, the patient protests, "I am radioactive and dangerous to others,"— then involuntary commitment in order to provide treatment would seem justified. The "thank you" name for the proposal came about when patients, fully recovered from their mental illnesses, recognize what has been done to help them and express gratitude to whatever person disregarded their wishes and insisted on providing the treatment, now seen as necessary. Whether or not the patient actually feels gratitude after the treatment (and many don't) seems a weak argument against the "thank you" proposition. The patient is out of the hospital and functioning at a more normal level. By most criteria, but not all, the action would seem to be serving the best interests of the patient and of society.

The American Psychiatric Association, in its model commitment proposal, a document designed to set standards for involuntary commitment, has adopted a somewhat modified form of Stone's proposal.

But what if the treatment proves ineffective, and the involuntary commitment leads to a prolonged hospitalization? Or what if circumstances develop, such as A. D. Brooks describes in his treatise *Law, Psychiatry, and the Mental Health System* (1974).

> "Emily Bronson, a widow, suffered two delusions: The first, that the restaurant at which she frequently ate, poisoned her food; and the second, that men were constantly planning sexual assaults upon her. These delusions were mild and harmless, and she continued to eat at the same restaurant, and her behavior with men seemed unaffected by her concerns. Her friends knew of her delusions, but they seemed to cause them or her no difficulty.

One day, Mrs. Bronson fell and injured her hip. She was brought to the emergency ward of a nearby hospital, where she remained for several days, during which time she spoke of her delusions. In this wholly fortuitous manner, she was perceived as a paranoid schizophrenic who needed treatment, and was transferred to a psychiatric hospital just as soon as her hip improved. She was subsequently committed involuntarily to a county facility, where she remained for five years before she saw an attorney. During that time, the hospital ordered her estate to pay for her psychiatric hospitalization."

Such a muddled state of affairs cannot be considered a rare occurrence when bureaucracy and involuntary commitment are brought together, supposedly to help a mentally ill person.

Dangerousness to Others. Here is what would seem to be a legitimate and socially responsible basis for committing a person with mental illness to a psychiatric hospital without the individual's consent. If other people, either family or strangers, might be killed or harmed (the meaning of dangerousness) by the mentally ill person, doesn't the protective system of society, in this case, the mental health system, have the duty of hospitalizing the individual, even if it has the stamp of incarceration?

The issue is not as easy to resolve as it might seem. The problem is that an impressive number of studies indicate that neither psychologists nor psychiatrists are able reliably to predict dangerousness. Most professionals would prefer not to be required to make decisions about the future dangerousness of a patient. Circumstances sometimes force them to express their best judgment.

There is a value judgment to be made here. Whose rights have a greater claim on protection, the individual held involuntarily in a psychiatric hospital on the basis of an evaluation that determines (perhaps inaccurately) the person to be dangerous, or a person in the community whose safety might now be in jeopardy because of the release of a person who is thought to be dangerous?

There is one study, conducted by Steadman and associates, that provides statistics to place in context any value judgment on the matter.

The U.S. Supreme Court ruled in 1967 that a large number of inmate/patients confined in prison hospitals in New York State be released. Despite the fact that they were adjudged in earlier psychiatric examinations to be criminally insane and potentially violent, should they be released, since they had been previously convicted of violence? The court ruled that incarceration violated their constitutional rights.

Steadman's group followed the released patients and reported four years later that only 2.7 percent of them had been arrested for assaultive behavior and been imprisoned again or been placed in a hospital for the criminally insane. One would judge that, with a history of violence, this population would be prime suspects for future violence, based on the belief that the best predictor of future behavior is past behavior. Yet in four years, according to the study, 97.5 percent of the group were not involved in behavior dangerous to anyone else. Perhaps the best that one can say is that predicting dangerousness is, from a professional point of view, a dangerous occupation. Any such prediction provides a weak basis on which to challenge basic human rights.

Dangerousness to Self. Although any threat of suicide should be taken seriously (and there is a fair number of multiple suicide attempts, some resulting in death), predicting which individuals will make those suicide attempts after such a threat is as unreliable as predictions about violence to others. Nevertheless, the involuntary commitment to a hospital of individuals who have threatened suicide seems a less critical violation of the individual's civil rights than other commitments. For one thing, it is usually a short-term commitment; it brings the individual into treatment, even if only for a short time; and later, when distress has subsided, is usually appreciated by the individual.

Grave Disability. When individuals are clearly so mentally impaired as to be unable to care for themselves, that is, to provide food, clothing, and shelter for themselves, a decision to commit the individual to a psychiatric facility seems the compassionate thing to do. Problems develop when the questions of the standard of care are raised. Freedom to be independent may be so valuable a possession that some individuals may decide, in preference to being hospitalized, to live at such a meager level as to cause social agencies to recommend commitment in a hospital. The decision to hospitalize an individual in such a case is a heart-breaking one, and family or other assistance should first be sought.

Level of Proof. One remaining consideration in protecting the rights of the mentally ill remains to be examined, which is the level of proof that criteria actually exist for an involuntary commitment. For example, this patient, it is alleged in a petition of involuntary commitment, is dangerous to others or to self. How convincing must the evidence be that dangerousness indeed exists, how absolute the judgments of those who make the decision, to justify denying personal freedom to any individual, whether it be the freedom of an open ward in a hospital or the freedom to live out in the community?

There are three levels of proof: 1. What has been called the 90-to 100-percent level of proof, known in legal circles as "beyond a reasonable doubt." Under the premise that a person is innocent until proven guilty, that level of certainty is required in criminal proceedings. Since individuals charged with a crime are in double jeopardy of losing their freedom and of being stigmatized as a criminal, that high standard is required. 2. At the other extreme when evaluating proof is the requirement that the preponderance of evidence favor a decision; that is, if evidence can be counted, it would presumably mean 51 percent of the evidence. Such a criterion of proof is considered adequate in civil courts dealing with money matters. 3. With respect to the issues involved in involuntary commitment, the Supreme Court, rejecting both the "beyond a reasonable doubt" criterion and the "preponderance of the evidence" standard, set an intermediate standard. It ruled that in involuntary commitment matters, the evidence must be "clear, unequivocal, and convincing." That is, to return to a quantitative statement, a 75 percent level of certainty should exist. It is that standard of proof which all states are now required to use as a standard in involuntary commitment matters.

TWO UNRESOLVED PROBLEMS

The long series of court rulings growing out of the mental health community's concern to protect the civil rights of the mentally ill, particularly those rights affected most by involuntary commitment, finally brought an Alabama court to a ruling that effectively established a bill of rights for hospitalized psychiatric patients in that state, and other states are attempting to abide by the parameters of that decision.

The case was a class action brought on behalf of a mentally retarded youth, not by a mentally ill person. In his decision, the judge reasoned that it was clearly a violation of due process to deny people their liberty on the grounds that they needed treatment and then to provide no treatment to them. The judge then went on to require, as a legally binding mandate, that all Alabama state mental institutions provide 1. an individualized treatment program for each patient; 2. skilled staff in sufficient numbers to administer such a program; and, 3. a humane psychological and physical environment.

In an extension of his ruling, he detailed the characteristics of a humane psychological and physical environment. For example, the requirements established the patient's right to privacy and dignity, described appropriate bathing and toilet facilities, and included the right to engage in interaction with members of the opposite sex.

The program outlined by the judge remains, to this day, more an ideal to strive toward than a reality; nevertheless, it does provide patients and their advocates a standard against which they can test any psychiatric institution, and, over the years, will bring significant improvement in the level of care provided.

The *Wyatt* v. *Stickney* decision (that is, the Alabama Case) was a hard-won and glorious victory for the mentally ill; nevertheless, two unexpected and troublesome consequences have resulted from the decision: the wholesale release back to unprepared local communities of mentally ill persons, and threatened interference in certain forms of professionally approved treatment.

Release of Patients. The judge in *Wyatt* v. *Stickney* placed heavy emphasis on adequate staffing which, to some extent, set an approved ratio of staff to patients. For most hospitals, that meant skyrocketing costs. Most budgets for public psychiatric facilities were hardly adequate for the minimal care that had been offered before this decision.

Hospital administrators had little hope that their budgets would be increased enough to meet the newly mandated standards. The only solution they could devise was to reduce the number of patients hospitalized, and the only way to do that was to release many of them into their communities. Under pressure from a citizen's tax protest, California led the states in this action. It closed many of its psychiatric hospitals and sharply reduced its mental health budget.

The decision to return psychiatric patients to their home communities had at least the veneer of sound public health policy. For some time prior to the release, there had been advocacy for closing the monstrously large state hospitals and placing patients in smaller community facilities, free of the bureaucracy and facelessness of the large institutions. The problem was that at the time of wholesale release of patients, few such community facilities had been established. What patients encountered were poorly supervised boarding houses in which the care offered was often worse than in the hospitals from which the patients had been released.

Many such patients soon chose to live in the streets, occasionally seeking refuge in massive public shelters set up only to give them overnight accommodations. This homeless population soon created impossible social problems for most urban communities and aroused irate reactions from their residents. A solution to this problem seems remote.

Interference in Therapy Programs. The problem here is a more subtle one. It arises from a conflict between two well-intentioned groups whose interpretations of a humane environment differ. No one can argue against protecting the mentally ill from forced labor, nor can anyone argue against granting patients accommodations that support their dignity and comfort. The conflict grows out of differing attitudes toward forms of therapy that professional staff consider beneficial in the care of long-term institutionalized patients, but which others—for example, some authorities in the courts—consider a violation of patients' rights.

Contingency Management. Two examples illustrate the conflict. In behavioral therapy, contingency management is considered an effective program for conditioning patients to live harmoniously in a community setting. The token economy is one form of contingency management. In a token economy, various listed desirable activities—for example, making one's bed—are reinforced by issuing a listed number of tokens, which can be spent either for certain privileges—for example, watching television—or for other material rewards that can be purchased in a canteen. The conflict arises when a complaint is made that the principle of a humane environment is violated when privileges or amenities, stated to be the right of the patient, are offered only as a reward for good behavior.

Aversive Techniques. A second example relates to the use of aversive techniques in behavioral therapy. In a well supervised hospital program, painful aversive techniques, such as nonlethal electric shock, are rarely used, and then only under supervision, in order to discourage seriously dangerous behavior, such as determined head banging. The court system has been alerted to the possibility of misuse of such techniques, and has set narrow limits for their use—too narrow, some therapists believe.

The criticism of aversive techniques has broadened to include physically painless aversive techniques, as well as electric shock; for example, the "time out" procedure. Here, a patient causing trouble is temporarily removed from a situation that might offer reinforcing satisfactions, such as undue attention, and placed alone by himself or herself. Here the courts, aware of the punishing use of solitary confinement in the prison system, have focused on "time out" to make sure that the technique is not misused to isolate a patient for long periods of time in a dismal setting.

Basically, the conflict with respect to the therapeutic approaches grows, not out of opposition to the proper use of the techniques, but out of the fear that they will be misused by untrained or unsupervised staff. The problem, of course, would probably be reduced significantly or even eliminated if hospitals were funded at levels sufficient to attract and train suitable staff.

COMMUNITY PSYCHOLOGY AND PREVENTION

Community Psychology, a relatively recently created division of the American Psychological Association, approaches mental illness in a way that takes account of the environment as a factor in mental health and encourages the use of community resources to eliminate conditions that may cause mental illness.

Clinical Psychology and Community Psychology

We can compare the different focuses of clinical psychology and community psychology by the ways in which they approach the problems of mental illness: individual patient versus environmental factors; attention to weakness (or disorders) versus building strengths; and cure versus prevention. We will, given present limitations in our knowledge of human behavior and the resources we have available for promoting mental health, need both approaches for a long time to come.

THE PATIENT VERSUS THE ENVIRONMENT

The word *clinical* derives from the Greek word for "physician who treats bedridden patients." Its use does highlight the primary (although not now exclusive) approach of the clinical psychologist, that is, a patient and a therapist. The community psychologist sees influencing the nature of inter-actions between the environment and human beings as an important long-range approach to promoting mental health. The clinical psychologist's efforts are to change a client's behavior; the community psychologist seeks to change the social environment affecting people.

FOCUS ON DISORDERS VERSUS FOCUS ON HEALTH

Clinical psychologists primarily have as their clientele people who are, before they get to the office, already disturbed by psychological problems. The community psychologist seeks to create environmental conditions that will promote healthy living, for example, family planning and parental training.

PREVENTION VERSUS CURE

The clinical psychologist certainly believes in the efficacy of preventive efforts and supports them, but ordinarily is preoccupied with the needs of individuals seeking immediate help. The community psychologist looks further into the future to consider what society, especially neighborhood communities, can do to keep its citizens healthy, and to guard against environmental factors that might cause psychological problems in the young.

Prevention of Mental Illness

Our focus throughout the earlier chapters has been principally on the work of the clinician. Here we consider the concerns of community psychologists, which are primarily preventive.

George Albee, a past president of the American Psychological Association, puts the importance of preventive efforts into perspective for us in the introduction to a book on preventive psychology.

> The number and distribution of persons with serious emotional problems in our society [are] far beyond what our resources, in terms of both personnel and institutions, [can] deal with on a one-to-one basis. I became convinced of the logic of the public health dictum that holds that no mass disorder is ever eliminated or brought under control by attempting to treat individuals. Every assessment of the distribution of disturbance in the society arrives at an estimate of approximately 15 percent of the population. And when we realize that in any given year only about seven million (of the more than 25 million who need help) are seen throughout the entire mental health system, we can appreciate the hopeless-ness of our present efforts.

Given those figures, we can judge how important a preventive effort is.

TYPES OF PREVENTION

In 1964, in a book setting out the principles of preventive psychiatry, Gerald Caplan distinguished three levels of prevention. His description is an adaptation of the medical model for preventing physical disease. It is now used widely in the field of mental health, and is outlined here.

Tertiary Prevention. Actually the most immediate preventive effort, tertiary prevention begins with the later phases of the treatment processes we have described in this book. Clinicians are increasingly coming to realize that what happens after treatment is a key component in preventing a relapse. Even a short stay in a psychiatric hospital leaves an individual uncertain and insecure about readjusting to the world outside—the longer the stay, the more difficult the readjustment.

Tertiary prevention is the effort to ease the problem by planning a network of supportive services prior to discharge. Studies demonstrate that the existence of an aftercare program and careful integration of the individual into it produce a significant lowering of the relapse rate, even in those who have gone through a serious mental illness such as schizophrenia. A typical aftercare program is the halfway house, in which individuals stay for a while after hospitalization, free to ease themselves back into the world, with help available along the way.

Even when the illness is not severe or of long duration, impulsive behavior may lead to drastic consequences—a street fight, a crime, a family argument. One may not be able to undo the immediate effects of such behavior, but tertiary prevention focuses on containment of the damage to the individual, the victim (if there is one), and to the immediate family. The goal is to prevent the development of a cycle of reinforcement for psychological problems.

Especially beneficial features of tertiary care are swiftness of response, the inclusion of persons affected by the situation but who might not reach out for help, availability of services in the neighborhood, and settings that don't have the aspects of an institution.

Secondary Prevention. The primary goal here is to detect psychological problems before they grow into disabilities. A child's sporadic truancy, for example, should suggest a family visit to offer early help. Secondary prevention is based on the maxim that any illness, including psychological illness, can best be treated if it is treated at its earliest stage. The principal approach of secondary prevention is outreach. Waiting until the individual is desperate enough or sufficiently discomforted to seek treatment on his or her own usually means that the illness has "settled in" and become that much more difficult to treat.

Modern mental health practice has found a number of successful ways of avoiding such a situation. All of them depend on increasing the visibility, convenience, and acceptability of helping services. Trained paraprofessionals, who may be closer in age, style of clothing, and use of language to the troubled individual, may be the best first contacts for attracting persons at risk. If their skill levels are high enough, they often serve at crisis intervention centers, where individuals can be helped on a walk-in basis and then followed up with short-term crisis therapy.

The goal of crisis intervention is to deal first with the psychological emergency. Once that is eased, the individual is more likely to be amenable to longer-range treatment efforts, and a stubborn illness is therefore prevented. The readily available "hot line," the mobile mental health van in the neighborhood, and on-the-street social workers all signal "help is here" and are being used increasingly in efforts at secondary prevention.

Primary Prevention. This long-range type of prevention is directed at communities and not at individuals. If the psychological disorders of communities can be treated, then so many more possible cases of mental illness can be prevented.

Growth of Outpatient Treatment. Two propositions support that approach. First, principally as a result of the community approach, between 1955 and 1983, the National Institute of Mental Health reports that outpatient treatment of psychiatric illnesses has increased from 27.6 percent of all psychiatric care to more than 70 percent of that care. Outpatient care is not only more economical, but more acceptable and effective. It has no doubt contributed to the larger numbers of the American population who now receive care for their psychological ills.

Inadequate Treatment Facilities. The second proposition suggests that despite the increased numbers now being cared for, so many more could lead happier and more productive lives if they could be persuaded to enter community psychiatric facilities. Mental health surveys indicate that more than 25 million people in any one year are in need of psychological help, yet less than 8 million are receiving it.

It is easy to agree with community psychologists that even with the increase in community-based services, it is unrealistic to count on a treatment mode to deal with the myriad problems of mental illness. What is needed is massive efforts to eliminate the conditions in the psychological environment that breed mental illness. Only through such large-scale preventive efforts can inroads be made on what may be the most significant public health problem today.

Goals of Community Change Programs

Three major environmental factors that breed psychological problems have been held up as targets for mental health efforts. They are racism, poverty, and drug abuse. The National Mental Health Association has spelled out four specific programs that have an immediate potential for attacking those targets and, in that way, reducing mental illness: a family focus approach, sex education, an educational thrust, and increasing popular knowledge of mental health resources.

FAMILY FOCUS PROGRAM

A stable and happy family can be a principal source of mental health. Sick families are the principal source of troubled emotions and psychological disorders. Families can be strengthened by providing increased family planning and prenatal services and by public information campaigns on good parenting practices and healthy family living.

SEX EDUCATION

A second proposed emphasis is the prevention of teenage pregnancies. The services needed to achieve that goal are sex education in the high schools, contraception and health services to teens, and help during the teen years with responsible decision-making.

THE EDUCATIONAL THRUST

School programs that find their way to helping children from unmotivating families to academic achievement sufficient to qualify them for entry-level jobs with a future are a principal need. Those programs must provide their students with interpersonal skills for building stable interpersonal relations—a tall order, indeed, but one that society cannot afford to neglect.

KNOWLEDGE OF COMMUNITY RESOURCES

The goal of this approach is to provide those in problem situations, such as teenage drug users, battered wives or families with an alcoholic problem, with information about community resources that are available to them. The presence of resources in the community that troubled people have never learned about is a waste of talent, both the staff's and the troubled person's, and a sure block to preventive efforts.

Few argue with this goal. The unsolved problem is to give it a sufficiently high priority so that financial support is provided to implement it. Mental health workers, who live close to the suffering created by a failure to do so, try to maintain a steady focus of public attention on the matter to get adequate action for these problems, and they need help from all of us.

THE MENTAL HEALTH COMMUNITY

Mental health has a constituency in America, but, unfortunately, its members have not yet grown large enough, its voice loud enough, nor its tactics effective enough, to stimulate a primary prevention program adequate to meet the needs. Yet there is reason to be hopeful. Over the past forty years, the power of those efforts to produce change has increased yearly, and the results of those efforts are now becoming apparent.

The mental health community exists at three levels: congressional sympathizers and government staff, professional associations, and volunteer groups.

Congressional and State Legislators

One example of this legislative power was the passage in 1946 of the first comprehensive national mental health bill. The bill authorized the establishment of the National Institute of Mental Health. It originally had one primary function: to serve as a center to stimulate mental health research and training.

Subsequently two other services were added to its original purpose: to provide assistance to communities in setting up locally based mental health programs, and to circulate information on mental health to mental health scientists and to the general public.

Implementing programs stimulated by the federal legislation is the responsibility of state and local governments. Federal funding has enabled them to do this. With that leadership at the national level, legislatures in a number of states have initiated their own programs in mental health with state funding.

Professional Associations

Organizations such as the American Psychological Association, the American Psychiatric Association, and associations of the social sciences, have, in the past, satisfied themselves principally with the setting of standards for training and practice in their respective fields. They have increasingly involved themselves in the promotion of social changes vital to the fostering of mental health.

The Volunteer Movement

In a most crucial sense, the mental health movement has attracted the support, energy, talent, and, to some extent, funding, of a large body of volunteers from all walks of life. The most well known of these volunteer groups is the National Association for Mental Health; a parallel group for the mentally retarded is the National Association for the Mentally Retarded. Professional mental health workers are well aware of the importance of this kind of grass-roots support and cooperate extensively with it. Indeed, they occasionally find it is the volunteer groups that take leadership roles in pushing for desirable social legislation and other supportive activities.

*B*eginning as early as 1834, English courts and the federal and state judiciary in this country have handed down decisions protecting the rights of the mentally ill. Courts in this country were particularly active in doing so during the 1970s. Court decisions have protected the rights of the psychologically disordered in five specific areas. They are as follows:

1. *The Insanity Plea.* In 1834, an Ohio court held that individuals could not be held responsible for their crimes if it could be established that, as a result of mental illness, they were unable to resist the impulse to commit a crime. Because of the impracticality of using that criterion, other criteria have been established over the years, the first of which was the McNaghten rule, which required that the individual at the time of the crime must have been aware of the nature of his or her behavior. In 1954, a federal district court significantly broadened that criterion, stating, in what has come to be called the Durham test, that if the crime was the product of mental disease or mental deficit the individual could not be held responsible. In 1972, the Durham test was replaced by a Supreme Court decision that stated that an individual could not be held responsible for a criminal act when, because of mental disease or mental defect, he or she lacked the capacity to appreciate the nature of the act or the capacity to control the impulse. It is that decision which largely governs the use of the insanity plea, which, as a matter of fact, has been used in only 2 percent of criminal trials and has been used successfully in less than 1 percent of felony cases.

The most recent development, arising out of John W. Hinckley's attempt to assassinate President Reagan, is the use of the verdict "not guilty by reason of insanity." An individual so judged avoids prison but is committed to a mental institution. Once committed, the Supreme Court ruled in 1983 that such a person might be hospitalized indefinitely.

2. *Competency to Stand Trial.* This issue deals not with the individual's mental state at the time of committing the crimes but rather with whether or not he or she is competent to cooperate with counsel in the trial. If determined to be incompetent, the individual must be committed to a mental institution.

3. *Civil Commitment.* Some mental health professionals advocate that before an individual is civilly committed to a mental institution, certain conditions be met. These are entitlement to a jury trial, protection against self-incrimination, and provision of legal counsel. In addition, the individual must manifest one or more of the following four conditions. They are: impaired judgment, need for treatment, dangerousness to self, and dangerousness to others.

4. In *Wyatt v. Stickney,* an Alabama court ruled that state mental institutions must provide their patients with an individualized treatment program, an adequate number of skilled staff, and a humane physical and psychological environment.

5. In the community at large, increased effort is now being directed to the prevention of mental illness and to the provision of neighborhood clinics designed to reach patients at an early point in their illness.

Selected Readings

Bacon, D. L. 1969. "Incompetency to Stand Trial: Commitment to an Inclusive Test." *Southern California Law Review*, 42: 444.

Livermore, J. M. and P. E. Meehl. 1967. "The Virtues of McNaghten." *Minnesota Law Review*, 51: 789-856.

Roth, L. A. 1979. "A Commitment Law for Patients, Doctors and Lawyers." *American Journal of Psychiatry*, 136: 1121-1127.

Steadman, H. J. 1981. "The Statistical Prediction of Violent Behavior: Measuring the Costs of a Public Protectionist versus a Civil Libertarian Model." *Law and Human Behavior*, 5: 263-274.

Stone, A. A. 1975. *Mental Health and Law: A System in Transition*. Rockville, MD: National Institute of Mental Health, Center for Studies of Crime and Delinquency.

Tardiff, K. and H. W. Koenigsberg. 1985. "Assaultive Behavior among Psychiatric Outpatients." *American Journal of Psychiatry*, 142(8): 960-963.

Weiner, B. A. 1985. "Mental Disability and the Criminal Law." in S. J. Brakel, J. Parry and B. A. Weiner (Eds.). *The Mentally Disabled and the Law*, 3rd ed. Chicago, IL: American Bar Foundation.

20

Research in Abnormal Psychology

*H*uman behavior, even behavior that varies from the norm, is something everyone can claim some knowledge of. Based on their own experiences and the casual observations that everyday living provides, people have their own notions about the causes of human behavior and, perhaps, especially about the causes of abnormal behavior. As an earlier chapter has indicated (chapter 1), those notions are often off the mark. Casual observation is an unreliable way of arriving at an accurate knowledge of normal or abnormal behavior.

Over the years, the study of abnormal behavior has adopted the rigor and controls of scientific methodology. This chapter examines first the characteristics, requirements, and vocabulary of scientific research. It then describes the research designs most frequently used in the study of abnormal behavior. Along the way, it describes basic concepts of statistical analysis.

Research on abnormal behavior is subject to limitations imposed by ethical considerations and practicality. An intervention introduced into an experiment in physics is a matter only of its usefulness in completing the experiment; an intervention in studying abnormal behavior must take into account any negative effects on the subject and must consider also any unrelated and confounding reactions it might arouse in those whose behavior is being studied, both control (a group unexposed to experimental conditions) and experimental groups.

THE GOALS OF SCIENTIFIC STUDY

There are three goals of scientific study: *description, prediction* and *understanding*.

Description

In pursuit of describing a psychological phenomenon, the basic activity of the scientist is *observation;* scientific observation requires special training. To give scientific significance to their activities, scientists usually limit their observations to the areas of their training and competence. Astronomers observing people's behavior would miss much of significance in the behavior of those they were observing, and psychologists would be equally handicapped in observing the celestial bodies.

On the basis of trained observation, scientists are able to describe the phenomena under study in great detail. They group similar phenomena into named categories and seek to discover relationships among the categories. They use various means to clarify their observations and make them more precise. Here are some examples from research in abnormal psychology: Psychologists-researchers make their observations many times (when they can), sometimes of the same person; at other times, by observing many people, frequently people in different settings. They use "instruments," such as psychological tests, questionnaires, rating scales, or checklists. They magnify their observations by viewing them with the help of electroencephalograms, or brain scans. The use of such supplements to observation increases the reliability (dependability) and comparability of repeated observations.

To make their observations as precise as possible, scientists define variables under study in *operational terms* by quantifying them. They describe results of their research and make comparisons in statistical values, such as measures of central tendency (means, modes, or medians), and measures of scatter or distribution, such as the standard deviation. To identify relationships between variables, they use coefficients of correlation. They compare or contrast the quantatively expressed results of their observations by a process called *statistical inference*. In that process, when they have taken two sets of measurements that differ from each other, they compute ratios to tell them whether or not such differences were a matter of chance variation or the result of true differences between the two phenomena that had been measured.

Prediction

The result of scientific observation and statistical treatment of measured observations is a statement that may lead to the prediction of future behavior or events, for example, a prediction of the likelihood of later development of criminal behavior.

Goldstein's 1968 research of the predictability of the later development of schizophrenia (see chapter 13) is an example of research leading to a prediction of future behavior. He and his associates found that there was a variation in the degree of communication deviance between parent and child in the homes of teenagers who were experiencing emotional problems. Using those differences in communication deviance, they predicted that the homes in which communication deviance was highest were most likely to produce children who would later develop schizophrenia. The researchers followed their subjects for fifteen years and were able to validate their prediction.

Understanding

This goal of scientific research means being able to identify a cause-and-effect relationship between two phenomena or events. Establishing a causal relationship requires that three conditions be met: 1. if one event is said to cause another, the two events must vary together, that is, for example, when one is absent, the other is absent; when one changes, the other changes; 2. the stated cause must exist or occur before the stated effect; and 3. there must be no other reasonable alternative cause for the perceived relationship between the two events.

The third condition is usually the most difficult to establish. An example of an early failure to meet the condition occurred in early studies of the schizophrenias. Researchers hypothesized that there might be measurable differences in the blood or urine chemistry of schizophrenics and non-schizophrenics. To test their hypothesis, they compared blood and urine in two sample populations, a group of hospitalized schizophrenics and a nonhospitalized normal population. They did find notable differences, but those differences resulted from *a confounding effect:* the difference between a hospital diet and an uncontrolled diet. The differences had nothing to do with schizophrenia.

Confounding Effects and Internal Validity

To draw a conclusion about causality, the two populations compared must differ significantly only in the variable under study. There cannot be more than one variable that could have caused the reported effect. When that condition has been established (and it is not always easy to accomplish), the study is said to have *internal validity*.

External Validity

The external validity of judgments about causation may be established by the conclusions generalizability, that is, does the same covariation occur when different groups are studied, in different situations, usually with different researchers? Establishing generalizability is possible only when the populations under study are representative of the universe they are designated to represent. If, for example, causal factors in the development of a conversion disorder (hysteria) are hypothesized only on the basis of patients seen in psychoanalytic therapy, drawn from the upper classes of a highly specific culture (Freud's practice), the sample on which the conclusion is based could hardly be considered representative of people generally, and the conclusions reached, without further research, might not be truly generalizable. Its *external validity* would therefore not have been established.

Representa-
tiveness

The *representativeness* of a sample is best assured by randomly selecting members of the group to be represented, that is, selecting them in such a way that each member of the population has an equal chance of being selected. The sample must also be large enough to be statistically reliable.

RESEARCH DESIGNS

There are six basic ways in which psychologists attempt to study abnormal behavior in a scientific way: 1. descriptive studies; 2. developmental designs, 3. correlational designs, 4. experimental designs, 5. analogue designs, and 6. experiments of nature.

Descriptive
Studies

The most basic design is one in which the researcher gathers data in such a way as to describe the phenomena under study. The researcher may want to describe a. the history of a phenomenon, that is, the events leading up to the present state of affairs, in which case the psychologist and associated psychiatrist, social worker, medical doctor, relatives, and friends, gather or provide the information that goes into a case history. The researcher may wish to describe b. the current state of affairs, principally the prevalence and distribution of one variable, for example, psychiatric illness, in a large, described population, in which case the survey method is used.

CASE HISTORY (SEE CHAPTER 5)

The earliest studies of psychiatric disorders were based on the life story and current symptomatology of patients in therapy. Such a history begins with the present and goes back to the earliest years that can be recalled by the patient or other knowledgeable persons. The patient's own interview account of those years is frequently supplemented by reports of friends, relatives, school and medical records, and whatever sources of information are available about the individual's life. Today, the case history usually includes a battery of psychological tests.

In a case history, the clinician or researcher may seek an understanding of a particular individual's illness, or, from a number of case histories of the same illness, the clinician may hope to understand the etiology of the disease itself and possible treatment approaches.

Freud's work provides abundant examples of both values of the case history. In the course of his treatment of a number of patients with what was then termed hysteria, he was able not only to demonstrate the value of his newly developed psychoanalytic method, but on the basis of the case histories of his patients, he came to an understanding of the illness itself. Freud concluded from his studies that repressed wishes were the cause of hysteria. Once his preliminary hypothesis was developed, he could test its validity by examining the case histories of a subsequent group of patients with the same disorder.

Kraeplin, principally on the basis of case studies, was able to provide the framework for a classification of psychiatric disorders that is still used today. Bleuler, in taking the case histories of a number of psychiatric patients, drew the conclusion that schizophrenia was not one but at least two quite different disorders.

EVALUATION OF THE CASE HISTORY

As a scientific method, the case history has both advantages and serious limitations.

Advantages of the Case Study. The case history offers three advantages: 1. The case history provides a description in its natural setting as the individual experienced it. In this way, it is superior, for example, to the experiment which introduces many artificialities not characteristic of real life. 2. The case history explores types of human behavior that, because of their bizarreness or rarity, cannot often be studied by other methodologies, for example, the survey or experiment. 3. The case history, thoughtfully considered, is a source of worthwhile hypotheses subject to future study and verification.

Disadvantages of the Case Study. There are three disadvantages of the case study: 1. Selectivity. The patient's recall of life experiences is not total. Memory, attitudes, the patient's expectations about what the therapist wants to hear, all cause the patient to be highly selective in what he or she includes in the case history. The described experiences are retrospective and colored by all that followed in the patient's life. The description of a childhood experience twenty years after it happened may not closely resemble the reality of the experience. 2. A life history is a one-time event. The experience of gathering it cannot be repeated in exactly the same way. A clinician's practice is ordinarily a varied one, embracing patients with a variety of illnesses. Repeatability (or replication) is ordinarily a requirement of the scientific method. It is a practical impossibility in using the case history. A clinician's practice cannot be drawn from a representative sample, not even a representative sample of all people suffering from the same psychiatric disorder. As has been described previously, Freud's patients, for example, were drawn from a very narrow cultural base: middle- and upper-class members of Viennese society during the Victorian period. Even when clinicians gather the case histories of many individuals, those histories would not be selected randomly. They are what might be called an opportunity sample whose characteristics were influenced more by the nature of the clinicians's practice than by random selection. 3. It is never possible, when constructing a case study, to exclude the possibility of other influential causes that have not been revealed by the patient. To find compelling evidence of causation, we would have to know that one event, the cause, was always followed by a described effect, and that when an effect was present, it had always been preceded by the hypothesized cause. But even many case histories may not provide that information.

THE SURVEY

A survey is essentially a counting of experiences, for example, the number of people in midtown Manhattan who have psychological problems, or the psychiatric disorder that accounts for the largest number of hospital admissions. The information is gathered from public records or from brief front door or telephone interviews with a sample population. Information that can be gathered in that way is valuable in planning mental health resources, but it tells us very little about etiology or effective treatment. However, it may lead to the development of hypotheses.

Characteristics of the Survey. H. B. Murphy (1968) provides an example of survey results that led him to an hypothesis about an environmental condition that possibly contributed to the development of schizophrenia. He summarized the results of a number of surveys, tallying the cases of schizophrenia by socioeconomic class. Murphy reported a disproportionately high rate of schizophrenia in the lower socioeconomic classes throughout much of the Western world. From this, he hypothesized a relationship between schizophrenia and poverty. The limitation in the survey method is indicated in his statement that from the data the direction of a causal relationship could not be determined.

He states, "It is not altogether clear what is the direction of causality in this relationship; whether the conditions of life of the lowest social classes are conducive to the development of schizophrenia, or schizophrenia leads to a decline in social class position."

Survey research is of two types: 1. reactive surveys, in which subjects are required to answer questions in an interview or on a printed questionnaire, and 2. nonreactive surveys, in which a survey uses available records, without seeking any reaction from members of the population being surveyed. The example cited above exemplifies a nonreactive survey. Nonreactive surveys use hospital, school, or other public records. The Midtown Mental Health Survey, in which data were gathered in door-to-door visits, is an example of a reactive survey.

In survey research, a representative sample of the population to be described is critical. Without representativeness of sample, survey results are meaningless. Scientific surveys carefully describe procedures used to obtain a random sample. In addition, they set the size of the sample required for reliable descriptions in accordance with statistical formulae for such purposes. In reporting results, they usually indicate the margin of error in their results. The larger the sample, the smaller the probable error.

Advantages of the Survey Method. The principal advantages are as follows: 1. They provide useful information on the incidence (number of new cases by time period, for example, annually) and its prevalence (number of cases in a described population). 2. Since a survey usually relates the psychiatric disorder to other information about the individual, the information provided helps identify individuals at risk and increases our understanding of point of onset and future course of the illness. 3. Statistical relationships uncovered in a survey often suggest hypotheses as to possible etiology. 4. Surveys are able to identify victims of particular disorders, not yet in therapy, who can be referred for treatment.

Disadvantages of the Survey Method. There are two possible hazards in survey research. They are as follows:

1. As mentioned previously, the value of a survey is dependent totally upon the representativeness of the sample. To assure that participants have been selected randomly, researchers have to state in advance how they will be selected so that each member of the population under study will have an equal chance of being selected. 2. In reactive surveys, the social desirability of an answer sometimes causes the respondent to give that answer rather than one that more accurately states the facts. Many adult individuals, for instance, might not be willing to state that they frequently have nightmares or often feel depressed. The researcher can often phrase questions in too forceful a way. The problem with doing so is that it might produce too many inaccurate positive answers.

Correlational Studies

In studying abnormal behavior, psychologists often go beyond simple descriptive studies, such as those provided by the case history or the survey, to consider how two aspects of the individual's behavior are related. They ask the question, for example, how do divorce and the presence of a psychological disorder correlate with each other? Or the psychologist may seek to test the hypothesis that poverty influences juvenile delinquency by recording delinquency rates and the prevalence of poverty in different sections of an urban community. He or she might then correlate those two prevalency levels. If the two correlated (varied together), one could say that poverty and delinquency were associated. On the basis of such a relationship, it would be premature to say that one caused the other.

THE COEFFICIENT OF CORRELATION

The coefficient of correlation is the statistical ratio used to assess the degree to which two events or conditions vary together. A coefficient of correlation may be positive (expressed in a positive number) and thus indicate that as one variable (a factor under study) increases, the second variable also increases. A perfect relationship, in which each variable increased to the same degree as the other, would be expressed by a coefficient of 1.00. Such a finding rarely, if ever, occurs when measuring human characteristics. The coefficient of correlation may be negative (expressed in a negative number), indicating that as one variable increases, the other decreases. For example, research reports that there is a negative correlation between time spent studying and failure rate. Some hard-working students may be disappointed to discover that the negative relationship is not minus 1.00, indicating a perfect negative relationship. Some students, despite hard work, still fail.

CORRELATION AND CAUSALITY

There is a temptation with covariation to believe a causal relation exists between the two variables. An important caveat is in order here: covariation does not demonstrate causality. Determining a causal relation demands more careful study than simply identifying a correlation between the two variables. For one thing, the time order between the two variables has to be considered. In Murphy's study (discussed above), the unanswered question was which came first, the poverty or the schizophrenia? Did the presence of the disorder lead to impoverishment, or did living in poverty increase the likelihood of schizophrenia?

Beyond that, the researcher must consider the possible presence of an independent third variable influencing or confounding both other variables. An odd example is often used in psychology classes to illustrate that possibility. It is pointed out that there is a moderately high correlation between the salaries paid to clergypersons in a community and the number of liquor stores in the community. Any conclusion concerning that relationship must take account of a third variable, the average income in the community. That third variable is likely to be the independent, confounding cause of the spurious correlation between the two variables. In studies of abnormal behavior, spurious correlations may also be found and conclusions drawn that ignore the presence of a third common influence on the two variables being studied.

Researchers attempt to eliminate the presence of a contaminating or confounding variable by matching the subjects under study in as many characteristics as possible. There are two problems with doing so: such matching sometimes results in the groups becoming so highly selected as to be unrepresentative. An example illustrating the danger, cited by Bootzin

(1988) follows: Matching senior citizens and college students on general health would lead to a most unrepresentative group of senior citizens since so many of them have health problems as they age.

Major Advantages of the Correlational Method. 1. A principal advantage of the method is that it allows the study of naturally existing groups when ethical or practical considerations would rule out the more rigidly structured experimental approach (to be discussed later). For instance, in studies of depression, it might be desirable to discover the relationship between dreaming and intensity of depression. The correlational method lends itself readily to such a study without undue interference in the life of the patient. Both variables, extent of nighttime dreaming and level of depression, are measurable. Obtaining a coefficient of correlation would at least demonstrate covariation between the two and lend preliminary encouragement to further study of the possibility that there might be a causal relationship.

Study of such a relationship might, in the first instance, be performed on natural groups in the population, for example, college students. Researchers label such studies *correlational research design.*

2. The correlational method provides a precise measurement of the covariation of any two measurable variables. There are many occasions in abnormal psychology when obtaining such a measurement would be helpful.

3. Correlational studies are free of the artificiality of laboratory research.

Disadvantage of the Correlational Method. As indicated previously, the correlational study does not allow the research to draw any definitive conclusions about causal relations. To counterbalance that disadvantage, it does encourage (or discourage) further research efforts to test out a speculative hypothesis.

Developmental or Longitudinal Studies

Following the course of an individual's development over many years offers many advantages, the principal one of which is establishment of a time-order relationship between life-time crises and psychiatric disorder, for example, in phobic reaction or depression. The methodology is essentially a variation of the correlational design and is subject to its limitations. The sequence of events, one event following upon another, by itself does not establish a causal relationship.

PROBLEMS IN LONGITUDINAL STUDIES

The developmental method has certain problems. Attrition of the population under study is one of them. A beginning population of one hundred subjects, over a period of five to ten years, because of the difficulty of maintaining contact with subjects, might become so small as to become unreliable for statistical analysis.

When the developmental study becomes a retrospective recall of early development on the part of the patient, it resembles the case study method. Such retrospective recall, as has previously been suggested, is highly unreliable.

A more scientific approach is to keep individuals under study through many years, preferably beginning at an early point in their life. Most often in abnormal psychology, a longitudinal study is likely to begin when the individual first comes to the attention of a clinic because of early signs of psychological difficulty. Such studies are called *high-risk research strategy*.

AN EXAMPLE OF A LONGITUDINAL STUDY

A research by Medwick (1968) is a good example of the developmental research design. The sample selected was 311 teenagers, made up of 207 children of schizophrenic parents, (the high-risk group) and a control group of 104 matched normal children. The study sought to identify some measurable sign detectable during early adolescence that would predict the later development of schizophrenia. Information collected initially included birth history, family history, school records, and various physical and psychological measurements. Both groups were followed for five years.

Premature recovery from shock produced by a startling stimulus (one test used by the study) was discovered to predict later development of schizophrenia. That response was also associated with such lifetime occurrences as birth complications and early separation from parents. The response was thus associated with both a genetic predisposition to schizophrenia (schizophrenic parents) and a difficult and disrupted early childhood. It was therefore considered compatible with a diathesis-stress formulation of the illness. (see chapter 10) That relationship to a theoretical way of thinking about schizophrenia seems to give the finding a form of external validity. Nevertheless, before the results can be accepted widely as substantially valid, it will have to be replicated by other researchers and with other subjects.

THE CROSS-SECTIONAL STUDY

A variation of the longitudinal or developmental research design is the cross-sectional study. A typical longitudinal study follows the same group of children over several years. In a cross-sectional study, at a single point in the study, groups of children representing a cross section of different ages are compared to trace the development of certain behavioral patterns. A study conducted by Jersild and Holmes in 1975 is a good example of a cross-sectional study. They identified children's fears at three periods, from ages one through six, and then attempted to relate them to specific developmental changes.

This method is more economical of time and effort than the longitudinal study. It has, however, more value in tracing developmental sequences than in identifying etiological factors in psychiatric disorders. But as with correlational studies, it tends to build (or weaken) hypotheses under consideration but does not crucially test them. Its weakness is that it ignores the effect of varying (and unmeasured) life experiences among the children studied. Its rationale for doing so is the assumption that a large enough sample will "wash out" individual differences.

The Experimental Research Design

A well-conducted experiment is an ideal model of the scientific method. As with all experiments, experimental research in abnormal behavior begins with a hypothesis. The experimenter's hypothesis usually relates to speculation about possible causes of a psychiatric disorder or possible therapies. It may have been formed on the basis of other research, tentative but suggestive. Such hypotheses grow out of findings in case studies or in correlational studies, sometimes even from surveys. Since the two most important goals of research in abnormal psychology are the identification of causes and the testing of hypotheses for effectiveness of treatment, hypotheses usually relate to those questions.

In all experimental research, there are two variables whose relationship is the prime concern of the researchers: an independent variable and a dependent variable. The independent variable is the hypothesized cause of a particular phenomenon; in abnormal psychology, for example, a specific form of therapy might be hypothesized as a cause of improvement in some psychiatric disorders, such as phobic disorder. In such cases, providing the therapy would be the independent variable.

A dependent variable is one whose occurrence is dependent on whether or not the independent variable preceded it. The most rudimentary experimental design may be illustrated as follows: pretest -experimental treatment -posttest. Here the experimental treatment is the independent variable; the dependent variable is any change between pretest and posttest. The experimental treatment might be an hypothesized therapy, described in specific, preferably quantative terms. A requirement of a good experiment is that both variables be operationally defined, that is, there should be a quantified or measured statement of the independent and dependent variables.

The design described here is a single-subject design in which the before-and-after comparison serves as a control. Relatively few conclusions in abnormal psychology are drawn from single-subject experiments. In most experiments, two groups are set up, one known as the experimental group, the other the control group. Such a two-group experiment may be diagrammed as follows:

Experimental Group:

Pre-test ⟶ Experimental Treatment ⟶ Posttest

Control Group:

Pretest ⟶ No Experimental Treatment ⟶ Posttest

If subjects in such an experimental design have been assigned randomly to each group so that each group is representative of the population being studied, and if the number of subjects is large enough to produce statistically reliable results, the researchers may conclude that any difference between the experimental group and the control group in the posttest would have been caused by the experimental treatment.

We can best illustrate the various steps in experimental research by describing a well-controlled experiment reported by Vogel in the *Archives of General Psychiatry* (1975). Here are the steps the researchers took:

Step 1. Developing an Hypothesis. The researchers were aware of two critical pieces of information: First, they knew that depressed patients who missed several nights of sleep, contrary to the way most of us would feel, felt less depressed. Secondly they knew that the medications regularly taken by the patients (which were helping their depression) tended, as a side effect, to reduce the amount of dreaming experienced by the individual. In a speculative leap, they hypothesized that reducing dream activity itself would lighten the depression. They then proceeded to test the hypothesis in an experiment.

Step 2. Operationally defining the independent variable. They described it as follows: In each of three weeks for three or four consecutive nights, the subjects in the experimental group were awakened whenever it was observed that they were dreaming, a fact that could be determined by observing the rapid eye movements (REM) that accompany dreaming.

Step 3. Measuring the dependent variable. The dependent variable in this experiment was level of depression, which was measured on a rating scale before and after the experimental treatment (all the circumstances of which had been described to the subjects before the experiment was attempted).

Step 4. Setting up a control group. Other depressed patients, selected to represent different types of depression but matched on other critical variables, experienced the same nocturnal awakenings in the same fashion as the experimental subjects, except that they were awakened during nondreaming periods (determined by the absence of rapid eye movements). Experimental and control groups, it may be confidently assumed, differed only in the amount of dreaming they did during a three-week period; only the presence of the independent variable distinguished the control and experimental groups.

Step 5. Drawing a conclusion. In an experiment, the critical finding is a statistically significant difference between the control and the experimental groups on their postexperimental treatment results. In the described experiment, only the endogenously depressed (a depression not caused by a life crisis) members of the experimental group showed a reduction in depressive symptoms. The authors concluded that dream deprivation lightens depressive symptoms in endogenously depressed patients; there was no evidence that it has a positive effect on other types of depression.

SPECIAL EXPERIMENTAL CONTROLS

There are two special precautions researchers take in running an experiment. They use what has become known as an ABAB research design, which seeks to measure the effectiveness of an experimental treatment by showing that the individual's behavior changes in opposite directions with alternating conditions of experimental treatment and no experimental treatment. A second requisite precaution is to eliminate both subject and experimenter bias by keeping both "blind" as to which are the experimental subjects and which the controls.

The ABAB Design. This design utilizes only one group of subjects. Instead of using an experimental and a control group, the experimenter sets up two experimental conditions, one with the experimental treatment and the other without. An ABAB research design can be diagrammed as follows:

Determination of Baseline ⟶ Experimental Treatment ⟶

Measurement of Change

A Return to Baseline ⟶ No Treatment

Measurement of Change ⟶

MEASUREMENT OF ANY CHANGE

If there is a change (alleviation of symptoms) after treatment, but no such change without treatment, the experimenter can conclude that the experimental treatment produced the change. Such a result when the experiment is a test of a specified therapy would cause experimenters to consider the treatment effective for the condition studied. The ABAB design is frequently called a reverse design experiment because any improvement in behavior after Condition I (with treatment) is likely to be reversed after Condition II (without treatment).

Here is an example of an ABAB design testing the effectiveness of a specific drug. During Condition I, for a three-week period, a number of depressed patients are given daily doses of the drug to be tested. At the end of the three-week period, the presence of depressive symptoms is rated by neutral and uninformed observers. A period of three weeks is allowed to elapse, and patients' symptoms return to their previous level. For a second period of three weeks, each day the subjects are given a placebo (a useless drug with the same external features as the actual drug). Again, at the end of the period, the researchers assess the depressive symptoms. If there has been improvement in the depression after Condition I but not after Condition II, the experimenter can judge the drug to be an effective agent for relieving depressive symptoms.

The Double-blind Experiment. Frequently described as an elegant design, the double-blind experiment is typically used in all major drug therapy research. In the double-blind experiment, some subjects (the experimental group) are given dosages of the drug under study; others (the control group) are given a placebo. In the experiment, both subjects and experimenters are kept "blind" as to which group individuals belong to until the experiment has been completed. Only after the results are completed are the control and experimental groups officially identified. The double-blind design eliminates any interfering effects from suggestibility in subjects and possible bias by experimenters.

Analogue Experiments. An experimenter may attempt to reproduce in a group of normal subjects behavior and feelings analogous to those that might be found in psychiatrically ill individuals. Although similar to the feelings and behavior seen in psychopathology, for ethical reasons the reactions produced must be milder than in a real illness and only of short duration. The condition produced can be considered the independent variable whose effect on future reactions of the subjects (the dependent variable) are then carefully observed and measured.

Analogue experiments, although they have their limitations, are especially helpful in research on abnormal behavior because it is infrequent that researchers have an opportunity of placing psychiatrically ill persons into the rigidities of an experimental design.

We describe here an example of a typical experiment conducted by Heroto and Seligman in 1975. Two groups of matched college students were initially given quite different experimental tasks. Each group was encouraged to feel that success in solving problems was a significant indicator of the individual's general ability. The control group first worked on a number of solvable problems; the experimental group faced a situation in which their failure was guaranteed. They were given a set of unsolvable problems on which to work. Naturally enough, they left that experience feeling at least discouraged, and probably mildly depressed. Their assigned task left them feeling helpless and ultimately hopeless. It was apparent that they felt quite differently about themselves than did the control group. The researchers set as the independent variable that difference in the feelings of the two groups. The experimental subjects were given self-feelings analogous to but much milder than the feelings of depressed patients.

The hypothesis the experimenters were testing was: depression is a learned form of helplessness. In the literature search leading to their hypothesis, they had learned that depressed patients did poorly in solving problems.

What was the experimenter's reasoning in testing their hypothesis? They began by defining the experimental condition (that is, having no success in solving problems under conditions of strong motivation) as "learned helplessness." If that state of mind caused the experimental group to do poorly on a second group of solvable problems when compared with the control group (which, indeed, turned out to be the case), they would therefore be showing signs of depression; that is, inadequate performance. With those findings, the experimenters could conclude that "learned helplessness" causes depression.

Since the disappointment in not solving experimental problems was trivial when compared to the intense suffering faced by pathologically depressed patients, the results can be considered only suggestive, possibly confirmatory, of other similar findings. Standing alone, it could not be considered the definitive establishment of a causal relationship between learned helplessness and depression.

Evaluation of Analogue Experiments. Analogue experiments have one principal advantage and one almost completely neutralizing disadvantage. They allow experimental conditions that could not ethically be imposed on psychiatric patients. To discourage and deflate the egos of a normal group of college students is allowable, especially if they were briefed about experimental conditions soon after the experiment, as they were.

Their disadvantage is that the analogous state produced by the experiment, of necessity, has to be a very pale version of the real illness. The basic criticism of the analogue experiment is that it is only analogous to, not identical with, real life. The intellectual leap from analogy to reality is a big one, and may not be justified in all cases.

Animal research offers a different kind of analogy, from animal to human. Although there are ethical and humane limits placed on animal research, many valuable insights into human behavior have been suggested as a result of using animals analogously in experimental designs in ways that would not be acceptable if the subjects had been human.

Experiments of Nature

Natural events, more often than not catastrophic events, such as floods, earthquakes, disastrous storms, and other such traumatic occurrences such as rape, airplane accidents, and military combat, provide occasions for studying certain types of abnormal behavior. Such unfortunate events have, for example, provided the basis for describing onset of post-traumatic stress disorder, its symptomatology, possible therapies, and even possible preventive measures. After such studies, the fully developed diagnostic criteria for that disorder were first presented in *DSMIII* (1980).

With such traumatic events, the striking, extreme, and all-encompassing nature of the event allows the researcher to conclude that any significant departure from previous levels of functioning can legitimately be considered an effect of the trauma.

That conclusion is a broad, global one, which does not specify what it is about the occurrence that causes the breakdown. There are many possibilities: suddenness, immediate threat of death, guilt about personal survival while relatives and friends did not survive. These are all psychologically disruptive experiences, possibly causative of a psychiatric breakdown. Psychological opinion suggests that the specific causal agent varies with the nature of the trauma.

In a sense, such catastrophic events can be labeled experiments of nature. From that point of view, the catastrophe is the independent variable and, for example, post-traumatic stress disorder would be the dependent variable. The psychological literature provides many examples of how studying the effect of natural catastrophes or other trauma increases our understanding of abnormal behavior. Catastrophes such as the following have been studied in follow-up: major flooding with many fatalities in the Buffalo Creek area of West Virginia in 1972; the Mount Saint Helen volcanic eruption in 1980; the Coconut Grove nightclub fire in Boston, in 1942, which took 491 lives; and the Vietnam war experiences of returned American soldiers.

Overall Evaluation of the Experimental Design

Two strong advantages of the experimental design, particularly since it can be conducted in a laboratory setting, have been identified by Rosenhan and Seligman (1989). To quote those authors, the experiment "is the foremost method for isolating causal elements." The careful control built into the experiment, which largely limits the operation of extraneous variables, is the principal factor giving the experiment that capability.

The second advantage is its repeatability; almost all significant experiments are replicated, sometimes on different populations, to test the generalizability of the experiment's conclusions.

A crucial limiting disadvantage of the experiment is its artificiality. The circumstances of the experiment signal to the subjects that they are a "special" group under study for scientific purposes. Attitudes created by that knowledge can cause them to behave in unnatural ways.

As society's interest in protecting the individual's rights increases, more limits are being placed on what can be done experimentally on humans and increasingly, as well, on animal subjects. For example, the early experiment performed by Watson and Raynor in 1920, in which they created a phobia in an eleven-month-old child whose parents unwisely allowed the research, would now be forbidden by law and by ethical considerations.

Because of an experiment's artificiality and the social and ethical limitations placed on certain types of experimentation, the study of abnormal behavior will continue to be dependent upon correlational studies and experiments of nature, and we will continue to look toward the case study as a source of promising hypotheses.

Abnormal psychology shares the goals of all science. Those goals are description, prediction, and understanding. The basic activity of the scientist is observation refined by special training and aided by the use of instruments. The abnormal psychology examples of instrumentation are psychological tests, rating scales, electroencephalography.

Research in abnormal psychology is principally interested in describing the individuals symptoms, understanding the causes of mental disorders and learning what therapies are helpful.

The basic requirements for scientific research in abnormal psychology are the absence of "confounding effects", they are extraneous factors that may influence the results (internal validity); generalizability to other populations by other researches (external validity) and the repre-sentativeness of the sample, that is the extent to which the sample is truly similar to the population being described.

There are six basic research designs in abnormal psychology. They are descriptive studies, developmental or longitudinal studies, correlational studies, experiments, analogue experiments, and "experiments" of nature.

DESCRIPTIVE STUDIES. There are two types. They are the case history and the survey.

DEVELOPMENTAL OR LONGITUDINAL STUDIES. Such studies may observe changing patterns of behavior in individuals or, in the cross sectional study, observe behavior in a cross section of different age groups.

CORRELATIONAL STUDIES. Here the researcher attempts to discover whether two types of behavior tend to be associated, that is, do they tend to vary together. The measure of that variation is the coefficient of correlation.

THE EXPERIMENT. Here the observation takes place in a laboratory setting in which the experimenter is able to control all significant variables. The experiment is set up so that the researcher can evaluate the effect of the independent variable (the variable under his or her control) on the depend-ent variable, that factor which, it is hypothesized, is dependent on the influence of the independent variable, which in an experiment must always precede the dependent variable.

There are five critical steps in experimental research. They are developing a hypothesis; quantifying the independent variable, that is providing an operational definition of it; setting up a control group, that is, one free of any influence from the independent variable; measuring the dependent variable for the experimental and control groups; drawing a conclusion.

ANALOGUE EXPERIMENTS. Here the experimenter will attempt to reproduce in a group of normal subjects behavior and feelings similar to those that might be found in psychiatrically ill individuals. The use of animal research also illustrates analogues experimentation.

EXPERIMENTS OF NATURE. Here the researcher studies the impact of some catastrophic natural occurrence (considered the independent variable) on the behavior of the surviving victims of the disaster (the dependent variable).

Each of the six research designs has specific advantages and disadvantages. Ethical and practical considerations frequently determine which design will be chosen.

Selected Readings

Baltes, P. B., H. W. Reese, and L. P. Lipsitt. 1980. "Life-span Developmental Psychology." *Annual Review of Psychology*, 31: 65-110.

Hersen, M., and D. H. Barlow. 1976. *Single Case Experimental Designs: Strategies for Studying Behavior Change.* New York: Pergamon Press.

Miller, N. E. 1972. "Comments on Strategy and Tactics of Research." in A. E. Begin and H. H. Strupp (Eds.) *Changing Frontiers in the Science of Psychotherapy.* New York: Aldine-Atherton.

O'Leary, K. D. and T. D. Borkovec. 1978. "Conceptual, Methodological and Ethical Problems of Placebo Groups in Psychotherapy Research." *American Psychologist*, 33: 821-830.

21

The Revised Diagnostic and Statistical Manual of Mental Disorders (DSM IIIR)

*O*riginally issued in 1952 by the American Psychiatric Association, the most recently published manual, familiarly known as DSM IIIR, was published in 1987.

It provides a means of classifying all recognized psychological disorders and evaluating their severity. The manual uses five axes to enable clinicians to be precise about diagnosis and evaluation. The axes are:

Axis I lists all the recognized clinical syndromes except developmental disorders and personality disorders which are classified under Axis II.

Axis III asks clinician to identify any physical conditions that might affect psychological functioning and any treatment.

Axis IV asks the clinician to rate the severity of any psychosocial stressors in the individual's life.

Axis V asks the clinician to rate the highest level of the individual's earlier functioning.

(The listing of clinical syndromes is reprinted from DSM IIIR with permission of the American Psychiatric Association.)

Axes I and II Categories and Codes

DEVELOPMENTAL DISORDERS USUALLY FIRST EVIDENT IN INFANCY, CHILDHOOD, OR ADOLESCENCE

Mental Retardation

317.00	Mild mental retardation
318.00	Moderate mental retardation
318.10	Severe mental retardation
318.20	Profound mental retardation
319.00	Unspecified mental retardation

Pervasive Developmental Disorders

299.00 Autistic disorder
    Specify if childhood onset
299.80 Pervasive developmental disorder

Specific Developmental Disorders
    Academic skills disorders
315.10 Developmental arithmetic disorder
315.80 Developmental expressive writing disorder
315.00 Developmental reading disorder
    Language and speech disorders
315.39 Developmental articulation disorder
315.31 Developmental expressive language disorder
315.31 Developmental receptive language disorder
    Motor skills disorder
315.40 Developmental coordination disorder
315.90 Specific developmental disorder

Other Developmental Disorders
315.90 Developmental disorder

Disruptive Behavior Disorders
314.01 Attention-deficit hyperactivity disorder
    Conduct disorder
312.20   group type
312.00   solitary aggressive type
312.90   undifferentiated type
313.80   oppositional defiant disorder

Anxiety Disorders of Childhood or Adolescence
309.21 Separation anxiety disorder
313.21 Avoidant disorder of childhood or adolescence

313.00 Overanxious disorder

Eating Disorders
307.10 Anorexia nervosa
307.51 Bulimia nervosa
307.52 Pica
307.53 Rumination disorder of infancy
307.50 Eating disorder

Gender Identity Disorders
302.60 Gender identity disorder of childhood
302.50 Transsexualism
    Specify sexual history: asexual, homosexual, heterosexual, unspecified
302.85 Gender identity disorder of adolescence or adulthood, nontranssexual type
    Specify sexual history: asexual, homosexual, heterosexual, unspecified
302.80 Gender identity disorder

Tic Disorders
307.23 Tourette's disorder
307.22 Chronic motor or vocal tic disorder
307.21 Transient tic disorder
    Specify: single episode or recurrent
307.20 Tic disorder

Elimination Disorders
307.70 Functional encopresis
    Specify: primary or secondary type
307.60 Functional enuresis
    Specify: primary or secondary type
    Specify: nocturnal only, diurnal only, nocturnal and diurnal

Speech Disorders Not Elsewhere Classified
307.00 Cluttering
307.00 Stuttering

Other Disorders of Infancy, Childhood or Adolescence
313.23 Elective mutism
313.82 Identity disorder
313.89 Reactive attachment disorder of infancy or early childhood
307.30 Stereotype/habit disorder
314.00 Undifferentiated attention-deficit disorder

ORGANIC MENTAL DISORDERS

Dementias Arising in the Senium and Presenium

Primary degenerative dementia of the Alzheimer type, senile onset

290.30   with delirium
290.20   with delusions
290.21   with depression
290.00   uncomplicated
(Note: code 331.00 Alzheimer's disease on Axis III)
Code in fifth digit:
1 = with delirium, 2 = with delusions,
3 = with depression, 0 = uncomplicated
290.1x   Primary degenerative dementia of the Alzheimer type, presenile onset
(Note: code 331.00 Alzheimer's disease on Axis III)
290.4x   Multi-infarct dementia
290.00   Senile dementia
Specify etiology on Axis III if known
290.10   Presenile dementia
Specify etiology on Axis III if known (e.g., Pick's disease, Jakob-Creuzfeldt disease)

Psychoactive Substance-Induced Organic Mental Disorders

Alcohol
303.00   intoxication
291.40   idiosyncratic intoxication
291.80   uncomplicated alcohol withdrawal
291.00   withdrawal delirium
291.30   hallucinosis
291.10   amnestic disorder
291.20   dementia associated with alcoholism
Amphetamine or similarly acting sympathomimetic
305.70   intoxication
292.00   withdrawal
292.81   delirium
292.11   delusional disorder
Caffeine
305.90   intoxication
Cannabis
305.20   intoxication

292.11   delusional disorder
Cocaine
305.60   intoxication
292.00   withdrawal
292.81   delirium
292.11   delusional disorder
Hallucinogen
305.30   hallucinosis
292.11   delusional disorder
292.84   mood disorder
292.89   posthallucinogen perception disorder
Inhalant
305.90   intoxication
Nicotine
292.00   withdrawal
Opioid
305.50   intoxication
292.00   withdrawal
Phencyclidine (PCP) or similarly acting arylcyclohexylamine
305.90   intoxication
292.81   delirium
292.11   delusional disorder
292.84   mood disorder
292.90   organic mental disorder
Sedative, hypnotic, or anxiolytic
305.40   intoxication
292.00   uncomplicated sedative, hypnotic, or anxiolytic withdrawal
292.83   amnestic disorder
Other or unspecified psychoactive substance
305.90   intoxication
292.00   withdrawal
292.81   delirium
292.82   dementia
292.83   amnestic disorder
292.11   delusional disorder
292.12   hallucinosis
292.84   mood disorder
292.89   anxiety disorder
292.89   personality disorder
292.90   organic mental disorder

Organic Mental Disorders associated with Axis III physical disorders or conditions, or whose etiology is unknown

293.00	Delirium
294.10	Dementia
294.00	Amnestic disorder
293.81	Organic delusional disorder
293.82	Organic hallucinosis
293.83	Organic mood disorder

Specify: manic, depressed, mixed

294.80	Organic anxiety disorder
310.10	Organic personality disorder

Specify if explosive type

294.80	Organic mental disorder

PSYCHOACTIVE SUBSTANCE USE DISORDERS

Alcohol
303.90	dependence
305.00	abuse

Amphetamine or similarly acting sympathomimetic
304.40	dependence
305.70	abuse

Cannabis
304.30	dependence
305.20	abuse

Cocaine
304.20	dependence
305.60	abuse

Hallucinogen
304.50	dependence
305.30	abuse

Inhalant
304.60	dependence
305.90	abuse

Nicotine
305.10	dependence

Opioid
304.00	dependence
305.50	abuse

Phencyclidine (PCP) or similarly acting arylcyclohexylamine
304.50	dependence
305.90	abuse

Sedative, hypnotic, or anxiolytic
304.10	dependence
305.40	abuse
304.90	Polysubstance dependence
304.90	Psychoactive substance dependence
305.90	Psychoactive substance abuse

SCHIZOPHRENIA

Code in fifth digit: 1 = subchronic, 2 = chronic, 3 = subchronic with acute exacerbation, 5 = in remission, 0 = unspecified

Schizophrenia,
295.2x	catatonic
295.1x	disorganized
295.3x	paranoid

Specify if stable type

295.9x	undifferentiated
295.6x	residual

Specify if late onset

DELUSIONAL (PARANOID) DISORDER

297.10	Delusional (Paranoid) disorder

Specify type:
  erotomanic
  grandiose
  jealous
  persecutory
  somatic
  unspecified

PSYCHOTIC DISORDERS NOT ELSEWHERE CLASSIFIED

298.80	Brief reactive psychosis
295.40	Schizophreniform disorder

Specify: without good prognostic features or with good prognostic features

295.70	Schizoaffective disorder

Specify: bipolar type or depressive type

297.30	Induced psychotic disorder
298.90	Psychotic disorder (Atypical psychosis)

MOOD DISORDERS

Code current state of Major Depression and Bipolar Disorder in fifth digit:
  1 = mild

2 = *moderate*

3 = *severe, without psychotic features*

4 = *with psychotic features (specify*
mood-congruent or
   mood-incongruent)

5 = *in partial remission*

6 = *in full remission*

0 = *unspecified*

For major depressive episodes, specify if chronic
and specify if melancholic type.

For Bipolar Disorder and Depressive Disorder,
specify if = seasonal pattern.

Bipolar Disorders

Bipolar disorder

296.6x	mixed
296.4x	manic
296.5x	depressed
301.13	Cyclothymia
296.70	Bipolar disorder

Depressive Disorders

Major Depression

296.2x	single episode
296.3x	recurrent
300.40	Dysthymia (or Depressive neurosis)

Specify: primary or secondary type
Specify: early or late onset

311.00 Depressive disorder

ANXIETY DISORDERS (or Anxiety and Phobic Neuroses)

Panic disorder

300.21 with agoraphobia
Specify current severity of agoraphobic
avoidance
Specify current severity of panic attacks

300.01 without agoraphobia
Specify current severity of panic attacks

300.22 Agoraphobia without history or panic
disorder
Specify with or without limited
symptom attacks

300.23 Social phobia
Specify if generalized type

300.29 Simple phobia

300.30 Obsessive compulsive disorder (or
Obsessive compulsive neurosis)

309.89 Post-traumatic stress disorder
Specify if delayed onset

300.02 Generalized anxiety disorder

300.00 Anxiety disorder

SOMATOFORM DISORDERS

300.70 Body dysmorphic disorder

300.11 Conversion disorder (or Hysterical
neurosis, conversion type)
Specify: single episode or recurrent

300.70 Hypochondriasis (or Hypochondriacal
neurosis)

307.80 Somatoform pain disorder

300.70 Undifferentiated somatoform disorder

300.70 Somatoform disorder

DISSOCIATIVE DISORDERS (or Hysterical Neuroses, Dissociative Type)

300.14 Multiple personality disorder

300.13 Psychogenic fugue

300.12 Psychogenic amnesia

300.60 Depersonalization disorder (or Depersonalization neurosis)

300.15 Dissociative disorder

SEXUAL DISORDERS

Paraphilias

302.40 Exhibitionism

302.81 Fetishism

302.89 Frotteurism

302.20 Pedophilia
Specify: same sex, opposite sex, same
and opposite sex
Specify if limited to incest
Specify: exclusive type or nonexclusive
type

302.83 Sexual masochism

302.84 Sexual sadism

302.30 Transvestic fetishism

302.82 Voyeurism

302.90 Paraphilia

Sexual Dysfunctions

Specify: psychogenic only, or psychogenic and
biogenic
(Note: If biogenic only, code on Axis III)
Specify: lifelong or acquired
Specify: generalized or situational

Sexual desire disorders
302.71   Hypoactive sexual desire disorder
302.79   Sexual aversion disorder
Sexual arousal disorders
302.72   Female sexual arousal disorder
302.72   Male erectile disorder
Orgasm disorders
302.73   Inhibited female orgasm
302.74   Inhibited male orgasm
302.75   Premature ejaculation
Sexual pain disorders
302.76   Dyspareunia
306.51   Vaginismus
302.70   Sexual dysfunction
Other Sexual Disorders
302.90   Sexual disorder

SLEEP DISORDERS

Dyssomnias

Insomnia disorder
307.42   related to another mental disorder (nonorganic)
780.50   related to known organic factor
307.42   Primary insomnia
Hypersomnia disorder
307.44   related to another mental disorder (nonorganic)
780.50   related to a known organic disorder
780.54   Primary hypersomnia
307.45   Sleep-awake schedule disorder
Specify: advanced or delayed phase type, disorganized type, frequently changing type
Other dyssomnias
307.40   Dyssomnia

Parasomnias

307.47   Dream anxiety disorder (Nightmare disorder)
307.46   Sleep terror disorder
307.46   Sleepwalking disorder
307.40   Parasomnia

FACTITIOUS DISORDERS

Factitious disorder
301.51   with physical symptoms

300.16   with psychological symptoms
300.19   Factitious disorder

IMPULSE CONTROL DISORDERS NOT ELSEWHERE CLASSIFIED

312.34   Intermittent explosive disorder
312.32   Kleptomania
312.31   Pathological gambling
312.33   Pyromania
312.39   Trichotillomania
312.39   Impulse control disorder

ADJUSTMENT DISORDER

Adjustment disorder
309.24   with anxious mood
309.00   with depressed mood
309.30   with disturbance of conduct
309.40   with mixed disturbance of emotions and conduct
309.28   with mixed emotional features
309.82   with physical complaints
309.83   with withdrawal
309.23   with work (or academic) inhibition
309.90   Adjustment disorder

PSYCHOLOGICAL FACTORS AFFECTING PHYSICAL CONDITION

316.00   Psychological factors affecting physical condition
Specify physical condition on Axis III

AXIS II[3a] PERSONALITY DISORDERS

Cluster A
301.00   Paranoid
301.20   Schizoid
301.22   Schizotypal
Cluster B
301.70   Antisocial
301.83   Borderline
301.50   Histrionic
301.81   Narcissistic
Cluster C
301.82   Avoidant
301.60   Dependent
301.40   Obsessive-compulsive

301.84   Passive-aggressive
301.90   Personality disorder

**V CODES FOR CONDITIONS NOT
ATTRIBUTABLE TO A MENTAL
DISORDER THAT ARE A FOCUS OF
ATTENTION OR TREATMENT**

V62.30   Academic problem
V71.01   Adult antisocial behavior
V40.00   Borderline intellectual functioning
         (Note: This is coded on Axis II.)
V71.02   Childhood or adolescent antisocial
         behavior
V65.20   Malingering
V61.10   Marital problem
V15.81   Noncompliance with medical treatment
V62.20   Occupational problem

V61.20   Parent-child problem
V62.81   Other interpersonal problem
V61.80   Other specified family circumstances
V62.89   Phase of life problem or other life
         circumstance problem
V62.82   Uncomplicated bereavement

ADDITIONAL CODES

300.90   Unspecified mental disorder (non-
         psychotic)
V71.09   No diagnosis or condition on Axis I
799.90   Diagnosis or condition deferred on
         Axis I
V71.09   No diagnosis or condition on Axis II
799.90   Diagnosis or condition deferred on
         Axis II

Glossary

adjustment disorder A disorder characterized by difficulty in adapting to a stressful event.

agnosia A disorder in which a person fails to recognize common items.

agoraphobia An irrational and intense fear of public or open spaces.

alcoholism A physical and psychological addiction to alcohol that results in impaired functioning.

Alzheimer's disease A type of dementia that results in progressive intellectual deterioration and memory impairment.

amnesia Loss of memory, either total or partial, that can result from physiological or psychological causes.

amniocentesis A test performed on pregnant women in which amniotic fluid is tested for chromosomal abnormalities.

amphetamines A central nervous system stimulant that produces a feeling of well-being and increased energy.

anorexia nervosa An eating disorder characterized by an irrational fear of obesity and an extremely limited intake of food.

antisocial personality disorder A chronic personality disorder characterized by impulsivity, superficial interpersonal relationships and an inability to accept responsibility.

anxiety A nonspecific, unpleasant feeling of apprehension and fear coupled with physiological arousal.

anxiety disorder This *DSM IIIR* classification encompasses panic disorders, phobic reactions, generalized anxiety disorder, and obsessive-compulsive disorder.

aphasia A language disorder resulting from brain injury in which the ability to communicate or to understand communication is impaired.

assertiveness training This cognitive-behavioral technique teaches a person to express his feelings and cognitions in an effective, nonaggressive manner.

attention-deficit disorder A behavioral disorder in children in which the child's ability to function is impaired by inattention, impulsivity and hyperactivity.

attribution This theory, from social psychology, deals with the way people assess and explain their behaviors.

autistic disorder This childhood disorder, classified as a pervasive developmental disorder in the *DSM IIIR,* is marked by severe communication difficulties, an inability to develop appropriate social relationships, and, frequently, cognitive impairment.

autonomic nervous system The part of the nervous system that regulates the internal environment including the endocrine glands, stomach, heart, and intestines.

aversion therapy This type of behavioral treatment attempts to modify behavior by pairing an unpleasant stimulus, such as electric shock, with the behavior that is to be changed.

avoidant personality This disorder is characterized by extreme sensitivity to social rejection, poor self-esteem, and social withdrawal.

barbiturate A drug that acts to depress many of the functions of the central nervous system. These types of sedatives can be physically and psychologically addictive.

baseline This term, used in behavior therapy, represents a person's level of response before any intervention is attempted.

behavior therapy This type of therapy focuses on overt behavior and attempts to modify this behavior through the use of classical and operant conditioning principles.

benzodiazepines A family of drugs used to decrease anxiety. Two of the most common are Librium and Valium.

biofeedback A system that allows a person to monitor certain physiological reactions and to achieve limited voluntary control over these reactions.

bipolar disorder This term replaced the term manic-depressive disorder and refers to a condition characterized by mood swings from mania to depression. This term can also be used to refer to a condition of mania without depression.

bisexual A person whose sexual orientation involves both heterosexual and homosexual activity.

borderline personality disorder This personality disorder is marked by unpredictable and unstable behavior.

bulimia This eating disorder is marked by uncontrollable binges during which enormous amounts of food are eaten.

case study An encompassing study of a single individual that utilizes observation and biographical information.

castration anxiety This term, central to Freud's Oedipus complex, refers to a fear in males of losing their penis as a punishment for their desires.

catharsis The release of emotional tension linked to childhood traumatic events through verbal expression.

cerebral cortex The surface layer or gray matter of the cerebrum.

cerebrum The largest part of the brain, the cerebrum regulates motor activities and is the center of learning and memory. It is divided into two hemispheres.

chlorpromazine The generic name for the antipsychotic medication marketed under the name Thorazine.

chronic This term refers to a long-lasting, often degenerative condition.

classical conditioning A basic learning theory, first described by Pavlov, in which a neutral stimulus is coupled with a response-producing stimulus. After many pairings, the neutral stimulus will elicit the same response by itself.

clinical psychologist A type of psychologist who has been trained at the doctoral level, and who specializes in the assessment and treatment of abnormal behavior.

cocaine This drug, derived from the coca plant, acts as a stimulant to the central nervous system and produces feelings of euphoria and extreme self-confidence. It can also be used to relieve pain.

cognition This term refers to the act of thinking and perceiving, and to the way in which we arrange our thoughts and attitudes about our environment.

cognitive-behavioral therapy A treatment modality which focuses on modifying behavior by changing faulty or maladaptive thoughts and beliefs.

community psychology The branch of psychology that recognizes the importance of environmental conditions on mental health and focuses on preventive intervention in the community rather than individual treatment.

compulsion The need to act in a repetitive, often senseless fashion in order to reduce feelings of anxiety.

concussion A brain injury, resulting from a blow to the head, that does not cause any permanent damage. Symptoms include mild confusion and short-term memory loss.

conduct disorder A type of disruptive behavior disorder of childhood that is characterized by a disregard for the rights of others and for the rules of society.

confabulation A false and often unlikely story that an individual will use to cover gaps in his memory. The individual believes these stories are accurate accounts.

confidentiality A guiding principle of many professions that makes it unethical for the professional to divulge information about his client to anyone else without the client's permission.

confounding effect An effect in an experiment that results from causes other than the independent variable.

congenital A condition present at birth but not as a result of heredity.

control group The group in an experiment who are not subjected to the experimental condition but in all other ways are similar to the experimental groups.

controlled drinking A behavioral treatment method that attempts to teach alcoholics to drink in a limited, controlled manner.

conversion disorder This disorder, formerly known as hysteria, results in impaired motor or sensory functioning even though no physical reason for this impairment can be found.

coping skills A cognitive-behavioral technique that teaches individuals a variety of ways to manage the stresses of everyday life.

correlational research A study that evaluates the relationship between two or more variables without explaining causal relationship between these variables.

counter-transference The feelings a therapist experiences toward a patient that are a result of the therapist's past experiences.

covert This term is used to describe behavior that is not readily observable and may include emotions and cognitions.

covert sensitization A cognitive-behavioral technique in which distressing imagery is paired with an unwanted behavior to decrease the occurrence of that behavior.

cyclothymic disorder An affective disorder characterized by mood swings of a less serious nature than those experienced in bipolar disorder. This disorder tends to be chronic.

decompensation A condition that occurs when an individual can no longer deal effectively with environmental stresses.

defense mechanism A psychoanalytic term that describes the unconscious process by which the ego prevents unacceptable anxiety-provoking conflicts from becoming conscious.

deinstitutionalization An approach that focuses on moving mental patients out of large institutions and maintaining them in the community.

delusions Inaccurate beliefs that are firmly held, even in the presence of factual and contradictory evidence.

dementia An impairment of cognitive functioning that results from a deterioration of brain tissue.

denial A psychoanalytic defense mechanism that prevents distressing realities from becoming conscious.

dependent personality disorder This disorder is marked by poor self-esteem and an inability to assume responsibility for one's life. These people cannot tolerate being alone for any extended period of time.

dependent variable	The part of an experiment that is hypothesized to change as a result of the application of the independent variable.
depression	This affective disorder, which is a common psychological difficulty, involves overwhelming sadness, loss of interest in previously enjoyable activities, poor self-esteem, and social withdrawal.
detoxification	Medical process that seeks to remove all alcohol from a person's body.
developmental disorder	A series of disorders in which a child's functioning is impaired. This impairment can be in many areas or may be limited to a very specific area of development.
diagnosis	The assessment and classification of specific behavioral disorders.
diathesis-stress model	Theory that explains abnormal behavior as a result of the combination of physical or psychological predisposition and environmental stress.
diazepam	The generic name for the antianxiety medication marketed as Valium.
disorientation	A confused cognitive state in which a person is unsure about his own identity and about time and place.
displacement	A psychological defense mechanism in which feelings about a person or object are shifted to a different, more acceptable person or object.
disruptive behavior disorders	A group of childhood disorders that includes attention-deficit disorder, oppositional-defiant disorder, and conduct disorder.
dizygotic twins	Fraternal but not identical twins who are the product of two separate eggs.
dopamine	A neurotransmitter substance that, when abnormalities are present, has been linked to the development of schizophrenia and Parkinson's disease.
Down's syndrome	A type of mental retardation resulting from an individual being born with 47 chromosomes.
Durham ruling	A landmark legal ruling that stated that an individual cannot be held responsible for a crime if that crime was a result of mental disease or deficit.
dyslexia	A type of learning disorder that impairs the ability to read.
dysthymia	An affective condition marked by chronic, moderate depression.
echolalia	The automatic repeating of the words and sounds of others.
ego	A term from psychoanalytic theory, Freud saw the ego as the part of a person's personality that is mostly conscious and manages the demands of the id, the superego, and reality.
ego-dystonic	Thoughts, ideas or values that are not acceptable to the ego.
ego-syntonic	Thoughts, ideas or values that are acceptable to the ego.

electro-convulsive shock treatment Also known as ECT, this treatment involves applying electric current to the patient's brain in order to produce a convulsion. This treatment is most frequently used with severely depressed patients who are a high risk for suicide.

empathy The ability to comprehend the feelings, needs, and desires of someone else.

empirical The use of experiments or observation to gather information.

encephalitis An acute inflammation of the brain commonly resulting from a viral infection.

encopresis A habit disorder involving loss of sphincter control and inappropriate bowel movements after the age of three.

endogenous Resulting from within a person rather than from external events.

endorphins Naturally occurring opiates, produced in the brain, that function as neurotransmitters and reduce pain.

enuresis A habit disorder, occurring most commonly in children, in which a person fails to achieve bladder control at a developmentally appropriate age.

epilepsy A nervous disorder marked by impaired consciousness sometimes accompanied by seizures.

epinephrine Also called adrenaline, this hormone is released in reaction to stress, resulting in a variety of physiological changes.

erogenous zones Those areas of the body that are sexually responsive.

etiology The determination of the causes of disease.

exhibitionism An abnormal sexual disorder in which a person receives gratification by exposing his genitals in public.

existential therapy A treatment approach that focuses on an individual's right to freely determine the course of his or her life and to accept responsibility for those choices.

exogenous Attributable to external causes, this term is frequently used to describe a type of depression.

experiment The basis for much scientific study, this investigative technique seeks to test a hypothesis by actively manipulating a variable under controlled conditions and observing what occurs.

external validity A measure of the ability of experimental results to be generalized to other situations and populations.

extinction A term used in behavior modification in which reinforcement is removed to weaken or eliminate the acquired response.

factitious disorder A self-limiting physical or psychological condition that is used to receive attention.

family therapy A group treatment approach that aims to facilitate communication among family members and to modify dysfunctional behavior.

fetal alcohol syndrome (FAS) This disorder results from an infant being exposed to alcohol during the mother's pregnancy. Characteristics include impaired cognitive functioning, restricted growth, and physical abnormalities.

fetishism A sexual disorder marked by the need to include an inanimate object in sexual activity in order to achieve arousal.

fixation A psychoanalytic term that describes an individual's inability to progress beyond a certain developmental stage.

flat affect An inability to experience a normal emotional response.

flooding A behavioral technique in which the client is subjected to a fear-inducing stimulus to decrease his conditioned response.

free association A psychoanalytic technique in which the patient says whatever comes to mind with no restrictions.

free-floating anxiety Generalized feelings of anxiety that cannot be attributed to a specific source.

functional disorder Any abnormal disorder for which there is no known organic basis.

galvanic skin response A measure of the changes in electrical resistance of the skin.

gender identity disorder A disorder marked by a conflict between an individual's physical characteristics and sexual identity.

general adaptation syndrome A three-stage reaction to stress, postulated by Selye, characterized by a physiological alarm reaction, defensive responses and exhaustion.

generalization An operant conditioning term in which a response will occur in the presence of a stimulus similar to the conditioned stimulus.

generalized anxiety disorder Anxiety experienced in situations in which there is no apparent anxiety-inducing stimulus.

genital stage The psychosexual stage of development when an individual develops the capacity for mature sexuality.

genotype The part of a person's characteristics that can be attributed to genetic factors.

gerontology The field of scientific study that focuses on the aging process and the interests and needs of older individuals.

gestalt therapy A humanistic model of treatment that emphasizes current concerns and the individual's perception of himself and his environment.

grand mal The most serious type of epileptic seizure during which an individual suffers extreme convulsions and loss of conscious functioning.

group therapy A treatment modality utilized by therapists of various orientations, in which two or more individuals are treated at the same time.

halfway house A temporary home provided for recently discharged psychiatric patients to ease their transition back to the community.

hallucination A false sensory perception that frequently is of a visual nature.

heredity An individual's characteristics that can be attributed to genetic makeup.

heroin An opiate that is derived from morphine and is addictive.

heterosexual Sexual preference for the opposite sex.

hierarchy of needs Theory developed by Maslow that postulates that an individual's basic needs must be met before higher level needs, such as self-actualization, can be addressed.

histrionic personality Disorder marked by excessive displays of emotion, dependency, self-centered behavior, and unstable sexual relationships.

homosexuality Sexual preference for a member of one's same sex.

humanistic perspective The view that emphasizes an individual's free will and responsibility to choose his or her own direction in life.

hypertension Abnormal high blood pressure that is frequently a result of psychological stress.

hypnosis A highly relaxed condition resembling a trance during which an individual is very open to suggestion.

hypochondriasis A chronic disorder marked by unfounded and excessive concerns about becoming ill.

hypothesis An unproved explanation for behavior that is evaluated in a psychological experiment.

hysteria The development of a physical problem that is not attributable to an organic factor.

id This Freudian concept is identified as the part of the personality structure governed by instinctual impulses and biological drives.

identification A psychoanalytic concept by which an individual achieves a higher stage of development by accepting the values and viewpoints of the same-sexed parent.

incest Sexual contact between family members.

independent variable The part of an experiment that is controlled by the investigator to determine its effect on the experimental subjects.

indoleamine A monoamine neurotransmitter linked to an organism's emotional state.

informed consent Guideline that requires that a patient be provided appropriate information before undergoing any treatment or experimental procedure.

insanity defense   A legal maneuver by which a defendant admits to committing a crime but pleads innocent because of mental disease.

insight therapy   A treatment modality that focuses on having the patient better understand the underlying reasons for their behavior.

insomnia   A disorder characterized by problems in falling asleep and staying asleep.

instrumental learning   A process in which a subject is reinforced for performing a designated response so that the frequency of this response will increase.

intellectualization   The repression of unacceptable emotions and the replacement of these emotions with a dry, intellectual explanation.

intelligence test   A standardized measure, usually administered by a psychologist, of evaluating an individual's level of intellectual functioning.

intermittent reinforcement   A method of reinforcing responses at periodic rates rather than after every response.

internal validity   The changes that occur in an experiment that can be attributed to the independent variable.

intrapsychic conflict   A Freudian term that describes the attempt by one area of the personality structure to resist thoughts, feelings or impulses from a different area.

introjection   Freudian term for the process by which an individual accepts and internalizes the values of another person or group.

isolation   Psychoanalytic concept in which the ego as a defense mechanism represses the emotions associated with a situation but not the memory of the situation.

in vivo treatment   A treatment technique that takes place in the actual situation.

irrational beliefs   Thoughts that rational-emotive therapists feel are self-defeating and lead to unproductive emotions and behaviors.

kleptomania   An abnormal condition in which an individual steals impulsively, even though there may be no need for that which is stolen.

Korsakoff's syndrome   A psychotic condition resulting from long-term alcoholism that is characterized by severe cognitive impairment.

lability   An unstable emotional state.

latency period   The development stage, as defined by Freud, during which sexual impulses are not important to an individual.

learned helplessness   The belief, developed in response to previous experiences, that one has no control over what occurs in life and is therefore helpless to make changes.

learning disabilities Difficulties learning arithmetic and reading, as well as speech problems, that can not be attributed to level of cognitive ability, physical impairment or psychological factors.

lesbian A female homosexual.

libido Freudian term for the sexual and instinctual drives harbored in the id.

Librium The trade name for chlordiazepoxide, an antianxiety medication.

lithium carbonate A medication, composed of chemical salts that is used to control the symptoms of bipolar disorder.

lobotomy An outdated method of treating severe mental disease in which nerve fibers in the brain are surgically severed.

locus of control Theory that suggests that people view situations in one of two ways; either they believe they have the ability to control the outcome of a situation or that they are powerless to control the outcome.

logotherapy A form of existential treatment, developed by Victor Frankl after his experiences in a concentration camp during World War II, that focuses on an individual's need to create a life that is productive and meaningful.

longitudinal study Method of investigation and research that focuses on observing and evaluating the same individuals over an extended period of time.

Luria-Nebraska Neuropsychological Battery A group of standardized tests that are used to evaluate brain damage and determine its location.

magical thinking A belief, common in young children, that thoughts and behaviors can affect situations in ways that cannot be explained by the laws of nature.

magnetic resonance imaging A relatively recent technique that employs the magnetic field around an individual's head to provide information about the functioning of the brain.

mainstreaming An educational concept aimed at providing handicapped students maximum exposure to a regular class setting.

major depression An affective disorder in which a person experiences severe depressive episodes but does not experience manic episodes.

major tranquilizers Medications used to treat psychosis.

maladaptive behavior Behavior that does not meet the demands of one's environment in an adequate manner.

malingering Faking a physical or mental disorder for personal gain.

mania A state of unfounded euphoria coupled with heightened cognitive and motor activity marked by pressured speech, poor judgment, and impulsiveness.

masochism   Disorder in which sexual gratification is achieved by being degraded or by having pain inflicted upon you.

medical model   An approach to the diagnosis and treatment of psychological disorders based on the approach medicine takes to physical disease.

monoamine oxidase (MAO) inhibitor   Group of antidepressant drugs that are effective with some depressed individuals.

narcissistic personality   A disorder marked by extreme self-involvement and an inflated sense of self-worth.

negative reinforcement   A behavioral technique in which the cessation of a noxious condition, such as electric shock, will increase the likelihood that a behavior will occur.

neo-Freudians   Theorists who accept many of the basic tenets of psychoanalysis but who have altered Freud's ideas in significant ways.

nervous breakdown   A general term used to describe a person's inability to maintain an adequate level of functioning in response to the stresses of the person's life.

neurology   The branch of science that studies the central nervous system.

neuropsychological assessment   A battery of tests designed to measure brain damage and its location.

neurotransmitter   A group of substances produced by the body that function within the central nervous system to facilitate the passing of impulses between neurons.

object relations   The internalized important relationships of the past that influence present social functioning.

obsessive-compulsive disorder   A disorder characterized by intrusive, unpleasant thoughts and irrational, ritualistic behaviors.

Oedipal conflict   Psychoanalytic term that describes a young boy's sexual desire for his mother and his wish to replace his father.

operant conditioning   Theory that posits that learning takes place when new behaviors are reinforced.

oppositional-defiant disorder   A conduct disorder of childhood characterized by argumentative and angry behavior directed mainly toward authority figures.

oral stage   One of the earliest stages of development, according to Freud, in which the infant's pleasures are focused on the mouth and feeding activity.

organic psychosis   An extreme cognitive disorder that results from actual physical impairment.

outpatient   In the context of psychological treatment, a patient who resides outside of the treatment center but makes visits to receive continued care.

overanxious disorder	An anxiety disorder of childhood marked by irrational fears, performance anxiety, and an excessive need for reassurance.
overt behavior	Behavior that can be readily seen by an observer.
panic disorder	An anxiety disorder in which a person experiences overwhelming fear and believes that he or she may go crazy or suffer a heart attack.
paranoid schizophrenia	A form of schizophrenia in which delusional ideation is prominent.
paraphilias	Sexual behavior in which unusual objects or scenarios are necessary to achieve sexual excitement.
parasympathetic nervous system	The part of the nervous system that controls bodily functions when the body is at rest.
Parkinson's disease	Disease caused by an inability of the brain to produce sufficient dopamine. Symptoms include muscle rigidity, lack of facial expression and tremors.
passive-aggressive personality disorder	Disorder in which underlying hostile impulses are expressed indirectly through the use of procrastination, forgetfulness and complaining.
pedophiliac	A person who achieves sexual excitement through physical contact with children.
perseveration	The act of persisting in a line of thought or activity when it is no longer functional or appropriate.
pervasive developmental disorder	A serious childhood disorder in which there is impaired functioning across many areas of development.
petit mal epilepsy	A mild type of epileptic disorder in which short periods of loss of consciousness take place.
phallic stage	The stage of development, according to Freud, during which the genitals are the focus of curiosity and pleasurable activity.
pharmacology	The study of drugs and their effects.
phobia	A fear for which there is no basis in reality.
placebo effect	A change or effect that takes place because a person believes and expects it will take place.
pleasure principle	The principle, according to Freud, that there are instinctual needs that strive to be gratified without concern about reality.
positive reinforcer	A reinforcer, in operant conditioning, that increases the likelihood that a behavior will occur.
posthypnotic suggestion	The suggestion proposed while the client is in a trance to be acted on after the trance is over.

post-traumatic stress disorder   Disorder in which a person experiences impairing symptoms resulting from an earlier distressing situation.

predictive validity   The extent to which a test can predict future performance.

premature ejaculation   Sexual dysfunction in which the male is unable to control ejaculation, so that it occurs before satisfying sexual relations can take place with his partner.

premorbid   Term that describes a person's level of functioning before psychological problems develop.

prognosis   Diagnostician's prediction on the direction an illness will take in the future.

projection   Psychoanalytic defense mechanism in which a person rejects thoughts or desires he is experiencing and attributes them to someone else.

projective tests   Measurement instruments composed of purposely ambiguous material that attempts to uncover an individual's unconscious thought processes.

psychoanalysis   Therapeutic technique, developed by Freud, that focuses on uncovering unconscious material as a way of understanding one's behavior.

psychomotor epilepsy   A form of epilepsy in which the person engages in behavior that is outside of his or her conscious control.

psychopathic personality   Personality disorder characterized by amoral behavior and superficial, exploitive social relationships.

psychopathology   The area of psychology that is concerned with deviant behavior.

psychopharmacology   The study of medications and their effects on psychological disorders.

psychophysiological disorders   Physical disorders that result in part from psychological causes.

psychosis   Extreme psychological disturbance in which thought processes are severely impaired and personality integration is disrupted.

psychotherapy   The systematic treatment of personality disorders or mental illness by psychological methods.

rape   An act of violence in which sexual intercourse takes place through the use of force.

rational-emotive therapy (RET)   Therapeutic techniques, developed by Albert Ellis, that focus on changing a patient's irrational beliefs.

reaction formation   A psychoanalytic defense mechanism in which a person replaces an unacceptable impulse with its opposite.

reality principle   A psychoanalytic term that describes the ego's efforts to mediate between the demands of the id and of the real world.

reinforcement In operant conditioning, the technique of following a response with a stimulus that will change the strength of the response.

reliability The ability of a test to consistently measure what it is designed to measure.

repression Psychoanalytic defense mechanism in which unacceptable thoughts or impulses are forced out of conscious awareness.

resistance A term from psychoanalytic therapy that describes the tendency of patients to avoid working on issues in treatment that make them anxious.

retrospective study A form of research that focuses on a subject's history when conducting an investigation.

Ritalin A stimulant drug that has the paradoxical effect of reducing hyperactive symptoms in children with attention- deficit disorder.

Rorschach test A projective test composed of ten bisymmetrical inkblots. The subject is asked to describe what the inkblots look like.

sadism Aberrant sexual behavior in which sexual excitement is achieved by inflicting pain upon one's partner.

schizo-affective disorder A severe psychotic disorder that combines symptoms of schizophrenia with depression or elation.

schizoid personality disorder Personality disorder in which a person is socially withdrawn, emotionally aloof, and indifferent to the feelings of others.

schizophrenia A severe disorder characterized by unusual behavior, distortion of reality, cognitive disorganization, and inappropriate affect.

school phobia A disorder of childhood in which a child becomes panicked at the thought of attending school.

seasonal affective disorder (SAD) Disorder characterized by the onset of depression in the Autumn and the remission of this depression in the Spring.

secondary gain The increased attention and other benefits that one receives when ill.

self-actualization Term, developed by Maslow, that describes a person functioning at his or her full capability.

sensate focus A technique of sexual therapy in which a couple is guided through a series of non-threatening sexual activities leading to mutually satisfying sexual intercourse.

separation anxiety disorder A childhood disorder in which a child is extremely fearful of being separated from his family.

sexual dysfunction Any impairment of a person's ability to desire sexual contact, to become sexually aroused or to achieve orgasm.

shaping An operant conditioning technique in which a complex response is taught by rewarding an incremental series of similar but less complex responses.

single-blind experiment A type of experiment in which the subject is unaware of whether he has received a placebo or the experimental condition.

social phobia Extreme anxiety about being observed in social situations.

somatoform disorder Disorder in which a person experiences physical symptoms that result from psychological rather than physiological causes.

statistical significance A statistical analysis that determines the probability of an experimental result occurring by chance.

statutory rape Sexual intercourse, usually consensual, with a legal minor.

stimulants A class of drugs that act upon the central nervous system to produce feelings of elation, confidence, and agitation.

stress A person's internal response to the demands of the environment.

stroke Impairment to the central nervous system resulting from blockage or total rupture of the blood vessels supplying nutrients to the area.

sublimation A psychoanalytic defense mechanism in which psychic energy is directed away from unacceptable outlets and directed toward socially desirable ones.

suicidal ideation Obsessive thoughts about ending one's life.

superego The part of the personality structure, according to Freudian theory, that has internalized the ethical and moral values learned from parents and other important people.

sympathetic nervous system That part of the nervous system that controls important bodily functions during times of stress.

systematic desensitization A behavioral therapy technique that utilizes relaxation training to reduce the anxiety evoked by certain situations.

Tardive Dyskinesia A side effect of phenothiazine medication that results in neuromuscular impairment.

test-retest reliability The extent to which a test, given to the same individuals at different times, will produce consistent scores.

thematic apperception test (TAT) A projective test in which the subject is asked to create stories about ambiguous pictures.

therapeutic community The structuring of a hospital setting so that all events and activities have a therapeutic value for the patient.

tic An involuntary muscle twitch, usually in the area of the face.

token economy A behavioral technique, frequently employed in residential settings, in which targeted behaviors are rewarded with tokens that can be used to purchase reinforcing objects or activities.

Tourette's syndrome An uncommon but severe disorder characterized by tics and involuntary verbalizations.

tranquilizers Medications that are used to alleviate anxiety and as antipsychotics.

transference A tendency on the part of patients, according to Freudian theory, to ascribe to the therapist the qualities of significant people in their lives.

transsexualism A psychosexual dysfunction in which an individual identifies with the opposite sex.

transvestism Sexual dysfunction in which an individual achieves sexual excitement by dressing as a member of the opposite sex.

tricyclic antidepressants A group of medications used to treat depression by prolonging the activity of neurotransmitters.

Turner's syndrome Abnormality in which females are born with one X chromosome instead of two X chromosomes. These girls do not develop sexually at puberty and have specific cognitive deficits.

type A personality Personality type characterized by aggressiveness, hostility, and an excessive drive to achieve. Some medical research links this personality type to an increased risk of heart disease.

unconditioned response A response to a stimulus that occurs naturally and without being taught.

unconditioned stimulus A stimulus that produces an unlearned, unconditioned response.

unconscious The part of a person's psychological makeup, according to Freud, that stores repressed thoughts, memories and impulses.

unipolar disorder An extreme emotional disorder characterized by depression without manic episodes.

validity The ability of a test to accurately measure what it is designed to measure.

vicarious conditioning Conditioning that takes place by observing the consequences of the behavior of other people.

voyeurism A sexual dysfunction in which sexual excitement is achieved by watching people undress or participate in sexual behavior.

Wechsler intelligence scales Standardized intelligence tests for preschoolers to adults that provide verbal and performance scale scores and a general IQ score.

word salad An incoherent, disorganized speech pattern that is often observed in psychotic patients.

xenophobia An irrational fear of any stranger.

zoophilia A sexual dysfunction in which sexual excitement is achieved by sexual contact with animals.

zoophobia An irrational fear of animals.

Index

OTHER BOOKS IN THE HARPERCOLLINS COLLEGE OUTLINE SERIES

ART
History of Art 0-06-467131-3
Introduction to Art 0-06-467122-4

BUSINESS
Business Calculus 0-06-467136-4
Business Communications 0-06-467155-0
Introduction to Business 0-06-467104-6
Introduction to Management 0-06-467127-5
Introduction to Marketing 0-06-467130-5

CHEMISTRY
College Chemistry 0-06-467120-8
Organic Chemistry 0-06-467126-7

COMPUTERS
Computers and Information Processing 0-06-467176-3
Introduction to Computer Science and Programming
    0-06-467145-3
Understanding Computers 0-06-467163-1

ECONOMICS
Introduction to Economics 0-06-467113-5
Managerial Economics 0-06-467172-0

ENGLISH LANGUAGE AND LITERATURE
English Grammar 0-06-467109-7
English Literature From 1785 0-06-467150-X
English Literature To 1785 0-06-467114-3
Persuasive Writing 0-06-467175-5

FOREIGN LANGUAGE
French Grammar 0-06-467128-3
German Grammar 0-06-467159-3
Spanish Grammar 0-06-467129-1
Wheelock's Latin Grammar 0-06-467177-1
Workbook for Wheelock's Latin Grammar
    0-06-467171-2

HISTORY
Ancient History 0-06-467119-4
British History 0-06-467110-0
Modern European History 0-06-467112-7
Russian History 0-06-467117-8
20th Century United States History 0-06-467132-1
United States History From 1865 0-06-467100-3
United States History to 1877 0-06-467111-9
Western Civilization From 1500 0-06-467102-X

Western Civilization To 1500 0-06-467101-1
World History From 1500 0-06-467138-0
World History to 1648 0-06-467123-2

MATHEMATICS
Advanced Calculus 0-06-467139-9
Advanced Math for Engineers and Scientists
    0-06-467151-8
Applied Complex Variables 0-06-467152-6
Basic Mathematics 0-06-467143-7
Calculus with Analytic Geometry 0-06-467161-5
College Algebra 0-06-467140-2
Elementary Algebra 0-06-467118-6
Finite Mathematics with Calculus 0-06-467164-X
Intermediate Algebra 0-06-467137-2
Introduction to Calculus 0-06-467125-9
Introduction to Statistics 0-06-467134-8
Ordinary Differential Equations 0-06-467133-X
Precalculus Mathematics: Functions & Graphs
    0-06-467165-8
Survey of Mathematics 0-06-467135-6

MUSIC
Harmony and Voice Leading 0-06-467148-8
History of Western Music 0-06-467107-7
Introduction to Music 0-06-467108-9
Music Theory 0-06-467168-2

PHILOSOPHY
Ethics 0-06-467166-6
History of Philosophy 0-06-467142-9
Introduction to Philosophy 0-06-467124-0

POLITICAL SCIENCE
The Constitution of the United States 0-06-467105-4
Introduction to Government 0-06-467156-9

PSYCHOLOGY
Abnormal Psychology 0-06-467121-6
Child Development 0-06-467149-6
Introduction to Psychology 0-06-467103-8
Personality: Theories and Processes 0-06-467115-1
Social Psychology 0-06-467157-7

SOCIOLOGY
Introduction to Sociology 0-06-467106-2
Marriage and the Family 0-06-467147-X

Available at your local bookstore or directly from HarperCollins at 1-800-331-3761.